THE

C000062463

London
Restaurants

2002 EDITION

There are more than two hundred Rough Guide
travel, phrasebook and music titles, covering
destinations from Amsterdam to Zimbabwe,
languages from Czech to Vietnamese, and musics
from World to Opera and Jazz

Rough Guides on the Internet

www.roughguides.com

Rough Guide Credits

Text editor: James McConnachie **Series editor**: Mark Ellingham
Production: Helen Prior, Julia Bovis, Ed Wright
Photography: Giles Stokoe

Publishing Information

This fourth edition published October 2001 by
Rough Guides Ltd, 62–70 Shorts Gardens, London WC2H 9AH.

Distributed by the Penguin Group

Penguin Books Ltd, 27 Wrights Lane, London W8 5TZ
Penguin Putnam, Inc., 375 Hudson Street, New York 10014, USA
Penguin Books Australia Ltd, 487 Maroondah Highway,
PO Box 257, Ringwood, Victoria 3134, Australia
Penguin Books Canada Ltd, 10 Alcorn Avenue,
Toronto, Ontario, Canada M4V 1E4
Penguin Books (NZ) Ltd, 182–190 Wairau Road,
Auckland 10, New Zealand

Typeset in Bembo and Helvetica to an original design by Henry Iles.
Printed in Spain by Graphy Cems.

About the Author

Charles Campion is an award-winning food writer and restaurant reviewer. He writes a restaurant column for *ES*, the *London Evening Standard* magazine, which won him the Glenfiddich "Restaurant Writer of the Year" award, and contributes to radio and TV food programmes, as well as a variety of magazines including *Bon Appetit* in the USA. His most recent book publication was *Real Greek Food*, which he wrote with chef Theodore Kyriakou.

Before becoming a food writer, Charles worked in a succession of London ad agencies and had a spell as chef-proprietor of a hotel and restaurant in darkest Derbyshire.

Help Us Update

We've tried to ensure that this fourth edition of *The Rough Guide to London Restaurants* is as up-to-date and accurate as possible. However, London's restaurant scene is in constant flux: chefs change jobs; restaurants are bought and sold; menus change. There will probably be a few references in this guide that are out of date even as this book is printed – and standards, of course, go up and down. If you feel there are places we've underrated or overpraised, or others we've unjustly omitted, please let us know: comments or corrections are much appreciated, and we'll send a copy of the next edition (or any other *Rough Guide* if you prefer) for the best letters. Please address letters to Charles Campion at:

Rough Guides, 62–70 Shorts Gardens, London WC2H 9AH or
Rough Guides, 4th Floor, 375 Hudson St, New York, NY 10014.

Or send email to: mail@roughguides.co.uk

Contents

Central London

The City & East London

North London

Contents

South London

West London

Index

Introduction

Welcome to the fourth edition of The Rough Guide to London Restaurants. If you used the first three, you will have noticed that the number of restaurants has stabilized around the 350 mark, but it is surprising how many openings and closures there have been within the space of a year. This edition has been extensively revised and as well as reassessing all the previous entries we have added a wide selection of new establishments. But the way we have organized the book has stayed the same. Anyone who has lived or worked in London knows that, while it may seem like one big metropolis to the outsider, it is really a series of villages. If you live in Clapham, you know about Clapham and Battersea, and maybe Brixton or Chelsea, while Highgate or Shepherd's Bush are far-off lands. And vice versa. Yet almost every other restaurant guide is divided up by cuisine, which assumes that this is your first criterion when choosing a place to eat. It shouldn't be. If you're meeting friends in Chiswick your best options might be Italian or Modern British; in Wembley or Tooting they might be Indian. But you want to know about that oddball great restaurant, too: whether it's an interesting newcomer like Mosaica in Wood Green, or a new gastropub like The Victoria in West Temple Sheen. This book divides London into five geographic sections (Central; City & East; North; South; West) and then breaks these down into the neighbourhoods, with restaurants arranged alphabetically in each section. Keep this guide handy and it will tell you where to eat well from Soho to Southall.

Another important thing to note about the restaurants selected and reviewed in this book is that they are all **recommended** – none has been included simply to make up the numbers. There are some very cheap places and there are some potentially pretty expensive places, but they all represent **good value**. The only rule we have made for inclusion is that it must be possible to eat a meal for £35 a head or less. In some of the *haute cuisine* establishments, that will mean keeping to the set lunch, while in some of the bargain eateries £35 might cover a blow-out for four. This guide reviews restaurants for every possible occasion from quick lunches to celebratory dinners. It also covers many different kinds of food – some fifty cuisines in all. In reality, we cover even more, as for simplicity we have used "Indian" and "Chinese" as catch-all terms.

Prices and credit cards

Price is one of the most difficult areas for any restaurant guide to master. Every review in this book has at the top of the page a **spread of two prices** (eg £12–£40). The first figure relates to what you could get away with – this is the minimum amount per person you are likely to spend on a meal here (assuming you are not a non-tipping, non-drinking skinflint). The second relates to what it would cost if you don't hold back. Wild diners with a taste for fine wines will leave our top estimates far behind, but the figures are there as a guide. For most people, the cost of a meal will lie somewhere within the spread.

For a more detailed picture, each review sets out the prices of various dishes. At some time in the guide's life these specific prices (and indeed the overall price spreads) will become out of date, but they were all accurate when the book left for the printer. And even in the giddy world of restaurants, when prices rise or prices fall, everyone tends to move together. If this book shows one restaurant as being twice as expensive as another, that is likely to remain.

The reviews also keep faith with original menu spellings of

dishes, so you'll find satays, satehs and satés – all of which will probably taste much the same. Hieroglyphics have been kept to a minimum, so opening hours and days are spelled out, as are the credit cards accepted. Where reviews specify "all major credit cards accepted", that means at least Amex, Diners, MasterCard and Visa. Acceptance of Visa and MasterCard usually means Switch and Delta, too; we've specified the odd exception, but if you're relying on one card it's always best to check when you book.

Getting off the fence...

Every restaurant reviewed in this book is wholeheartedly recommended...but it would be a very strange person who did not have favourites, so here are some of my "six of the bests".

Best Newcomers

Best Chinese and Southeast Asian

Best French

Best New-Style Indian

Best Old-Style Indian

Best Italian

Introduction

Best Eccentric Restaurant

Best Gastropub

Best Vegetarian Meal

Best Budget Meal

Best for Business

Best for Lively Atmosphere

Best Local

Best-value Set Lunch

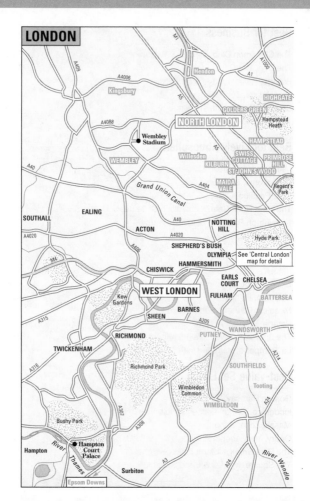

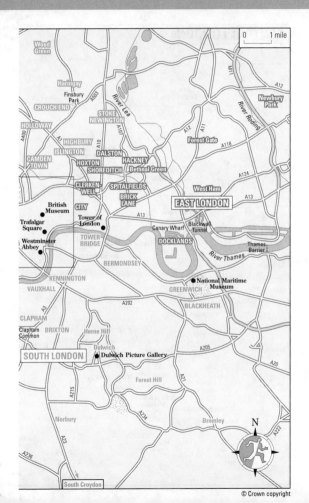

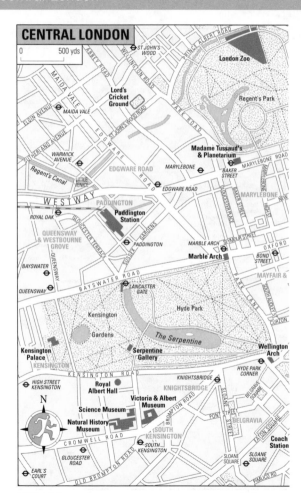

CENTRAL LONDON

0   500 yds

ST JOHN'S WOOD

London Zoo

Regent's Park

Lord's Cricket Ground

ELGIN AVENUE

MAIDA VALE

SUTHERLAND AVENUE

WARWICK AVENUE

Regent's Canal

LITTLE VENICE

Madame Tussaud's & Planetarium

MARYLEBONE

BAKER STREET

MARYLEBONE

EDGWARE ROAD

EDGWARE ROAD

WESTWAY

PADDINGTON

Paddington Station

ROYAL OAK

QUEENSWAY & WESTBOURNE GROVE

PADDINGTON

MARBLE ARCH

OXFORD

BOND STREET

BAYSWATER

Marble Arch

QUEENSWAY

MAYFAIR

BAYSWATER ROAD

LANCASTER GATE

Hyde Park

CURZON

Kensington Gardens

The Serpentine

Serpentine Gallery

Wellington Arch

Kensington Palace

KENSINGTON

KENSINGTON ROAD

KNIGHTSBRIDGE

HYDE PARK CORNER

HIGH STREET KENSINGTON

Royal Albert Hall

KNIGHTSBRIDGE

BELGRAVE SQUARE

N

Science Museum

Victoria & Albert Museum

BROMPTON ROAD

PONT STREET

SLOANE STREET

BELGRAVIA

Natural History Museum

SOUTH KENSINGTON

Coach Station

CROMWELL ROAD

SOUTH KENSINGTON

SLOANE SQUARE

EARL'S COURT

GLOUCESTER ROAD

OLD BROMPTON ROAD

PIMLICO RD

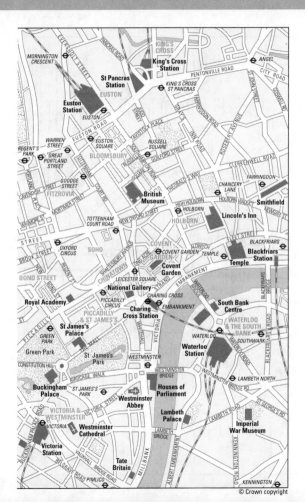

© Crown copyright

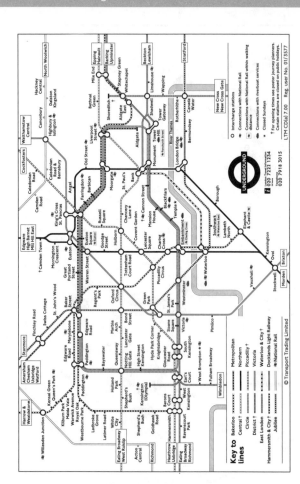

Central

Bloomsbury & Fitzrovia

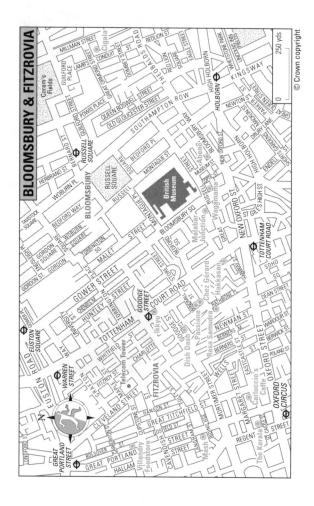

Abeno

Abeno claims to be Europe's only specialist okonomi-yaki restaurant, and it may well be. London has plenty of teppan-yaki restaurants – where the chef cooks gourmet morsels for you on the teppan hotplate that is sunk into the table in front of the diners – but, as yet, okonomi-yaki hasn't swept to prominence, perhaps because it is an altogether messier, more grass-roots sort of experience. Even the finest okonomi-yaki does look a bit like road-kill. Imagine a sloppy pizza crossed with a solid omelette then layered with all manner of odds and ends. Then imagine it being assembled and cooked on the table in front of you. Abeno is saved by the gentle and friendly service, the freshness of the ingredients, the charm of the cooks, and the low, low prices. And it's fun.

| Cost | £7–£30 |

Address 47 Museum St, WC1
T 020 7405 3211
Station Tottenham Court Road
Open Mon–Sat noon–10pm, Sun noon–8pm
Accepts MasterCard, Visa

JAPANESE

You could try yaki-soba, a fried noodle dish with chicken, squid or pork (£6.95). Or soba-rice, a natty combination of rice and noodles which is all the rage in Kansai – try it with pork and kimchi (£8.95). You could even try the teppan-yaki (£8.80), an upscale fillet-steak-and-chicken sort of affair. But you're here for the okonomi-yaki. The base is cabbage, egg and dough, with spring onions and tempura batter; all this is piled onto the hot plate. You specify whether you want deluxe or super deluxe, trad or wholemeal base, and off they go. Try tofu, corn and extra spring onion (£6.70/£8.70); or Osaka mix – pork, kimchi and prawn (£6.95/£8.95); or spicy Tsuruhasi – kimchi and an extra egg (£6.70/£8.70); or Abeno special – pork, bacon, konnyaku, asparagus, squid, prawn and salmon, topped with an egg (£13.80); or London mix – pork, bacon, cheese and salmon (£8.80/£10.80). These dishes are very tasty, and it's fun to watch the layering at work. And there are nice side dishes that will serve as starters, such as ika itame – squid with garlic and soy (£2.80), and miso soup (£2.20). Set menus take the angst out of ordering.

Don't visit this place in the height of summer, as the red-hot tabletop in front of you chucks out a fierce amount of heat. By the same token, keep your elbows, your newspaper and the menu well away from it – unless the smell of scorching stimulates your tastebuds.

Carluccio's Caffe

When Antonio Carluccio first ambled across our television screens, it was in his role as chef-proprietor of the upscale Neal Street Restaurant and ultra-passionate mushroom hunter. Carluccio's Caffe is a much more businesslike, mainstream concern than Neal Street, and it's also an extremely busy place, which makes for a great atmosphere. The downside is having to queue. The front of the premises is a delicatessen-cum-shop; the mid-section is a bar; the rear is a café-restaurant. A commendable effort has been made to incorporate all that is admirable about Continental coffee shops and so often missing in our own. Carluccio's is open throughout the day. Proper meals are available at all hours. The coffee is notably good. Children are welcome.

Cost	£8–£25
Address	8 Market Place, W1
T	020 7636 2228
Station	Oxford Circus
Open	Mon–Fri 8am–11pm, Sat & Sun 10am–10pm
Accepts	All major credit cards except Diners
W	www.carluccios.com

In the morning the temptations are croissants (£1.50) and coffee: caffè ristretto (£1.15); cappucino (£1.60); double espresso (£1.40) – pukka stuff. This segues into the main menu, on which there are always a couple of good soups to be had: zuppa di funghi (£3.75) or pasta e fagioli (£3.85) – note the fair prices. There's a good "bread tin" (£2.75) with sweet stuff at breakfast time and some moody Italian regional breads at meal times. There are sound antipasti, including Sicilian arancini di riso (£3.50), which are crisp, deep-fried rice balls filled with mozzarella or ragu. There are salads. Main courses range from calzone (£4.75) to a trad osso buco (£9.85); and from ravioli (£5.50) to fegato e polenta (£8.95). Puds major in ice cream – gelati artiginali (£3.50). For a restaurant serving so many customers, the cooking is very good. Dishes are well-seasoned; service is quick and the prices are fair.

Beware the shopping zone lest you be tempted by the gleaming Piaggio Vespa ET2 50cc. You'll find it listed on the menu under "Transport" and described as a "fully automatic scooter, carefully made and imported from Italy" – and priced at £1,599.

Chez Gérard

When the inner prompting shouts for steak frites you can't do better than turn to Chez Gérard. Though today there are more than a dozen branches of this popular brasserie spread throughout London, the Charlotte Street branch is the original and, some say, the best. When it opened, twenty years ago, this type of French restaurant – where the steak is good and the frites are fabulous – was a novelty in London; today, Chez Gérard feels reassuringly old-fashioned. Along with the fine steak frites, you'll find salade de crottin tiède, French onion soup, snails and crème brûlée. The bread is crusty, the service Gallic, and the red wine decent. It's not cheap, but the food is always good, and in summer you can eat alfresco at one of the pavement tables.

Cost	£20–£50

Address 8 Charlotte St, W1
T 020 7636 4975
Station Goodge Street
Open Mon–Fri noon–3pm &
6–11.30pm, Sat 6–11.30pm,
Sun noon–3pm & 6–10.30pm
Accepts All major credit cards
W www.sante-gcg.com

FRENCH

Start with rock oysters (£6.50 for six; £9.75 for nine; £13 for twelve), pâté de campagne (£4.75), or, for a real belt of nostalgia, a dozen snails in garlic butter (£5.30). The steaks come in all shapes and sizes – Châteaubriand is for two people (£31.50), while côte de boeuf rib-eye (£14.50) is now cooked "per person" rather than to share. There's a 9oz fillet steak (£16.55) and an entrecôte (£13.35). This is also one of the few places in London where you can get onglet (£9.95), a particularly tasty French cut. Everything from the grill comes with pommes frites and sauce Béarnaise. There is also space on the grill for salmon, sea bass and chicken, and on the menu for a couple of vegetarian options. But don't kid yourself – you're here for the steak frites. Salads, side orders of vegetables, desserts – including tarte Tatin (£4.50) – and a decent selection of regional French cheeses (£4.25) are all nicely in tune with the Gallic ambience. So too are the house wines (£9.50), which are so good that you can almost disregard the wine list.

There is also a very sound menu prix fixe available from Monday to Saturday evening and at Sunday lunch – just £15.95 for three courses. Gravadlax; onglet; pud makes pretty good reading.

CENTRAL

Cigala

SPANISH

Jake Hodges, previously one of the founders of Moro (see p.198), opened Cigala just before Christmas 2000. The fussy decor of the neighbourhood brasserie which stood on the site previously has given way to a spartan, clean-cut dining room, and the tired French food has made way for blissfully straightforward Iberian dishes. Within a couple of months of opening Cigala had a hatful of glowing reviews and, which is more unusual, the kitchen deserved them! This is a very good restaurant. Look out for simple dishes. Strong flavours. Fresh ingredients. Real passion.

Cost	£18–£60

Address 54 Lamb's Conduit St, WC1
T 020 7405 1717
Station Russell Square
Open Mon–Fri 12.30–2.30pm & 6.30–10.30pm
Accepts All major credit cards except Diners

The menu changes daily. It is dependent on the markets and what the chef can find that looks good. This makes for seasonal dishes, and that is a huge plus. So a winter menu might start with sopa de castana (£4.50), a simple and gratifyingly rich chestnut and pork soup. Or a rare roast beef salad with ratte potatoes, thyme, parsley and garlic (£5.50). Or lengua a la Aragonesa (£5) – ox tongue with pepper and sherry sauce. Or clams with garlic parsley and Manzanilla (£5). All these dishes are simple, well-seasoned and have good combinations of flavour. Mains deliver in much the same fashion. Fabadas Asturianas (£13) is a rich, comforting bean stew with good, spicy chorizo, the Spanish blood sausage called morcilla and rashers of fat bacon. Delicious. Sea bass a la plancha (£16.50) comes with deep-fried artichokes and a Romesco sauce. Roast skate (£12.50) comes with broccoli and anchovies. Puddings lie in wait: the walnut tart (£4) is actually a substantial walnut and chocolate pie. The wine list doffs its cap to a goodly selection of sherries, and features a good range of well-chosen Spanish wines. The cooking here is very adept and Mr Hodges has the sense to stick to simple, unpretentious dishes and simple, unpretentious presentation. This guarantees some very enjoyable meals.

There's a good set lunch here. Two courses cost £15 and three courses cost £18 – and you get three choices for each course.

Dish Dash

Don't let yourself be put off by the name – Dish Dash is an attractive, groovy space. It opened in 2000, and in a neighbourhood of old-fashioned trattorias and sandwich shops this modernist Persian restaurant makes a welcome change. Half of the establishment is all concrete, communal tables and wooden chairs, with the kitchen open to view, while the other half has chrome fittings, low-hanging silk-covered lights, a leather-clad lounge area and a well-stocked bar. The atmosphere is distinctly different on either side of the dividing wall. Pick whichever suits your mood.

Cost	£20–£50
Address	57–59 Goodge St, W1
☎	020 7637 7474
Station	Goodge Street
Open	Mon–Fri noon–3pm & 6–11.30pm, Sat 6–11.30pm, Sun noon–3pm & 6–10.30pm
Accepts	All major credit cards

The menu is divided into first courses and mains, and these in turn are broken down into hot and cold soups, called mazzas, then kebabs or "mish mash". Though you can order just one or two mazzas (£3.50 each), they are designed for sharing, with special plates to hold a selection of five (£12.50) or seven (£18). You'll find the classics – hummus, baba ghanoush and felafel – alongside less common offerings like muhammura – a red pepper, walnut and pomegranate dip; Persian Gulf-style curried prawns; or little black sesame-coated fishcakes. There's plenty of variety in texture and taste. Breads are served and charged separately. In the kebab section, alongside the ubiquitous kofta (£9) and chicken (£8.50), there are versions using swordfish (£13.50), sardines (£9.50) and vegetables (£6.50). Each comes with an appropriate garnish, be it rice, couscous or sumac chips. The "mish mash" section is given over to everything else, from a green bean and chicken khoresh stew (£9), to dolma (£8) – stuffed peppers. Desserts are happily simple dishes such as glazed figs with marscapone (£4.25), and baklava with honey ice cream and toasted nuts (£4).

There's a short wine list, but the main bulk of the drinks list is given over to cocktails, which are professionally made and agreeably strong. This means that Dish Dash is popular with a drinking crowd and tends to get loud and boisterous towards the end of the week.

Hakkasan

CHINESE

As you nod to the doorman and walk down the green slate tunnel that is the staircase, you could easily think that you were entering a super-plush theme park ride. Hakkasan opened in April 2001 and is as impressively designed as only the judicious application of more than £3 million can achieve. There is a double-smart cocktail bar. You

Cost	£18–£80
Address	8 Hanway Place, W1
T	020 7927 7000
Station	Tottenham Court Road
Open	Daily noon–4pm & 5.30pm–midnight
Accepts	All major credit cards

expect to find some awestruck architecture students gawping at the majestic toilets. And inside an elegant and ornate carved wooden cage is the large dining area. Top-name designers from the worlds of film and fashion have given their all and it has worked: this is a smart and elegant place. The food is novel, well-presented, fresh, delicious and, in strangely justifiable fashion, expensive.

The starters are called "small dishes" and lean heavily towards fish, seafood and luxury ingredients. The three style vegetarian roll (£6) teams a mooli spring roll with a bean curd puff and a yam roll. Good, but not great. The claypot crab with Kwantung Mijiu (£10.50), however, is a triumph: a large, fresh crab is perfectly steamed and tastes as good as you would find anywhere in Chinatown. The main dishes are innovative and delicious: the stir-fried jellyfish, squid and Chinese chives (£8.50) has rich, multiple textures and delicate flavours. Abandon any lingering jellyfish prejudices and try this one. Or there is steamed Mori-naga tofu with prawn and wolfberry (£9.50) – these are nests of the lightest, meltingest steamed tofu with the texture of fine panna cotta, each with a crunchy, large prawn. Memorable. Or there's a dish of roast organic pork with red rice, ginger and Shao Hsing wine (£11.50). Or a very good braised chicken with dried shitake and chestnuts (£11.50). By way of a staple, try the Hakka vermicelli (£6.50), which is a simple noodle dish that comes with a bowl of chive consommé to moisten the noodles down.

The lunch menu combines slightly ritzy dim sum – such as fried cod roll (£4.50) and baked venison puffs (£4.50) – with satisfying noodle dishes, rice dishes and congee. Traditional congee is sloppy and often bland rice porridge – it's a good bet that this is the first time the world has seen "lobster congee with ginger, served with roast peanut" (£7.50).

Ikkyu

🍴 Busy, basic and full of people eating reliable Japanese food at sensible prices – all in all, Ikkyu is a good match for any popular neighbourhood restaurant in Tokyo. What's more, it's hard to find, which adds to the authenticity. Down the steps and through the twine fly screen and you've made it. The first shock is how very busy the place is –

Cost	£10–£40
Address	67a Tottenham Court Rd, W1
T	020 7636 9280
Station	Goodge Street
Open	Mon–Fri noon–2.30pm & 6–10.30pm, Sun 6–10.30pm
Accepts	All major credit cards

you are not the first person to discover what must be about the best-value Japanese food in London.

Nigiri sushi is good here and is priced by the piece: tuna (£2); yellow tail (£2.10); salmon (£1.70); mackerel (£1.40); cuttlefish (£1.70). Or there's sashimi – which runs all the way from mackerel (£4.50) to sea urchin (£13), with an assortment for £13.50. Alternatively, start with soba (£3.60) – delicious cold brown noodles. Then allow yourself a selection of yakitori, either a portion of assorted (£5), or mix and match from tongue, heart, liver, gizzard and chicken skin (all £1 a stick). You will need a good many skewers of the grilled chicken skin, which is implausibly delicious. Moving on to the main dishes, an order of fried leeks with pork (£7.20) brings a bunch of long, onion-flavoured greens – which may well be chives, although they're not so pungent – strewn with morsels of grilled pork. Whatever the green element is, it is certainly not leeks. Or there's grilled aubergine (£3.40), or rolled five vegetables with shrimp (£7.70), which is like a Swiss roll made with egg and vegetable with a core of prawn.

Ikkyu's menu rewards experimentation, as it has a good many delicious secrets, though the Japanese-favoured drink, shouchu and soda (£3.50), is perhaps not among them – shouchu is a clear spirit which tastes like clear spirit and the addition of soda does little to make it palatable. Asahi and Kirin beers (both £2.70) are a much better choice. Another doubtful order would be fermented soya beans topped with a raw egg (£3.10), which in Japan is thought to be the perfect way to start the day, but is unlikely to woo you away from cornflakes.

The Kerala

In 1935, Gough Brothers opened Shirref's wine bar at 15 Great Castle St at a time when such establishments were something of a novelty. Shirref's stood the test of time and became a favourite watering hole for musicians and actors working around the corner at the BBC in Portland Place. At the end of the 1980s it was taken over by

Cost	£8–£22
Address	15 Great Castle St, W1
T	020 7580 2125
Station	Oxford Circus
Open	Daily noon–3pm & 5.30–11pm
Accepts	All major credit cards

David Tharakan and continued to prosper – a good deal of wine was consumed and there was even a short menu of pub food favourites. The big changes came at the end of 1997, when David's wife Millie took over the kitchen and changed the menu. Shirref's started to offer Keralan home cooking, with well-judged, well-spiced dishes at bargain-basement prices. Since then The Kerala restaurant – which is what it has become – has gone from strength to strength.

To start with, you must order a platoon of simple things: cashew nut pakoda (£2.75), potato bonda (£2.50), lamb samosa (£2.75), chicken liver masala (£3.75), mussels ularthu (£3.75). These are honest dishes, simply presented and at a price which encourages experimentation. Thereafter the menu is divided into a number of sections: Syrian Christian specialities from Kerala; coastal seafood dishes; Malabar biryanis; vegetable curries; and special dosas. From the first, try erachi olathiathu (£4.95), a splendid dry curry of lamb with coconut. From the second, try meen and mango vevichathu (£4.95), which is kingfish cooked with the sharpness of green mango. From the biryanis, how about chemmin biryani (£5.95) – prawns cooked with basmati rice? Avial (£3.25) is a mixed vegetable curry with yoghurt and coconut. The breads are fascinating – try the lacy and delicate appams (two for £2.60) made from steamed rice-flour.

This is a very friendly place, completely at odds with the hectic rush of nearby Oxford Street. The people who run The Kerala are intensely proud of their country and its cuisine, and will be happy to help you discover glorious new dishes. The Kerala would be good value in the suburbs, but being hidden behind Oxford Circus makes it a contender for bargain of the age.

Malabar Junction

The cuisine at Malabar Junction is that of Kerala – the home province of the proprietor – and it is served up from two entirely separate kitchens and brigades of chefs, vegetarian and non-vegetarian, kept completely separate to comply with religious requirements. But however busy it may be down in the kitchens, inside the restaurant all is calm. This is a top-quality Indian restaurant, fully licensed, with a spacious dining room with comfortable chairs and a conservatory roof. None of which elegance is hinted at by the rather unprepossessing frontage at the Tottenham Court Road end of Great Russell Street.

Cost	£14–£29
Address	107 Great Russell St, WC1
T	020 7580 5230
Station	Tottenham Court Road
Open	Daily noon–3pm & 6–11.30pm
Accepts	All major credit cards except Diners

Kerala is the spice centre of India, and all the Malabar dishes tend to be spicy and nutty – curry leaves, cinnamon, coconut, chilli and cashew nuts prevail. There is also a good deal of fish. To start with, try the spinach vadia (£3.50) – small chickpea doughnuts made with spinach and ginger, deep fried and served crunchy with two dipping sauces of yoghurt and tamarind. Or there's uppuma (£4), a kind of eastern polenta, which is semolina fried in ghee with onions, spices and cashew nuts. The special poori masala (£5) takes the form of two balloon-shaped puffed breads with a potato cake that's not a million miles from pricey bubble and squeak. For a main course, try some fish or seafood: the fish moilee (£7.50) runs the gamut of cinnamon, cloves, cardamom, green chillies, garlic, coconut and curry leaves, while the Cochin prawn curry (£9.50) is more tomatoey, and comes with huge prawns. Chicken Malabar (£8) applies much the same Keralan spice palate to chicken. From the array of vegetable dishes, try avial (£4.50), a combination of all sorts of vegetables with a host of woody and aromatic spices, or a plate of green bananas (£4.50), tangy and delicious.

You'll also find all the traditional Southern Indian vegetarian favourites listed on the menu here, including rava dosa (semolina pancake), uthappam (crisp lentil pancake) and iddly (rice and lentil cakes). This may well be the perfect restaurant for a mix of vegetarians and fish or meat eaters.

CENTRAL

MODERN EUROPEAN

Mash

Mash is certainly modern – and it will probably go on looking modern for the next twenty years. Like its antecedent in Manchester, London Mash combines a brewery with bar, deli and restaurant. The brewery stands at the back of the low and busy bar, while the deli, always busy, is open for breakfast and sells takeaway packed lunches. Occasionally a restaurant has an indefinable something which guar-antees it success, and London Mash has been full since the day it opened. If you like the buzz, and the crowds of other people who like the buzz, you will be happy here. There are moments when the food is very good, and it seldom slips much below OK. There is a wood-fired oven and a wood-fired grill. And lots and lots of wood-fired food.

Cost	£18–£38
Address	19–21 Great Portland St, W1
T	020 7637 5555
Station	Oxford Circus
Open	Mon–Fri noon–3pm & 6–11pm, Sat noon–4pm & 6–11pm
Accepts	All major credit cards

The reasonably priced starters range from the Mediterranean charcu-terie plate (£6.50/£11), through aromatic spiced prawns and glass noodle salad with ginger and mirin (£6.50), to warm garlic-roasted peppers, mizuna leaves, goat's cheese and crostini (£6). To follow, there are fish dishes, meat dishes, pasta and vegetarian options, pizzas from the wood-fired grill, and sides. Pizzas are of the new breed, with toppings such as confit duck, plum sauce, Mozzarella, cucumber and bok choi (£9.90), or roast courgette, spinach, artichoke cream, tomato and Idiazabel cheese (£9.50). Pastas are likewise, with such temptations as tortelloni of ricotta, Mozzarella and basil with tomato sauce (£9.50). And then there are the fish dishes: grilled marlin steak stir-fry with wonder beans and udon noo-dles, and a Thai basil and black bean sauce (£13.70); or whole roasted sea bass with sun-dried tomato mayonnaise (£15). Carnivores will appreciate pan-fried venison, Swiss chard, roast sweet potatoes and shallots (£14). If dishes such as these sing out to you, you'll be very happy here, as they are confidently cooked and well presented.

The four beers made on the premises are probably an acquired taste – though anyone drinking enough of the fruit beer to acquire a taste for it deserves some sort of commendation for fortitude. There's a decent wine list for people who don't get along with the beer. Beer anoraks, how-ever, can book in for a tour of the microbrewery – a tutored tasting and three-course meal costs £30.

Passione

You may not have heard of Gennaro Contaldo, but you will certainly have heard of his protégé, Jamie Oliver, aka the Naked Chef, whose scooter-driving, drum-bashing antics keep a swath of middle England foodies firmly glued to their television screens when they could be out having a nice

Cost	£24–£50
Address	10 Charlotte St, W1
T	020 7636 2833
Station	Goodge Street
Open	Mon–Fri 12.30–2.30pm & 7–10.30pm, Sat 7–10.30pm
Accepts	All major credit cards

dinner. Many of Oliver's "revolutionary" methods stem from the time he spent working as a commis in a brigade headed by Contaldo. That was in the days before Contaldo achieved his ambition and opened his own place, Passione. This is a good restaurant. Simplicity, an unpretentious feel to the place, seasonal ingredients and a great deal of care and ability in the kitchen: these are sure bets when it comes to eating. Be sure not to miss the splendid breads, including Contaldo's fabled focaccio – the bread which the Naked One is always banging on about.

You owe it to yourself to have four courses here, and the portions are geared towards being able to manage such a splurge – how nice it is to have four delicious platefuls and not feel overstuffed. The menu changes daily, and there is a constant procession of specials. Among the antipasti, zuppa maritata (£6.50) is a soup of cannellini beans, broad beans and peas; while caponata con le uova di quaglie (£7.50) is a dish combining slow-cooked aubergine with quail's eggs. Then there are pastas and risotti – tagliatelle con tartufo (£9/£11) is suffused with the heady scent of truffles, while risotto all'accetosella (£9/£11) has the tasty tang of wild sorrel. Mains are rich and satisfying: coniglio con rosmarino e patate saltate (£15.50) is a simple dish of rabbit with rosemary served with sauté potatoes. Or maybe pesce san pietro con filetti di pomodoro e olivio taggiasca (£17) tempts? It's another simple dish – John Dory with tomatoes and olives. The service is slick here; this is a place where they understand the art of running a great restaurant.

Puddings (all £5.50) are serious stuff, though it has to be said that the delicious gelato Passione, a swirl of zesty limoncello ice with a splash of wild strawberry folded into it, is for all the world a grown-up's raspberry ripple.

Bloomsbury & Fitzrovia

Rasa Samudra

Rasa Samudra is the latest in a long line of restaurants to occupy this site. After many years as a smart English fish restaurant, it became a haute cuisine establishment where the cooking was good enough to win a Michelin star. Now it represents the "smart fishy" sector in Das Sreedharan's burgeoning restaurant portfolio (see Rasa, p.296;

Cost	£18–£40

Address 5 Charlotte St, W1
T 020 7637 0222
Station Goodge Street
Open Mon–Sat noon–3pm & 6–11pm
Accepts All major credit cards
W www.rasarestaurants.com

Rasa W1, p.83; and the latest, Rasa Travancore, p.297). The food served at Rasa Samudra is sophisticated fish cookery, the kind of stuff that would be more at home in Bombay than in London, consisting as it does of classy South Indian fish dishes – a million miles from curry-house staples.

At first glance the menu may seem heart-stoppingly expensive, partly due to a strange and exclusively British prejudice that no curry should ever cost more than a fiver, even if made from the kind of top-quality ingredients that are worth £15 in a French restaurant. Note, however, that all the more expensive choices – which are often based on fish, usually the most pricey of ingredients – come complete with accompaniments. This makes them substantial enough to allow all but the greediest of diners to dispense with starters, except perhaps for the samudra rasam (£5.95), a stunning shellfish soup, or the array of pappadoms, papparvardi and achappam (£4). Plus wicked pickles (£2.50). And maybe the meen cutlets (£4.50), which are like fishcakes made with tuna and cassava. For main course, koonthal olathiathu (£9.95) – squid cooked with onion, curry leaves, ginger and fresh coconut – is well offset by pooris (£2.50) and spicy potatoes (£5.25) as side dishes. Other good choices include koyilandi konju masala (£12.95) – crab cooked dry with ginger; fish moily (£10.50) – a curry of king fish cooked in coconut milk; and arachu vecha aavoli (£10.95) – tilapia cooked with shallots, red chillies and tamarind, a dish which is well complemented by beetroot curry (£6.25) and a chapati. The cooking is well-judged and the spices well-balanced.

If you are still nervous of the bill, don't be – the food is worth it. Serious gastronauts should opt for the Kerala feast (seafood £30; vegetarian £22.50). This takes the worry out of ordering.

Villandry Foodstore

As both foodstore and restaurant serving breakfast, elevenses, lunch, tea and dinner, Villandry began in more fashionable but cramped surroundings in Marylebone High Street. Its success brought the need for larger premises and, thus installed in Great Portland Street, a handsome foodstore gives onto a modern and rather stark dining room.

Cost	£22–£55
Address	170 Great Portland St, W1
T	020 7631 3131
Station	Great Portland Street
Open	Daily 8.30am–10.30pm
Accepts	Amex, MasterCard, Visa

MODERN BRITISH

Passing displays of some of Europe's most extravagant ingredients may jangle the nerves and alarm the wallet, but if you're serious about your food, and you have time to wait for careful preparation, Villandry won't disappoint.

The menu changes daily, so you won't necessarily find all – or indeed any – of the dishes mentioned here. But as you'd expect at the back of a foodstore that caters for the well-heeled sector of the foodie faithful, ingredients are scrupulously chosen and prepared with care. At its best, this kind of "informal" menu is surprisingly demanding on the cook – and exact cooking is crucial to ostensibly simple dishes. To start, you may be offered a leek and potato soup with truffle oil (£5.25); ricotta with Piedmontese peppers and rocket (£7.50); grilled langoustines with aioli (£8.50); seared scallops with salsify and globe artichokes (£8.50); or a small dish of bang bang chicken (£7.25). Main courses are often hugely impressive: slow-cooked shoulder of lamb with roasted root vegetables (£15.25); fillet of brill with watercress, new potato, shallots and beurre blanc (£15.25); roast loin of organic pork with Puy lentils, pancetta, mustard and roast carrots (£14.50); fish stew of monkfish, sea bass and John Dory, with fennel and chickpeas (£15). Desserts include moist chocolate cake (£5.50) and, as you'd expect from the array in the shop, there's an extensive if expensive cheeseboard (£10.50), served with terrific walnut and sourdough breads.

Wine prices, like the food, are distinctly West End, though there are reasonably priced house selections. Overall, standards are high, and the balancing both of flavours and of the menu itself suggests that the kitchen brigade knows what it's doing and isn't afraid to buck the trends. Lunch prices are a tad easier on the wallet.

Wagamama

Wagamama has been trendy – and packed – since the day it opened, and its popularity shows no signs of falling off. Which is fair enough, because this is as good a canteen as you'll find, serving simple and generally rather good Japanese food at very reasonable prices. What it's not is a place for a relaxed or intimate meal. The basement interior is cavernous and minimalist, and diners are seated side by side on long benches. At regular eating times you'll find yourself in a queue lining the stairway – there are no reservations. When you reach the front, you're seated, your order is punched into a hand-held computer, then the code numbers for your dishes are written on the low-tech placemat in front of you – a legacy of the day when the radio-ordering system failed. There's beer and wine available, as well as free green tea.

Cost	£6–£15

Address 4 Streatham St, WC1
T 020 7323 9223
Station Tottenham Court Road
Open Mon–Sat noon–11pm, Sun 12.30–10pm
Accepts All major credit cards
W www.wagamama.com

Dishes arrive when they're cooked, so a party of four will be served at different times. This system doesn't favour sharing – what you order is yours. Generally that means ordering a main dish – noodles in soup, fried noodles or sauce-based noodles – or a rice dish. Plus a side dish, which can also be pressed into service as a sort of starter. The mains include a splendid chilli beef ramen (£7.50) – slivers of sirloin steak in a vat of soup with vegetables and noodles (it's good etiquette to slurp these). Also good is the yasai katsu curry (£5.55) – boiled rice with a light curry sauce and discs of deep-fried vegetables; and ebi katsu (£5.05) – very tasty deep-fried king prawns with chilli and garlic sauce. A couple of interesting sides are gyoza (£3.70) – chicken dumplings, fried and delicious; and the rich, pan-fried noodles known as yaki soba (£4.90). If this all sounds confusing, that's because it is. To enjoy Wagamama you'll need to go with the flow.

It's not often that a restaurant offers a glossary that includes its own name. Wagamama is described as "Willfulness or selfishness: selfishness in terms of looking after oneself, looking after oneself in terms of positive eating and positive living". It seems to work here and at the numerous other branches scattered around town.

Chinatown

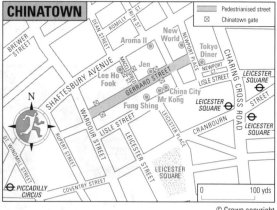

© Crown copyright

Aroma II

Ken and Kitty Lee, the people behind Aroma II, have an unusually long track record on the Chinese restaurant scene. Previously at Aroma I, and before that at Harbour City, they now run this bright, modern restaurant, a comfortable place if somewhat fussy in decor. The menu is exhaustive, sweeping from trad dishes to some rather interesting and authentic Mandarin treats that hail from Peking. But, not to be left out, there are also Cantonese specialities, barbecued meats, and traditional hand-pulled noodles that are well worth investigation. Now there's the excellent Aroma III as well, at 39 Gerrard St, W1 (℡020 7439 0534).

Cost	£8–£55
Address	118 Shaftesbury Ave, W1
T	020 7437 0370
Station	Leicester Square/ Piccadilly Circus
Open	Daily noon–11.30pm
Accepts	All major credit cards
W	www.aromares.co.uk

CHINESE

The breadth of the menu at Aroma II means that it is targeted directly at you whatever kind of meal you are after. For a bargain lunch you can't do better than the noodles: stir-fried hand-pulled noodle with seafood or king prawn (both £7), Singapore fried rice noodle (£4.20), or braised soft egg noodle with chives and ham (£7.50). For a no-holds-barred banquet, there is braised shark fin superior (£68), braised abalone with oyster sauce (£28), or even braised sea slug and spring onions with shrimp roe (£14.80). Perhaps the best strategy is to make up an order that combines the cheapest and the most expensive, and includes dishes you know and love along with more adventurous options. So have the sautéed king prawn, scallop and squid in light wine sauce (£9), and the roast crispy chicken with red beancurd flavour sauce (£11 half), but save room for the deep-fried marinated pork chitterling (£8), a dish of crispy tubes whose pungent flavours wouldn't be out of place in rural France. Or you could team prawns Kung Po (£9) with bang bang chicken (£5.50), and play deep-fried eel fillet with spicy salt and pepper (£9) as your adventure.

This is one of the more accessible of London's finer Chinese restaurants and staff are happy to give advice. Or go for one of the well-judged set menus: the seafood option (£22 per person, minimum two people) brings fish slice and crabmeat soup, sautéed lobster with hand-pulled noodles, stir-fried king prawn and scallops, fish in garlic sauce, Kung Po squid, braised mushrooms and rice.

Chinatown

China City

White Bear Yard lies off Lisle Street to the north. There's a large gate and an archway; go through the arch, cross the courtyard, and you'll come to a large, glass-fronted Chinese restaurant which seats five hundred diners on three floors. Go early. You will see the restaurant change from cavernously empty to bustling and packed. The service is "Chinatown-brusque", but a combination of good flavours, large portions and sensible pricing keeps the clientele coming back for more. The menu stipulates a "minimum charge of £10 per person", but don't be put off – this is not an expensive restaurant and you will have to go some to spend a lot more.

Cost	£10–£25
Address	White Bear Yard, WC2
T	020 7734 3388
Station	Leicester Square
Open	Mon–Sat noon–midnight
Accepts	All major credit cards

Both home-style dishes and less familiar exotic dishes are good here. This is a place in which to spread your wings and try something new. Naturally, the menu includes sweet and sour pork, platters of mixed appetizers and crispy duck with attendant pancakes, but why not start instead by trying the mixed seafood with fish straw soup (£3.50)? It's rather like that old workhorse, "crab meat and sweet corn soup", but altogether more delicate. Whatever fish straw may be – and you cannot tell from the evidence in the bowl – it is certainly delicious. Then sample some chicken: steamed with ginger and spring onion sauce (£8.50), it produces astonishingly rich flavours and satisfying chunks of meat. Alternatively, look in the section on hot-pot dishes: mixed seafood with bean curd in hot pot (£7) is a casserole containing fresh scallops, huge prawns, crisp mangetout and bean curd, all in a terrific sauce. The simpler dishes are good too: try fried ho fun with beef, dry (£4.50) – wide noodles with tender beef and a rich brown sauce – very comforting. And just to see something green on the table and so appease your conscience, order choi sum in oyster sauce (£4.50).

"Seasonal price" is a caption to strike fear into the heart of even the most experienced diner. At China City you'll find them alongside all the lobster dishes. These include deep-fried lobster with garlic and chilli, and baked lobster with cheese and garlic. Ask the price, you'll get a straightforward answer – and it may just prove surprisingly accessible.

Fung Shing

Fung Shing was one of the first restaurants in Chinatown to take cooking seriously. Twenty or so years ago, when it was still a dowdy little place with a mural on the back wall, the kitchens were run by the man acknowledged to be Chinatown's number one fish cook, chef Wu. When he died, in 1996, his sous-chef took over. The restaurant itself has changed beyond recognition and now stretches all the way from Lisle Street to Gerrard Street, ever bigger and ever brassier. Even if there has been a slight decline in overall standards here, the menu is littered with interesting dishes, the fish is still very fine and portions are large. Unfortunately, prices are creeping ever upwards, and you need to pick carefully to ensure good value.

Cost	£18–£55
Address	15 Lisle St, WC2
T	020 7437 1539
Station	Leicester Square
Open	Daily noon–11.30pm
Accepts	All major credit cards
W	www.fungshing.com

By Chinese restaurant standards, the menu is not huge, topping out at around 160 dishes, but the food has that earthy, robust quality which you only encounter when the chef is absolutely confident of his flavours and textures, whatever the cuisine. To start, ignore the crispy duck with pancakes (half for £11.50) – good but too predictable – and the lobster with noodles (£20 a pound, with noodles £2 extra) – too expensive. Turn instead to the steamed scallops with garlic and soya sauce (£2.60 each) – nowhere does them better. Or the spare ribs with chilli and garlic (£8) or barbecued (£8). The prosaically named mixed meat with lettuce (£8.50), is also good – a wonderfully savoury dish of mince with lettuce-leaf wraps. You could also happily order mains solely from the chef's specials: stewed belly pork with yam in hot pot (£9.50); crispy spicy eel (£10.95); cold spice- and herb-boiled chicken with jellyfish (half £14) – suspend your doubts, for it's amazingly delicious. The other dishes are good too – the perfect Singapore noodle (£6), crispy stuffed baby squids with chilli and garlic (£8.95), braised aubergine with black bean sauce (£7).

The Fung Shing has always been a class act, but what is unusual, certainly in Chinatown, is the gracious and patient service. This is a place where you can ask questions and take advice with confidence.

Jen

Jen burst onto the scene in 1998. The restaurant is bright and light, and in the spring of 2001 it underwent its first refurb. The menu proclaims that the restaurant's objective is to serve "the best Hong Kong style food available" and, for once, this is no idle boast. Only navigate your way past the pages of rather dull set menus and you'll find yourself among some interesting dishes. What's more, the service is friendly, the cooking is adept and the prices are accessible. This is a very good place to broaden your knowledge of Chinese cuisine, and to try those dishes that have made you curious.

Cost	£15–£50

Address 7 Gerrard St, W1
T 020 7287 8193
Station Leicester Square
Open Mon–Sat noon–3am,
Sun noon–10.30pm
Accepts All major credit cards

Start with deep-fried squid in hot and spicy salt (£6) – perfectly cooked squid coated in a mixture redolent of chilli. Or treat yourself to a whole crispy soft-shell crab in the same sauce (£4.50 each) – delicious. You eat the whole thing – just bite some off and chomp it up. Or perhaps this will be the place you first try pepper-flavoured ducks' wings and tongues (£3) – if ducks' tongues were bigger and less fiddly to eat then they would be a candidate for dish of the century. Take a look at the fish and seafood listings – sautéed fillet of eel with spicy yellow bean sauce (£9) is a thoroughly successful combination of flavours. Fresh fish is prepared in a variety of ways: steamed fresh Dover sole with ginger and spring onion (£15); steamed eel in black bean sauce (£9); deep-fried crispy red snapper fillet with sweet corn (£8). Or maybe the fragrant yam duck (£8) appeals? Or steamed minced pork with salted fish (£7)? Or the house speciality – which really is special – crispy roasted chicken with soya sauce (whole £14, half £8)? Or double-cooked Szechuan pork (£5.50)? Or perhaps some veg? Sautéed asparagus (£7) is served wonderfully crunchy, while pan-fried eggplant is stuffed with minced shrimp in black bean sauce (£6).

You may not feel quite ready for shredded pig's stomach in spicy sauce, served cold (£3), or stewed frog's leg with bitter melon in black bean flavour (£7). But make yourself a promise that when you come to Jen you will order one dish that is an outlandish experiment, something you have never had before, or even dreamed of. You may be surprised how much you enjoy it.

Lee Ho Fook

Encouraged by the glowing reports in the guidebooks, lots of tourists set out to eat at Lee Ho Fook on Macclesfield Street but never actually manage to find it. This is a genuine Chinese barbecue house – small, spartan and cheap, with the food good of its kind. But the restaurant is not so helpful

Cost	£5–£12
Address	4 Macclesfield St, W1
T	020 7734 0782
Station	Leicester Square
Open	Daily 11.30am–11pm
Accepts	Cash only

as to have a sign in English. Thus many potential non-Chinese diners find themselves at the larger, grander, more tourist-friendly Lee Ho Fook around the corner on Gerrard Street. These, then, are the directions: Macclesfield Street runs from Shaftesbury Avenue in the north to Gerrard Street in the south; on the west side is a backstreet called Dansey Place and, on the corner, with a red and gold sign in Chinese characters and a host of ducks hanging on a rack, is Lee Ho Fook. Inside there's a chef chopping things at a block in the window and four or five waiters. Sit down and you get tea, chopsticks and a big bottle of chilli sauce placed in front of you. Tables are shared and eating is a brisk, no-nonsense business.

The main focus of the short menu is an array of plated meals – a mound of rice with a splash of soy sauce "gravy" and a portion of chopped barbecued meat balanced on top. Choose from lean pork loin, crisp, fatty belly pork, soya chicken or duck (all £4.10), or suckling pig (£6.50). You can also mix and match – half pork, half duck, say – or order a "combination" of mixed roast pork, soya chicken and duck with rice (£5.60). Some choose to order the meats without rice – perhaps a whole duck (£18) or a portion of suckling pig (£7). There's also a thriving takeaway trade.

Because of the specialized nature of this place, the other menu items are all too easily overlooked. Try adding a plate of crisp vegetables in oyster sauce (£3.80) to your order. And, before the main event, perhaps choose a bowl of won ton soup (£2.20) or the even more substantial won ton noodle soup (£2.80). The extension into the shop next door has doubled the number of seats but, aside from that, this establishment continues to do a simple thing very well, which is not as easy a trick to pull off as it sounds.

CHINESE

Chinatown

Mr Kong

You have to wonder whether the eponymous Mr Kong flirted with the idea of calling his restaurant King Kong. Despite its marathon opening hours, at all regular mealtimes it's full of satisfied customers who would support such an accolade. Going with a party of

Cost	£7–£20
Address	21 Lisle St, WC2
T	020 7437 7923
Station	Leicester Square
Open	Daily noon–3am
Accepts	All major credit cards

six or more is the best plan when dining at Mr Kong, as that way you can order, taste and argue over a raft of dishes. You can share, and if there's something you really don't like, you can exile it to the other end of the table. If there's something wonderful, you can call up a second portion. It's a canny strategy which means that you can never be caught out.

There are three menus here: the main menu, with 160 or so dishes; the "Chef's Specials", with seventy more; and the "Today's Chef's Specials", with another ten. The main menu is rather safety-first, but sliced pork, salted egg and vegetable soup (minimum two people; £2.10 each), something of a house speciality, is worth a try. It's very good and rich, and the salted egg tastes pleasantly cheesy. Then try deep-fried crispy Mongolian lamb (£6.50), from "Today's", which is a very crisp breast of lamb with a lettuce-leaf wrap – avoid the accompanying hoi sin sauce, which is very sickly. Also from "Today's", there is braised shin of beef with fresh lotus root in hot pot (£6.50). Then turn to the "Chef's Specials" for sautéed dragon whistlers with dried scallops (£11), made with fresh pea shoots. Back to the main menu for a good, spicy Singapore noodle (£4.20); Kon Chin king prawn (£7.50) – an interesting prawn dish in a spicy tomatoey sauce; and Chinese broccoli in oyster sauce (£4.60) – dark green, crunchy and delicious. On the "Chef's Specials" you'll find steamed fresh razor clam with garlic at "seasonal price" – when available that's about £2.50 each. They're tender, well flavoured and worth every penny. Order a couple per person by way of an extravagance.

Portions are generous and, even when dishes contain exotic ingredients, prices are reasonable. Just ignore the decor, which falls somewhere between ordinary and grubby.

New World

When the 1990s saw the arrival of the mega-restaurants, giant two- and three-hundred-seater emporiums, the proprietors of this long-established Chinese restaurant were right to feel aggrieved and ask what all the fuss was about. The New World seats between

Cost	£6–£18
Address	1 Gerrard Place, W1
T	020 7734 0396
Station	Leicester Square
Open	Daily 11am–midnight
Accepts	All major credit cards

four and six hundred people depending on how many functions are going on at any one time. This is probably the largest single restaurant in Europe and it can comfortably swallow up a couple of huge Chinese wedding parties as well as getting on with the daily business of feeding thousands of people. When you arrive you invariably have to wait in a sort of holding pen just inside the door until the intercom screeches with static and you are sent off to your table. The menu, leather-bound and nearly twenty pages long, features everything you have ever heard of and quite a lot you haven't. In any case, you don't need it – go for the dim sum, which are served every day from 11am until 6pm.

The dim sum come round on trolleys. First catch the eye of a waiter or waitress with a bow tie, to order drinks, and then you're at the mercy of the trolley pushers. Broadly speaking, the trolleys are themed: one has a lot of barbecued meat; another is packed with ho fun – broad noodles; another with steamed dumplings; another with soups; another with cheung fun – the long slippery rolls of pastry with different meats inside; and so on. A good mix would be to take siu mai (£1.70) and har kau (£1.70) from the "steamers" trolley. Then char sui cheung fun (£2.80) – a long roll with pork. Then some deep-fried won ton (£1.50) – little crispy parcels with sweet sauce. Or perhaps try something exotic like woo kwok (£1.70) – deep-fried taro dumplings stuffed with pork and yam. And something filling like char sui pow (£1.70) – steamed dough-nuts filled with pork; or nor mai gai (£2.80) – a lotus-leaf parcel of glutinous rice and meats.

If you arrive after 6pm, you're on your own: there are literally hundreds of dishes on the main menus. However, Chinese functions apart, New World is really best as an in-and-out dim sum joint. It's about eating and not, as the sticky carpet immediately declares, design and fripperies.

Chinatown

Tokyo Diner

Tokyo Diner offers conclusive proof that you needn't take out a second mortgage to enjoy Japanese food in London. Stacked up on three floors of a block that clings to Chinatown's silk skirts, this is a friendly eatery that shuns elaboration in favour of fast food, Tokyo-style. The place was actually set up by a

Cost	£8–£25

Address 2 Newport Place, WC2
T 020 7287 8777
Station Leicester Square
Open Daily noon–midnight
Accepts All major credit cards

Nipponophile Englishman, but the kitchen staff are all Japanese and its Far Eastern credentials bear scrutiny. The decor, crisp and minimalist, leaves the food to do the talking, which it does fluently – if the number of Japanese who walk through the doors are any indication. If you don't know your teppan-yaki from your kamikaze, or your sushi from your sumo, you'll be glad of the explanatory notes on the menu. When your food arrives, pick a set of chopsticks, snap them apart – the menu recommends that you rub them together to rid them of splinters – and get stuck in.

Top seller is the soba noodle soup (£6.10), thin brown buckwheat noodles in a soya broth. It's pleasant, filling and very popular with the drop-by lunchtime trade. Don't be afraid of slurping it – as the menu explains, slurping is OK. Or try the set lunch in a bento box: rice, noodles, sashimi and your choice of teriyaki, all for around £12. The bento will dispel once and for all the misconception that Japanese food is just for picking at, though watch out for the little green mound of wasabi which will blow your head off if you're not careful – it should be mixed in a saucer with soy sauce, and used to dunk a morsel into. Other bento favourites include the ton katsu bento (£11.50), which is a kind of superior breadcrumbed pork escalope. If you don't have appetite enough for a full-on bento box, skip the curries – as the menu admits, they're a bit like school food – and head straight for the sushi and sashimi. They too come in "sets": try the nine-piece nigiri set (£14), which is very good value, or the hosi-maki set (£4.90), which comprises six pieces of salmon, three pieces of cucumber and three pieces of pickled radish.

To wash it all down, the Japanese beer Asahi (£1.99) is good, or there's complimentary Japanese tea. For a special treat, try the rich, sweet plum wine (£2.99 for 125ml), which is surprisingly moreish and quite delicious.

Covent Garden & Holborn

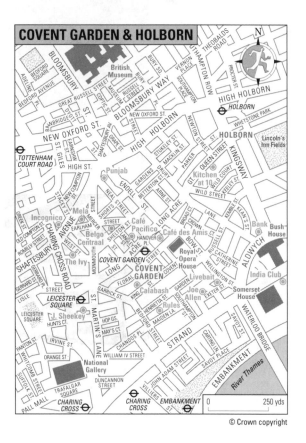

COVENT GARDEN & HOLBORN

© Crown copyright

Bank

A good many foodists believe that this restaurant is the closest London gets to re-creating the all-day buzz and unfussy cuisine of the big Parisian brasseries. Bank opens for breakfast (Continental, Full English, or Caviar), lays on brunch at the weekend, does a good-value pre-theatre (5.30–7pm) and lunch prix fixe (both are £15.50 for two courses, £17.90 for three), and has a bustling bar ... and then there's the other matter of lunch and dinner for

Cost	£20–£60

Address 1 Kingsway, corner of Aldwych, WC2
T 020 7379 9797
Station Holborn
Open Mon–Fri 7–11.30am, noon–3pm & 5.30–11.30pm, Sat & Sun 11.30am–3.30pm & 5.30–11.30pm (Sun 10pm)
Accepts All major credit cards
W www.bankrestaurants.com

several hundred. Whatever the time of day, the food is impressive, especially considering the large numbers of people fed, and if you like things lively you will have a great time. If you're leaving after 10pm, incidentally, and want a taxi, go for the cabs arranged by the doorman; black cabs are rare as hen's teeth around here after the Drury Lane theatres empty.

The menu changes seasonally, so dishes may come and go. Start with something simple – simple to get wrong, that is – a Caesar salad (£6.50), say, or a smoked haddock and ricotta tart (£6.50); or push the boat out with a well-made terrine of foie gras and plum chutney (£11). Or go for shellfish. A key role in Bank's history was played by one of London's leading catering fishmongers, so crustacea such as cold lobster in shell (half £15.50, whole £29) or dressed crab with ginger and wasabi dressing (£12.50) should be reliable. The fish dishes are equally good, from the ambitious – roast red mullet, tapenade and Provençale vegetables (£16.50) – to the traditional – Bank fish and chips, featuring halibut, mushy peas and tartare sauce (£18.50). Meat dishes are well-prepared brasserie fare such as grilled calves' liver, bacon, sage and onion mash (£16.50), and glazed belly of French pork with Chinese cabbage (£12.50). Puds include a trio of crème brûlées (£5.40); a chocolate tart with vanilla ice cream (£5.50) and a self indulgent pear and Amaretto gratin (£5.50).

Breakfast specialists may find themselves turning to the "Caviar" breakfast. You have to suspect that 7.30am is only the right time to be spending £87 on 50g of Oscietra with a potato waffle and crème fraîche if you haven't been to bed. Which surely would make it late supper?

CENTRAL

BELGIAN

Belgo Centraal

The Belgians invented mussels, frites and mayonnaise – and Belgo has done all it can to help the Belgian national dish take over London. The Belgo group's flagship restaurant is a massive metal-minimalist cavern accessed by riding down in a scissor-powered lift. Turn left at the bottom and you enter the restaurant (where you can book seats); turn right and you get seated in the beerhall, where diners share tables. With 95 different beers, some at alcoholic strengths of 8–9%, it's difficult not to be sociable.

Cost	£5–£30
Address	50 Earlham St, WC2
T	020 7813 2233
Station	Covent Garden
Open	Mon–Thurs noon–11.30pm, Fri & Sat noon–midnight, Sun noon–10.30pm Restaurant closed but beerhall open 3–5.30pm
Accepts	All major credit cards
W	www.belgorestaurants.com

Belgo offers the best mussels in town and no mistake. A kilo of classic moules marinières served with frites and mayonnaise (£10.95) has fresh mussels that have clearly been cooked then and there. Other varieties on offer include classiques – with cream and garlic; moutarde – with grain mustard; and Provençal – with tomato, herbs and garlic (all £11.95). And there are many alternatives for the non-mussel eater. Try carbonnade Flamande (£9.95) – beef braised in Geuze beer with apples and plums and served with frites; or escalope de thon grillé à la Liègoise (£10.95) – marinated tuna steak with new potatoes and haricots verts. There are also two different asparagus dishes (both £6.95), and sausages made with Chimay beer (£8.95). Desserts, as you might expect, are strong on Belgian chocolate. They include, among many others, crème brûlée aux fraises (£3.95), and traditional Belgian waffles with ice cream, cream and chocolate sauce (£4.75). Belgo delights in special offers, too. There's a £5 lunch – boar sausages with Belgian mash and a beer, or half a kilo of mussels and salad. The Belgo Complet (£15.50), always available, comprises a mini salade Liègoise followed by a kilo of moules served with frites, and a choice of Brugs tarwebier of Maes pils, soft drink or ice cream.

Belgo offers value, atmosphere and very sound food. But it's the awesome beer list that makes it a must-visit. There are other branches at Belgo Noord, 72 Chalk Farm Rd, NW1 (☎020 7267 0718), and Belgo Zuid, 124 Ladbroke Grove, W10 (☎020 8982 8400).

Café des Amis

This is the latest incarnation of an old-established restaurant just around the corner from the newly resurrected Opera House. Where once it was Gallic shabby, all is bleached, blond wood. All is modern, all is clean and bright. The resuscitated menu sits uneasily with its French section headings – "Les plats", "Specialités des amis" – as it darts from influence to influence: Thai red fish cakes meet venison carpaccio and potato gnocchi. The venerable clientele, many of whom used to have half a meal before the opera, and a dessert in the interval, are in shock. However, from a food point of view, there's only good to report. In the hands of a predominantly French team, the bistro menu has been shaken into the new millennium. Service is efficient and friendly, while the set menus, served all day, are a real bargain – two courses £12.50, three courses £15.

Cost	£12–£35
Address	11–14 Hanover Place, off Long Acre, WC2
T	020 7379 3444
Station	Covent Garden
Open	Mon–Sat 11.30am–11.30pm
Accepts	All major credit cards
W	www.cafedesamis.co.uk

MODERN EUROPEAN

The menu changes regularly, but you might start with a dish like venison carpaccio with pickled girolles and wild rocket (£8.50). Or there's Bayonne ham with roasted figs and lemon oil (£7.50). Between starters and mains you'll find dishes that can be served as either – Caesar salad (£5.50/£8.50); grilled artichoke risotto with smoked Mozzarella and oven-dried tomatoes (£6.95/£9.95); or papardelle with cep cream and a sauté of wild mushrooms (£7.50/£11.50). The "main" kind of main courses run the gamut from braised shank of lamb with "haricots blanc", garlic and thyme jus (£14.25); through seared loin of tuna, glazed bok choi and fermented black bean dressing (£14.95); to Scotch rib-eye steak with fries, onion rings, grilled tomatoes, tarragon and shallot butter (£16.95). The set menu (three courses £15) features starters such as squid bisque with croutons and rouille; mains such as fillet of plaice with cumin crust, mint tabouleh, oregano and fresh basil; and desserts such as chocolate truffle cake with sauce Anglaise. The cooking is well judged, the presentation on the plate is good, and the prices are reasonable.

The wine-bar under the restaurant is as dark and cavernous as the restaurant above is light and bright. And so it should be!

CENTRAL

TEX-MEX

Café Pacifico

The salsa is hot at Café Pacifico – both types. As you are seated, a complimentary bowl of searing salsa dip with corn chips is put on your table. As you eat, hot salsa music gets your fingers tapping. The atmosphere is relaxed and you're soon in the mood for a cold Tecate (£2.90) or Negro Modelo (£2.90) beer. There are nine Mexican beers, a good selection of wines and dozens of cocktails. Parties can enjoy a pitcher of Margaritas to serve eight people for £27.95. But Pacifico's tequila list is the highlight. There are more than sixty varieties, ranging from £2.60 to £100 a shot, and including some very old and rare brands.

Cost	£15–£30
Address	5 Langley St, WC2
T	020 7379 7728
Station	Covent Garden
Open	Mon–Sat noon–midnight, Sun noon–11pm
Accepts	All major credit cards except Diners
W	www.cafepacifico-laperla.co.uk

The menu is a lively mixture of old-style Californian Mexican and new Mexican, so, while favourites like fajitas, flautas and tacos dominate, there are also some interesting and unusual dishes. Portions are generous and spicy, and many main courses come with refried beans and rice. Refried beans at Café Pacifico are smooth and comforting, and just the thing to balance the spicy heat. Try nachos rancheros (£7.95, £6.75 vegetarian) for starters and enjoy a huge plate of corn chips with beans, cheese, guacamole, onions, sour cream and olives. Excellent for sharing. Taquitos (£4.50) – filled fried baby tacos – are very tasty, too, as are smoked chicken quesadillas (£5.50) – flour tortillas with chicken, red peppers and avocado salsa. Main courses include degustación del Pacifico (£9.75), which includes a taste of almost everything. The burrito especial (£9.15) gives you a flour tortilla filled with cheese and refried beans covered with ranchero sauce and a choice of roast beef, chicken or ground beef. Roast beef is slow-cooked and falling-apart tender. Look out for their modern Mexican dishes like fillet steak (£13.95) – these are available from 6pm.

Café Pacifico has been a place to party since 1978 and claims to be London's oldest Mexican restaurant. And, yes, they do have a bottle of mescal with a worm in it.

Calabash

🍴 The Calabash is a very cool place, in the old-fashioned, laid-back sense of the word. The restaurant, deep within the bowels of the Africa Centre, is at once worthy, comfortable and cheap. The same complex features a splendidly seedy bar, a live music hall, and African arts and crafts for sale. The food is genuine and somewhat unsophisticated, and the menu struggles bravely to give snapshots of the extraordinary diversity of African cuisine. They manage dishes from North, East and West Africa, as well as specialities from Nigeria, Ivory Coast, Senegal and Malawi. So if you're looking for a particular dish you may be out of luck. However, if you want a cheerful atmosphere, a small bill, and wholesome, often spicy and usually unfamiliar food, the Calabash is worth seeking out.

Cost	£10–£25
Address	The Africa Centre, 38 King St, WC2
T	020 7836 1976
Station	Covent Garden
Open	Mon–Fri noon–2.30pm & 6–10.30pm, Sat 6–10.30pm
Accepts	MasterCard, Visa

Starters include familiar dishes like avocado salad and hummus (both £2.20) along with interesting offerings such as aloco (£2.30), which is fried plantain in a hot tomato sauce, and sambusas (£2.95), a vegetarian cousin of the samosa. Those with an enquiring palate will pick the gizzards (£2.95), a splendid dish of chicken gizzards served in a rich, spiky pepper sauce. Grilled chicken wings (£2.60) are less exotic but very good nonetheless. Main courses are marked according to origin. From Nigeria comes egusi (£6.95), a rich soup/stew with spinach, meat and dried shrimps, thickened with melon seed. Yassa (£6.50) is grilled chicken from Senegal, while doro wot (£6.95) is a pungent chicken stew from East Africa, served with injera, the soft and thin sourdough bread. From Malawi there is nyamam yo phika (£7.75), a rich beef stew made with sweet peppers and potatoes and served with rice. Drink whichever of the African beers is in stock at the time you visit.

One of the best dishes, simply called "chicken" (£6.25), takes the form of superb fried chicken served with fried plantain, sweet potato chips, mixed salad and ferocious hot sauce. The chef who handles the frying is a master craftsman who manages to get the outside perfectly crisp and the inside perfectly tender. Order this to get an inkling of what the Colonel has been striving for all these years.

Incognico

On the rear of the menu is a picture of Michelin-bespangled chef Nico Ladenis (for he is the Nico in question), kitted out as Zorro. So there you have it, the name of this eatery is a play on words, and one so ponderous as to reveal its Gallic heritage – the French have never really grasped puns. Fortunately the French are pretty good at dishing up sensible food, and when you

Cost	£17–£70
Address	117 Shaftesbury Ave, WC2
T	020 7836 8866
Station	Covent Garden/ Tottenham Court Rd
Open	Mon–Sat noon–3pm & 5.30pm–midnight
Accepts	All major credit cards

are talking about classic French cooking they have few equals. The dining room is comfortable and done out in dark brown tones, the only cavil being that some of the tables are packed in a bit tightly, so that you could whisper in a loved one's ear and still share the billing and cooing with your neighbours. This restaurant won "best new restaurant" at the 2001 Moet & Chandon Restaurant Awards.

The cooking is very sound here. The menu is a long one and, while not actually being old-fashioned per se, there are enough old favourites to please the stickiest stick in the mud. Starters such as endive pear and Roquefort salad (£9.50), New Zealand mussels with garlic butter (£10.50), and terrine of foie gras with green peppercorns (£15) strike a chord. As do mains like ossobuco (£14.50), which is delightfully rich and served with a Parmesan risotto. And veal kidneys in mustard sauce (£12.50). Or wing of skate with capers (£13.50). Or grilled baby Dover sole with tartare sauce (£14.50). Puddings (all £5.50) carry on the theme successfully: rice pudding; crème caramel; apple tart. Be warned: your wallet may hate the wine list.

The set menu (available at lunch and 5.30–7pm) changes daily and is an outstandingly good deal. For £12.50 you get three courses and, joy of joys, there is an equally priced pichet of vin rouge (£7.50 for 50cl). There are two choices per course and the dishes are appealing. The choice may be between smoked salmon and horseradish cream, or ravioli of goat's cheese with red peppers and basil oil; followed by breast of guineafowl with lentils, or grilled sea bass with basil puree and red pepper oil; culminating in crème brûlée with soft Italian cheese and red fruit, or vanilla bavarois with blackcurrant coulis. This is a very good meal indeed.

India Club

When the India Club opened in 1950, the linoleum flooring was probably quite chic; today it has a faded period charm. Situated up two flights of stairs, sandwiched between floors of the grandly named Strand Continental Hotel (one of London's cheaper hotels), the Club is an institution, generally full, and mostly with regulars, as you can tell by the stares of appraisal given to newcomers. The regulars, in love with the strangely old-fashioned combination of runny curry and low, low prices, don't mind traipsing downstairs to the hotel reception to buy themselves a cold bottle of Cobra beer – they quite understand the inflexibility of English licensing arrangements. These stalwart customers can be split into two categories: suave Indians from the nearby High Commission, and a miscellany of folk from the BBC World Service, hanging on precariously to their old Central London base down the road in Bush House.

Cost	£6–£12
Address	143 Strand, WC2
T	020 7836 0650
Station	Charing Cross
Open	Mon–Sat noon–2.30pm & 6–10.50pm
Accepts	Cash or cheque only

INDIAN

The food at the India Club predates any London consciousness of the different spicings of Bengal, Kerala, Rajasthan or Goa. It is Anglo-Indian, essentially, and well cooked of its kind, although to palates accustomed to more modern Indian dishes it is something of a symphony to runny sauce. Mughlay chicken (£5.20) is a wing and a drumstick in a rich, brown, oniony gravy, garnished with two hard-boiled eggs; while scampi curry (£6) is runny and brown, with fearless prawns swimming through it. Masala dosai (£3.60) is a well-made crispy pancake with a pleasantly sharp-tasting potato filling. Dhal (£3.30) is yellow and... runny. The mango chutney (40p) is a revelation: thick parings of mango, each three inches long, are chewy and delicious. Breads – paratha (£1.60), puris (two for £1.80) – are good, while the rice is white and comes in clumps (£2).

You should heed the kindly warning of your waiter about the chilli bhajis (£2.60), a dish as simple as it is thought provoking. Long, thin, extra-hot green chillies are given a thick coating of gram-flour batter and then deep-fried until crisp. These are served with a coconut chutney that has a few more chopped chillies sprinkled through it. Eating this actually hurts. Console yourself by remembering that, however bad, chilli burn lasts only ten minutes.

The Ivy

The Ivy is a beautiful, Regency-style restaurant, built in 1928 by Mario Gallati, who later founded Le Caprice. It has been a theatreland and society favourite ever since – Noël Coward was a noted regular – and never more so than today. The staff, it is said, notice recessions only because they have to turn fewer people away. And that's no joke: The Ivy is booked solid for lunch and dinner right through the week. Its clientele include a lot of face-familiar actors and media folk, and to get a booking it helps to proffer a name of at least B-list celebrity. That said, there are tables to be had here if you book far enough ahead, try at very short notice or ask for a table in the bar area (nice enough, if your legs aren't over-long). It's also less busy for the weekend lunch – three courses for a bargain £16.50 plus £1.50 service charge, with valet parking thrown in.

Cost	£25–£60

Address 1 West St, WC2
T 020 7836 4751
Station Leicester Square
Open Daily noon–3pm (Sun 3.30pm) & 5.30pm–midnight
Accepts All major credit cards

And once you're in? Well, first off, whether you're famous or not, the staff are charming and unhurrying. Second, the food is pretty good. The menu is essentially a brasserie list of comfort food – nice dishes that combine simplicity with familiarity and which are invariably well cooked. You could spend a lot here without restraint; surprisingly little if you limit yourself to a single course and pudding. You might start with caramelized onion tart (£6.75); or the famous risotto nero (£8.50/£12.75), black with squid ink; or the eggs Benedict (£5.75/£10.75). Then there's kedgeree (£10.25); corned beef hash with double fried egg (£9.50); and well-made versions of classic staples: calves' liver and bacon (£16.75); the Ivy hamburger with dill pickle and club sauce (£9); shepherd's pie (£10.75); salmon fishcakes (£11.75). Even the vegetable section is enlivened with homely delights like bubble and squeak (£2.75) and medium-cut chips (£3). For dessert you might turn to Bakewell tart (£5.50) or Eton mess (£9.50), or perhaps finish with a savoury such as Scotch woodcock (£3.25).

The Ivy's present incarnation is the result of a 1990 makeover that meticulously restored the wood panelling and leaded stained glass. It also involved a roll call of British artists. Look around and you may notice works by, among others, Howard Hodgkin, Peter Blake, Tom Phillips and Patrick Caulfield.

J. Sheekey

Sheekey's is one of a handful of restaurants which had shambled along since the war – the First World War. Then, in the late 1990s, it was taken over by the team behind The Ivy and Le Caprice (see p.38 and p.98). After a good deal of redesign and refurbishment it emerged from the builders' clutches as J. Sheekey, with much the same attitudes and style as its senior siblings, but still focused on fish. The restaurant may be new, then, but it certainly seems old, and its series of interconnecting dining rooms gives it an intimate feel. The cooking is accomplished, the service is first-rate, and the fish is fresh – a good combination!

Cost	£17–£65

Address 28–32 St Martin's Court, WC2
T 020 7240 2565
Station Leicester Square
Open Mon–Sat noon–3pm & 5.30pm–midnight, Sun noon–3.30pm & 5.30pm–midnight
Accepts All major credit cards

The long menu presents a seductive blend of plain, old-fashioned, classic fish cuisine – lemon sole belle meunière (£16.25) – with more modernist dishes – yellow-fin tuna with arrocina beans (£16.50). There are always hand-written dishes on the menu, "specials" which change on a weekly basis. To start with, there are oysters, crabs and shellfish, plus everything from jellied eels (£4.75) and potted shrimps (£9.75) to seared rare tuna (£8.50) and char-grilled razor clams with chorizo and broad beans (£10.75). Main courses, like roasted scallops with tarragon mash and spring peas (£18.50), or pan-fried wing of skate with slow baked tomatoes and capers (£14.75), or Cornish fish stew with rouille (£19.75), are backed up by classics such as herb-crusted cod (£13.50) and Sheekey's fish pie (£9.75). Puddings go from spotted dick with butter and golden syrup (£5.25) to raspberry trifle (£5.75) and mirabelle jelly with Jersey cream (£6.75).

The set menus are good value. At the weekend, lunch costs just £10.75 for two courses, or £14.50 for three (plus a £1.50 cover charge in the main dining room). You could tuck into Italian black figs with Parma ham; then escalope of salmon with mixed courgettes and tomato vinaigrette; and finish with chocolate and Grand Marnier tart. In a further bid to make life at the weekend hassle-free, the restaurant operates a valet parking system on Sunday.

Joe Allen

By some inexplicable alchemy, Joe Allen continues to be the Covent Garden eatery of choice for a wide swath of the acting profession. It is a dark, resolutely untrendy place which dishes up American comfort food. So saying, you can never have anything better than exactly what you want and, if your heart is set on a Caesar salad, chilli con carne or eggs Benedict, this is a great place to come. Joe Allen also has a splendid attitude to mealtimes: the à la carte runs all day, so you can have lunch when you will, and there's a special menu offering two courses for £12 and three for £14 (noon–4pm), plus a pre-theatre menu (Mon–Sat 5–6.45pm) which delivers two courses for £13 and three for £15.

Cost	£16–£35
Address	13 Exeter St, WC2
T	020 7836 0651
Station	Covent Garden
Open	Mon–Fri noon–12.45am, Sat 11.30am–12.45am, Sun 11.30am–11.30pm
Accepts	All major credit cards except Diners

The food is the kind of stuff that we are all comfortable with. Starters include salmon and cod fishcake with grain mustard sauce (£5.50), chopped chicken liver (£5), and bang bang chicken (£6). They are followed on the menu by a section described as salads/eggs/sandwiches in which you'll find some of Joe Allen's strengths: Caesar salad (£4.50); roast chicken salad with penne, cherry tomatoes and pesto dressing (£8); and eggs Joe Allen (£8), a satisfying combination of poached eggs, potato skins, Hollandaise sauce and spinach. Main courses range from grilled swordfish with Niçoise salad and citrus dressing (£13); through barbecue spare ribs with rice, wilted spinach, black-eyed peas and corn muffin (£11); to pan-fried calves' liver with bubble and squeak and red onion marmalade (£12.50). The side orders are most attractive: mashed potatoes with gravy (£2.50), broccoli with toasted almonds (£2.50). And the desserts are serious – go for the brownie (£4.50), with hot fudge sauce as an extra (£1.50).

Joe Allen is also home to its very own urban legend. The hamburger is very highly rated by aficionados everywhere, but you have to be in the know to order one, as it has never been listed on the menu.

Livebait Restaurant & Bar

This large, bustling restaurant is an offshoot of the original Livebait, at 41 The Cut, SE1 (☎020 7928 7211), behind Waterloo station, and the group is now bent on world domination with branches all over London and in Birmingham, Leeds and so on. You'll find the same black-and-white tiling and rather cramped diner booths in each. Things have calmed down a bit since the early days, when the kitchen was all eccentricity, and some of the wilder combinations of ingredients have been tamed. The emphasis, however, remains on superb crustacea and fish so fresh you expect to see it flapping on the slab. The breads are still a feature and service is friendly. The hand of big business is apparent, but the Livebait ethos is so irrepressible that this remains one of the most succesful fish restaurants in town.

Cost	£20–£50

Address 21 Wellington St, WC2
T 020 7836 7161
Station Covent Garden
Open Mon–Sat noon–3pm & 5.30–11.30pm
Accepts All major credit cards
W www.sante-gcg.com

As an amuse-gueule you get a few fresh prawns to munch on, along with an amazing array of bread – anything from a sourdough bread to a yellow bread with tumeric. If you continue with seafood, you've any number of treats to choose from: vast, Saudi, white crevettes with mayonnaise (£2.65 each); whole Dorset brown crabs, cracked with mayonnaise (£7.75 each); winkles, cockles, clams, oysters – maybe it is best to go for it, and have the Livebait platter (£48.50), which includes Nova Scotian lobster. The cooked starters are often complex: they might include such combinations as Livebait fishcakes with tagine of vegetables, coriander, preserved lemons and harissa oil (£5.75); or roast octopus, chilli yam stew, smoked tomato sauce, thyme and garlic croutons (£6.95). If you were not hugely hungry, you'd do well to order one for starter and another for your main course. Which is not to knock the mains, which fall into two categories. Catch of the day features varying fresh fishes, either grilled or pan-roasted, and priced according to the market. The more adventurous main dishes include charred zander fillet with pumpkin and sweet-potato Colcannon, salsa verde and oven-dried tomatoes (£13.95); or monkfish Wellington with chilli and coriander, plus globe artichoke, asparagus and wild mushroom fricassée (£16.50).

Livebait's food is exciting and the wine list is carefully chosen. But the wide range of beers is a particular delight.

Mela

In the colourful brochure, Mela is described as "Indian cuisine – Country style". What they really mean is "Indian cuisine – Indian style". This is one of the new breed of Indian restaurants that doesn't follow the time-honoured tradition of Bangladeshi restaurants, with their familiar dishes carefully developed solely for the Brits. At Mela the attitude is more "If it's good enough for Delhi… ". The result is a restaurant serving very attractive and remarkably good-value Indian food. Mela may even have cracked the great lunch conundrum – Indian restaurateurs find it very difficult to persuade Londoners to eat curry for lunch. There's a "Paratha Pavilion" at lunchtime, which may sound a bit kitsch but lists a variety of delicious set lunches, from the insubstantial at £1.95, to the jolly good at £4.95. Stellar value in WC2.

Cost	£4–£35
Address	152–156 Shaftesbury Ave, WC2
T	020 7836 8635
Station	Covent Garden
Open	Mon–Sat noon–11.30pm, Sun noon–10.30pm
Accepts	All major credit cards
W	www.melarestaurant.co.uk

At lunch the set meals revolve around bread – parathas to be precise – much as in Delhi's famous Parathey Wali Gali, which is snackers' heaven. Choose bread made from maize, sorghum, millet, whole-wheat flour, or chilli- and coriander-flavoured chickpea flour. The latter is particularly good. They come with dal or curry of the day for £1.95! Or with a savoury stuffing at £2.95. There are other breads, too, such as roomalis (large and thin, wholemeal handkerchief bread), puris (fried chapatis), uttapams (rice flour pancakes) and naans. Dosas come in at £3.95. At these prices you can experiment. The main menu, which is available at lunch but comes into its own in the evening, is full of good things. Calamari paktooni (£3.95) is fiery chilli squid; and tandoor dishes like chukandar kalam ke kebab (£7.95) – a boned chicken leg marinated in beetroot and chillies – are very tasty indeed. There is also a good Allepey seafood curry (£9.95), and an exemplary rara gosht rojganjosh (£7.95).

The decor here is on the bright side, but this is a large and modern restaurant that disowns the flock wallpaper tradition and bustles along, happily dishing out good, fresh food to happy customers. It is also located in the West End, and open throughout the afternoon, which is something of a boon. Service is slick and friendly.

Punjab

In 1951, Gurbachan Singh Maan moved his fledgling Indian restaurant from the City to new premises in Neal Street in Covent Garden, his plan being to take advantage of the trade from the nearby Indian High Commission. It was a strategy that has worked handsomely. Today, his grandson Sital Singh Maan runs what is one of London's oldest curry houses, though one which

Cost   £15–£35

Address 80–82 Neal St, WC2
T 020 7836 9787
Station Covent Garden
Open Mon–Sat noon–3pm & 6–11.30pm, Sun noon–3pm & 6–10.30pm
Accepts All major credit cards
W www.punjab.co.uk

INDIAN

has always been at the forefront of new developments – in 1962 the Maan family brought over one of the first tandoor ovens to be seen in Britain, and in 1989 they added the then-exotic chicken jalfrezi to their repertoire. Despite these forays into fashion, the cuisine at the Punjab has always been firmly rooted where it belongs – in the Punjab. This is a Sikh restaurant, as you'll realize straightaway from the imposing, turbaned waiters.

Punjabi cuisine offers some interesting, non-standard Indian dishes, so start by ordering from among the less familiar items on the menu. Kadu and puri (£2.10), for instance, a sweet and sharp mash of curried pumpkin served on a puri; or aloo tikka (£2.10), which are described as potato cutlets but arrive as small deep-fried moons on a sea of tangy sauce. Or chicken chat (£2.60), which is diced chicken in rich sauce. To follow, try the acharri gosht (£7.50), or the acharri murgha (£7.80) – the first is made with lamb, and the second with chicken. The Maan family are very proud of the acharri; the meat is "pickled" in traditional Punjabi spices and, as a result, both meat and sauce have an agreeable edge of sharpness. Chicken karahi (£7.10) is good, too – rich and thick. The anari gosht (£7.50) combines lamb with pomegranate, while from the vegetable dishes, channa aloo (£4) offsets the nutty crunch of chickpeas with the solace of potatoes. For refreshment, turn to a satisfyingly large bottle of Cobra lager (£3.60), which originated in Bangalore but is now, rather more prosaically, "brewed in Bedford".

On the menu you'll also find benaam macchi tarkari (£7.50), a "nameless fish curry, speciality of chef". This curry may be nameless but it is certainly not flavourless, with solid lumps of boneless white fish in rich and tasty gravy.

Rules

The Americans have a word for it. When something is so clichéd that it starts to parody itself they rather unkindly refer to it as "schlock". Rules would be "schlock" but for one essential saving grace – all the fixtures and fittings and studied eccentricities that look as if they have been custom-made in some modern factory are real. Rules is the genuine article, a very English restaurant that has been taking its toll of tourists for two hundred years. Dickens, Betjeman, H.G. Wells, Thackeray, Graham Greene, King Edward VII ... just a few of the celebs who have revelled in Rules. In 1984 the restaurant passed into the hands of John Mayhew, who sourced some of its game from his estate – Lartington Hall Park in the High Pennines – and, in 1997, brought in David Chambers as head chef. Rules' proud boast is: "We specialise in classic game cookery". Indeed they do, and now the restaurant has become more of a bustling brasserie than the mausoleum it once was, despite instituting a resolute non-smoking policy which has upset as many people as it has pleased.

Cost	£25–£65
Address	35 Maiden Lane, WC2
T	020 7836 5314
Station	Covent Garden
Open	Mon–Sat noon–11.30pm, Sun noon–10.30pm
Accepts	All major credit cards
W	www.rules.co.uk

First of all you should note that Rules is open from noon till late, which is very handy when circumstances dictate a four o'clock lunch. There is also a competitive pre-theatre offer – £19.95 for two courses. Start with a warm salad of smoked haddock, quails eggs, potato and truffle (£9.95); a mussel and scallop soup with saffron (£6.95); or an outstanding terrine of foie gras and pigeon with walnut and raisin bread (£10.95). Go on to game in season: whatever the time of year, you'll find something good here. The menu changes with the seasons but, aside from game, the steak and kidney pudding with mash (£16.95) is a banker. As are the grilled Dover sole for two (£37.90) and the Aberdeen Angus roast rib of beef for two (£39.90). Also noteworthy is the poached Finnan haddock in a mussel and saffron sauce (£17.95). Puddings, such as treacle sponge or sticky toffee (both £6.75), are merciless. Why not go for the traditional blue Stilton cheese with celery and a glass of port (£11.95)?

And all this in a beautiful Victorian setting. Should you face entertaining out-of-town relations, foreign visitors in search of something old and English, or even yourself, Rules is a good place to indulge your nostalgia to the full.

CENTRAL

Sway

The Connaught Rooms used to be a very staid and stuffy sort of place which specialized in banqueting – school reunion dinners, yawningly long speeches, white-gloved waiters, murky gravy. In early 2001 a great chunk of this formidable building took on a new role as home to something a tad more hip and happening. Sway is what granny would have called a nightclub. It's a nest of bars,

Cost £9–£35

Address 61–65 Great Queen St, WC2
T 020 7404 6114
Station Covent Garden/ Holborn
Open Mon–Sat noon–1am, Sun 11am–7pm
Accepts All major credit cards

MODERN BRITISH

there are places to dance, and there's a modern and stylish 150-seat restaurant which is to be commended for getting two things absolutely spot on. It is single minded – there is a rotisserie with row after row of slowly turning, gently roasting chickens. And there is a communal table down the centre of the room. To find two grand ideas in one new restaurant is rare indeed.

If that were not enough to have the public beating down the doors, prices are reasonable and the chickens are well-chosen. There are starters to be had, such as a somewhat dodgy Caesar salad (£2.95/£5.75), and the focaccia are good, although very much in the chain-restaurants' school of garlic bread. Try the garlic and herb (£1.75); Provençale tomato (£1.85); or red onion chutney and cheese (£1.95). But don't expend much valuable appetite – go straight for the chicken. The chickens are free range and grown by a Mr Herman, who will have booked his place in heaven already due to his unusual kindness to the hundreds of fowl that he raises lovingly and organically. The chicken comes on a platter with a stand, accompanied by chips and sauces: half chicken (£8.75); breast and wing (£6.95); leg and thigh (£5.95); whole chicken (£16.95). The chicken is delicious. The best sauces – some are deeply dodgy, like the curried lychee and mango – are honey and grain mustard, Béarnaise, and candied lemon, thyme and garlic butter. The chips are good and the mash is less good. There are other dishes, too: pork and herb bangers served with mash (£7.95); 18oz Scotch T-bone (£17.95); even tempura rock lobster (£19.95). But the chicken is the thing here.

The prices on the wine list are not shy, the puds are so-so, the room is "designed" and arty, but the twin beacons of a decent roast chicken and the charm of a shared refectory table shine on through.

Euston & King's Cross

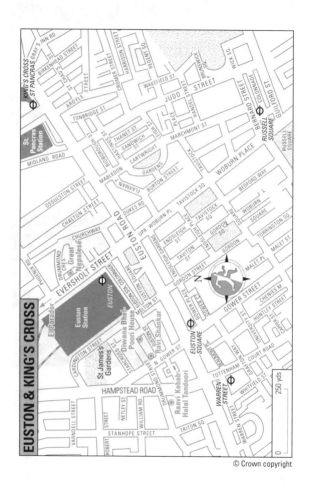

EUSTON & KING'S CROSS

© Crown copyright

Diwana Bhel-Poori House

🍴 All varnished pine and shag-pile carpets, the Diwana Bhel-Poori House puts you in mind of a late-1970s Wimpy bar. Only the Indian woodcarvings dotted around the walls give the game away – that and the heady scent of freshly blended spices. It's a busy place, with tables filling up and emptying at a fair crack, though the atmosphere is convivial and casual rather than rushed.

Cost	£5–£18

Address 121 Drummond St, NW1
T 020 7387 5556
Station Euston
Open Daily noon–11.30pm
Accepts All major credit cards
W www.diwana restaurant.com

There's no licence, so you can bring your own beer or wine (corkage is free) and a full water jug is supplied on each table. This, the low prices (the costliest dish will set you back just £6.20), a chatty menu listing "tasty snacks", and fast, friendly service combine to create a deceptively simple stage for some fine Indian vegetarian cooking. There's even a set lunch buffet at £5.10.

Starters are copious, ladled out in no-nonsense stainless steel bowls. The dahi bhalle chat (£2.30) is a cool, yoghurty blend of chickpeas, crushed pooris and bulghur wheat, sprinkled with "very special spices". The dahi poori (£2.30) is a fragrant concoction of pooris, potatoes, onions, sweet and sour sauces and chilli chutney, again smothered in yoghurt and laced with spices. Stars of the main menu are the dosas, particularly the flamboyant paper dosa (£4.60), a giant fan of a pancake with coconut chutney, potatoes and dhal nestling beneath its folds. Also superb is the house speciality, thali annapurna (£6), a feast of dhal, rice, vegetables, pickles, side dishes, mini bhajees and your choice of pooris or chapattis – divine but unfinishable, especially if you make the mistake of ordering some monstrously proportioned side dishes as well.

Whatever feast you put together, do leave room for dessert, as there's a heavenly kulfi malai (£1.70) to dig into – a creamy pyramid of frozen milk flavoured with kevda, nuts and herbs. A rich but less sweet-toothed option is the shrikhand (£1.60), a Western Indian dish with cheese, spices and herbs counteracting the sugar. Alternatively, try the Kashmiri falooda (£2.20) – cold milk with china grass and rose syrup topped with ice cream and nuts. Though strictly speaking a drink, this is surely pudding enough for anyone.

Euston & King's Cross

Great Nepalese

This bit of London behind Euston station is distinctly seedy, and the shops that are neighbours to the Great Nepalese offer strange products for probably quite strange people. The restaurant, however, is now the proud possessor of a bright new shop front and inside everything is reassuringly normal, if a little old and faded – like the giant wall photo showing the Queen and Prince Philip standing with the five living Gurkha holders of the Victoria Cross. This is a place that manages to combine friendly and homely service with authentic Nepalese food and, in case your nerve falters, the menu also has a buffer zone littered with standard curry house favourites like chicken tikka masala and lamb rogan josh – the latter helpfully subtitled "a very popular lamb curry".

Cost £8–£22

Address 48 Eversholt St, NW1

T 020 7388 6737

Station Euston/Euston Square

Open Mon–Sat noon–2.45pm & 6–11.30pm, Sun noon–2.30pm & 6–11.15pm

Accepts Amex, Diners, MasterCard, Visa

Don't order the lamb curry unless feeling profoundly unadventurous. It may be a very nice, popular lamb curry but the authentic Great Nepalese dishes are nicer still. Start with masco bhara, a large frisbee-shaped doughnut. It is made from black lentils, but without their black skins, so the result is a nutty-tasting, fluffy white mass with a crisp outside. It comes with a bowl of curry gravy for dipping (£3.50 plain, £3.85 with a hidden core of shredded lamb). Or try haku choyala (£3.75), diced mutton with garlic, lemon juice and ginger. It's spicy and agreeably sharp. For mains, the staff direct you to the dumba curry (£4.95), a traditional Nepalese-style curry, reliant on the same rich gravy as the masco bhara, or the chicken ra piaj (£5.20), with onions and spices. Both are highly recommended. Another very typical Nepalese dish is the butuwa chicken (£5.20). It combines ginger and spices with garlic and green herbs and is delicious. And if you like dhal, you shouldn't miss the kalo dal (£2.95), nutty and dark with black lentils.

A single note of caution. Beware the Coronation rum from Kathmandu. This firewater was first distilled in 1975 for the coronation of his majesty, the late King Birendra Bir Bikram Shah Dev, and it comes in a bottle shaped like a glass kukri. You probably have to be a Gurkha to appreciate its finer points.

El Parador

El Parador is a small, no-frills Spanish restaurant and tapas bar, slightly stranded in the quiet little enclave around Mornington Crescent, between King's Cross and Camden. It serves very tasty tapas at very reasonable prices and has a friendly, laid-back atmosphere, even on busy Friday and Saturday nights. It's a good place to spend a summer evening, with a lovely garden out the back, though this is no secret and the sought-after tables here should be booked in advance.

Cost	£8–£20
Address	245 Eversholt St, NW1
T	020 7387 2789
Station	Mornington Crescent
Open	Mon–Thurs noon–3pm & 6–11pm, Fri noon–3pm & 6–11.30pm, Sat 6–11.30pm, Sun 7–10.30pm
Accepts	All major credit cards

As ever with tapas, the fun part of eating here is choosing several dishes from the wide selection on offer, and then sharing and swapping with your companions. The plates are small, so allow yourself at least two or three tapas a head – more for a really filling meal – and go for at least one of the fish or seafood dishes, which are treats. Highlights include chipirones salteados (£3.90) – baby squid pan-fried with sea salt and olive oil; gambas al pil-pil (£4.60) – nice fat tiger prawns pan-fried with parsley, paprika and chilli; and salteado de pez espada (£4.90) – fresh swordfish sautéed with garlic and coriander. Carnivores shouldn't miss out on the jamón serrano (£4.80), delicious Spanish cured ham, or the morcilla de Burgos (£4.20), sausages that are a cousin of black pudding. Also good is the potaje de cordero con lentejas (£4), a classy lamb stew with lentils. The numerous vegetarian tapas include judias salteadas (£4) – green beans sautéed with braised leeks, red peppers and wine; paella del Parador (£3.80) – a vegetable paella with peas, corn and green beans; and buñuelos de patatas (£3.80) – mashed potato cooked with sun-dried tomatoes, cumin and Manchego cheese. Desserts keep up the pace: marquesa de chocolate (£3) is a luscious, creamy, home-made chocolate mousse; flan de naranja (£2.80) is a really good orange crème caramel.

Try a glass of the dry Manzanilla (£2) to start or accompany your meal. It's a perfect foil for tapas. Or delve into El Parador's strong selection of Spanish wines. Enjoyable choices include Muga crianza '97 (£14.50), a smooth white Rioja, and the Guelbenzu crianza '95 (£14), a rich and fruity red.

Raavi Kebab Halal Tandoori

This small restaurant has been a fixture for more than 25 years, during which time Drummond Street has become one of the main curry centres of London. Competition here is more than just fierce, it is ludicrous, as well-established vegetarian restaurants compete to offer the cheapest "eat-as-much-as-you-can" lunch buffet. It is lucky that vegetables are so cheap. But the Raavi is not just about bargain prices – or vegetables, come to that. It is an unpretentious Pakistani grill house that specializes in halal meat dishes, and on the menu shyly offers "probably the best grilled and cooked items in London". And indeed, when you fancy tucking into an item, this is a great place to come.

Cost	£3–£10
Address	125 Drummond St, NW1
T	020 7388 1780
Station	Euston/Euston Square
Open	Daily 12.30–10.30pm
Accepts	All major credit cards

The grills here are good but hot – hot enough for the wildest chilli-head. Seekh kebab (£2) – juicy and well-flavoured, straight from the charcoal grill in the doorway – is hot. Chicken tikka (£2.10) is hot. Mutton tikka (£2.20) is hot. And with the kebabs comes a khaki-coloured dipping sauce that is sharp with lemon juice, strongly flavoured with fresh coriander and, as you'd expect, hot with fresh chillies. Lamb quorma (£4.25) is not so fierce – a rich sauce with fresh ginger and garlic is topped with a sprinkle of shaved almonds. Chicken daal (£3.25) brings chunks of chicken on the bone, bobbing on a sea of savoury yellow split-pea dhal. Thoroughly delicious. Nan breads (90p) are light and crispy. In 1999, a new arrival, nihari (£4.50) – the traditional Muslim breakfast dish of slow-cooked curried mutton – dislodged haleem from its spot as best seller here. Haleem (£3.20) is a dish whose origins are shrouded in mystery. Some say that it was invented in the Middle East, which is certainly where it is most popular today; other devotees track it back to Moghul kitchens. The recipe is arduous. Take some meat and cook it, add four kinds of dhal, a good deal of cracked wheat, and two kinds of rice, plus spices. Cook for up to seven hours, then add some garam masala. The result is a gluey slick of smooth and spicy glop from which any traces of the meat have all but disappeared.

And how does it taste? You'd be hard pushed to be more enthusiastic than "not bad".

Ravi Shankar

As a hotbed of Indian dining, Drummond Street is still a magnet for curryholics and anyone else seeking a good, cheap meal. The Ravi Shankar opened in the 1980s, and its decor is still firmly wedged in an era when plain enough was good enough. The Ravi Shankar may look ordinary, and the

Cost	£4–£15
Address	133 Drummond St, NW1
T	020 7388 6458
Station	Euston
Open	Daily noon–10.45pm
Accepts	MasterCard, Visa

seating may not be ultra-comfortable, but the food is very honest and very cheap. Which is something that weighs heavily with a loyal clientele which makes it a busy place even while the waiters in some more orthodox (and more expensive) curry houses elsewhere on Drummond Street are kicking their heels.

On a Monday, the daily special consists of cashew nut pillau rice and cauliflower curry, served with salad and mint yoghurt chutney for the princely sum of £3.50. There are not many £3.50 meals left anywhere in London, let alone a meal at such a price that is well-cooked and satisfying. The cashew nut pillau is rich and nutty, and the cauliflower curry has been made substantial by the addition of chunks of potato. On Tuesday, there's vegetable biryani with curry (£3.95), Wednesday brings aloo palak with chapatti (£3.50), and the specials wind onwards to the extravagance of chana batura (£4.25) on Saturday – a delicious fried bread with a chick pea curry. The main menu starters fall into two categories. There are hot snacks from Western India, including samosas (three for £1.95), bhajia (£1.95) and potato bonda (£2.25) – a solid, tasty, deep-fried sphere made from potato and lentils. Then there are cold "snacks and chat", billed as coming from Bombay's famed snack city, Chowpatty beach. At Ravi Shankar there are bhel puri (£1.95), pani puri (£1.95) and potato puri (£1.95). Try the pani puri – a plate of tiny spherical shells arrives with a bowl of cooked chickpeas in tamarind and date sauce. You punch a hole in the top of the puri then add a spoonful of chickpeas. Good fun. Breads are good – treat yourself to an ace stuffed paratha (£1.95).

Or try a thali – these complete meals come on stainless steel trays, and range from rice and dal (£3.50) to the Shankar thali (£6.95) – start with dhal soup, then four different curries with rice, raita, a pappadom, puris or chapatis, and finally a dessert.

Kensington

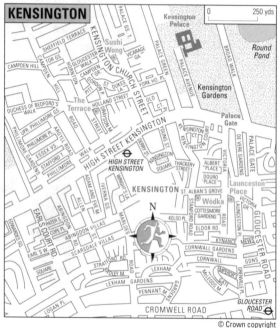

KENSINGTON

0   250 yds

Launceston Place

Launceston Place is one of those small, chic streets where you cannot help feeling a pang of envy for anyone rich enough to live in the slick little houses. As the road curves you'll find a sprinkling of high-ticket shops on one side and the Launceston Place restaurant on the other. The restaurant sprawls its way through a nest of rooms and is pleasantly formal. Or perhaps that should be formal and pleasant. Service is efficient but not in your face and there is

Cost	£18–£65

Address 1a Launceston Place W8
T 020 7795 6533
Station High Street Kensington
Open Mon–Fri 12.30–2.30pm & 7–11.30pm, Sat 7–11.30pm, Sun 12.30–2.30pm
Accepts All major credit cards except Diners

a traditional feel to everything. This is a neighbourhood restaurant but one that is the product of a very swish neighbourhood, which makes some sense of the fact that a couple of years after opening here the team went on to create Kensington Place (see p.451) – another establishment very much in tune with its surroundings.

The menu changes on a seasonal basis and dishes match traditional combinations with fashionable ingredients in an unstuffy way. Starters range from a stunning dish of potato gnocchi with girolles, broad beans, tomatoes and mint dressing (£7.50 starter, £12 main) – great complimentary textures; to pear Gorgonzola and French bean salad with spicy pecans and oak leaf (£6.50); and asparagus with poached egg, crispy pancetta and Hollandaise sauce (£8) – not wildly original but very good. Mains range from plain dishes such as grilled sea bass with basil mayonnaise (£18.50), or pan-fried John Dory with a gooseberry Hollandaise (£16.50), to more complicated offerings such as crispy duck confit with chorizo, peas and saffron risotto (£16.50), and on to the formidable – grilled veal chop with red onions and melted goat's cheese (£18). The dessert menu ticks all the appropriate boxes: there's buttermilk panacotta (£6), and warm chocolate pudding with vanilla ice cream (£6.50). The wine list is strong in traditional areas, so think French.

The set lunch is much beloved by local ladies-who-lunch and is priced reasonably at £15.50 for two course and £18.50 for three. Seafood risotto, grilled duck breast with cherry compote, mascarpone parfait with figs, coffee, a tsunami of chilled white wine and gossip – just about perfect.

Sushi Wong

Sushi Wong is the kind of name you either love or hate but, whichever side you take, you have to concede that it is certainly slick – just like this deceptively sized restaurant. On the ground floor there's a modernist Japanese restaurant-cum-sushi-bar seating about 25 people. Downstairs there's a teppan-yaki table and room for a further sixty diners. Looking in from the

Cost	£15–£35

Address 38c-d Kensington Church St, W8
T 020 7937 5007
Station High Street Kensington
Open Mon–Sat noon–2.30pm & 6–10.30pm, Sun 6–9.30pm
Accepts All major credit cards

street it's hard not to admire the stark bright-yellow and blue colour scheme, and the tables, each topped with ground glass backed by a blue neon tube. In the face of all this brightness and modernity, the service is so low-key that it almost seems timid, but Sushi Wong is a confident and efficient place for all that.

Sushi is delicious here. Ordering the sushi matsu set (£19) brings a round lacquer tray with six pieces of salmon or tuna roll flanked by ten pieces of various sushi. The chef's selection. The fish is fresh, the wasabi strong, the gari delicious and the sushi well prepared. A good array at a fair price. The menu emphasizes hosomaki (roll sushi), ranging from edo (£4.20) – crab meat, salmon and cucumber – to "Kensington roll" (£3.80), which is a crispy salmon and asparagus concoction "specially made for Kensington dwellers!" There is also a wide range of à la carte selections: starters like agedofu dengkaku (£3.90), which are thick-sliced tofu grilled on skewers; deep-fried soft-shell crab (£6.20); yakitori (£4.90); and age-gyoza (£4), which are deep-fried dumplings. Mains include stir-fried lobster tail (£10.80); chicken teriyaki (£8.80); pork tonkatsu (£8.80); and the Sushi Wong tempura selection (£12.80), which includes king prawns, fish and vegetables. Among the noodle dishes you'll find nabeyaki udon (£7.50) and Sushi Wong ramen (£6.50) – egg noodles with chicken, prawns, egg and vegetables in miso broth.

The set menus make life simpler. The Geisha gets you five courses for £23. The Sakura gets you sashimi, tempura, salmon steak or beef teriyaki, rice and miso soup, plus dessert for £26. There's also a seven-course Sushi Wong Dinner (£36). Or book one of the hibashi tables for a teppan-yaki dinner cooked in front of you – five courses for £33.

The Terrace

The Terrace is a small, modern restaurant hidden among the residential streets north of Kensington High Street. Its dining room is small but, as the name proclaims, there is a terrace fronting onto the street, where a handful of tables await any diners who have the nerve to brave the British weather. The food is simple, seasonal and modern.

Cost	£18–£30

Address 33c Holland St, W8
T 020 7937 3224
Station High Street Kensington
Open Mon–Sat noon–2.30pm & 7–10.30pm, Sun 12.30–3pm
Accepts All major credit cards

Presentation is unfussy and the standard of cooking is generally high. Elsewhere you would probably expect the prices to be a tad lower, but here – in Kensington on the way to Holland Park – they represent quite decent value.

The menu changes regularly. Starters like warm smoked haddock brandade with beef tomato salad and marjoram dressing (£8.50) are well executed, while the pan-fried foie gras (£11), a huge portion of liver served with caramelized pears, is an impressive bargain of a dish, and not to be trifled with. Or there's a scallop and red onion marmalade tart (£8.50), served with a wild leaf salad and an orange and thyme beurre blanc. The Terrace salad (£5) could be anything from a competently made Caesar to a combination of grilled spiced aubergines, plum tomatoes and goat's cheese. Soups veer towards the exotic, such as watercress and lime with crème fraîche (£5). At first glance the main courses look like standard fare – cod, tuna, chicken, lamb – but they're all made from fresh ingredients which deliver good, strong flavours. Pan-fried fillet of pork with an apple and ginger purée with melted gorgonzola and Pommery mustard sauce (£14.50) is particularly good; roast rack of grass-fed Welsh lamb (£19.50) comes with a herb and mustard crust, potato gratin and mint Béarnaise. Or there's char-grilled blue-fin tuna (£18.50), accompanied by a Niçoise salad; and a fine wild mushroom risotto (£10.50), which comes with a splash of truffle oil and plenty of Parmesan. The dessert section ranges from chocolate mousse with vanilla cream (£5.50), via gooseberry fool (£5.50), to raspberry crème brûlée (£5.50).

Regulars are easily spotted: they're the ones tucking into the excellent-value (and constantly changing) set lunches – £12.50 for two courses, £14.50 for three.

Wódka

Wódka is a restaurant that lies in wait for you. It's calm and bare, and the food is better than you might expect – well cooked, and thoughtfully seasoned. The daily lunch menu represents extremely good value at £10.90 for two courses and £13.50 for three, a large proportion of the dishes being refugees from the evening à la carte. Where, you wonder, is the streak of madness that helped the Polish cavalry take on German tank regiments with sabres drawn? On the shelves behind the bar, that's where – in the extensive collection of moody and esoteric vodkas which are for sale both by the shot and by the carafe.

Cost	£14–£42
Address	12 St Albans Grove, W8
T	020 7937 6513
Station	High Street Kensington
Open	Daily 12.30–2.30pm & 7–11.15pm
Accepts	All major credit cards

The soup makes a good starter: Ukrainian barszcz (£3.90) is a rich, beetrooty affair. Blinis are also the business: they come with smoked salmon (£6.90/£8.90), aubergine mousse (£5.50/£6.90), foie gras (£9.90/£14.90) or 40g of Oscietra caviar (£23.50). A lunchtime selection will get you all except the caviar. Also good is the kaszanka (£6.90) – grilled black pudding with pickled red cabbage and pear puree. For a main course, the fish cakes (£10.90) with leeks and a dill sauce are firm favourites with the regulars (many of whom are from nearby Penguin Books). In line with the Polish love of wild game, when partridge is available it is roasted and served with a splendid mash of root vegetables – the mashed potato is also worthy of special praise. Or there may be haunch of venison with sour cherries and honey-roasted pears (£13.50). Puddings tend to be of the oversweet, under-imaginative gateaux variety, but the vodka will ensure that you won't be worrying about that.

Consider the vodka list with due attention – there is a host of them: Zubrówka (made with bison grass); Okhotnichya (for hunters); Jarzebiak (that's rowan berries); Cytrynówka (lemon); Sliwowica (plum); Sliwówka (plum, but hot and sweet); Czarna Porezecka (blackcurrant); Ananas (pineapple); Krupnik (honey, and served hot); Roza (rose petals); Goldwasser (made with flakes of gold and aniseed); Soplica (which is a mystery). They cost from £2.25 to £2.75 a shot, and from £33.90 to £37.90 per 50cl carafe. Remember this simple test: pick any three of the above names and say them quickly. If anyone shows signs of understanding, you need another shot.

Knightsbridge & Belgravia

KNIGHTSBRIDGE & BELGRAVIA

HYDE PARK CORNER

Foliage

KNIGHTSBRIDGE

Osteria d'Isola

KNIGHTSBRIDGE

La Tante Claire

TREVOR SQ

TREVOR SQUARE

RAPHAEL ST.

LANCELOT PL

HOOPS CT

STREET

TREVOR PLACE

TREVOR ST.

DUPLEX ROW

SEVILLE ST.

WILLIAM ST.

WILTON PLACE

OLD BARRACK YD

WILTON ROW

WILTON CRESCENT

GROSVENOR CRESCENT

N

KNIGHTSBRIDGE

MONTPELIER MEWS

BROMPTON

BROMPTON PL.

HANS RD

BEAUFORT GS

BEAUCHAMP PLACE

PONT ST

WILTON PL

BASIL

HANS CRESCENT

HARRIET ST.

WILLIAM M.

WILLIAM M.

LOWNDES

SQUARE

MOTCOMB ST.

WILTON STREET

BELGRAVE MW. N.

BELGRAVE SQUARE

WALK

SLOANE

PAVILION

HANS

HANS ST.

COTTAGE WALK

WEST HALKIN ST.

LOWNDES ST.

CADOGAN

BELGRAVE M.W.

CHESHAM PLACE

BELGRAVIA

ROAD

PONT

STREET

CADOGAN

PLACE

CHESHAM STREET

CHESHAM PL.

LYALL MEWS

LOWNDES PLACE

WALTON

HASKER ST.

DUNSTON ST.

LENNOX GDN MWS

LENNOX GARDENS

CLABON MEWS

LENNOX

CADOGAN SQUARE

CADOGAN SQUARE

CADOGAN LANE

LYALL

PLACE

EATON

PR. MEWS NORTH

EATON MEWS NORTH

EATON SQ.

MILNER ST.

To Sloane Square

0   250 yds

© Crown copyright

Foliage

Foli-aaage – rather irritatingly the Mandarin mandarins presume to correct our pronunciation of their restaurant's name – has a terrific view of Hyde Park. When it reopened in 2000, rebranded with the posh new name, it had been completely refurbished. In the main, critics and commentators took against the new decor, and some even found the service to be a little over the top. But, in respect of the food, such comments were drowned out by deafening murmurs of appreciation. The chef is Hywel Jones and he is a very good cook. This is a restaurant that has set out its stall to pursue the highest gastronomic honours and it may yet achieve them.

Cost	£30–£120

Address Mandarin Oriental Hyde Pk, Knightsbridge, SW1
T 020 7201 3723
Station Knightsbridge
Open Mon–Fri noon–2.30pm & 7–10.30pm, Sat 7–10.30pm
Accepts All major credit cards

FRENCH

The main menu offers eight starters and up to a dozen mains. The tariff is £42.50 for three courses, and the cooking is classical French, with the occasional modernist twist or addition. A great deal of effort goes into the presentation – rumoured to be a direct route to any Michelin inspector's heart. When the restaurant opened there was a stunning starter of roast scallops, turnip purée, creamed parsley, verjus glaze, and fricassée of ceps and snails. Exceptionally sophisticated and genuinely earthy at one and the same time. Or how about salad of crushed cauliflower and spiced quail, Banyuls reduction; or rabbit and foie gras terrine with warm sweetcorn pancakes; or poached Scottish lobster, Cornish crab, confit tomatoes and caviar vinaigrette? Mains are also impressive: roast fillet of gilthead bream, pumpkin ravioli, salsify, sage and brown butter vinaigrette; or venison fillet, beetroot gratin, fricassée of white beans and oxtail. For those in love with the great classic combinations there may be roast "Label Anglais" chicken, new season morels, asparagus and Gewürzträminer cream. Desserts are elegant and greed inspiring: hot Cuban chocolate fondant, whisky ice cream, and pistachio craquelin; baked coconut soufflé and passion fruit sorbet. The wine list keeps pace with everything else, and starry vintages get starry prices.

The cooking here is "worth a detour" and perhaps the best way to access it is via the lunch menu, which offers three courses for £24. Chicken liver and foie gras parfait with warm Muscat grapes, followed by grilled red mullet, saffron risotto and deep-fried squid, then bitter chocolate tart, coffee ice cream and walnut wafers. Sounds pretty good.

Osteria d'Isola

There are two restaurants at this swanky Knightsbridge address. Upstairs there is Isola, which is exceedingly smart, and downstairs there is the Osteria d'Isola, which is less formal and accommodates a large bar that breathes life into the space. In the kitchen (which serves both venues) is a highly regarded Frenchman called Bruno Loubet. So far so good; nice place, great chef. Most critics and commentators then go on alarmingly about the perils of expecting a Frenchman to cook Italian food. Why? There are enough Englishmen cooking good French food. And Bruno Loubet is an outstanding chef. So, service is friendly. The dining room is comfortable. Prices are tolerable. There's a wood-fired oven. The food is delicious. And the chef is French. Carry on.

Cost	£20–£45

Address 145 Knightsbridge, SW1

☎ 020 7838 1055

Station Knightsbridge

Open Mon–Fri noon–3pm & 6–11pm, Sat noon–3.30pm & 6–11pm, Sun noon–3.30pm & 6–9pm

Accepts All major credit cards

The menu changes regularly to reflect the seasons and what's good at the market. It is a four-stage affair, with antipasti, pasta, pesci and carni, and dolci. Start with a classic like farinetta di ceci, rucola e ricotta di bufala (£7.50); or insalata di polpi e carpaccio di tonno (£8.50). Or there is a serious platter of Italian cured meats with Parmesan (£17 for two people to share). Pasta dishes might include ravioli Isola alla barba-bietola (£8/£12) – beetroot ravioli; or an old friend like spaghetti puttanesca (£7/£14). You won't find better in Italy. Main course dishes might include a stuffato di polpi e baccala' con ceci e pomodoro (£17); cotechino di maiale con lenticche di Castelluccio e pesto (£16); or sea bass which has been roasted in the wood-fired oven (£19.50). Or how about the spiedini di agnello da latte, carciofi e polenta (£17.50) – milk-fed lamb served with artichoke and polenta? Puds are equally Italian, such as the zabaglione made with Strega (£6.50) or dangerous delicacies like torroncino al frutto della passione e macedonia (£6) – nougat meets fruit salad. The bread is good here. The wine list is extensive and delves deeply into far corners of Italy; gratifyingly, there is a huge range served by the glass.

In common with most other local establishments, Osteria is less busy at lunch and, as a consequence, there is a typical set lunch to tempt you – two courses for £17.50 and three for £19.50.

La Tante Clare

At the end of 1998, Pierre Koffman gathered up his kitchen brigade and moved them all to a new location within the purlieu of the Berkeley Hotel in Knightsbridge. How the owners of this hostelry must have rubbed their hands with glee – now they had not only Vong on one flank but also Koffman on the other. The Michelin people, however, showed their disapproval of restaurants gadding, and promptly docked Tante Clare a star. Things have settled down now, and the new Tante Clare has regained form and is as sublime as ever. Perhaps it is his Gascon heritage, but Koffman's food pulls off an amazing treble whammy: it is sophisticated but earthy and rich in flavour; dishes are both elegant and satisfying; things look good but they taste better. There is only one way to find out how he does it, and that is to go and eat. Every chef with aspirations should try the set lunch here – £28 for three courses, coffee and petits fours.

Cost	£35–£150
Address	Wilton Place, SW1
T	020 7823 2003
Station	Hyde Park Corner
Open	Mon–Fri noon–2pm & 7–11pm, Sat 7–11pm
Accepts	All major credit cards

What an amazing deal! There are two choices for both starter and main, so you might find yourself agonizing between a salade Niçoise – a large bowlful with small potatoes and runny egg, marinated tuna, capers, and anchovies – and a chicken liver parfait with Sauternes jelly. Choosing the main is no easier – herb-crusted cod versus perfect rack of lamb with ratatouille. If these dishes sound simple, that is because they are. They are also perfectly judged, strongly flavoured, well balanced and well presented. Come back at dinner and prices move briskly upwards. There are usually five starters, five fish and six meats on offer. Starters like bouillon de volaille et pain blanc, garni de haricots et truffe noir (£22), and coquilles St Jacques grillés, sauce a l'encre de seiche, pointe de poivrons et d'ail (£25) pave the way for agneau des Pyrénées (£29) – roast leg of baby lamb with a gratin of ceps; and canard de Challans (£29) – roast duck with a spice and herb sauce. Or perhaps you should try Koffman's signature dish, the pied de cochon farci aux morilles (£28), and see the fabled dish from which so many chefs have drawn inspiration for so long.

The service here is slick and unobtrusive, the petits fours are good and the puddings are amazing. There's also a minimum charge of £50 a head in the evening, plus a 12.5% service charge and a wine list that starts sensibly and ends up stratospheric. All in all this is the real thing. So start saving now and treat yourself.

Marylebone

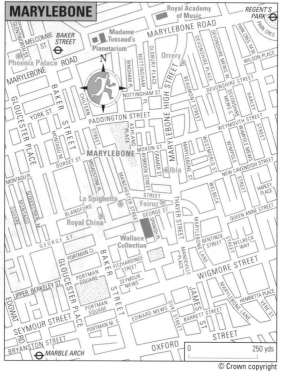

MARYLEBONE

REGENT'S PARK

Royal Academy of Music

MARYLEBONE ROAD

Madame Tussaud's Planetarium

MELCOMBE ST.   BAKER STREET

Phoenix Palace   ROAD

MARYLEBONE

GLENWORTH ST.

PARK CRES. M.W.

PARK CRES.

DEVONSHIRE MEWS S.

DEVONSHIRE PLACE

WILSON PLACE

Orrery

BINGHAM PL.

NOTTINGHAM STREET

OLDBURY PLACE

MARYLEBONE HIGH STREET

BEAUMONT STREET

DEVONSHIRE STREET

DEVONSHIRE MEWS S.

HARLEY STREET

WIMPOLE MEWS

N

CHILTERN STREET

NOTTINGHAM ST.

NOTTINGHAM PL.

WESTMORELAND STREET

WEYMOUTH STREET

WIMPOLE STREET

GLOUCESTER PLACE

BAKER STREET

YORK ST.

MONTAGU M.

PADDINGTON STREET

ASHLAND PLACE

MOXON ST.

AYBROOK STREET

CRAMER ST.

MARYLEBONE ST.

NEW CAVENDISH STREET

MARYLEBONE

DORSET ST.

Ibla

HARLEY PLACE

MONTAGU PL.

MONTAGU SQUARE

BROADSTONE PL.

MANCHESTER STREET

STREET

WELBECK STREET

La Spighetta

BLANDFORD STREET

Fairuz

THAYER STREET

QUEEN ANNE STREET

Royal China

GEORGE ST.

SPANISH PL.

BENTINCK STREET

MARYLEBONE LANE

WELBECK WAY

GEORGE ST.

Wallace Collection

FITZHARDINGE STREET

MANDEVILLE PLACE

PORTMAN CL.

PORTMAN SQUARE

SEYMOUR MEWS

WIGMORE STREET

UPPER BERKELEY ST.

GLOUCESTER PLACE

BAKER STREET

PORTMAN SQUARE

JAMES ST.

HENRIETTA PLACE

MARYLEBONE LANE

VERE ST.

EDGWAT

PORTMAN M.S.

EDWARD MEWS

DUKE STREET

BARRETT STREET

SEYMOUR STREET

BRYANSTON STREET

MARBLE ARCH

OXFORD

STREET

0   250 yds

© Crown copyright

Fairuz

Squeezed in between Stephen Bull on one side and a hip and groovy bistro on the other, Fairuz happily carries on doing its own thing, which is Lebanese cooking. As you open the front door, jolly souk music, the smell of Eastern spices and the light of the warm, mud-coloured room assault and beguile the senses.

Cost	£15–£35
Address	3 Blandford St, W1
T	020 7486 8182
Station	Bond Street
Open	Daily noon–11pm
Accepts	All major credit cards

LEBANESE

The menu is set out in traditional style. There's an epic list of mezze, both hot and cold, to start, followed by a selection of charcoal grills and a couple of oven-baked dishes. You can leave the selection up to the restaurant and order a set mezza (minimum two people, £16.95 per head), or a set menu (minimum two people, £24.95 per head) which combines a mezza with a mixed grill "specially made to regret being a vegetarian" – with a glass of fiery arak thrown in. The set mezza delivers eight or ten little dishes, plenty for lunch or a light supper. But if you prefer to make your own selection, the menu lists 39 different mezze for you to choose from: cold dishes all cost £3.95; hot dishes £4.75. Particularly recommended are the wonderfully fresh and herby tabbouleh; the warak inab – stuffed vine leaves; the hummous Beiruty; and makanek – spicy lamb sausages. Even that most dangerously indigestible of delicacies, the felafel, is fine here. Main course grills are generous and well prepared. Kafta khashkhash (£9.95) – lamb minced with parsley and grilled on skewers – is unexpectedly delicate and fragrant, but stands up well against its accompanying chilli sauce, while the shish taouk (£9.95) – chicken marinated in garlic and lemon – really is finger-licking good. Round off your meal with excellent baklava (£3.50), and real Turkish coffee (£2).

Fairuz is a comfortable place, full of sleek and contented Marylebonians. It's not the most authentic, the cheapest or the best Lebanese food that you'll eat in town (best head to the nearby Edgware Road for that). But the ambience at Fairuz is better suited to novice Westerners – the staff are friendly and helpful, and the wine list, though short, is offered willingly. If you can, get there early to secure one of the nook and crannyish, tent-like tables. A second branch is planned for Bayswater.

Ibla

🍴 At first glance, Ibla looks unpromising. The interior is a touch on the dark side, and there have been murmurings amongst the critics that the food might not be so much "authentic Italian" as "modern Italian". But persevere – it will be worth it. Along with well-laid dining tables at the front, there is a nod to the shop-like premises with a small attempt to sell smart packets of pasta and the like. If possible, ask for a

Cost	£18–£50

Address 89 Marylebone High St, W1
T 020 7224 3799
Station Baker Street/ Regent's Park
Open Mon-Fri noon-2.30pm & 7-10.15pm, Sat 7-10.15pm
Accepts Amex, MasterCard, Visa

table in the back room, a pretty yet functional square space, and settle down for some excellent Italian food.

The menu – uncompromisingly Italian – changes weekly and works on a set-price basis. You choose from the à la Carte and pay £30 for two courses or £35 for three. There is also a special set lunch with limited choice (just a couple of options for each course) – two courses at £15 and three at £18. Starters may include courgette flowers and crab with tomato and basil sauce; marinated red mullet with orange, fresh chilli and mango; or asparagus, rocket and Parmesan salad. Primi piatti are often inspired: fish ravioli with home-made bottarga; cannelloni of rabbit ragout, Taleggio and truffle sauce; or quail risotto with wild mushrooms. Main courses split into piatti di pesce and piatti di carne – the former along the lines of grilled sea bass with grilled vegetables and balsamic sauce; or monkfish fillet with sweet tomatoes, mussels and clams. Piatti di carne might be grilled pork fillet with stuffed aubergines and tomato sauce; or roast breast of duck with timbale of ham and chickpeas, lemon and fig sauce. The less Italian-sounding dishes, such as salmon with herb crust, are in general less interesting, but the chef really knows his stuff and all will be zingily fresh, well seasoned and perfectly presented. Puddings are good, though they do suffer somewhat from coming at the end of a filling Italian meal.

Picky diners might take issue with the all-Italian wine list, which will be confusing to anyone but a connoisseur, and the service, which has more attitude than you might enjoy. But on the positive side, the staff are perfectionists, and will only take as many customers as the kitchen can cope with. This is no bad thing, after all, as a kitchen that's not over-stressed is a kitchen that is at its best.

Orrery

There is no doubt that Sir Terence Conran has gone to great lengths to ensure that the public don't see a "formula" in his restaurants. There are large ones, small ones, short ones, tall ones; Italian, French, British; loud music, no music. Even so, Orrery stands out. This is a very good restaurant indeed, driven by a passion for food, and the mainspring is the head chef, Chris Galvin. It may be part of a large group, but they still change the menu daily if need be. Centralized buying might make economic sense, but Orrery still cherishes its own small local suppliers, going for large, line-caught, sea bass above their smaller, farmed cousins, and selecting the best poulet noir, Bresse pigeon and Scottish beef. The service is slick and friendly, the dining room is beautiful, the cheeseboard has won prizes, the wine list is exhaustive. And the cooking is very good indeed. All of the above is reflected in the bill. For once, you do get what you pay for.

Cost	£29–£90

Address 55 Marylebone High St, W1
T 020 7616 8000
Station Baker Street/ Regent's Park
Open Mon–Sat noon–3pm & 7–11pm, Sun noon–3pm & 7–10.30pm
Accepts All major credit cards
W www.orrery.co.uk

What a pleasure to see such a short menu, with simple starters like cep consommé (£7.50) served with Jerusalem artichoke and chestnut agnolotti; or a first-rate terrine of foie gras (£16.50) served with Sauternes jelly and toasted sourdough; or cannelloni of Dorset crab with Banyuls vinaigrette (£12.50). Mains feature well-judged combinations of flavours: assiette of veal with Marsala sauce (£22); Anjou pigeon with ravioli of cèpes, pigeon confit and Savoy cabbage etuvée (£22.50); pavé of Scottish halibut with seared sea scallop, Puy lentils and Burgundy jus (£23). Presentation is ultra-chic, flavours are intense – this is serious stuff. Puddings span the range from classics such as baked chocolate fondant (£8) to the nouvelle delice of liquorice and pear (£9).

One way to eat well here is to rely heavily on the set menus: the three-course menu du jour is £23.50; while Sunday dinner, also three courses and including a glass of champagne, costs £28.50. The Menu Gourmand (which must be ordered by the entire table) brings six courses, coffee and petits fours for £45, rising to £75 when you opt for the specially matched glasses of wine. A stress-free bargain.

Marylebone

Phoenix Palace

The Phoenix Palace burst onto the scene in 2000. Brand new Chinese restaurants are few and far between, and to find a large, bright, busy one to the north of the Marylebone Road is very unusual. This site was formerly an Indian eatery called the Viceroy of India and, in the transition, the rather smart Indian carvings have been left behind. The result is a large room with some tables on a raised dais running around the room, the obligatory feng shui fishtank, and the

Cost	£12–£45

Address 3–5 Glentworth St, NW1
T 020 7486 3515
Station Baker Street/ Marylebone
Open Mon–Sat noon–11.30pm, Sun 11am–10.30pm
Accepts All major credit cards except Diners

little wooden idols looking down. This is a very North London sort of place; it may be only just over the river of traffic that flows past Madame Tussaud's, but it has North London attitudes and North London punters.

The menu is a huge one, and stretches off into the farthest corners of Chinese chefly imagination. The food is well-presented and portions are large – something for which we must thank those North London attitudes? Starters include all the old favourites, but steamed fresh scallops at £3 each are no bargain. Stick to chicken wrapped in lettuce leaf (£5.50), which is well-flavoured, if a little short on lettuce leaves. Or order a main-course portion of the deep-fried squid in light batter (£8), which makes a fine opening move. The menu chunters on for over two hundred dishes and is worth a careful read, as there are some interesting discoveries to be made. Salt-baked chicken (£10/£20) is a wonderful, savoury roast chicken with juicy meat and crisp skin. The fried minced pork cakes with salted fish (£6.50) are very classy, the salt-fish seasoning the pork mix successfully. The dual seasonal greens with curry (£5.50) is a novelty item – baby sweetcorn and broccoli lurk in a yellow and pretty fierce curry sauce. Very inscrutable. The stewed beef flank (£5.50) is that old favourite, braised brisket – very dark and very rich. The range of noodle dishes is extensive.

The standard of cooking here is good and would not be out of place in the better Chinatown eateries, even if the decor might raise an eyebrow. The Phoenix Palace deserves to do well and may yet cheer up a whole tranche of North London.

Royal China

Like its elder sibling – at 13 Queensway, W2 (☎020 7221 2535) – this branch of the Royal China is a black-and-gold palace. The effect is a kind of cigarette-packet chic and smacks of the 1970s. But don't let that put you off. The food is not as expensive as the decor would have you believe, the service is efficient and brisk (rather than that special kind of rude and brisk you may encounter in Chinatown), and the food is really good. One knowledgeable chef-critic describes the Royal China's sticky rice wrapped in a lotus leaf as the "best ever".

Cost	£12–£25

Address 40 Baker St, W1
T 020 7487 4688
Station Baker Street/
Bond Street
Open Mon–Sat noon–11pm,
Sun 11am–10pm; dim sum
served daily until 5pm
Accepts All major credit cards
except Diners

You could eat well from the Royal China's full menu, but it is the dim sum that is most enticing here. Like everything else in the Royal China, the small booklet that holds the dim sum menu is bound in gold. It goes from "Today's Chef Special" through dim sum to lunchtime noodle and rice dishes. The most famous dim sum here is the roast pork puff (£1.80) – unusual, in that it is made from puff pastry; it is very light and has a sweetish char sui filling. From the "specials", try the lobster dumpling (£3.50) and Thai-style fish cake (£2.30), both of which are tasty. Also worth noting are the prawn and chive dumpling (£2.20), pork and radish dumpling (£1.80), and seafood dumpling (£2.20) – or a selection of three. The glutinous rice in lotus leaves (£3) really is the best ever – rich and not too gamey; two parcels come in each steamer. The Royal China cheung fun (£2.70) is another sampler providing one of each filling – prawn, pork and beef. They take their cheung fun seriously here, with a total of eight variants including mushrooms and dry shrimp (£3). The fried rice dishes and the noodles are well-priced (£5 to £7).

This may well be the place finally to take the plunge and try chicken's feet. Spicy chicken feet (£1.80) come thickly coated in a rich, spicy goo and, to be frank, this sauce is so strong that – were it not for the obvious claw shapes – you could be eating almost anything.

La Spighetta

Walk past La Spighetta and you could be forgiven for thinking that this is the least popular small pizza and pasta joint in London. You will see five or six tables, generally deserted, and you'll be lucky if there is a member of staff within sight. But venture inside and down the stairs and you will discover a large basement restaurant buzzing with activity. At lunchtime there is the Marylebone office crowd (advertising, Marks & Spencer staff); at dinner it's more local (young professionals). The decor is more practical than elegant, with terracotta and cream walls, and banquette seating, while the kitchens are open-plan, with a magnificent pizza oven dominating the room. But it's the food – well cooked and well priced – that you're here for.

Cost	£25–£40

Address 43 Blandford St, W1
T 020 7486 7340
Station Bond Street/Baker Street
Open Mon–Fri noon–2.30pm & 6.30–10.30pm, Sat noon–2.30pm & 6.30–11pm, Sun 6.30–10.30pm
Accepts Amex, MasterCard, Visa

Even if you had planned to drop in for just a bowl of pasta, it's worth considering La Spighetta's first courses. Carpaccio di spada affumicato con insalata di finocchi al limone (£6.90) is a light, fresh and simple dish of smoked swordfish, while Mozzarella di bufala con melanzane grigliate (£6.90) reminds you what Mozzarella really can taste like. A smallish choice of pastas and a full list of pizzas follow, alongside some main courses. But the pastas and pizzas are so good that you'd be advised to stick to them. Especially good are the linguine alle vongole e peperoncino (£7.50), a dish which is dressed with fine olive oil and actually tastes of clams, and the tagliatelle di castagne con funghi e erbe (£7.40), a flavoursome chestnut pasta. Pizza Napoli (£7) really tastes of tomato, anchovies and capers, while the chef's pizza (£9) is a well-judged combination of Mozzarella, rocket, fresh tomato, Parmesan and Parma ham. The other mains are standard Italian restaurant fare – fegato di vitello con zucchine brasate all erbe (£10.50), say, or tonno alla griglia con rucola e pomodoro (£10.90). Puddings are workmanlike classics. If you have room, try the tiramisù (£6).

La Spighetta is the perfect local pizza and pasta joint – simple food at sensible prices, a good buzz at most times of night, and no real need to book. If it has a fault, it's that the service is a bit rushed and can be forgetful. But at these prices, that's hardly a gripe.

Mayfair & Bond Street

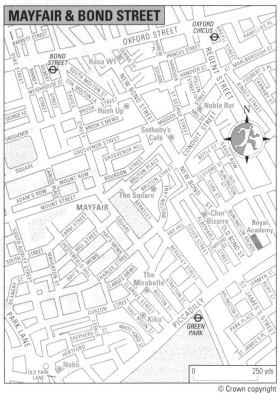

MAYFAIR & BOND STREET

OXFORD CIRCUS

RAMILLIES PL.

ARGYLL STREET

BARRETT STREET

OXFORD STREET

DUKE STREET

DERING ST.

HARLEY PL.

PRINCES STREET

GT MARLBOROUGH ST.

FOUBERT'S PL.

BOND STREET

Rasa W1

HANOVER SQUARE

HANOVER STREET

REGENT STREET

KINGLY STREET

CARNABY ST.

BINNEY ST.

GILBERT ST.

WEIGHHOUSE ST.

SOUTH MOLTON ST.

STH. MOLTON LA.

STREET

BROOK STREET

DAVIES STREET

Hush Up

BROOK'S MEWS

NEW BOND STREET

ST GEORGE STREET

MADDOX STREET

PULLEN PL.

MILL ST.

Noble Rot

GEORGE YD

Sotheby's Café

CONDUIT STREET

N

GROSVENOR

GROSVENOR STREET

GROSVENOR HILL

BOURDON STREET

BOYLE ST.

SAVILE ROW

SQUARE

CARLOS PLACE

MOUNT ROW

BOURDON STREET

BRUTON PLACE

CLIFFORD ST.

BURLINGTON

ADAM'S ROW

MOUNT STREET

The Square

BRUTON STREET

BRUTON LANE

CORK ST.

BURLINGTON GDNS

MAYFAIR

BERKELEY SQUARE

NEW BOND ST.

Chor Bizarre

ALBEMARLE

STAFFORD ST.

OLD BOND ST.

BURLINGTON ARCADE

Royal Academy

SOUTH AUDLEY STREET

FARM STREET

HILL STREET

HAY'S MEWS

HAY HILL

DOVER STREET

CHESTERFIELD HILL

WAVERTON ST.

CHARLES STREET

HAY'S MEWS

DEANERY ST.

SOUTH AUDLEY STREET

CLARGES MEWS

The Mirabelle

STRATTON ST.

BERKELEY STREET

ST JAMES'S ST.

BURY ST.

JERMYN ST.

CURZON STREET

CLARGES STREET

BOLTON ST.

ARLINGTON ST.

PARK PLACE

PARK LANE

HALF MOON ST.

Kiku

WHITE HORSE ST.

GREEN PARK

PICCADILLY

ST JAMES'S STREET

SHEPHERD STREET

HERTFORD

Nobu

OLD PARK LANE

ST. JAMES'S PL.

| 0 | 250 yds |

© Crown copyright

Chor Bizarre

Chor Bizarre is something of a novelty in London as one of a handful of Indian restaurants that has a "head office" in India. Indeed the London Chor Bizarre is a straight copy of the one in the Broadway Hotel in Delhi. Its name is an elaborate pun (Chor Bazaar translates as "thieves' market") and, like the Delhi branch, the London restaurant is furnished with an amazing clutter of Indian antiques and bric-a-brac. Every table, and each set of chairs, is different, and you may find yourself dining within the frame of an antique four-poster bed. The food is similarly eccentric, but very well prepared and strikingly authentic. Care is taken over the detail, and wine expert Charles Metcalfe has devised a striking wine list. Chor Bizarre does, however, carry the kind of price tag you'd expect of Mayfair.

Cost	£24–£45
Address	16 Albemarle St, W1
T	020 7629 9802 or 8542
Station	Green Park
Open	Mon–Sat noon–3pm & 6–11.30pm, Sun 6–10.30pm
Accepts	All major credit cards
W	www.chorbizarre.net

INDIAN

Start with simple things such as pakoras (£4.50), which are tasty vegetable fritters, or samosas (£4.50), which are fresh, full of potato and peas, and served with fine accompanying chutneys. Kebabs are taken seriously here, too: gilawat ke kebab (£6) is a Lucknow speciality made with lamb. Gazab ka tikka (£11), a best-seller in Delhi, is a kind of chicken tikka deluxe. Then, for your main course, choose dishes like baghare baingan (£8), a Hyderabadi dish combining aubergine, peanuts and tamarind. Or one of the dum pukht dishes, where the food is cooked slowly in a sealed pot – the chooza dum pukht (£14) is made with chicken. Breads are also impressive, including an excellent naan (£2.50); pudina paratha (£2.75) – a mint paratha; and stuffed kulcha (£2.75) – choose from cheese, potato or mince.

The many imposing set menus are a good way to tour the menu without watching your wallet implode. South Indian Tiffin (£24) features chicken Chettinad, Kerala prawn, porial, and sambal, served with rice and Malabari parathas on a banana leaf. Kashmiri tarami (£24) is a copper platter with goshtaba, mirchi korma, rajmah, al Yakhni, tamatar chaaman and nadru haaq on rice, preceded by a starter of dry-cooked lamb ribs. Or there is the Royal Repast (£24, or £22 vegetarian) – two starters, one item from the tandoor, two non-vegetarian main courses, three vegetarian mains, two breads, rice, two desserts and coffee!

Hush Up

Hush is one of a growing number of ultra-screaming-trendy night-club/members' clubs where the management has turned its attention to the quality of the grub. After the bars, the ambience and the beauty of the customers had been attended to, food had to make it to the top of the pile one day. Downstairs at Hush there is a bar/brasserie, on the top floor there is a members-only private dining and in between is the public resto. It's an elegant enough room, complete with a large bar, and the decor is suitably clubby. Hush Up is comfortable for lunch but fashionably dark in the evening, so the aged and infirm (that is to say anyone over thirty) may need to take a torch so that they can read the menu. The chef is Henry Harris, who joined, towards the end of 2000, from the Fifth Floor Restaurant at Harvey Nichols, Knightsbridge.

Cost	£27–£75
Address	8 Lancashire Court, Brook St, W1
T	020 7659 1500
Station	Bond Street
Open	Mon–Fri noon–3pm & 7–10.30pm, Sat 7–10.30pm
Accepts	All major credit cards

At dinner the menu usually offers seven starters, seven mains and seven puds. The cooking is the kind of stuff Harris made his name with: a beguiling combination of sophisticated and robust. Starters like red wine and duck risotto (£9); hot foie gras, "French toast", sauce Bigarade (£12.50); and potato velouté with fresh truffles (£10) are typical. Mains range from calf's kidney, smoked black pudding and mushroom croute with mustard sauce (£15); to rack of lamb "au poivre", Roquefort and spinach salad (£38 for two); and fillet of John Dory with a spinach risotto and Caesar dressing (£19). Puds are taken seriously, from the familiar – sticky toffee pudding with toffee sauce (£6) or coffee icebox pudding with chocolate Armagnac sauce (£6.50) – to the exotic, such as lemon rice pudding, mango and chilli sorbet (£5.50). The wine list has a decent selection but at Mayfair prices.

By day the kitchen takes a deep breath and simplifies everything. The lunch menu changes on a weekly basis and offers real value at £22 for two courses and £25 for three. Expect good, well-flavoured starters like a smooth and silky ham, vegetable and white bean soup; or a fricassée of chicken livers with stracci di pasta and Marsala vinaigrette. Main courses may include saffron papardelle with baby leeks and spinach; or roast rib-eye of beef, champignol potatoes, Savoy cabbage and Yorkshire pudding.

Kiku

There's no doubt it sounds like a bit of a porky. Kiku is a Japanese restaurant (translates as pricey), deep in the heart of Mayfair (translates as very pricey) and one that serves top class sushi with a classical ambience – without charging the earth. Your bill will prove it. In helpful, Oriental fashion it lists the huge number of sushi portions you are alleged to have consumed and then the average price. On one occasion in 2001 this figure was an awesomely low £2.93 per dish. What's even more appealing is that Kiku is laid out around a traditional sushi bar where you can sit and wonder at the dexterity of the knife man, who effortlessly keeps pace with the appetites in his section. Go along smack on opening time, snatch a seat at the counter and go for it.

Cost	£16–£55

Address 17 Half Moon St, W1
T 020 7499 4208
Station Green Park
Open Mon–Sat noon–2.30pm & 6.30–10.15pm
Accepts All major credit cards

JAPANESE

Knowledgeable Japanese folk always start a meal of sushi with tamago (£1.50) – the sweetish, omelettey one which allows the diner to properly assess the quality of the rice before getting serious with the fishy bits. Who knows? The toro – tuna belly (£5) is good; the suzuki – sea bass (£2.70) is good; the amaebi – sweet shrimp (£2.30) is … sweet. Hiramei – turbot (£2.70) is very delicate. You must have the hotate (£2.70) – slices of raw scallop, translucent and subtle, very good indeed. From the rolled sushi section, pick the umeshiso maki (£3.20), made from rice perked up by pickled plums and fresh green shiso leaves. There are so many good things here that you might feel emboldened to try some of the more challenging sushi, like akagai – ark shell (£3), or uni – sea urchin roe (£4.50). Verging on the "experts" category is tobiko (£2.70), which is flying fish roe and really rather good. A successful strategy might be to try a few sushi and then turn to the main menu: perhaps tempura moriawase (£9.50), which is mixed tempura; or sake teriyaki (£6.80), which is grilled teriyaki salmon. Drink the very refreshing Asahi beer and only venture into the realms of sake if you understand it.

If you feel your nerve breaking, there is a grand assortment of sushi combinations such as tokujyo nigiri (£27) or jyongiri (£20). You can share these to minimize the risk.

The Mirabelle

Anyone hoping to open their own restaurant should have lunch at The Mirabelle. It's not just the touch of Marco Pierre White, London's own culinary Rasputin; the whole operation is superlative. Forgive them the mind-numbingly arrogant and extensive wine list – which climaxes with an 1847 vintage Chateau d'Yquem at £30,000 – and concentrate on the food, which is quite reasonably priced for this kind of cooking. The ingredients are carefully chosen. The presentation on the plate is stunning. The surroundings are elegant, and the service attentive. There's a very elegant bar, too, which really does invite a pause for a drink before and maybe after a meal. Go on, splash out.

Cost	£25–£110

Address 56 Curzon St, W1
T 020 7499 4636
Station Green Park
Open Mon–Fri noon–2.30pm & 6–11.30pm, Sat & Sun noon–3pm 6–10.30pm
Accepts All major credit cards
W www.whitestarline.org.uk ·

Start with a classic: omelette "Arnold Bennett" (£9.50). It's no wonder that Arnold liked these so much – they're rich, buttery and light, made with smoked haddock. Or there's ballotine of salmon with herbs (£8.95). Or fresh asparagus with sauce mousseline (£10.50). Step up a level for some triumphant foie gras "en terrine" dishes: with green peppercorns, gelée de Sauternes and toasted brioche (£16.95); or "parfait en gelée" with toasted Poilane bread (£9.95). Believe it or not, these two are actually bargains. For a fishy main course, what about fillet of red mullet Niçoise with pommes safranes (£16.95)? Or the classical grilled lemon sole served on the bone with sauce tartare and creamed potatoes (£18.95)? In the meat section, there's pot roast of pork with spices and fresh ginger (£14.95); or escalope of calves' liver and bacon, sauce diable (£15.95); or grilled cutlet of veal à la forestière (£17.95). Puddings (all at £7.50) are deftly handled. The star is dark chocolate fondant with milk ice cream.

Choose the set lunch, don't let the wine list sneak up on you (there's a decent enough Montes Sauvignon Blanc for £16) and you could be enjoying a fine meal of terrine of pork knuckle with lentils and mustard dressing; followed by mousseline of salmon with new potatoes and langoustine velouté; and finally a ginger and lemongrass crème brûlée. Monday to Saturday, two lunchtime courses go for £16.50, and three for £19.95; at Sunday lunch three courses cost £19.50.

Noble Rot

When marketing consultants hold seminars on the importance of choosing the perfect name they probably don't start with a slide recommending Noble Rot. This establishment is sibling to 1 Lombard Street (see p.181), and the man responsible for the name is a Dane called Soren Jessen. The resto is called Noble Rot because of Jessen's passion for classic dessert wines – botrytis cinerea is the mould whose dessicating effects put the £££s into Chateu D'Yquem, amongst other top drops. Noble Rot is very much New Mayfair, New Money. After a slightly dodgy start, it has matured into a restaurant that, albeit expensive, offers well-presented, carefully considered dishes with a gratifying seasonal bias.

Cost	£18–£90

Address 3–5 Mill St, W1
T 020 7629 8877
Station Oxford Circus
Open Mon–Sat noon–3pm & 6–11pm
Accepts All major credit cards
W www.noblerot.com

FRENCH

In a strange way, the menu is influenced by the wine list, rather than the other way around. Starters may include a stunning and technically very accomplished foie gras and smoked eel terrine with apple jelly and toasted brioche (£11.95). Or an elegantly plated spiced Dorset crab salad with avocado relish and white tomato sorbet (£11.95). Or another foie gras dish, perhaps a terrine with piquillo peppers (£11.95)? All suitable dishes have a dessert wine suggestion appended. Main courses lean towards the classic: there may be osso buco; or choucroute garnie; or sirloin of beef. Roast skate may come with mash, oyster fritters and a laverbread sauce (£15). Halibut may be tea-smoked and served with rosti, girolles and sauce Bordelaise (£17.50). Richness is not shunned, quite the reverse – consider the poached and truffled chicken breast with morels and Riesling cream sauce (£17.50). Or roast rabbit, black pudding, mushy peas and foie gras tortellini (£17). Geese must be pretty frightened of the kitchen here. Puds are grandstand affairs and, in keeping with the ongoing theme, there is even a Valrhona chocolate and foie gras terrine, pineau des Charentes, caramel (£6.95) – although this reads like the crassest of publicity gimmicks it actually tastes rather good.

There is an epic selection of nearly thirty dessert wines by the glass, and a good many more by the bottle or half bottle. If you have £44 you can toy with a small glass of Chateau D'Yquem 1990. Or for £1725 there's a half litre of Tokaji Aszu, 6 Puttonyos 1912 – just the thing to indulge that sweet-tooth moment.

Nobu

It's hard to know just what to make of Nobu. On the face of it, a restaurant owned by Robert de Niro, Drew Nieporent and Matsuhisa Nobuyuki sounds like the invention of a deranged Hollywood producer. And then there is the cocoon of hype: the restaurant is exclusive, it's within the mega-cool Metropolitan hotel, it's amazingly expensive and it's full of famous people. As is often the case with hype, some of the above is gossip and some is gospel, but which is which? Don't worry – concentrate on the food, which is innovative and superb. Ingredients are fresh, flavour combinations are novel and inspired, and presentation is elegant and stylish. See for yourself – breeze in for the lunchtime bento box, which includes sashimi salad, rock shrimp tempura, black cod, oshitashi, vegetable spicy garlic, assorted sushi and miso soup, all for £25. There is now a second Nobu, called Ubon, at 34 Westferry Circus, E14 (☎020 7719 7800)

Cost	£30–£95
Address	19 Old Park Lane, W1
T	020 7447 4747
Station	Hyde Park Corner
Open	Mon–Thurs noon–2.15pm & 6–10.30pm, Fri & Sat noon–2.15pm & 6–11pm, Sun 6–9.30pm
Accepts	All major credit cards

Chef Matsuhisa worked in Peru, and South American flavours and techniques segue into classical Japanese dishes – some of the dishes here puzzle even stalwart Japanese foodies and defy classification. There are lists of Nobu "special appetisers" and "special dishes"; the problem is where to begin. Tiradito "Nobu" style (£10.50) is a plate of wafer-thin scallop slices, each topped with a dab of chilli, half a coriander leaf and a citrus dressing – delicate and utterly delicious. The sashimi is terrific; salmon is sliced and just warmed through to "set" it, before being served with sesame seeds (£10) – the minimal cooking makes a superb texture. The black cod with miso (£22.50) is a grandstand dish – a piece of perfectly cooked, well-marinated fish with an elaborate banana-leaf canopy. Other inspired dishes are the rock shrimp tempura (£8.75), and, for dessert, the chocolate and almond parfait with red berry compote (£7.95).

Nobu is probably the only place in London where none of the customers fully understands the menu. No one on their first visit could hope to make sense of it. For once it is no cop-out to opt for the omakase (chef's choice) menu, which costs £70 in the evenings and £50 at lunch. Do not be intimidated: book your table well in advance and settle back for a stunning gastronomic experience.

Rasa W1

Rasa W1 is a multiple contradiction: a Keralan restaurant that is pricey, elegant, fashionable, upmarket and still strictly vegetarian. When they opened in 1998, the management proudly claimed that this was the only non-smoking Indian restaurant in Britain. Rasa is a place completely at ease with itself, and with good reason – this is an off-shoot of the hugely

Cost	£12–£40

Address 6 Dering St, W1
T 020 7629 1346
Station Bond Street
Open Mon–Sat noon–3pm & 6–11pm, Sun 6–11pm
Accepts All major credit cards
W www.rasarestaurants.com

successful Rasa in Stoke Newington (see p.296) and it continues the tradition of superb cooking and friendly service that has kept North London diners blissfully happy for the last few years. The menu is littered with unfamiliar and homely dishes and they are all worth investigation. Lean heavily on the sound advice available.

Start with the pre-meal snacks (£4) and you will never be satisfied by a few curling popadoms again. Five different variations on the popadom theme are accompanied by seven fresh chutneys. Of the snacks, the acchappam is a fascinating three-dimensional honeycomb affair, while the chena upperi are root vegetable crisps. The chutneys, too, are stunning – there's a garlic pickle of genuine virulence, and what is described by Das, the proprietor, as "Mum's special" – a terrific concoction made from sharp green mangoes. Don't miss these. Highlights on the starters menu are banana boli (£4.25) – deep-fried plantain fritters; Mysore bonda (£4.25) – potato, ginger and curry-leaf cakes; and cashew nut pakoda (£4.25) – a kind of peanut brittle made with cashews. With the main courses (which in the evenings are served the traditional way, on banana leaves), try as many of the different rices as possible: tamarind, lemon and coconut (all £3.75). The curries are fascinating and unusual: cheera parippu curry (£6.25) is made with spinach, toor dall, garlic, cheese and tomatoes; bagar baingan (£6.25) is rich with aubergines; moru kachiathu (£6.25) is an unusual combination of sweet mangoes and green bananas. Also look out for the nadan parippu (£6), which is a Keralan lentil curry.

Going for the set menu often seems like an easy option, but this is one place where you'd be foolish not to consider it. The Kerala feast costs a not insubstantial £22.50 a head, but brings waves of dishes, each one seemingly better than the last. There are also likely to be a few off-menu delights – Mum's specials – which really are special.

Mayfair & Bond Street

Sotheby's Café

If you like the idea of eating in an art collection attached to a famous auction house, and rubbing shoulders with international art dealers and collectors, you will enjoy Sotheby's Café. Quintessentially English, it manages to retain an air of peace despite being sited on one side of the main hall of Sotheby's. For once, mumblings about an oasis of calm are entirely appropriate. The Café is also that rarity among London restaurants nowadays – a place where you can get a proper English afternoon tea.

Cost	£12–£35

Address 34–35 New Bond St, W1
T 020 7293 5077
Station Bond Street
Open Mon–Fri 9.30–11.30am, noon–3pm & 3–4.45pm (tea)
Accepts All major credit cards

The lunch menu is short, and changes daily with seasonal variations. Warm asparagus with citrus butter (£5.95) is very fresh and there's a good tang of lemon in the butter, while the cream of courgette soup with lemon crème fraîche (£4.95) is smooth, creamy and subtle. You may find halibut starring in a risotto of poached halibut and fresh peas with white truffle oil (£14.50). Lobster club sandwich (£12.50) makes for an ideal light lunch – the large chunks of fresh lobster are served in a club sandwich with fresh mayonnaise – but has proved so popular that it's worth ordering it in advance. Puddings include strawberry ice cream, fresh strawberries and lemon biscuits (£4.95), and a delightfully fresh-tasting pear and almond tart with clotted cream (£4.95). There is also a large range of teas, herbal teas and other infusions. Wines are chosen by Serena Sutcliffe, the Master of Wine who also runs Sotheby's wine auction department, and are well suited to the dishes that they accompany.

For afternoon tea you can choose dishes like Welsh rarebit (£4.75), Dumfries smoked salmon with brown bread (£6.75), and chicken club sandwich (£6.95). There are also set tea menus at £5.25 and £10.95; the latter includes chicken, tarragon and egg sandwiches and home-made cakes. Breakfast extends to scrambled eggs with toast (£3.50), and Scottish smoked salmon bagel with cream cheese (£6.95), but sadly no bacon and eggs. Whatever time of day, visitors who come just for the food are made very welcome – there's no pressure to feel that you need to go home with a paperweight or an old master. However, in keeping with the reverential atmosphere, a notice whispers "please, no smoking or mobile phones".

The Square

In 2001, The Square won the best French restaurant category at the Moet & Chandon London Restaurant Awards, and the wheel had turned full circle. After a century of French chefs being the only kind that mattered, Philip Howard (a rosbif!) had steered his brigade to the prize for best French restaurant. And The Square is very French: food is terribly important here. The finest ingredients are sought out and then largely classical technique ensures that each retains its essential character and flavour. Eating here is a palate-expanding experience.

Cost	£25–£110
Address	6–10 Bruton St, W1
T	020 7795 7100
Station	Green Park
Open	Mon–Fri noon–3pm & 6.30–10.45pm, Sat 6.30–10.45pm, Sun 6.30–9.30pm
Accepts	All major credit cards

FRENCH

This is a very gracious restaurant. Service is suave, silent and effortless. Dishes use the very best seasonal produce. Seasoning is on the button. Presentation is elegant. The wine list seems boundless in scope and soars to the very topmost heights (where mortals dare not even ask the price). Go for lunch and experience real excellence. For £20 you might have an assiette of duck and foie gras, or a risotto of pea and morels with scallops; followed by either roast salmon with a ragout of Jersey royals, mussels, saffron and leeks, or navarin of lamb with creamed potato and spring vegetables. Add the extra fiver and go on to chocolate fondant with malted milk ice cream. In the evening three courses cost £50 (plus a few supplements for the wildest extravagances). The menu changes on a broadly seasonal basis but you are likely to choose from eight starters – dishes like velouté of globe artichokes with chanterelles and a soft-poached truffled egg; or a warm salad of red mullet with Parmesan, pine nuts, fennel and lemon oil; or ballotine of duck and foie gras "à l'Orange". Then nine mains, which may include roast turbot with haricot beans, Savoy cabbage, lardons and a grain mustard velouté; sauté of monkfish and artichokes with hand-rolled macaroni, cauliflower purée and black truffles; or herb-crusted saddle of lamb with shallot purée, artichokes, roast garlic and rosemary. Puddings are classics with a bit extra – a caramelized lemon tart, perhaps, or a prune and Armagnac soufflé. Howard is an able man and Michelin's two-star measure of his worth is an underestimate. Dishes are deceptively simple, honest, and very, very good to eat.

There's also a six-course "taster" menu for £65 (for the entire table only). Book now. This is one treat you will never regret.

Paddington & Edgware Road

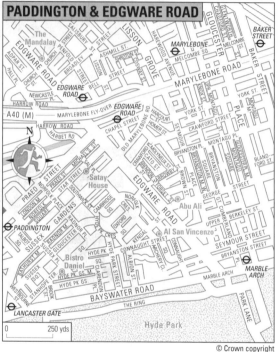

PADDINGTON & EDGWARE ROAD

© Crown copyright

Abu Ali

You can only suppose that, in the Lebanon, going out to eat is man's work. That certainly seems to be the case around the Oxford Street end of the Edgware Road, where you'll find Abu Ali's bustling café. This is an authentic place, the Lebanese equivalent of a northern working man's club: a bit spartan in

Cost	£7–£25
Address	136–138 George St, W1
T	020 7724 6338
Station	Marble Arch
Open	Daily 9.30am–11.30pm
Accepts	Cheque or cash only

LEBANESE

appearance, with honest, terrific-value food and pavement tables where men gather to smoke a pipe or two and discuss the world. Although you are unlikely to find many Lebanese women here, female diners get a dignified welcome. There's nothing intimidating about the place or its clientele.

You will want a selection of starters. Tabouleh (£2.50) is bright green with lots of fresh parsley, lemon juice, oil and only a little cracked wheat – it even tastes healthy. Hommos (£2.50) is rich and spicy, garnished with a few whole chickpeas and Cayenne pepper. Warak inab (£3) are stuffed vine leaves served hot or cold, thin and pleasantly sour. Kabis is a plate of tangy salt and sour pickles – cucumber, chillies and red cabbage – that comes free with every order. For main dishes there's kafta billaban (£5.50) – minced lamb kebabs served hot under a layer of sharp yoghurt and with a sprinkling of pine kernels. Or there's kibbeh bissiniyeh (£5), which is a strange dish: a ball of mince and pine kernels coated with a layer of mince and cracked wheat, then baked until crispy in the oven. The plain grilled meats are also good: try the boned-out poussin – farrouge moussahab (£7). To drink, there is mint tea (£2) – a Lipton's teabag and a bunch of fresh mint in every pot – or soft drinks.

Inside and outside Abu Ali's, the air is full of the sweet scent of bubble pipes. They cost £5 a go, and you can have either apple or strawberry. The long strands of black tobacco are mixed into a squelchy mess with chopped fruit and then covered with a piece of foil, on top of which is placed a chunk of blazing charcoal – you are on your way to clouds of sweet-smelling smoke. Some of the cognoscenti take this procedure a step further and replace the water through which the smoke bubbles with ice and Appletise. It certainly makes for a perfumed environment from which to watch the world go by.

Bistro Daniel

Bistro Daniel is the baby brother of Daniel Gobet's smarter restaurant, Amandier. The bistro occupies the basement while the restaurant is on the ground floor. Both are dedicated to French gastronomy with a Provençal bias and they share the same kitchen. Daniel served in the kitchens of Mon Plaisir before opening his own place, La Ciboulette in Chelsea, which gained an enviable reputation in a very short space of time. Both establishments were resolutely French; Bistro Daniel, while still offering accomplished cooking, introduces some less traditional touches. It is an informal restaurant and the cool basement makes for an intimate atmosphere.

Cost	£15–£50

Address 26 Sussex Place, W2
T 020 7723 8395
Station Paddington
Open Mon–Fri noon–2.30pm
& 6.30–10.30pm, Sat
6.30–10.30pm
Accepts All major credit cards

Starters might include home-made country style terrine and gherkins (£4.50); half a dozen snails in their shells with garlic parsley butter (£5.30); a pukka French onion soup with croutons and cheese (£4); and a tartare of avocado and Atlantic prawns (£5.40). Main courses may include braised knuckle of lamb, carrots and thyme jus (£10.95); fricassée of Scottish scallops and fine tagliatelle with a herb butter sauce (£12.95); and duck leg confit with Puy lentils and gravy sauce (£8.95). There's also coulibac of salmon with chive butter sauce (£7.95); pan-fried Scottish sirloin steak with a peppercorn sauce (£12.50); and, on a lighter, vegetarian note, fricassée of fine tagliatelle with chanterelle mushrooms (£7.50). Side dishes of gratin Dauphinois, pommes frites and carrots with cumin seeds (all £1.95) are generous and tasty. Puddings (all at £3.95) include pear and ginger bread-and-butter pudding; profiteroles and vanilla ice cream; and chocolate cake with pistachio ice cream. Trifling with the selection of French cheese will set you back £5.

Bistro Daniel shares a wine list with the Amandier restaurant upstairs. So you can venture all the way from sensible to serious: listed here are wines as grand as Bâtard Montrachet Grand Cru for £110 or even a Château Latour at £350, if the fancy takes you and your wallet concurs. At Amandier, there's a daily set lunch at £9.95 for two courses and £12.95 for three – an economical way to taste the sophisticated dishes upstairs.

The Mandalay

In the Edgware Road desert – north of the Harrow Road but south of anything else – Gary and Dwight Ally, Scandinavian-educated Burmese brothers, have set up shop in what must be an ex-greasy spoon. The resulting restaurant is rather bizarre, with just 28 seats, the old sandwich counter filled with strange and exotic ingredients, and greetings and decoration in both Burmese and Norwegian. Gary is in the kitchen and smiley, talkative Dwight is front of house.

Cost   £6–£16

Address 444 Edgware Rd, W2
T 020 7258 3696
Station Edgware Road
Open Mon-Sat noon–2.30pm & 6–10.30pm; closed bank holidays
Accepts All major credit cards
W www.bcity.com/mandalay

BURMESE

The Ally brothers have perhaps correctly concluded that their native language is unmasterable by the English, so the menu is written in English with a Burmese translation – an enormous help when ordering. But the food itself is pure unexpurgated Burmese, and all freshly cooked. The local cuisine is a melange of different local influences, with a little bit of Thai and Malaysian, and a lot of Indian, and a few things that are distinctly their own. To start there are popadoms (two for £1.20) or a great bowlful of prawn crackers (£1.90), which arrive freshly fried and sizzling hot (and served on domestic kitchen paper to soak up the oil). First courses range from spring rolls (from £1.90 for two) and samosas (£1.90 for four), to salads like raw papaya and cucumber (£3.90) or fermented tea leaf (£3.90), which is a great deal better than it sounds. There are soups, noodle soups and all manner of fritters as well. Main courses are mainly curries, rice and noodle dishes, spiced with plenty of ginger, garlic, coriander and coconut, and using fish, chicken and vegetables as the main ingredients. The cooking is good, flavours hit the mark, portions are huge, and only a handful of dishes costs over £6.50. Vegetable dishes are somewhat more successful than the prawn ones, but at this price it's only to be expected.

Even with its eccentric setting, tiny room and rigorous no-smoking policy, The Mandalay has built up a loyal following over the years. The tables are minuscule and the acoustics are good, so be careful what you talk about and keep your ears open – you are just as likely to sit next to a dustman as an expat Burmese diamond dealer.

Al San Vincenzo

Al San Vincenzo is not a cheap restaurant. But then you'll find it smack bang in the middle of a patch of serious affluence near the bottom end of the Edgware Road, so the local clientele are not over bothered. This is a very passionate place with a small dining room, and a single-minded chef in the kitchen, which perhaps accounts for the mercifully simple dishes and good seasonal food. The front-of-house attitudes are more relaxed, but if there were a motto over the door it would probably read "No compromise". The pricing is straightforward: two courses may be had for £27.50 and three courses cost £33.50; supplements are rare but some of the more expensive ingredients, like fresh fish, can bump the price up a bit.

Cost	£35–£65

Address 30 Connaught St, W2
T 020 7262 9623
Station Marble Arch
Open Mon–Fri 12.15–3pm & 7–11pm, Sat 7–11pm
Accepts Visa, MasterCard

The menu changes to reflect the seasons, but there are usually six or seven starters to choose from. Dishes range from the plain but satisfying, such as potato and lentil soup, to interesting and unusual combinations like slivers of breast of goose with a pomegranate sauce and rocket salad. Flavours are intense and presentation gloriously unfussy. The perfect example is "fresh eels pan fried with chilli, onions and lemon" – the richness of the boneless eel fillets is cut by the lemony tang and a belt of chilli. This tastes as good as it sounds. Main courses are in similar vein: fillet of brill with mussels, saffron and potato puree; rack of venison with red cabbage and green beans; or risotto of cannellini beans, celery and Parmesan cheese. Vegetarians are well-served here, and one of the starters (a lasagne of porcini mushrooms, buffalo Mozzarella and pumpkin) is particularly fine. The dessert menu ranges from the expected – vin santo with biscotti – to more surprising puds such as fresh dates stuffed with marzipan, rolled in pistachio and served with a bitter chocolate sauce and vanilla ice cream.

The wine list covers the mid-ground well, with a well-chosen series of Italian wines priced at between £15 and £35. Look out for the light and bright Vernaccia, which is a good option at lunch. Beer lovers will be intrigued by the full flavoured Ichinusa beer from Sardinia – this is a real treat.

Satay House

Why is it that starters always seem to have the edge on main courses? This depressingly accurate rule of thumb can be explained in part by the fact that you get to the starters first – when your appetite is still a contender. The Satay House breaks this rule. Here the starters are pretty pedestrian and the satay, for which the establishment was named,

Cost	£14–£36

Address 13 Sale Place, W2
T 020 7723 6763
Station Paddington
Open Daily noon–3pm &
6–11pm
Accepts All major credit cards
W www.satayhouse.com

MALAYSIAN

particularly ordinary. But do not be downcast, for the main courses are spectacularly good. Simply adjust your expectations and ordering policy to suit. This is one of the few Malaysian restaurants in London that is actually Malaysian-run (most are owned by Chinese restaurateurs cashing in on something new) and, in consequence, the Satay House attracts a knowledgeable Malaysian clientele. Service is friendly and the light, bright dining room is usually full.

Order the satay (£5.20 for six sticks) if you must – the sauce is chunky but under-seasoned. It's much better to make a start elsewhere on the menu, perhaps with a murtabak (£5.50), off the bread list. This is an eggy Malaysian bread wrapped around minced meat and served like a small plump pillow, with bright-orange, sweet pickled onions – it is very delicious indeed and the onions have an almost addictive quality. Continue with nasi lemak (£7) – rice cooked in coconut milk, topped with crisp whole peanuts, still in their little red jackets, and slivers of deep-fried anchovy. You could also go for one of the excellent noodle dishes such as kway teow goreng (£5.50) – with meat, prawns, egg and vegetables. Among the main dishes, standouts include the rendang daging (£7) – beef cooked for days and served almost dry but spectacularly tender; and the ayam goreng beriada (£5.50) – chicken pieces on the bone covered in chilli paste and fried. Try some specials, too: an order of sambal belacan (£3) produces fiercely salty and fishy chillies, fish paste and cucumber; cincalok (£2.50) brings you shrimps cooked Mallacan style.

The Malaysian customers drink odd fluorescent-coloured drinks made from sugar cane, or soya beans, or lychees, or guava, or else dark brown tea with condensed milk and ice. Happy experimenting.

Piccadilly & St James's

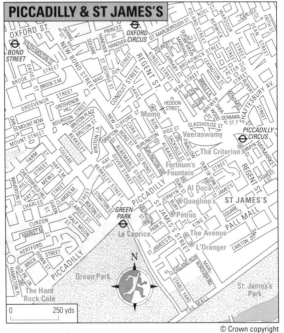

PICCADILLY & ST JAMES'S

© Crown copyright

The Avenue

The Avenue was one of the first banker-led restaurants in London – owner Chris Bodker got a bunch of City chums to join him in setting up the kind of restaurant where he and they would choose to eat. Now he has a sprawling empire, including Kensington Place (see p.451). This is a stark yet stylish barn of a place, with white walls and pale cherry-wood chairs, and an enormous video wall of moving images around the bar seating area. Entrance is through a glass door, part of a great glass plate fronting the restaurant, and greeting is by designer-clad hosts. Inside it's very noisy, with an upbeat atmosphere. There is not much subtlety about this place – wear your choicest clobber to feel most at home and do not be afraid to gawp.

Cost	£25–£50
Address	7–9 St James's St, SW1
T	020 7321 2111
Station	Green Park
Open	Mon–Thurs noon–3pm & 5.45pm–midnight, Fri & Sat noon–3pm & 5.45pm–12.30am, Sun noon–3.30pm & 7–10pm
Accepts	All major credit cards
W	www.theavenue.co.uk

Cooking is well executed and the menu is a fashionable mix of English and Italian. First courses are generally salads and pastas: tomato and Mozzarella salad (£5.95); gravlax with spinach and mustard salad (£6.50); or a leek and truffle cheese tortellini (£6.25/£11), offered in two sizes to give more choice to vegetarians, who may otherwise feel the choice here is a little cramped. Main courses are generally more substantial, and lean towards nursery food: fish fingers (£11.75); smoked haddock fish cake with mustard sauce (£12.95); or calves' liver with lentils and Tuscan salami (£15), which is a posh liver and bacon with mash. Anyone watching their weight might like to try the rare seared tuna with red onion and parsley salad (£15.50). And for those with a traditionalist bent there's loin of pork with parsnip mash (£14.95). Puddings – white chocolate "cannelloni" with mixed berries (£5.75), lemon curd cheesecake (£5.75) and sticky toffee pudding with cream (£5.75) – are generally unchallenging, and will appeal to those with a seriously sweet tooth.

The Avenue is huge, so even if you haven't booked it's likely you'll get a table for dinner. Call to check if there have been any cancellations. At lunchtime there's a good set menu at £17.50 for two courses, and £19.50 for three. The same menu is available pre- or post-theatre (5.45–7.30pm and 10.15pm–midnight), at £14.50 and £16.50.

Le Caprice

Cost	£25–£55

Address Arlington House, Arlington St, SW1
T 020 7629 2239
Station Green Park
Open Daily noon–3pm (Sun 4pm) & 5.30pm–midnight
Accepts All major credit cards

No socialite in London worth their salt is not a regular at this deeply chic little restaurant behind the Ritz – everyone from royalty downwards uses it for the occasional quiet lunch or dinner. That's not because they'll be hounded by well-wishers or because photographers will be waiting outside. They won't. This restaurant is discreet enough to make an oyster seem a blabbermouth. It's not even particularly plush or comfortable, with a black-and-white tiled floor, a big black bar and cane seats. What keeps Le Caprice full day in, day out is its personal service, its very good, properly prepared food and a bill that holds no surprises.

The much-copied menu is enticing from the first moment. Plum tomato and basil galette (£6.75) is simplicity itself, but with decent ingredients that taste of what they should. Crispy duck comes with watercress salad (£8.75), while dressed Cornish crab with landcress (£13.75) is so fresh and clean it makes you wonder why other restaurants can't manage this. In season, there's usually game, such as a grouse salad with elderberries (£13.50) – perfectly hung breast of grouse with tender salad leaves. Or perhaps char-grilled squid with Italian bacon (£13.50) tempts; or braised beef in Barolo with creamed macaroni (£9.75); or deep-fried haddock with minted pea puree, chips and tartare sauce (£14.75). If you are still up for pudding, try the sherry trifle with summer fruits (£5.75) or the blackberry summer pudding (£6.50) to see just what classic English puds are about. In the winter there is an array of more solid rib-stickers.

Expense aside, the only trouble with Le Caprice is the struggle to get a table. It is so permanently booked up that they only really accept reservations from people they know, or people who book well in advance. If you are able to plan far enough ahead, you should go just for the experience, otherwise you'll have to befriend a regular. But this has its advantages, too. It's too chic and grown up to attract the fly-by-night fashion people, and you won't find wall-to-wall hip designer-wear. All you need to look the part is a Continental tan, a little jewellery, Italian clothes and a few old-fashioned laughter lines.

The Criterion Brasserie

The Criterion is one of London's most beautiful restaurants. Covered up and used as a shop for decades (it was a 24-hour Boots branch for years), in its latest incarnation it has been restored to its full-on *belle-époque* glory. Dining areas are divided by classical arches, and the impossibly high ceiling is decorated with gold mosaics and flower-like lamps. And a trip to the loo is de rigueur, simply to be able to walk the whole length of the room viewing the romantic paintings on the walls. Tables are laid with linen and silver in a modern version of traditional perfection, and are set far apart from each other. Diners are a mix of young romantic couples, middle-aged gourmets and a few business people clearly plotting the next billion-pound deal. All of them hope that while Marco Pierre White doesn't cook here personally, he's keeping an eye on the food.

Cost £28–£55

Address 224 Piccadilly, W1
T 020 7930 0488
Station Piccadilly Circus
Open Mon–Sat noon–2.30pm
& 5.30–11pm, Sun 6–10.30pm
Accepts All major credit cards
except Diners

Start with the warm salad of smoked eel, bacon and pommes sautées with creamed horseradish (£9.50), or the risotto with crab, clams and parsley (£9.50), and you will see how a reputation is earned. Main courses are created from simple combinations of good ingredients – ingredients that have been combined so that each enhances the other. Try turmeric-roasted brill, which is served with a mussel and clam fondue (£14.75); braised shank of lamb with broad bean puree and rosemary jelly (£15.75); smoked haddock and poached egg with Colcannon bonne Nantaise (£13.95); or sautéed calves' liver with lime jus and spiced pommes écrasées (£14.95). Puddings (all £7.50) include sticky toffee pudding with caramel ice cream; tarte Tatin of Cox's apples (for two); orange ravioli with citrus gratin; truffle au chocolat; and fresh strawberries in a red wine and basil jelly. You'll find that overindulgence seems strictly necessary.

The Criterion doesn't come cheap. With wines up to £225 on the ordinary list (there is a fine wine list at much higher prices) you could blow your monthly salary here, but there are some bargains too. The daily set lunch at £14.95 for two courses and £17.95 for three is good value, considering the quality and venue. Booking for dinner is essential.

ITALIAN

Al Duca

This restaurant hit the West End scene, to warm applause, in 2000. High quality, sophisticated food, agreeable setting, slick service – and all at prices that represent real value. What you get here seems to be far more than you pay for. It's unlikely, however, that Al Duca makes a loss, being part of talented restaurateur Claudio Pulze's mini-group. What seems more likely is that prices elsewhere may be a tad higher than they should be. The formula here is a simple one: at lunch, two courses cost £16.50, three cost £19.50, and four £22.50. In the evening the prices go up to £19, £22, and £25. A four-course dinner for £25 within stumbling distance of Piccadilly? More like this please!

Cost	£20–£40

Address 4–5 Duke of York St, SW1
T 020 7839 3090
Station Piccadilly Circus
Open Mon–Thurs noon–2.30pm & 6–10.30pm, Fri noon–2.30pm & 6–11pm, Sat 12.30–3pm & 6–11pm
Accepts All major credit cards except Diners

Anyone who eats out regularly in London might feel cynical about such an offer, doubtful that the cooking and portion sizes could remain uncompromised by the low prices. But do not think London, think Italy. Such regularly changing menus are commonplace there. There are usually six starters at Al Duca: dishes like poached egg with organic polenta and Fontina cheese; or salad of spinach, goat's cheese and roasted red onions. Then there are six dishes under the heading pasta: boccoli all'ortolane (garden vegetables); linguine with clams; or reginette with peas and bacon. Followed by six main courses: pan-fried salmon with fennel salad and lemon vinaigrette; fillet steak; roast leg of duck with lentils and aromatic leaves. Finally, six desserts ranging from an indulgent tiramisù to a classic, simple plate of fresh pear and Pecorino cheese. The standard of cooking is high, with dishes bringing off that difficult trick of being both deceptively simple and satisfyingly rich. The home-made pasta and polenta are fresh and good. The fish is perfectly cooked. Overall there is much to praise here, and the slick service and stylish ambience live up to the efforts in the kitchen.

As seems to be the case with every "all-in" menu, the dreaded supplements do put in an appearance, but they are on the small side and seem fair – £4 extra for the sea bass, £2 for a starter made with buffalo Mozzarella and goose ham.

Fortnum's Fountain

The main entrance to Fortnum's Fountain Restaurant is at the back of the store on the corner of Jermyn Street. This makes it a draw for those working and shopping in the surrounding area, though the core clientele of this rather traditional English restaurant are well-to-do retired folk who use Fortnum & Mason to shop, or wish that they still could. The Fountain reflects their taste and is utterly dependable, delivering just what you expect – and indeed hope for – in its well-prepared, very English, breakfasts, lunches, teas and early dinners. The ingredients, as you'd expect of London's smartest and most old-fashioned food shop, are top-class. And the Fountain itself is a very pretty room, with classical murals all around.

Cost	£15–£30

Address 181 Piccadilly, W1
T 020 7973 4140
Station Piccadilly Circus/
Green Park
Open Mon–Sat 8.30–11.30am
breakfast, 11.30am–3pm
lunch, 3–5.30pm tea,
5.30–8pm dinner
Accepts All major credit cards

The Fountain is deservedly famous for its selection of Fortnum's teas and coffees accompanied by cream teas and ice cream sundaes, and on any given afternoon you will see small children being treated to their idea of heaven by elderly relatives. And beware, the splendid Knicker-bocker glory (£4.75) has a terrifying ability to turn even grumpy middle-aged men into small children. But the restaurant also serves a very decent breakfast: the full English, called Fortnum's Farmhouse Breakfast (£12.95), is rather better than that found in many hotels, and the grilled kipper with brown toast (£7.95) will gladden the dourest heart. The dishes on the Fountain Menu (which serves for both lunch and dinner) reflect the ingredient-buying power of the food department and, sensibly enough, tend to the straightforward. The excellent London smoked salmon with soda bread (£13.25) is a real treat, as is Fortnum's Welsh rarebit on Cheddar bread with grilled tomato, back bacon or poached egg (£8.75). There are also simple classics such as grilled Dover sole with side salad and new potatoes (£19.50); grilled sirloin steak with peppercorn sauce and chips (£14.75); and Highland scramble (£10.25), which teams scrambled eggs with smoked salmon.

The restaurant is always busy and, though they turn tables, you will not be hurried. The downside is that there is no booking. That's great for shoppers, but anyone on a schedule should avoid the lunchtime peak. Give breakfast serious consideration.

The Hard Rock Café

The Hard Rock Café is a genuine celebration of rock'n'roll, which makes its location, in Hyde Park's trad hotel strip, all the more strange. Perhaps it was chance, or clever marketing, as the bulk of the café's customers are tourists. Whatever the reason, this is the original Hard Rock Café, here since the 1970s, and it's the original theme restaurant. As such, it's a hard act to follow. The queue to get in is legendary – there is no booking and you will find a queue almost all day long, every day of the year – and it kind of adds to the occasion. Once in, there is a great atmosphere, created by full-on rock music, dim lighting and walls dripping with rock memorabilia. The Hard Rock food is not bad, either, predominantly Tex-Mex and burgers.

Cost	£8–£35
Address	150 Old Park Lane, W1
T	020 7629 0382
Station	Hyde Park Corner
Open	Daily 11.30am–12.30am (Sat 3am)
Accepts	All major credit cards
W	www.hardrock.com

They like their paperwork here. As well as three separate menus – one in the shape of a life-size guitar, another that lists seasonal specials and a bar menu which also lists the merchandise available – there is a memorabilia catalogue, the Hall of Fame, which also displays the floor plan of this rock'n'roll museum. The menus are peppered with rock'n'roll vocabulary. B.B. wings (boneless bodacious wings – £5.25) are graded classic rock (medium) or heavy metal (hot). The burgers (£7.25) knock spots off those at the high-street chains and cover the spectrum from natural veggie burger (£7.25) to "pig sandwich" (£7.35). Among the Tex-Mex dishes, the grilled fajitas (£11.55) are pretty good. Choose from chicken, beef or vegetarian; all come with bits and pieces for parcelling up with sour cream and guacamole. Puddings are self-indulgent: the hot fudge brownie (£4.25) elevates goo to an art form.

Elderly Lords and Ladies who have tottered up Piccadilly in search of the branch of Coutt's bank that stood on the opposite corner from 150 Old Park Lane will be deeply puzzled to find that it is now the Hard Rock's memorabilia shop (perhaps they could try for a T-shirt and cashback?). Meanwhile, connoisseurs of the quainter vagaries of restaurant design will be upset that the refurbishment of the downstairs at the Hard Rock has meant the demise of the "Elvis Stairs" – one of London's more eccentric shrines.

Momo

Momo is an attractive and very trendy Moroccan restaurant tucked away in a backwater off Regent Street. For dinner, you usually have to book at least a week in advance and to opt for an early or late sitting. If you apply for the late shift, be prepared for a noisy, night-club ambience, especially on Fridays and Saturdays. The design of the place is clever, with bold geometric kasbah-style architecture, decked out with plush cushions and lots of candles. Down-stairs there's an even more splendid-looking Moorish bar, annoyingly reserved for members only – a shame, as Momo is the kind of place where you could happily carry on the evening, especially if you're booked in for the earlier (7–9pm) of its two dining slots.

Cost	£30–£50
Address	25 Heddon St, W1
T	020 7434 4040
Station	Piccadilly Circus/ Oxford Circus
Open	Mon–Fri noon–2.30pm & 7–11.30pm, Sat 7–11.30pm, Sun 6.30–9.45pm
Accepts	All major credit cards

NORTH AFRICAN

Whenever you arrive, get into the mood with a Momo special (£6), a blend of vodka, lemon juice and sparkling water, topped with a pile of chopped mint. While you're downing that, you can check out the starters. Briouat de haddock fumée aux pignons, emulsion des poivrons rouges (£7) are mouthwatering little parcels of paper-thin pastry filled with smoked haddock and pinenuts, while salade Méchouia (£6.50) is made with grilled peppers, tomatoes, cumin and coriander. Or you might try filet de sardines marinées, aumonière de legumes croquants (£7.50), marinated sardines in a filo pastry basket with stir-fried vegetables. For main course, there are six tagines to choose from; these are North African-style stews served in a large clay pot. Try the tagine of confit duck with persimmon (£15.50) – not something you'd find in Morocco, but delicious all the same. Alternatively, opt for couscous: brochette de poulet (£14) combines the staple with marinated spicy chicken and a pot of vegetables; couscous Méchoui (£32 for two) adds roasted spiced lamb. Or treat yourself to the Fès speciality of pastilla (£10), the super-sweet pigeon pie in millefeuille pastry – a main course that has been relegated to the starters list. Desserts (all around £5.50) include a pastilla made with chocolate, and an orange salad with orange-blossom syrup.

Finally, even if you don't make it into the seclusion of the member's bar, don't miss a trip to the toilets downstairs – the men's urinal is an installation of some beauty.

Piccadilly & St James's

L'Oranger

From the outside, L'Oranger looks like a very expensive French restaurant dedicated to expense-account diners. While it's not cheap, the inclusive menus do bring serious cooking within reach. At lunch you pay £20 for two courses or £24.50 for three, and dinner is set at £39.50 for three courses. For your money you can expect modern Provençale cooking of a high standard. The saucing leans towards light olive oil bases rather than the traditional "loadsa-cream" approach and, for cooking of this quality, it is most competitively priced.

Cost	£28–£70
Address	5 St James's St, SW1
T	020 7839 3774
Station	Green Park
Open	Mon–Fri noon–2.30pm & 6–11pm, Sat 6–11pm
Accepts	All major credit cards

Starters may include Provençale chickpea soup; open ravioli of lamb and tomatoes; lamb consommé; steamed salmon boudin stuffed with a mousse of scallops with Niçoise leeks; and braised Swiss chard served in a veal broth with bone marrow and herbs. They are beautifully realized and well-judged combinations of flavours. For main courses, try roasted duck magret with fondant potato and foie gras sauce – delicious, and not as rich as you might imagine. There's also roasted monkfish tail rolled in black pepper and crushed with spinach in sauce Antiboise (tomato, basil and pistou); canon of lamb with braised fennel, artichoke and confit of tomato; pan-fried fillet of sea bass with courgettes, tomato, black olive vinaigrette and basil (£3 supplement); and roasted loin of pork wrapped in bacon and sage with confit of celery. Puddings include lemon and thyme crème caramel; warm chocolate fondant; and baked apple pudding with orange zest. It's one of those menus where you want everything, even though some of the more elaborate dishes carry a small supplement. Side dishes of seasonal vegetables are also served. The wine list is encyclopedic, starting at £16 for a Chardonnay and going up to £450 for a bottle of La Tâche de la Romanée-Conti. But there's plenty of good choice at the lower prices.

L'Oranger is refined and elegant with attentive service but a relaxed and unstuffy atmosphere. There's also a secret outside courtyard, which is open at dinner only, and a private function room for twenty. The set prices policy turns what would be an expensive treat menu into accessible dining. More restaurants copy please.

Pétrus

🍴 St James's, which once used to bristle with stuffy clubs for English gentlemen, has achieved a new role as something of a restaurant centre. As the older restaurants – some of which, like Prunier's and Overton's, had been around since the war – upped sticks, so modern establishments arrived. And now, despite the terrible shortage of parking, there's a small coterie of restaurants offering fine

Cost	£30–£90
Address	33 St James's St, SW1
T	020 7930 4272
Station	Green Park
Open	Mon–Fri noon–2.45pm & 6.45–10.45pm, Sat 6.45–10.45pm
Accepts	All major credit cards

dining. This site's transformation has not been simple: the first restaurant here, 33, opened to fanfares in 1996, but never quite made it, and at the beginning of 1999, after a serious refurb, it reopened with new owners as Pétrus.

This is a restaurant that, despite being a relative newcomer, manages to give the impression of being old-established, and it has built up a suitably St James-ish clientele. Head chef Marcus Wareing is a skilled cook. Dishes have a grand intensity of flavour, presentation is aimed squarely at the tyrefolk inspectors, and each dish is a well-balanced affair – both in terms of taste and texture. Even more miraculous, dishes here have a quirk of originality about them. Meals are straightforwardly priced at three courses for £45. Starters are often elaborate and "haute cuisine": sautéed scallops with tortellini of leek and onion, ginger and horseradish cream; or ballotine of confit foie gras with celeriac and apple salad, baby artichokes, sliced truffle and cream vinaigrette; or pan-fried red mullet served with marinated red peppers, confit of new potatoes and tapenade. Main courses may include a roasted fillet of turbot with brandade of salt cod, braised fennel and red wine sauce; or saddle of venison, sautéed ceps and baby spinach with potato galette and Madeira truffle jus; or braised halibut, caramelized orange, chicory, sautéed girolles and Sauternes sauce. The puddings and pastrywork are accomplished: apple and date crisp with crème fraîche ice cream and caramel sauce; or Earl Grey tea cream with raisin biscuits, Chantilly and vanilla butter sauce.

There's a terrific set lunch – how about pressed terrine of game and sweetbreads with a game jus, vinaigrette and toasted brioche; then braised fillet of brill with crab ravioli, cos lettuce, gnocchi, asparagus and velouté of crab; and finally bitter chocolate tart with caramel ice cream? And for £26? Outstanding.

Quaglino's

In 1929 Giovanni Quaglino opened a restaurant in Bury Street which became an instant success. He was a daring innovator and is reputed to have been the first person to serve hot dishes as hors d'oeuvres. The thing his new restaurant had, above all else, was glamour. When Sir Terence Conran redesigned and reopened Quaglino's, more than sixty years later, his vision was

Cost	£16–£70
Address	16 Bury St, SW1
T	020 7930 6767
Station	Green Park
Open	Mon–Sat noon–3pm & 5.30pm–midnight, Sun 5.30–11pm
Accepts	All major credit cards
W	www.conran.com

essentially the same. Love it or loathe it, Quaglino's is glamorous, and when it first opened it attracted a sophisticated crowd. Inevitably, with such a huge restaurant, that early exclusivity is a fading memory. And although the food is no longer in the first division, the ambience is still at the top of the Premiership: the elegant reception, the sweeping staircase into the bar which overlooks the main restaurant, and the second stairway one down to restaurant level. If this kind of thing rings your bell you will be happy here.

The menu is simple, classy and brasserie-style, with very little to scare off the less experienced diner. Given the size of the restaurant, it is best to go for the simpler dishes that need less finishing and exactitude – with this number of people to feed, the head chef is not going to have a chance to get to every plate. The fabulous display of seafood at the far end of the restaurant makes it tempting to stick to the plateau de fruits de mer (£30 per person), which is as good as you would hope, or whole lobster mayonnaise (£29). Fish and chips (£13.50) is served with home-made chips and tartare sauce and is excellent, while entrecôte Béarnaise (£18.50) is a treat when served, as it is here, properly cooked. Puddings are straightforward and agreeably sweet – apple tart with caramel ice cream (£6); double chocolate pudding (£6.50).

Quaglino's staff can be brusque, but then marshalling large numbers of glamour-seekers is a testing enough job which would make anyone a little tetchy. You can avoid this altogether by staying in the bar, which offers highlights from the menu – including all the seafood. Furthermore, Quaglino's is open late, which makes it perfect for a genuine after-theatre dinner. There's a prix fixe menu at lunch and pre- or post-theatre: two courses for £12.50, three for £15.

Veeraswamy

Veeraswamy is Britain's oldest-surviving Indian restaurant, founded in 1927 by Edward Palmer following a successful catering operation at the British Empire Exhibition. Its next owner was Sir William Steward, who pulled in the rich and famous throughout the postwar boom – their numbers included the King of Denmark, whose penchant for a glass of Carlsberg with his curry is said to have first established the link between Indian food and beer. The latest owner is Namita Panjabi, who also owns Chutney Mary (see p.404) and Masala Zone (see p.128). She has swept Veeraswamy into the modern era: the old and faded colonial decor has gone, along with the old and faded dishes. In their place there's an elegant, fashionable restaurant painted in the vibrant colours of today's India, and an all-new menu of bold, modern, authentically Indian dishes of all kinds, from street food to regional specialities. It's a bit of a shock to find an Indian restaurant like this – but a pleasant one.

Cost	£20–£50
Address	Victory House, 101 Regent St, W1
T	020 7734 1401
Station	Piccadilly Circus
Open	Mon–Sat noon–2.30pm & 5.30–11.30pm, Sun noon–3pm & 5.30–10.30pm
Accepts	All major credit cards
W	www.realindianfood.com

You'll need to adjust your pattern of ordering. Main dishes come as a plate with rice, and sometimes vegetables too. They're not designed for sharing, and you will definitely need one each. Street food makes great starters: pani puri (£5.25) – rich with tamarind; or ragda pattice (£5.25) – spiced potato cakes with chickpea curry. Or there's machli ki tikki (£5.75) – fish cakes; or fresh oysters, exquisitely stir-fried with Keralan spices (£7.50). The main-dish curries are well spiced and have a good depth of flavour. Apple dopiaza (£13) is lamb curry with chillies, caramelized onions and apples. You could also try the Malabari lobster curry (£16.50), with fresh turmeric and raw mango; or chicken salaan (£13), hot with black pepper – a Keralan dish. The biryanis are a revelation, too, and particularly good is the moghlai masala biryani (£12), a dish of lamb and rice cooked slowly in a sealed pot with lots of green herbs and nuts. Vegetarian dishes are also grandstand affairs and include such as tarkari Hyderabadi biryani (£11) – vegetables and mushrooms slow cooked with rice.

Like its sister restaurant, Chutney Mary, Veeraswamy does an excellent Sunday lunch, and there is also a "tasting menu" at £29.50 per person.

Queensway & Westbourne Grove

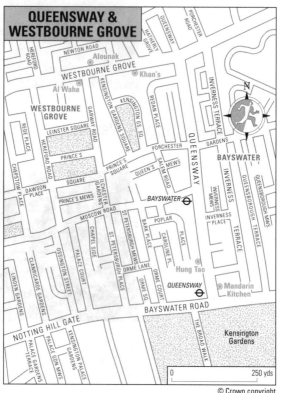

QUEENSWAY & WESTBOURNE GROVE

© Crown copyright

Al Waha

Anissa Helou, who has written the definitive book on Lebanese cuisine, nominates Al Waha as London's best Lebanese restaurant. And after cantering through a few courses here you will probably agree with her. Lebanese restaurants are all meze-obsessed and Al Waha is no exception. What is different, however, is the way in which the chef at Al Waha is obsessive about the main course dishes as well. And when he won the award for best Middle Eastern restaurant, in 2001, he gave the credit to his Mum's recipes!

Cost	£12–£37
Address	75 Westbourne Grove, W2
T	020 7229 0806
Station	Bayswater/Queensway
Open	Daily noon–midnight
Accepts	All major credit cards

When you sit down a dish of fresh, crisp crudités will be brought to the table. It includes everything from some quartered cos lettuce through to a whole green pepper. Get the healthy eating part over early. As always with Middle Eastern food, choosing is the problem – there are 22 cold starters and 24 hot ones. Go for a balance and always include one that you have never had before – hummus (£3) is good here; tabouleh (£4) is heavy on the parsley; the kabees (£3) are moreish if you like the Lebanese style of heavily salted (and so very salty) pickles. The foul moukala (£4) is good, despite its name – it's a dish of broad beans with garlic, coriander and olive oil. From the hot section, try manakeish bizaatar (£3.75), which is a freshly baked mini-bread topped with thyme, like a deluxe pizza, or maybe haliwat (£4.50), a dish of grilled sweetbreads with lemon juice and herbs. Or there's batata harra (£3.75), which combines potatoes with garlic and peppers. The makanek ghanam (£4.50) are tiny Lebanese lamb sausages, like a very refined cocktail sausage. For main courses, grills predominate, and they are all spanking fresh and accurately cooked. Tasty choices include shish taouk (£8.75), made with chicken, and samakeh harrah (£18), with sea bass. Star turn is kafta khashkhash (£8.75), a superb cylinder of minced lamb with parsley, garlic and tomato. The bread here is fresh and delicious. Drink the good Lebanese beer or the very good Lebanese wines.

Al Waha's greatest strength is in its superb home-style dishes of the day. Monday means dajaj mahshi – stuffed chicken with rice and pine nuts. Tuesday gets you a good artichoki mozat, which is lamb stewed with artichoke bottoms. Friday is fish – sayadieh is a fillet of fish cooked with herbs and rice. They are all priced at £9.

Alounak

Westbourne Grove has always had a raffish cosmopolitan air to it, which makes it the perfect home for this, the second branch of Alounak (actually the third, if you count its early years in a Portakabin opposite Olympia station). Don't be put off by the dated sign outside – this place turns out really good, really cheap Iranian food. The welcoming smell of clay-oven-baked flat bread hits you the moment you walk through the front door, creating a sense of the Middle East that's enhanced further by the gentle gurgling of a fountain, and the strains of Arabic music.

Cost	£8–£20
Address	44 Westbourne Grove, W2
T	020 7229 0416
Station	Bayswater/ Queensway
Open	Daily noon–midnight
Accepts	All major credit cards

The sizeable contingent of Middle Eastern locals dining here testifies to the authenticity of the food on offer. As an opening move, you can do no better than order the mixed starter (£8.40), a fine sampler of all the usual dips and hors d'oeuvres, served with splendid, freshly baked flat bread. And then follow the regulars with some grilled meat, which is expertly cooked. Joojeh kebab (£6.90) is melt-in-the-mouth baby chicken, packed with flavour. The kebab koobideh morgh (£6.90) is a tasty kebab made from minced chicken "reassembled" into long cylinders. As you would expect from a Middle Eastern restaurant, lamb dishes feature heavily, and the good quality lamb, simply grilled without fuss or frills, has undeniable charm. A good way to try two-in-one is to order the chelo kebab koobideh (£11.10), marinated lamb fillet coupled with minced (lamb) kebab, which is deliciously rich and oniony. For those with an inquisitive bent there is the innocuous-sounding "mixed grill' (£30), which brings a vast platter best summed up as grilled everything. It seems hard to believe that there is a single way of kebabbing lamb that doesn't make it onto the platter. It's worth looking out for the daily specials, too – especially good on a Tuesday, when they offer zereshk polo (£6.20), a stunning chicken dish served on saffron-steamed rice mixed with sweet-and-sour forest berries.

Round things off with a pot of Iranian black tea (£3), sufficient for six and served in ornate glass beakers. Infused with refreshing spices, it does a great job of cleaning the palate, leaving you set for a finale of select Persian sweets. Beware, however, of musty-tasting yoghurt drinks with unpronounceable names.

Hung Tao

It is easy to find the Hung Tao: just look out for the much larger New Kam Tong restaurant, and two doors away you'll see this small and spartan establishment. They're actually part of the same group, as is another restaurant over the road (which is where all those singularly appetizing ducks hanging up in the windows of the three establishments are roasted). The reason to choose the Hung Tao above its neighbours is if you fancy a one-plate (or one-bowl) meal. Despite a long and traditional menu, featuring mainly Cantonese and Szechwan dishes, its strengths lie in barbecued meat with rice, noodle dishes and noodle soups. All attract the hungry and are keenly priced.

Cost	£4–£20
Address	51 Queensway, W2
T	020 7727 5753
Station	Bayswater/ Queensway
Open	Daily 11am–11pm
Accepts	Cash and cheques only

The very first thing on the menu is delicious – hot and sour soup (£1.90). Uncannily enough, this is both hot, with fresh red chillies in profusion, and sour. There are also a dozen different noodle soups, priced between £4.50 and £5. Then there are twenty dishes that go from duck rice (£4.50) to shrimps and egg with rice (£5.25). Plus about thirty noodle, fried noodle, and ho fun dishes, priced from £3 to £6. The fried ho fun with beef (£4.50) is a superb rich dish – well-flavoured brisket cooked until melting, on top of a mountain of ho fun. And the barbecued meats displayed in the window are very tasty, too – rich, red-painted char sui; soya duckling; crispy pork and duck – all shuttled across from the kitchens of the sister restaurant over the road.

Towards the front of the menu, and hailing from Canton, you'll find a succession of congee dishes. Congee is one of those foods people label "interesting" without meaning it. It is a thick, whitish, runny porridge made with rice: stunningly bland and under-seasoned, but tasting faintly of ginger. Plunge in at the deep end, and try thousand years egg with sliced pork congee (£4.50). As well as containing pork, there's the "thousand year" egg itself, the white of which is a translucent chestnut brown and the yolk a fetching green. Inscrutably, it tastes rather like an ordinary hard-boiled egg. Pundits will tell you that far from being a thousand or even a hundred years old, these eggs acquire their bizarre, slightly cheesey taste after being buried for just one hundred days.

Khan's

🍴 If you're after a solid, inexpensive and familiar Indian meal, Khan's is the business. This restaurant, in busy Westbourne Grove, is a long-standing favourite with students and budget-wary locals who know that the curries here may be the staples of a thousand menus across Britain, but they're fresh, well cooked and generously portioned. Just don't turn up for a quiet evening out. Tables turn over in the blink of an eye, service is perfunctory (this isn't a place to dally over the menu), and it's really noisy. Try to get a seat in the vast, echoey ground floor, where blue murals stretch up to the high ceilings – it feels a bit like dining in an enormous swimming pool. The basement is stuffier and less atmospheric. Wherever you sit, be prepared to be fed briskly and hurried on your way.

Cost	£6–£20

Address 13–15 Westbourne Grove, W2
T 020 7727 5420
Station Bayswater
Open Mon–Thurs noon–3pm & 6–11.45pm, Fri–Sun noon–midnight
Accepts All major credit cards
W www.khansrestaurant.com

There are some tasty breads on offer. Try the nan-e-mughziat (£1.60), a coconut-flavoured affair with nuts and sultanas, or the paneer kulcha (£1.45), bulging with cottage cheese and mashed potatoes. You might also kick off with half a tandoori chicken (£2.75), which is moist and well cooked, or a creditable chicken tikka (£3.80). For main dishes, all those curry house favourites are listed here – meat madras or vindalu (£3.20), prawn biryani (£5.25), chicken chilli masala (£3.20), king prawn curry (£6.20) – and they all taste unusually fresh. Especially good is the butter chicken (£4.70), while for lovers of tikka masala dishes, the murgh tikka masala (£3.70) will appeal. There's a typical array of vegetable dishes too: bhindi (£2.70), sag aloo (£2.60) and vegetable curry (£2.60). Desserts include kulfi (£2.15), chocolate bombe (£1.60) and various ice creams – or you could try the lemon or orange delight (£1.70). A pint of lager will set you back £1.90, and there's a small selection of wines: a bottle of Chardonnay costs £8.50, or you can get a glass of house white or red for £1.60.

Cast your eye around the tall, tiled ground floor and front windows and you'll find enough architectural clues to confirm that this was once a Kardomah coffee bar. On a more enterprising note, this is one of very few curry houses that has a special children's menu. Excellent, start them young.

Mandarin Kitchen

London has its fair share of French fish restaurants, and there are famous English fish restaurants, so why does it seem odd to come across a Chinese fish restaurant? Part of the mystique of the Mandarin Kitchen, which you'll find at the Kensington Gardens end of Queensway, is the persistent rumour

Cost	£15–£35
Address	14–16 Queensway, W2
T	020 7727 9012
Station	Queensway
Open	Daily noon–11.30pm
Accepts	All major credit cards

that they sell more lobsters than any other restaurant in Britain. (When questioned about this myth, the management will confirm that they regularly have 100-lobster days!) This is a large restaurant, busy with waiters deftly wheeling four-foot-diameter table tops around like giant hoops as they set up communal tables for large parties of Chinese who all seem to be eating … lobster. What's more, as the menu observes, "we only serve the finest Scottish wild lobsters, simply because they are probably the best in the world".

Whatever you fancy for the main course, start with as many of the steamed scallops on the shell with garlic soya sauce (£1.80 each) as you can afford. They're magnificent. Then decide between lobster, crab or fish. If you go for the lobster, try ordering it baked with green pepper and onion in black bean sauce (it is priced at about £15 per pound depending on the season), and be sure that you order the optional extra soft noodle (£1.20) to make a meal of it. The crab is tempting, too. Live crabs are shipped up here from the south coast, and a handsome portion of shells, lots of legs and four claws baked with ginger and spring onion is a pretty reasonable £12. Fish dishes require more thought – and an eye to the per-pound prices, which do reflect the gluts and shortages of the fish market. The menu lists "the fish we normally serve" as sea bass, Dover sole, live eels, live carp, monkfish, Chinese pomfret and yellow croaker. Sea bass comes steamed whole at £17–19 per pound, depending on season. The roast eel fillets with garlic and chilli (£7.90) are notable, and strongly flavoured. The monkfish (£9.90) is meaty and delicious.

After seafood, the never-ending menu wanders off down a road of old favourites, and even features a number of veal dishes such as roasted veal chop with Mandarin sauce (£9.90) – so a seafood allergy is no reason for you to miss out.

Soho

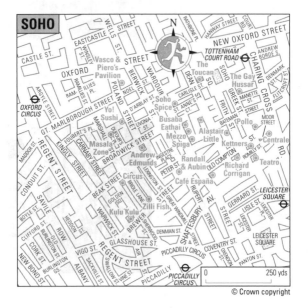

SOHO

WELLS STREET
EASTCASTLE STREET
CASTLE ST.
WINSLEY
OXFORD STREET
Vasco & Piero's Pavilion
RAM- ILLIES PL.
ARGYLE STREET
OXFORD CIRCUS
GT. MARLBOROUGH STREET
POLAND STREET
BERWICK STREET
WARDOUR STREET
DEAN STREET
NEW OXFORD STREET
TOTTENHAM COURT ROAD
ANDREW BORDE ST.
The Toucan
CHARING CROSS ROAD
DENMARK
The Gay Hussar
GREEK ST.
MANETTE STREET
FLITCROFT ST.
Soho Spice
CARLISLE ST.
ST. ANNE'S CT.
D'ARBLAY ST.
NOEL ST.
Yo! Sushi
LIVONIA ST.
FRITH ST.
Busaba Eathai
Pollo
BATEMAN ST.
MOOR STREET
INGPOUR ST.
Alastair Little
Kettners
Centrale
MARSHALL STREET
FOUBERT'S PL.
BROADWICK STREET
Masala Zone
Mezzo
Spiga
ROMILLY ST.
CARNABY STREET
KINGLY STREET
Andrew Edmunds
INGESTRE PLACE
Randall & Aubin
OLD COMPTON STREET
Richard Corrigan
Teatro
Circus
PETER ST.
LEXINGTON STREET
Café España
GREAT WINDMILL STREET
RUPERT STREET
WARDOUR STREET
GERRARD STREET
LEICESTER SQUARE
REGENT STREET
CONDUIT STREET
BEAK STREET
GOLDEN SQ.
BRIDLE LANE
SHAFTESBURY AV.
LISLE ST.
LEICESTER SQUARE
MADDOX ST.
SAVILE
BOYLE ST.
Kulu Kulu
WARWICK ST.
BREWER STREET
Zilli Fish
SHERWOOD ST.
DENMAN ST.
COVENTRY ST.
LEICESTER SQUARE
CLIFFORD ST.
OLD BURLINGTON ST.
HEDDON ST.
GLASSHOUSE STREET
AIR ST.
PICCADILLY CIRCUS
DENMAN ST.
PANTON ST.
CORK ST.
BURLINGTON GS.
VIGO ST.
REGENT STREET
SACKVILLE ST.
SWALLOW ST.
ALBANY
NEW BOND ST.
SAVILLE ST.
JERMYN ST.
PICCADILLY
PICCADILLY CIRCUS

0   250 yds

© Crown copyright

Alastair Little

This restaurant was Alastair Little's first, opened back in those days when the London eating public was moving hesitantly out of a world where visiting an Italian restaurant meant gasping at the size of the peppermills and the clever way that the straw-wrapped chianti flasks had been

Cost	£30–£65
Address	49 Frith St, W1
T	020 7734 5183
Station	Leicester Square
Open	Mon–Fri noon–3pm & 6–11pm, Sat 6–11pm
Accepts	All major credit cards

transformed into lamps. The sparse decor and unfussy, modern lines of Little's Frith Street joint seemed little short of revolutionary at the time. Today, the place looks much the same as every other trendy eatery. Most importantly, Alastair Little was the man who showed us a new style of Mediterranean food: simple, strong flavours; fresh produce; joyful meals. And today his two restaurants continue to fly the flag for these admirable values (you'll find the other one reviewed on p.444).

Unlike the decor, the menu changes twice a day. Not radically, although there may be one extra starter or main course to choose from at dinner. Pricing is simple: at lunch £27 buys you three courses; at dinner £35 gets you three courses. The wine list is a largely sub-£30-a-bottle affair, with a sprinkling of more ambitiously priced famous names. The menu runs the gamut – the charcuterie may come from Spain, and there will be French classics mixed in with resolutely Italian dishes – but everything is seasonal. So starters may include nettle soup with crème fraîche; cacciucco Livornese – a Tuscan fish casserole; or that old dinner party faithful beloved of Delia Smith – Piedmontese peppers. Or how about grilled pigeon breast, French beans, sautéed potatoes and pancetta? The main courses are in a similar vein, featuring roast breast of chicken with peas, broad beans and button onions; or calves' liver with potato cake and braised endive. And, perhaps most accomplished of all, roast plaice steak with mash and shrimp sauce. It's a difficult business, cooking a large tranche of plaice – the fish has to be really fresh to stop it disintegrating into mush. And the sweetish sauce served here is a wonderful accompaniment for this good white fish.

To end your meal there are splendid puds like panna cotta with apricot sauce, or chocolate torta with espresso ice cream – but how much better to call for a plate of British cheeses with oatcakes.

Andrew Edmunds

Andrew Edmunds' wine bar, as it is called by Soho locals, has been an institution in the area for some fifteen years – a long time when you consider how speedily so many restaurants come and go. It all started when the lease on the wine bar next door to his print gallery became vacant and he decided that as he wanted to go on eating there himself, he should take it on. The restaurant now

Cost £20–£35

Address 46 Lexington St, W1
T 020 7437 5708
Station Oxford Circus
Open Mon–Fri noon–3pm &
6–11pm, Sat 1–3pm &
6–11pm, Sun 1–3pm &
6–10.30pm
Accepts All major credit cards

has a loyal band of regulars who like the imaginative bistro-style dishes. It's cosy, dark and very crowded, a place where people wave to friends across the room.

The menu changes daily and combines solid favourites with bright new ideas, so that regular diners can either comfort themselves with the familiar or head off into the unknown. Start with skate wing rillettes with crème fraîche, cucumber and fried capers (£4.75) – a remarkably accomplished way to deal with skate; or the creamy, rich duck liver pâté and tomato cruda (£4.25). Main courses include stalwarts like lamb casserole with saffron rice (£9.50), and roast guinea fowl with mustard sauce, green vegetables and roast garlic (£9.50), as well as lighter ideas like roast flat mushrooms with egg noodles, vegetable julienne and peanut dressing (£7.50), and seared swordfish steak with black-eyed beans, French beans and chilli oil (£10). The lamb is rich, robust and deeply satisfying, and the huge mushrooms are tender, sweet and flavoursome. Puddings include chocolate mousse cake (£3.50), the ubiquitous tiramisù (£3.50), and plum and almond tart (£4). The first two are ruinously rich, the last crisp, sharp and nutty.

Wines are a passion with Andrew Edmunds. The constantly changing, broker-bought list is long and special and, because of his policy of not marking up much, you get massive bargains in the higher-priced wines, especially French and Californian. Many are priced at little more than wine shop prices. There is an additional list of halves of sweet wines as well. Daily special wine offers are chalked on a blackboard, and there are excellent sherries and other aperitifs. Expect to pay a bit more and get much more in return. Booking, especially for the tiny upstairs dining room, is essential.

Busaba Eathai

Busaba occupies a West End site that was once a bank – you remember the days when banks were conveniently positioned all over the place? Former customers stumbling into 106 Wardour St would be more than a little surprised by the dark, designery, and implacably trendy Thai eatery that is now bedded in. One of the gents behind this new establishment is the brains behind the original Wagamama (see p.18), and regulars there will find all sorts of echoes and resonance at Busaba Eathai. There's the same share-a-table and no bookings policy, and there's the same half-cod philosophy: "sanuk is busaba's living ethos. Based upon traditional Bhuddist values… " You need read no further. The place is saved by serving pretty decent Thai food at low prices, and with consummate lack of pretension. For all the fake Zen this is a jolly and energetic restaurant and you will probably have a very good time.

Cost	£8–£20

Address 106–110 Wardour St, W1
T 020 7255 8686
Station Piccadilly Circus
Open Mon–Thurs noon–11pm, Fri & Sat noon–11.30pm, Sun noon–10pm
Accepts All major credit cards except Diners

Food, grouped into categories, veers towards one-pot dishes, and vegetarians are particularly well served. If you want starters you need to peruse the side dishes – choose from such things as a good green papaya salad (£5.60); or po-pea jay (£2.90), which are vegetable spring rolls; or fish cakes (£4.50); or Thai calamari (£3.90), which are not unlike everyone else's calamari. There are four curries: prawn and pineapple (£8.20); green chicken (£6.90); green vegetable (£5.90); and red salmon (£7.50). You'll find genuine Thai veg like pea aubergines with sweet basil and lime leaves, although these dishes do tend to be on the sweet side. Or there's phad Thai (£5.90), and thom yum chicken (£5.50). Stir fries range from char-grilled duck in tamarind sauce with Chinese broccoli (£6.90); scallop and asparagus (£8.50); khuen chai stir-fry (£6.90), which is baby squid with Thai pepper and garlic; and deep fried cod with chilli and basil sauce (£7.50).

The power juice phenomenon has reached Busaba. Nam polamai (£2.70) is organic, and combines carrot, apple and celery with dandelion and nettle extract – just the thought of it should be enough to make you repent all those hard days and long nights.

Café España

🍴 Situated as it is at the heart of Soho's pink strip, at the Wardour Street end of Old Compton Street, and nestled among the hard-core shops and video stores, Café España is a remarkably balanced restaurant. From the outside it looks rather small and shabby – not very prepossessing at all, in fact, and much like the more tourist-focused trattorias. But once through the door,

Cost	£10–£20
Address	63 Old Compton St, W1
T	020 7494 1271
Station	Piccadilly Circus/ Tottenham Court Rd
Open	Mon–Sat noon– midnight, Sun noon–11pm
Accepts	MasterCard, Visa

tripping over the dessert trolley, you can sense you're in for something good. You'll be greeted by a friendly maître d' and led up the stairs to join a hubbub of hungry Soho folk with a nose for a bargain.

The menu does give a nod to the trattoria, with a short list of pastas, but it is Spanish, not Italian cooking that you should be going for here – and if you are anything less than seriously hungry, it's best to stick with the tapas. Mejillones a la marinera (£4.50) delivers enough mussels for a small main course; a portion of tortilla (£4) is the size of a saucer and is likely to be cooked especially for you; ordering the jamón serrano (£6.25) brings a decent portion at a price you'd be hard to match wholesale. For something more substantial there's plenty of choice, mostly in the form of simple grills. Try chuletas de cordero a la brasa (£9.95) – lamb chops; higado de ternera (£8.95) – calves' liver and bacon; or rodaballo a la plancha (£12.95) – grilled turbot. Or there are the traditional paellas, Valenciana and marinera (£22, to feed two), though these are slightly less exciting. Service is swift, if a little harassed. Keeping food prices this low means a rapid turn-around of custom, but the waiters are nonetheless friendly and polite. And given the number of people in the place, you can be sure that whatever you are eating is freshly prepared – the volume of ingredients they get through must be huge.

To enjoy Café España to the maximum, go mob-handed and allow yourself the luxury of running amok with the tapas selections before pouncing on the paella. But be warned: it is very unwise to try and re-create the glorious abandon of your last Iberian holiday here – the sangria is a dark and dangerous West End concoction that is really quite horrid.

Centrale

🍴 In a grid of streets full of bottom-dollar belly-fillers, Centrale stands out, with an idiosyncratic charm beloved by its clued-in regulars. But don't be misled by its down-at-heel exterior – there's something special about sweeping through the plain glass door and sliding into one of its cracked vinyl banquettes, forced into cosy, chatty

Cost	£5–£15

Address 16 Moor St, W1
T 020 7437 5513
Station Leicester Square/ Tottenham Court Road
Open Mon–Sat noon–9.30pm
Accepts Cash and cheques only

proximity with strangers across a narrow red Formica table. Maybe it's the tininess of the place, maybe it's the crush of students, maybe it's just the cappuccino in smoked-glass cups, but Centrale is not only effortlessly friendly but also strangely glamorous. Odd, really, when this is basically a place to line your stomach with cheap pasta before going on to a pub or club.

Centrale's menu is artless – orange juice (£1) appears as a starter – and the portions are substantial. Appetizers include home-made minestrone (£2.25), salame (£3.75), and pastina in brodo (£2.25) – short pasta snippets in a clear, slightly oily soup. There's a fair spread of diner staples to follow, including pork chop (£4.75) and fried scampi (£4.75), each partnered by an inevitable sprinkling of chips, but the main event here is the pasta. The Bolognese dishes – spaghetti, tagliatelle, rigatoni and ravioli (all £3.75) – are equally dependable, adequately spicy and chewily meaty, and the lasagna al forno (£4.25) reassuringly button-popping, but the specials list holds more adventurous temptations. Standouts include the spaghetti vongole (£4.50), with its shoal of baby clams in a garlic, chilli and tomato sauce, and the rigatoni Alfredo (£4.25), a pungent swirl of cream, mushrooms, cheese, tomato and lots and lots of garlic. Rather than a small salad (£1.75), a side order of spinach (£2.25) adds a pleasantly slippery counterpoint to the solid bulk of the pasta.

The menu gives up the ghost a bit when it comes to dessert, sticking to just three old favourites: banana split (£1.75), apple pie (£1.75) and ice cream (£1.50), the last being a tripartite scoop of chocolate, strawberry and vanilla. Still, you're not here for puds. You're here for a fix of cheap food – and cheap wine. There's no licence, so you can bring your own bottle for 50p corkage (£1 for a big bottle). You'll find a couple of off-licences just around the corner in Old Compton Street.

BRITISH

Circus

When it opened towards the end of the 1990s, Circus was everything a fashionable fin-de-siècle restaurant should be. The decor was cool shades of black and white, there was a de rigueur members bar downstairs, open till the wee hours, and there were spiky "statement" flower arrangements. The service was efficient and good looking, the food competent, clean and very much of the moment. It took little time for Circus to become a destination restaurant for media and design professionals. A few years and several trends later, Circus has proved that it can stand the test of time. It still has the attributes with which it started, it's still pulling the punters in, and it still has a gloss of confidence that rubs off on its customers.

Cost	£16–£60
Address	1 Upper James St, W1
T	020 7534 4000
Station	Oxford Circus
Open	Mon–Fri noon–3pm & 5.45pm–midnight, Sat 5.45pm–midnight
Accepts	All major credit cards
W	www.circusbar.co.uk

The menu works hard to offer something for everyone. Tucked in amongst the modish salt beef and mustard salad (£5.75), and the aged Feta, aubergine and pepper terrine (£5.75), you'll find starters as diverse as pea and ham soup (£4.50) – for those coming in from the cold – or 30g of Iranian caviar with trimmings (£50) - for serious celebrations. Main courses offer the traditional – roast rump of lamb (£15.50), rib-eye steak with Dauphinoise potatoes (£18.50) – as well as more modern dishes such as fried squid with bok choy, chilli and tamarind (£13.50). It would be very surprising, given the style of restaurant and clientele, not to find decent vegetarian options, and indeed the menu always carries a seasonal risotto or pasta dish. Everything about this place suggests that whatever you choose will be well executed, professional and pleasing to the eye. The kitchen is obviously at ease, cooking good quality ingredients properly and with predictable results. This being an expense-account eatery ideal for business lunches and dinners, desserts are often skipped. Which is a shame, as the pastry chefs obviously delight in flights of fancy.

Be aware that the sometimes ambitiously priced wine list can further inflate an already not inexpensive dinner bill, but a meal at Circus needn't always be a costly affair. There's a competitively priced set lunch (£17.50 for two courses, £19.50 for three) available throughout the week and an early/late dinner which at £10.50/£12.50 is a positive steal.

The Gay Hussar

As you walk in off the street, the ground floor dining room of the Gay Hussar stretches before you: there are banquettes; there are waiters in dinner jackets; there is panelling; the walls are covered with political caricatures. "Aha!" the knowledgeable restaurant-goer murmurs, "How very retro – some fashionable designer has replicated an entire 1950s restaurant dining room." Not

Cost	£18–40
Address	2 Greek St, W1
T	020 7437 0973
Station	Tottenham Court Road
Open	Mon-Sat 12.15–2.30pm & 5.30–10.45pm
Accepts	All major credit cards
W	www.gayhussar.co.uk

so. The Gay Hussar is the real thing. Granted, it has been spruced up, and the room is clean, neat and comfortable, but that is *the* photo of a naked Christine Keeler.

Perhaps the politicos like the food, which is solid, dependable, comfortable and tasty. It's also good value: at lunch there is a prix fixe – two courses for £15.50; three for £18.50. In the evening, dishes get a trifle more complicated. Starters include a well made disnó sajt (£3.90) – pressed boar's head; and hási pástétom (£3.90) – a fine goose and pork pâté; but the most famous (a house speciality that has featured in various novels) is the chilled wild cherry soup (£3.80), which is like a thin, bitterish, sourish yoghurt and is rather good. Main courses are blockbusters – try the hortobagyi palacsinta (£13.40), a pancake filled with a finely chopped veal goulash and then sealed, deep-fried and served with creamed spinach. Very tasty. Or there are fish dumplings (£11.85), which are served with rice and a creamy dill sauce. From the side dishes, try the tarhonya (£2.70), described as egg barley – perhaps because it is an egg pasta and each piece is the size of a grain of barley. Or there's cigány gyors tal (£13.90), billed as a gypsy fry-up of pork and peppers. The food here is tasty and filling, and best eaten in the chill of winter. Puds are also fierce – poppy-seed strudel comes with vanilla ice cream (£4.15). The home made liptoi (£3.50), a savoury amalgam of cream cheese, herbs, paprika and a whiff of onion, is very good. The wine list is gently priced – try the good, dry Hungarian whites like the Castle Island Furmint (£14.50).

Sometimes, there are questions that just have to be asked: "Does the Transylvanian mixed grill (erdély fatányéros, £35 for two people) include a stake?"

PIZZA/BURGERS

Kettners

Owned by Soho restaurateur Peter Boizot, the man who introduced pizza to Britain in the 1960s, Kettners takes its tone from the Pizza Express chain that he founded and later sold. Over the years it has built up a loyal following that starts out the evening in the champagne bar then moves on to a pizza in the restaurant across the hall. Going to the bar beforehand (or indeed the restaurant after) isn't obligatory. But do at least one or the other. Kettners is a gorgeous old restaurant and part of the fabric of Soho.

Cost	£14–£35
Address	29 Romilly St, W1
T	020 7734 6112
Station	Leicester Square
Open	Daily noon–midnight
Accepts	All major credit cards

The pizzas are amongst the best in London, their crusts biscuit-thin and crispy, their topping thick, rich and tasty. What more could you ask from a pizza? If you don't want one at all, however, there are additional choices like Kettners' special hamburger (£8.75), chilli con carne (£7.70) and sausage mash and onion gravy (£7.85). Given that you'll probably spend a tenner or more on champagne in the bar (though you could pay up to £865 for a twenty-bottle Nebuchadnezzar of Pol Roger), this makes for a delightful paradox of cheap staple food and expensive luxury drink. The pizza list includes all the standards like American hot (£9.75), margherita (£8.50) and Napoletana (£9.10), plus unusual ideas like the King Edward (£8), which has a potato base. As at Pizza Express, the Veneziana (£9.10) comes with onions, capers, olives, pine kernels, sultanas, Mozzarella and tomato, and every time you buy one 50p is passed on to the Venice in Peril Fund – this initiative has just passed the £1 million mark.

A trip to Kettners isn't just for the pizzas, though they're good. You're here as much for the venue. Decorated in *belle-époque* style, the building was founded as a grand hotel in 1867 by Auguste Kettner, chef to Napoleon III. Stories also have it that the hotel was used by the then king, Edward VII, to woo and bed his mistress. Upstairs rooms sport numbers on the doors to remind you of the racy past, and some can be booked for private parties of between eight and eighty. The main room, however, doesn't accept bookings and you are advised to get there early.

Kulu Kulu

Kulu Kulu is a conveyor-belt sushi restaurant which pulls off the unlikely trick of serving really good sushi without being impersonal or intimidating. It is light and airy and there are enough coat hooks for a small army of diners. The only thing you might quibble over is the design of the rather low stools, which are so heavy they feel fixed to the floor – anyone over six feet tall will find them-

Cost £10–£30

Address 76 Brewer St, W1
T 020 7734 7316
Station Piccadilly Circus
Open Mon–Fri noon–2.30pm
& 5–10pm, Sat noon–3.45pm
& 5–10pm
Accepts MasterCard, Switch,
Visa

selves dining in the tuck position favoured by divers and trampolinists. The atmosphere is Japanese utilitarian. In front of you is a plastic tub of gari (the rather delicious pickled ginger), a bottle of soy and a small box containing disposable wooden chopsticks. After that, as they say at Bingo, it's eyes down, look in, and on with the game.

The plates come round on the kaiten, or conveyor, and are coded by design rather than colour, which could prove deceptive: A plates cost £1.20, B plates are £1.80, C plates are £2.40, and D plates £4. All the usual sushi favourites are here, and the fish is particularly fresh and well presented. Maguri – tuna – is a B; Amaebi – sweet shrimp – is a C; Hotategai – scallops – is a C, and very sweet indeed. Futomaki – a Californian, cone-shaped roll with tuna – is a B. Ds tend to be the ritzier fishes like belly tuna. The wasabi/eye-watering factor, however, is a bit hit or miss. Just as you're wishing for a bit more wasabi, you bite into something that makes you long for a bit less. As well as the sushi, the conveyor parades some little bowls of hot dishes – one worth looking out for combines strips of fried fish skin with a savoury vegetable puree (it counts as an A). The bowl of miso soup is also an A. To drink there is everything from Oolong tea (£1.50) through Kirin beer (£2.60) to Urku shochu – a particularly dangerous Japanese white spirit (£1.80).

Kulu Kulu also offers a range of set options which represent excellent value and take the strain off keeping your eye fixed on the conveyor belt. They include mixed sashimi (£10) and mixed tempura (£8.60). Look behind the bar and you may see a stack of cardboard cases containing sake supplies. It is strange but true that one of the premium sakes is made in the Rocky Mountains – in America!

Masala Zone

Masala Zone, which opened in May 2001, is impossible to pigeonhole. The food is Indian, but modern Indian, with a commendable emphasis on healthy eating – as would be the norm in India, there's a long list of attractive vegetarian options. The dining room is smart and large, but the prices are low. There are fast-food dishes on the menu, but they tend to be the roadside snacks of Bombay rather than junk dreamt up in the US. And the playlist was put together by one of India's top club DJs. In all, this is an informal, stylish and friendly place, serving food that is simple and delicious.

Cost	£5–£18
Address	9 Marshall St, W1
T	020 7287 9966
Station	Oxford Circus/ Piccadilly Circus
Open	Daily noon–2.30pm & 5.30–11.30pm
Accepts	All major credit cards

The gentle informality extends to the menu, which begins with small plates of street food, almost all priced at £2.50. There are sev puris, dahi puris, samosas, a particularly fine aloo tikki chaat, and tokir chaat – an amazing potato basket filled with veg, salad and fruit. Don't worry if things are unfamiliar, pick several dishes and graze your way along – at these prices it doesn't matter if there's the occasional miss amongst the hits. At lunch there are some splendid Indian sandwiches, including a giant masala chicken burger (£4) and a superb Bombay layered-vegetable grilled sandwich (£3). There are half a dozen curries that are well balanced and richly flavoured – served simply, with rice, they cost between £4.50 and £6.50. But you should move straight on to the thalis, which are what you would be offered in an Indian home. At Masala Zone these are steel trays with seven or eight little bowls containing a vegetarian snack (to whet the appetite), a curry, lentils, a root vegetable, a green vegetable, yoghurt, bread, rice and pickles. You just choose the base curry and a complete, balanced meal arrives at table. Choose from chicken thali (£8), lamb thali (£8.50), prawn thali (£9), vegetarian thali (£7.50), or chicken and lamb thali (£10).

The wall decorations are striking. After the surface had been rendered with a close approximation to mud, two tribal artists were flown in to do the painting. The mural depicts their people's history from hunters, to gatherers, to farmers selling to the cities. The artists have also featured their trip to London – look out for the stretch limo, which impressed them quite as much as Buckingham Palace.

Mezzo

When Sir Terence Conran unveiled Mezzo in 1995, people came to look at it just because it was there, and just because it was so ... big. Nobody had opened a restaurant in London with space for six hundred diners in decades, and this was on a grand scale, encompassing a bar, an "informal" ground-floor restaurant (Mezzonine), and a full-on restaurant (Mezzo) at the bottom of a sweeping staircase with a stage for performers. All of these areas have been busy ever since. This is not a place for a quiet night out. The restaurant tables are packed close and there's a fashionable mayhem of noise. But if you like a buzz with your meal, Mezzo has few rivals – and the food, considering the huge numbers of covers, is sound enough.

Cost	£15–£50
Address	100 Wardour St, W1
T	020 7314 4000
Station	Piccadilly Circus
Open	Mon & Tues 6pm–midnight, Wed–Thurs noon–3pm & 6pm–midnight, Fri noon–3pm & 6pm–1am, Sat 6pm–1am, Sun 12.30–3pm & 6–11pm. Crustacea bar open Fri & Sat till 3am
Accepts	All major credit cards

The Mezzo menus send out different signals for each session. Thus you can have two courses of a short lunch or pre-theatre menu for £12.50 (three courses for £15.50); a set Sunday brunch menu of three courses also costs £15.50. Or you can spend a good deal more ordering à la carte. And there is a large seafood and crustacea bar targeted at your wallet. Whichever you go for, expect a mix of trad favourites and novel twists – you may see dishes like confit duck leg with braised brown lentils and Madeira jus (£14.50) vying for attention with Portobello mushroom with couscous and eggplant caviar (£14). But things can get a lot more elaborate, and grandstand dishes may include pan-fried foie gras and grilled pineapple (£13.50); monkfish saltimbocca (£19, minimum two people); or roast scallops, parsnip puree and crisp pancetta (£16.50). The grills and rotisserie section has some particularly attractive items such as roast loin of pork with Armagnac prunes and crackling (£12.50). Beware the cost of veg: a side order of French beans is not cheap at £3.50. And leave space for the puds, which are rich and greed-provoking: pain perdu, poached pear, and chocolate ice cream (£5.50); apricot Vacherin with vanilla cream (£5.50); tarte Tatin with crème fraîche (£6).

Mezzo has live music every evening, mostly jazz, and it's often very good. You pay a £5 charge for a seat to watch the shows not bad value if that's what you're here for.

Pollo

You won't find haute cuisine at Pollo, but you do get great value for money. As at its neighbouring rival, Centrale (see p.123), this is comfort food, Latin-style – long on carbohydrate and short on frills. Sophistication is in short supply, too – the interior design begins and ends with the lino floors and tatty pictures. But no matter, devotees return time and again for the cheap platefuls of food and the friendly, prompt service. Diners are shoehorned into booths presided over by a formidable Italian mama who tips you the wink as to what you should order. Downstairs there's more space, but you still might end up sharing a table.

Cost	£4–£15
Address	20 Old Compton St, W1
T	020 7734 5917
Station	Leicester Square
Open	Daily noon–midnight
Accepts	Cash or cheque only

The spotlight of Pollo's lengthy menu falls on cheap, filling pasta in all its permutations. Tagliatelle, rigatoni, ravioli, pappardelle, tortelloni and fusilli are all available. Your choice is basically down to the pasta type, as most of them are offered with the same selection of sauces. The tortelloni salvia (£3.60), which comes with a wonderfully sagey butter sauce, is very good, as is the tagliatelle melanzana (£3.40), whose rich tomato sauce is boosted by melt-in-the-mouth aubergine. Meat courses are less successful: anchovies, for instance, are few and far between in the bistecca alla pizzaiola (£5.80) – steak in capers and anchovy sauce. But vegetarians are very well catered for here. Meat-free highlights include spaghetti aglio, olio e peperoncino (£3.30), a hot mix of garlic, olive oil and chilli. Meanwhile, a hearty plateful of gnocchi (£3.60) would curb even the most flamboyant appetite. Then there are pizzas – perhaps not the elegant, wood-fired-oven type that are all the rage, but solid and substantial nonetheless, like the Regina (£3.90) – a hammy, cheesy, mushroomy kind of experience. There is even a selection of risotti to choose from (all £3.50). A carafe of house wine is a bargain at £5.95; and so are the puddings, at £1.60. After a substantial hit of pasta, the imposing portion of tiramisù is a challenge for even the greediest diner.

As if Pollo wasn't cheap enough as it is, it offers the same menu as takeaway; on which all the pasta dishes cost just £3.

Randall & Aubin

Formerly a butcher's, Randall & Aubin has been recast as a sharp restaurant – as its seafood counter and champagne buckets groaning with flowers suggest – but it's also a rotisserie, sandwich shop and charcuterie to boot. It's the oysters that draw you in, along with the 1900s shop decor. The

Cost	£12–£38

Address 16 Brewer St, W1
T 020 7287 4447
Station Piccadilly Circus
Open Mon–Sat noon–11pm,
Sun 4–10.30pm
Accepts All major credit cards

SEAFOOD/ROTISSERIE

original white tiles have been cleverly adapted with touches of the French and American diner – cool, marble table tops and high stools that look characterful, though they don't exactly lend themselves to relaxed dining. But that's part of the plan – Randall's serves good food speedily to folk without a lot of time. In summer, the huge sash windows are opened up, making this a wonderfully airy place to eat, especially if you grab a seat by the window. The formula works so well that there is now a second Randall & Aubin at 329–331 Fulham Rd, SW10 (T020 7823 3515).

There's an extensive menu. An eclectic choice of starters roams the globe with soupe de poisson (£3.90), Japanese fish cakes (£5.95), and smoked salmon and caviar blinis (£9.10). Main courses range from "original" Caesar salad (£7.75), through spit-roast herb chicken (£9.50), and sausages and mash with onion gravy (£9.75), to sirloin steak with sauce Béarnaise and pommes frites (£12.50). There are also some interesting accompaniments, such as pommes Dauphinoise (£2.75), or zucchini frites with basil mayonnaise (£3.95). If you don't mind crowds, drop in at lunchtime for a hot filled baguette (£6.70 to £7.70): the salt beef, sauerkraut and gherkin variety, served with pommes frites (£7.70) is authentic. Also available in the evening, the baguettes provide an inexpensive yet satisfying meal. The list of fruits de mer offers well-priced seafood, ranging from a whole dressed crab at £9.50 to delicious, panfried scallops and sauté chilli potatoes (£15.85), and whole roast lobster, garlic butter and pommes frites (£24). Puddings all cost £3.95 and range from tarts and brûlées to the more adventurous pear and caramel galette, or chocolate truffle cake. Many of these dishes are also on the inexpensive takeaway menu, which makes for exciting picnicking.

Hard-core traditionalists with a penchant for chewing gobbets of resilient rubber which taste remarkably like the aroma of pumped-out bilge water will relish the fresh whelks with lemon and vinegar (£7.50).

Richard Corrigan at The Lindsay House

Even among chefs – not usually held to be overly calm and level-headed people – Richard Corrigan is regarded as something of a wild man. He arrived at this deservedly Michelin-starred restaurant in Soho via a spell bringing haute cuisine to a dog track in the East End, and at The Lindsay House

Cost	£30–£90
Address	21 Romilly St, W1
T	020 7439 0450
Station	Leicester Square
Open	Mon–Fri 12.30–2.30pm & 6–11pm, Sat 6–11pm
Accepts	All major credit cards

he seems to have found his niche. The restaurant is split into a series of small rooms, the service is attentive, and the food is very good indeed. The menus are uncomplicated and change regularly to keep in step with what is available at the market. Dinner means a choice of seven starters, six main courses and six puddings and costs £44, while at lunch the line-up is a tad smaller, as is the price – a real bargain at £23 for three courses.

Only a fool would try to predict what dishes Richard Corrigan will have on his menu tomorrow, but you can be sure that they will combine unusual flavours with verve and style. Starters surprise – a ballotine of suckling pig, sour apple and sage jelly – or are lusciously opulent – warm oysters, salsify, caviar and chive butter. Or there are combinations that seem familiar but come with a twist, like poached scallops, crab tortellini and saffron pistou. Main courses follow the same ground rules (or lack of them!), so you might be offered baked brill, celery and truffle broth; or organic pork, black pudding, crubeen and choucroute – pork from England, trotters from Ireland, cabbage from Alsace. Or, on a more classical note, red mullet, barigoule cream and artichoke vinaigrette. The puddings soar towards dessert lover's heaven with such as "orange and its variations", millefeuille of rhubarb, spiced mango compote, or chocolate croquettes with passion fruit jelly and white chocolate velouté. The wine list is extensive and expensive.

If there is one thing that marks out the cuisine at the Lindsay House, it is Corrigan's love affair with offal. Sweetbreads, kidneys and tongue all find their way onto the menu, in dishes that perfectly illustrate his deft touch with hearty flavours.

Soho Spice

Soho Spice is the new face of Indian restaurants. It's large – seating one hundred in the restaurant and forty in the bar – and takes bookings only for parties of six or more. It's busy, with loud music and late opening at the weekends. The decor is based around a riot of colour. And it is very, very successful. Which must be mainly down to food that is a large step away from curry house staples. The main menu features contemporary Indian cuisine, while a regularly changing special menu showcases dishes from particular regions. What's more, when you order a main course it comes on a thali – with pulao rice, naan, dhal and seasonal vegetables of the day – which makes ordering simple and paying less painful.

Cost	£10–£28
Address	124–126 Wardour St, W1
T	020 7434 0808
Station	Leicester Square/ Piccadilly Circus
Open	Mon–Thurs 11.30am– 12.30am, Fri & Sat 11.30am– 3am, Sun 12.30–10.30pm
Accepts	All major credit cards

On the main menu, starters include rampuri seekh kebab (£3.75) and mahi lasooni tikka (£5.25), which is salmon cooked in the tandoor. Or there's chicken tikka (£3.75), or methi bhaji (£3.25), which is a mixture of onion and potato that has been dosed with fenugreek and deep-fried. Main courses represent good value, given their accompaniments. Good choices are the pudina lamb chops champ (£12.50) – spicy lamb chops marinated with mint; or achaari gosht (£9.95) – a dish of lamb marinated overnight in pickling spices, Rajasthani style. Or how about the Bengal fish curry (£11.95) – fillets of tilapia cooked with tomatoes and onions and given bite by mustard seeds? Gentler palates will enjoy the Lucknow korma (£11.95), a milder curry made with coconut and poppy seeds. Desserts offer a nice range of kulfis (£2.95) – an Indian ice cream made with boiled milk – and that sweetest of comfort foods, gulab jamun (£3.25), a dumpling soaked in rose syrup.

The special regional menu, called "Seasonal Colour", changes every month – so it may be recipes from Rajasthan or dishes from Bengal. For example, when the chosen region was the North West Frontier there were starters like gilafi kebab – lamb dumplings with pearl onions and button mushrooms. Mains included the celebrated murg malai Peshwari – a kebab of chicken breast and cheese; and Kandhari pasanda – lamb with onions, tomatoes, almonds and saffron. Deals proliferate – special lunch and pre-theatre menus cost £7.20 for two courses. And there's a three-course set meal that costs £16.95, including tea or coffee.

Soho

Spiga

Spiga has an impeccable pedigree. It comes from the same stable as Aubergine, L'Oranger and Zafferano, and has that piece of kit that long identified any Italian restaurant as serious – a wood-fired oven. But despite its credentials you don't need to pay a king's ransom to eat here, nor do you have to dress up. This is a pleasantly casual affair. The atmosphere is lively – some-

Cost	£14–£30

Address 84–86 Wardour St, W1

T 020 7734 3444

Station Leicester Square

Open Sun–Tues noon–3pm & 6–11pm, Wed–Sat noon–3pm & 6pm–midnight

Accepts All major credit cards

times the music is too lively – and the look is cool. Spiga may have cut the prices but they haven't cut corners – the tableware is the latest in Italian chic. In 2001, a second Spiga opened at 312 King's Rd, SW3 (☎020 7351 0101).

Menus change monthly, with occasional daily specials, but there's a definite pattern. Starters will get you in the mood. The buffalo Mozzarella is served with marinated peppers, olives, capers and basil (£6). Or try something like the prosciutto affumicato di cervo (£6.50), which is smoked venison ham, or the legumi griglia (£6/£9). But the home-made pasta course is where it's really at. What's good is that, like the starters, most pasta dishes come in large or small portions. Think Italian and enjoy an extra course, such as gnocchi di ceci, scamorza e pomodorini (£6.50/£8.50), or ravioli di ricotta affumicata e radicchio (£7/£9), a dish of pasta stuffed with smoked Ricotta cheese and served with a radicchio salad. Then consider a pizza – thin crust, crispy and the size of a dustbin lid. Pizza buffala (£9) is rich with genuine Mozarella; pizza spinaci, stracchino e cotto (£8) comes with Mozarella and Stracchino cheeses, cooked ham and spinach. Alternatively, main courses offer up char-grilled and pan-fried dishes, like merluzzo con olive neri e pomodorini (£13.50), which teams cod with black olives and cherry tomatoes; or palliard di pollo con patate e spinaci (£12.50), a simple but good char-grilled chicken breast. And, if you aren't already full, the pudding section is well worth a look, too. Highlights include a wickedly indulgent lemon and mascarpone tart (£5.50) and an excellent tiramisù (£6.50).

Full marks to the person who can identify the weirdly thought-provoking loofah-like objects hanging on the walls.

Teatro

This restaurant has both celebrity owners (Lee Chapman and Leslie Ash) and celebrity customers. The latter may be spotted not only hiding in the members' bar but plying the knife and fork in the main arena. Given such potential distractions, the food is remarkably good and not too extravagantly priced. In 2001 John Newton took over the kitchens from the original head chef, Stuart Gillies, and we finally saw the demise of the charming concept of "foie gras de jour".

Cost	£30–£70
Address	93–107 Shaftesbury Ave, W1
T	020 7494 3040
Station	Leicester Square
Open	Mon–Fri noon–3pm & 6–11.45pm, Sat 6–11.45pm
Accepts	All major credit cards

Paying homage to diners who weight-watch (or who like the idea of four courses), the menu starts with salads such as warm salad of smoked mackerel, horseradish and Puy lentils (£6.95), and Asian pear, shaved fennel and Pecorino (£6.50). Starters are more substantial, with favourites like smoked haddock fishcake with creamed leeks (£7.50), which is very smoky and sweet. Or if you're a foie gras fan, try it pan-fried with honey-glazed cipolline onions (£16.50). For fish lovers there's lightly cured salmon served as a ceviche (£7.50), and a red mullet and saffron soup with gruyère croutons (£7.50) which easily eclipses many more traditional fish soups. Main courses take the favourites theme further, with confit leg of Barbary duck with a cassoulet of Swiss chard, coco beans and smoked bacon (£15.50), and home-made venison sausage with honey roast parsnips, raspberry and chocolate jus (£13.50). These dishes work extremely well. The duck, in particular, has more taste and texture than you'd expect from confit. Puddings (all £6.50) veer towards the rich and comforting, with dishes like creamed rice pudding with Seville orange marmalade; banana tarte Tatin with coconut sorbet; and warm chocolate fondant with chocolate sauce and crème fraîche. The wine list, which starts at £13.50 for a house bottle and climbs doggedly to £250 for a Chateau Margaux 1989, is well chosen, with some bargains in the £20 to £40 region. There are twenty wines by the glass (from £3.50 to £9.50) and 17 cigars (£4.70 to £22). The Bolivar Tubos No1 at £11, we are told, is "not for the faint hearted".

Like many smart restaurants, Teatro now has a bargain corner. Between noon and 7.30pm there's a special set lunch or pre-theatre menu at £11.50 for two courses, £14 for three. For cooking of this standard this is very good value.

Soho

The Toucan

When they opened The Toucan the proprietors' first priority was to approach Guinness and ask if they could retail the black stuff. They explained that they wanted to open a small bar aimed single-mindedly at the drinking public, just like the ones they had enjoyed so much in Dublin. Guinness replied that, providing they could shift two barrels a week, they'd be happy to put them on

Cost £7–£14

Address 19 Carlisle St, W1
T 020 7437 4123
Station Leicester Square/
Tottenham Court Road
Open Mon–Sat 11am–11pm
Accepts MasterCard, Visa
(over £10)
W www.thetoucan.co.uk

the list. Neither party imagined that the regular order would end up at more like thirty barrels a week! It's an impressive intake, but then The Toucan is an impressive place, serving home-made, very cheap, very wholesome and very filling food, along with all that Guinness. Its success has meant expansion from the original hot, dark, cellar premises to include the ground floor – and the establishment of a Toucan Two at 94 Wimpole St, W1 (☎020 7499 2440).

Start with six Galway Bay oysters (£7), or the vegetable soup with bread (£2). Go on to a large bowl of Irish stew with bread (£4.50), or Guinness pie and champ (£5.50) – champ is a kind of supercharged Irish mashed potato with best butter playing a leading role alongside the spring onions. It features in a couple of novelty items – you can have chilli and champ (£4.95), or ratatouille and champ (£3.75) – these two are also available with rice. The JPs (jacket potatoes) come with various fillings, and there's an array of sandwiches. There's also a great-value smoked salmon plate (£6). One thing to bear in mind if you've come here hungry is that there are times when The Toucan becomes so packed with people that you can scarcely lift a pint. At those times, all attempts at serving food are abandoned.

Of course, if things have got out of hand, you could spend a happy evening at The Toucan without actually eating. As some Irish sage once remarked, "There's eating and drinking in a pint of Guinness". And if it's a chaser you're after, then be aware that The Toucan also makes a feature of Irish whiskies – including some exotic and stratospherically expensive Tullamore Dews – 38, 41 and 42 year olds. If you have to ask how much it costs, you cannot afford it.

Vasco and Piero's Pavilion

Very much a family-run restaurant, the Pavilion has been a Soho fixture for the past twenty years. But there's nothing old or institutional about the cooking or decor. Vasco himself cooks for his regulars, and the establishment has long been a favourite with diners who appreciate his food, which is fairly simple but made with top-class ingredients.

Cost	£20–£32

Address 15 Poland St, W1
T 020 7437 8774
Station Oxford Circus
Open Mon–Fri noon–3pm & 6–11pm, Sat 7–11pm
Accepts All major credit cards
W www.vascosfood.com

ITALIAN

Dishes are biased towards Umbrian cuisine. Customers include the great and the good, and the Pavilion's modern yet comfortable atmosphere guarantees them anonymity.

There's an à la carte menu at lunch only, but the basic deal at the Pavilion is that you choose either two courses for £18.50 or three for £21.50. Given the quality, freshness of ingredients and attention to detail, this proves exceptional value, and reverses the Soho trend towards bargain lunches and à la carte evenings. A starter of carpaccio of roast pink lamb, rucola and Parmesan is a moreish and clever variation on traditional carpaccio. Or there may be a simple bruschetta with garlic, tomato and basil. Duck salad, mixed leaves and mostarda di Cremona is plate-wipingly good, with the duck shreds crispy yet moist. Pastas, all home-made, are excellent, too, particularly the spaghettini with fresh tomato and basil – perfectly cooked and with a sauce that is prepared from fresh ingredients and tastes like it. Or perhaps tagliatelle with fresh tomatoes and Fossa cheese? Simple is good. For carnivores, however, there is nothing to beat the calves' liver with fresh sage – paper-thin liver that literally melts in the mouth, with just a hint of sage, and crisp vegetables that have been cooked at that moment rather than reheated. Piscivores should turn to the grilled swordfish with a kick of fresh chilli and cannellini beans.

Puddings continue the theme – simple and top quality. A panna cotta that is gelatinously creamy, a praline semi-freddo that is rich and soft as well as being crunchy, and a torta della nonna that reveals buttery sponge pastry and custard – flavours that remind you of bread and butter pudding and ambrosia. There is a good selection of the less usual Italian wines, as well as some good Italian pudding wines.

Yo!Sushi

When Yo!Sushi burst upon the scene it was to fanfares and a tidal wave of publicity. This was an event beyond just another kaiten (conveyor-belt) sushi bar. Robotic sushi-makers, robotic drinks trolleys, video screens – not many restaurants credit "sponsors" like ANA, Sony and Honda. In among all this there is even some food and, while purists may shudder, it's more consistent than the hype would have you suspect.

Cost	£8–£25

Address 52 Poland St, W1
T 020 7287 0443
Station Oxford Circus/ Piccadilly Circus
Open Daily noon–midnight
Accepts All major credit cards
W www.yosushi.co.uk

Plates are marked in lime (£1.50), blue (£2), purple (£2.50), orange (£3) and pink (£3.50): when satiated you call for a plate count, and your bill is prepared. You sit at the counter with a little waiters' station in front of you – there's gari (pickled ginger), soy and wasabi, plus some little dishes and a forest of wooden chopsticks. Kirin beer costs £3, a small warm sake £3, and unlimited Japanese tea is £1. You're ready to begin. Yo!Sushi claim to serve more than one hundred sushi, so be leisurely and watch the belt – and, if in doubt, ask. The nigiri sushi range from fruit and crabstick (both £1.50); through salmon, French bean and mackerel (at £2); and tuna, prawn and squid (at £3); and so on up to yellowtail and fatty tuna – which carry the warning that they are "as available" and a pink price tag of £3.50. There are about twenty different maki rolls (with vegetarians well catered for), at all prices. The seven different sashimi and seven different gunkan all command the higher orange and pink prices. As do the handrolls – which are nori funnels, Californian-style. Dining at Yo!Sushi does call for some restraint and deft mental arithmetic – the tower of brightly badged empty plates building up in front of you can end up costing more than you expected.

Yo!Sushi is at the forefront of restaurant merchandising and no age group is safe. There are Yo!Sushi T-shirts, fleeces, coats, and even baby-gros. Webbists can even buy badged mouse mats. You'll find other branches of Yo!Sushi within The Fifth Floor Food Market at Harvey Nichols in Knightsbridge; in Selfridges on Oxford Street; in Whiteley's Bayswater; at 95 Farringdon Rd; and deep within the O2 centre on the Finchley Road.

Zilli Fish

Bright, brittle and brash, Zilli Fish is a companion to Aldo Zilli's other Soho venues – Signor Zilli, at 40 Dean St, W1 (℡020 7734 3924) and the Zilli Bar, next door. In a hectic atmosphere, it serves a modern Italianate fish menu to London's media workers and the rest of the young Soho crowd. Tables are close and everything is conducted at a racy pace. Not ideal for a secret conversation or for plighting your troth, unless you want the whole place to cheer you on.

Cost	£25–£45

Address 36–40 Brewer St, W1
T 020 7734 8649
Station Piccadilly Circus
Open Mon–Sat
noon–11.30pm
Accepts All major credit cards
W www.zillialdo.com

ITALIAN/FISH

The menu starts with the modestly entitled section, "what we are famous for". These are dishes like char-grilled tuna steak with Caesar salad (£15); spaghettini with fresh lobster (£19); and wild salmon stuffed with crab and spinach and steamed in ginger and soya (£15). Or simple sea bass fillet baked with cherry tomatoes, ginger, garlic, basil, olive oil and lemon dressing (£15). Dishes like whole roast lobster with garlic butter and herbs, served with chips (£22), demonstrate admirable restraint. From the side orders, rocket and Parmesan salad is simple but well made (£4.50). While the list is dominated by fishy favourites, in keeping with the name, there are some modern Italian vegetarian and meat options as well, including risotto with wild and field mushrooms and white truffle oil (£9.90), and fillet of beef tagliata served on roasted vegetables (£18). Puddings include a lime and marscapone tart with white chocolate ice cream (£5); a home-made tiramisù with Pavesini (£5); and, rather incongruously, a fried banana spring roll with vanilla ice cream.

Aldo Zilli has built up a reputation in Soho that guarantees that his bar and restaurants are almost always packed. Zilli Fish offers good food, but also good fun. In keeping with so many restaurants nowadays, Signor Zilli is quite happy to give away his secrets, so signed copies of his latest book are always available in the restaurant. Gastronauts will probably wish to visit Zilli Fish on a Sunday, when the suckling pig is the special of the day.

South Kensington

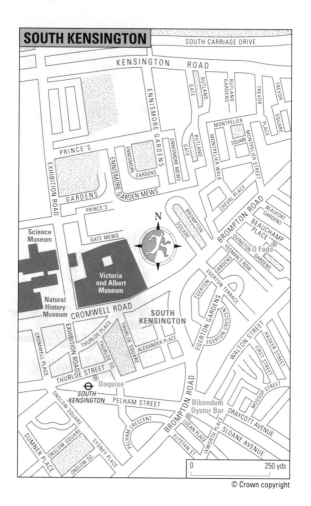

Bibendum Oyster Bar

Bibendum Oyster Bar is one of *the* places to eat shellfish in London. The 1911 building, a glorious tiled affair that was a former garage for the French tyre people, is Conranized throughout, but the oyster bar is housed in what looks like the old workshop on the ground floor and they've done precious little to it. On the old forecourt stand two camionettes: one is used as a shellfish stall, selling lobsters, oysters and crabs to the good people of Chelsea; the other is a flower stall, with lilies, ginger flowers and roses rather than carnations. It all looks rather quaint, but it's very attractive, and it gives a much-needed initial splash of colour which stays with you in the plain oyster bar, with its cream walls, marble tables and stone floor.

Cost	£12–£30

Address Michelin House, 81 Fulham Rd, SW3
T 020 7589 1480
Station South Kensington
Open Mon–Sat noon–10.30pm, Sun noon–10pm
Accepts All major credit cards
W www.bibendum.co.uk

The menu is a shellfish lover's heaven. Here you'll find three different types of rock oysters (£7.50 to £8 per half-dozen) – you can choose your favourite or order a selection to find out the difference. The crab mayonnaise (£9) comes in the shell, giving you the enormous fun of pulling it apart and digging through the claws. Or you can have it done for you in a crab salad (£9.50) – probably just as good, but not nearly so satisfying. If you're really hungry, there's a particularly fine plateau de fruits de mer (£27.50 per head, minimum two people), which has everything – crab, clams, langoustine, oysters, prawns and shrimps, as well as winkles and whelks. There is plenty of choice for those less inclined to use claw crushers, though surprisingly there is practically nothing that uses this wealth of crustacea in hot dishes. Instead there are simple classics such as cold pink veal with artichoke salad and anchovy dressing (£12), and ham and pease pudding with parsley salad (£11.50). The daily-changing set menu follows the same lines – grilled chicken breast with chorizo and potato salad (£12); Greek salad with hummus and pitta bread (£9). Desserts are simple and seasonal – raspberries and Jersey cream (£5.50); a selection of cheeses (£5.50); and the inevitable crème brûlée (£5.50).

Given the nature of the place, there's a really sensible wine list, mostly given over to white wine and champagne, with a decent smattering of half-bottles and wines by the glass.

Daquise

Daquise is more old-fashioned than you could possibly imagine. High ceilings, murky lighting, oilcloth table covers, charming service, elderly customers – the full Monty. During the day it serves coffee, tea and rather good cakes to all comers, breaking off at lunchtime

Cost	£8–£25
Address	20 Thurloe St, SW7
T	020 7589 6117
Station	South Kensington
Open	Daily 11.30am–11pm
Accepts	MasterCard, Visa

and in the evening to dispense Polish home cooking, Tatra Zwiecka beer, and shot glasses of various vodkas. Several novels have been completed here by penniless writers seeking somewhere warm to scribble – buying a cup of coffee gets you a full ration of patience from the management, all you need supply is a little inspiration. The food is genuine here, and does evolve, albeit at a glacial pace. Regulars were disappointed when the wild mushroom stew fell off the menu and also when the magnificent "herrings with potato" became the almost as good "herrings with bread". Portions are serious here, but prices are very reasonable, even if you don't take advantage of Daquise's hospitality to while away the day.

Start with Ukrainian barszcz (£2.50), rich and red, or the new starter, herrings with bread (£3.50) – the herring fillets are amazingly good here. Thick cut, pleasantly salty, and with a luxurious smooth texture. Go on to the kasanka (£6), a large buckwheat sausage, cousin to black pudding, made using natural skins. Or, for the fearless, there is giant golonka (£8.80), a marinated pork knuckle which is boiled and served with horseradish sauce. Also welcome back an old friend, Vienna schnitzel with a fried egg on top (£9.50). And it is hard not to be tempted into ordering an extra dish of potato pancakes (£5.50), which are large, flat and crispy, and come with sour cream or apple sauce. The other side-dish options are a strange sauerkraut (£1.50), served cold and very mild; cucumbers in brine (£1); and kasza (£1.60), the omnipresent buckwheat. For purists there's also that classic Central European dish, a simply cooked trout (£8.50).

Since the first edition of this guide we have reported on the planning wrangles which crop up every now and then when a speculator proposes to redevelop this entire chunk of Thurloe Street. On such occasions the locals and regulars band together to defend the Daquise. Thankfully, to date they have always been successful.

O Fado

O Fado seems somewhat out of place in the chic environs of Beauchamp Place. In a street lined with some very pretentious establishments, this Portuguese restaurant flies the flag for simpler things. O Fado is owned, staffed and largely frequented by Portuguese, though the waiters also need to speak Japanese, or at least refer to the food glossary on the wall when taking orders from the regulars, who come here for the seafood. Pretty in pink, and bedecked with hand-painted azulejos, it is quite a romantic restaurant, seductively lit with a few nooks and crannies that are bagged quickly – so book well ahead.

Cost	£18–£35

Address 45–50 Beauchamp Place, SW3
T 020 7589 3002
Station Knightsbridge
Open Daily noon–3pm & 6.30pm–1am
Accepts All credit cards except Diners
W www.ofado-restaurant-fsnet.uk

The menu and wine list are both exhaustive. Favourite dishes among Japanese diners include octopus salad (£6.50), and arroz de marisco (£25 for two) – the Portuguese take on paella. But those wanting to get in the mood for their summer holiday should try the crisp and salty grilled sardines (£3.85), or caldo verde soup (£3.50), followed by a spicy piri piri chicken and fries (£8.90) that should send French chefs scuttling for their cooking manuals. Finish off with the comfortingly named pudin flan (£3.50) – crème caramel Portuguese-style. More sophisticated options are the shellfish crêpe with brandy sauce (£4.60), and the mussels with a twist – served in olive oil and coriander together with the usual wine and garlic (£5.50). The range of salt cod specialities is popular with Portuguese families for Saturday lunch: Bacalhau a catalana (£12.95) is a dish of salt cod and clams, pressure-cooked in a rich tomato sauce, and it's surprisingly delicious. Look out for daily specials such as suckling pig (£15), but ask the price first, as they can prove expensive. If you still have room after the sumo-wrestler portions, try the arroz doce (£2.80), a wonderful rice pudding. The tarta da laranja (£2.80) – a moist, eggy orange cake – and Molotof (£3.20) – not a bomb but an egg-white soufflé – are both good as well. To accompany your meal, the Borba VQPRD 1996 is delicious, and a snip at £11.90.

This place is called O Fado for a reason: mid-evening the house singer begins the haunting, lyrical strains of fado ballads, with guitar accompaniment, and diners listen appreciatively if they know what's good for them. It's all a lot quieter at lunchtime.

Victoria & Westminster

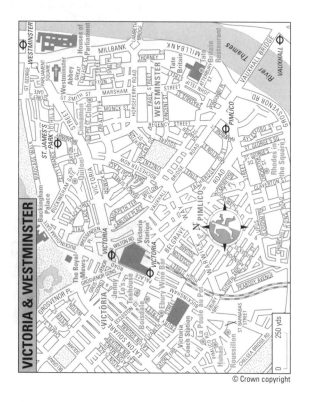

VICTORIA & WESTMINSTER

© Crown copyright

Boisdale

Boisdale is owned by Ranald Macdonald, who is next in line to be the Chief of Clanranald, and if that information gives you a premonition of what the restaurant is like you are probably thinking along the right lines. This is a very Scottish place, strong on hospitality, and with a befuddlingly large range of rare malt whiskies. Fresh produce – cor-

Cost	£15–£50

Address 15 Eccleston St, SW1
T 020 7730 6922
Station Victoria
Open Mon–Sat noon–1am
Accepts All major credit cards
W www.boisdale.co.uk

rection, fresh Scottish produce – rules wherever possible, and it is no wonder that the clubby atmosphere and reliable cooking makes this a haven of choice for local businessmen, who are also likely to be found in the ultra-Scottish back bar, home to the formidable malt whisky collection.

There are three Boisdale menus, one of which is the admirably simple "Flying Scotsman" lunch menu – for £14, diners can enjoy leek and potato soup or soused mackerel, followed by crofters pie, salmon kedgeree or breast of chicken with stoved potatoes, and finally rhubarb crumble. Or there's the "Boisdale" menu – a choice of six starters and seven mains for £17.45 (yes, just like the rebellion!). Starters range from Hebridean lobster bisque and mini roast Macsween haggis to the slightly less Scottish salad of vine tomatoes and Feta cheese with basil dressing. Main courses veer from Aberdeen Angus beef stew, through smoked haddock and cod fish cakes to, you've guessed it, roast Macsween haggis. The à la carte includes a good many luxury ingredients: as well as Lochcarnan smoked salmon from South Uist (£9.90), and Rannoch Moor smoked venison with black truffle dressing (£9.90), there's spiced potted lobster with rocket and warm toasted brioche (£10.50). Commendably, the mains feature fresh fish of the day, fresh offal of the day, and today's roast game. Plus various Aberdeen Angus beef steaks: fillet with Béarnaise sauce and chips (£19.90), or rib-eye with black truffle, pommes Dauphinoises, spinach and wild mushrooms (£20).

Sensibly enough, you can mix and match all of these menus as you work towards an after-dinner malt, or malts. Perhaps in the Macdonald bar and cigar club, next door, which features jazz every evening from Monday to Saturday (cover charge £3.95)?

The Cinnamon Club

It had to happen. Those brave people who set up smart new restaurants were eventually bound to run out of bank premises to convert. It seems we are entering the next phase, as the Cinnamon Club occupies what was formerly Westminster Library. Banks and libraries have a good deal in common – lofty ceilings, large doors, old wood floors, plenty of panelling – just the stuff to make a cracking formal restaurant.

Cost	£25–£70

Address Old Westminster Library, Great Smith St, SW1
T 020 7222 2555
Station St James/ Westminster
Open Mon–Fri noon–3pm & 6–11pm, Sat 6–11pm, Sun noon–3pm
Accepts All major credit cards
W www.cinnamonclub.com

The Cinnamon Club is an elegant, substantial, very pukka restaurant. Service is polished and attentive, the linen is snowy white, the cutlery is heavy, the ashtrays stealably elegant, the toilets opulent, and there are huge flower arrangements. The cooking at this restaurant is accomplished, and each dish offers a finely judged combination of flavours, every one distinct. There's an informed wine list. And yes, unlikely as it may sound, this is an Indian restaurant.

From the "Appetisers" section of the menu, char-grilled sea bream with pomegranate extract (£6.50) is worth noting – a thick-cut, meaty chunk of fish is marinated in a gently spiced yoghurt and then grilled; it contrasts perfectly with the ruby-red pomegranate sauce, heavily reduced to concentrate the flavour. Or there is loin of rabbit with cottage cheese and dried fruit (£7.50). This is a grand dish – a kind of Indian spiced ballotine sits proud on a bed of pickled sweet onions, the whole dish lifted by pungent yellow mustard oil and onion seeds. Or perhaps the home-smoked lamb kebabs (£5.25) – lamb tikka and seek kebab dragged into the twenty-first century. Mains are also well thought out: Goan spiced duck with curry leaf-flavoured semolina (£12.70) is a whole spiced duck breast, simply cooked, sliced and presented with a small mound of semolina. An accurately cooked turbot comes with a rich and spicy Keralan curry sauce, spinach and lemon rice (£17.50). Go for the basket of breads (£3) as a side dish – a selection of unusual parathas, nans, and rotis. Desserts are elegant: try the layered coconut cake (£5.50), or the steamed mango rice cakes (£4.50), which come with a deep-purple berry sorbet.

Politicos have already been sighted here prowling amongst the grazing foodies. Perhaps this is a sign that refined and elegant Indian food will soon take its place as the lobbyist's weapon of choice?

Ebury Wine Bar and Restaurant

Ebury may call itself a wine bar, but the food is not the kind of stuff that springs to mind when wine bars are mentioned. The regulars – from those swingeingly expensive houses in Belgravia and the offices around Victoria – come for a bottle of decent claret in the front area or to eat at the restaurant out the back. They overlook the rather chintzy decor and the closely packed tables, they will even overlook the somewhat uncomfortable chairs. They pitch up for the food, and to enjoy the rather old-fashioned but undeniably friendly service.

Cost	£18–£35

Address 139 Ebury St, SW1
T 020 7730 5447
Station Victoria
Open Daily noon–3pm & 6–10.30pm (Sun until 10pm)
Accepts All major credit cards

The food is well cooked, adventurous and always interesting – in an almost radical counterpoint to the decor. The menu changes regularly, but starters might include salt cod brandade with smoked eel (£5.75); or a duck liver parfait with red onion jam and toasted brioche (£6.50); or spicy fish cakes with peanuts and sweet chilli cucumber (£6/£9.50). Rare meats like kangaroo, ostrich and emu all make the occasional guest appearance, and there is a magnificent "plate of savouries" (£6.75) offering a complete tour around tastes and textures. Then there's a menu section devoted to salads – in tune with the local customers – which offers the likes of a warm salad of saucisson, new potatoes and poached egg (£5), or the whimsically but descriptively named Asian prawnslaw (£6). The more orthodox (only slightly more orthodox!) main courses are also inventive: smoked haddock with scotch egg, leeks and Gruyère cream (£11.75); baked onion, Puy lentils and cauliflower puree (£10); braised duck in Sauternes (£13.75); New Zealand venison, mash and red wine jus (£15); Cumberland sausages with mash and onion gravy (£10). These are good dishes, well presented and made with well-chosen ingredients.

Desserts are equally moody – such as banana and fig tarte Tatin (£5), and a dish that has had a generation of chefs arguing over who invented it first. The Mars bar spring roll (£4) – aka the deep-fried Mars bar – was probably (it's worth stressing the "probably" as there's a good deal of debate around the subject) first devised some years ago by Josh Hampton, who's in charge of the kitchens here.

Hunan

The Hunan is the domain of Mr Peng. As you venture into his restaurant you put yourself into his hands, to do with you what he will. It is rather like being trapped in a 1930s B-movie. You order the boiled dumplings ... and the griddle-fried lettuce-wrapped dumplings turn up, "because you will like them more". And most likely you will.

Cost	£25–£40
Address	51 Pimlico Rd, SW1
T	020 7730 5712
Station	Sloane Square
Open	Mon–Sat noon–2.30pm & 6–11.30pm
Accepts	All major credit cards except Diners

Probably at least ninety percent of Mr Peng's regular customers have given up the unequal struggle, submitting themselves to the "feast" – a multi-course extravaganza, varied according to the maestro's whims and the vagaries of the market, that might include pigeon soup. Or goose. Or a dish of cold, marinated octopus. This fine food and attentive service is matched by the Hunan's elegant surroundings – but be warned: the prices are Pimlico rather than Chinatown, and the soaring rent rises Mr Peng faced in 2001 will soon be working their way through to drive them even higher.

If you want to defy Mr Peng and act knowledgeable, you could actually try asking for the griddle-fried lettuce-wrapped dumplings (£5.50), which are exceedingly delicious. Or there are frogs' legs in rich and hot Hunan sauce (£6); or fried crab claws (£10); or grilled salt and peppery beef (£5.50). Alternatively, try the camphor-wood and tea-smoked duck (£18 for a half, £33 for a whole) – once again, this dish is as interpreted by Mr P, so as well as a southwestern Chinese version of crispy duck (with pancakes etc) there's a sweet and sourish sauce (apparently his regulars felt that it was "too dry" without). Other standouts include spicy-rich beef in Hunan sauce (£6), and stir-fried squid "any style" (£7), which is accurately cooked. Also on offer are sizzling prawns (£7), braised scallops (£7) and spicy braised eggplant (£4.80).

However, for all but the strongest wills, resistance is useless and you'll probably end up with what is described on the menu as "Hunan's special leave-it-to-us-feast – minimum two persons, from £28 a head. We recommend those not familiar with Hunan cuisine and those who are looking for a wide selection of our favourite and unusual dishes to leave it to the chef Mr Peng to prepare for you his special banquet. Many of the dishes are not on the menu." Quite so.

Jenny Lo's Teahouse

Jenny Lo's Teahouse in Victoria is the complete opposite of those typically stuffy, overdesigned Chinese restaurants. This place is bright, bare and utilitarian – and stylish and fashionable, too. From the blocks of bright colours and refectory tables to the artifice of framing the emergency exit sign like a picture over the door, this is a somewhat smart – but comfortable – place to eat.

Cost £7–£22

Address 14 Eccleston St, SW1
T 020 7259 0399
Station Victoria
Open Mon–Fri 11.30am–3pm & 6–10pm, Sat noon–3pm & 6–10pm
Accepts Cash or cheque only

CHINESE/NOODLES

And that just about sums up the food too. Service makes you think that you're in the politest cafeteria in the world and the prices don't spoil the illusion. Although portion sizes and seasoning can vary, the food is freshly cooked and generally delicious. All of which meets with unqualified approval from a loyal band of sophisticated regulars.

The menu is divided into three main sections: soup noodles, wok noodles and rice dishes. Take your pick and then add some side dishes. The chilli beef soup ho fun (£6.95) is a good choice. A large bowl full of delicate, clear, chilli-spiked broth which is then bulked out with yards of slippery ho fun – ribbon noodles like thin tagliatelle – plus slivers of beef and fresh coriander. The black bean seafood noodles (£6.95) are an altogether richer and more solid affair, made from egg noodles with prawn, mussels, squid and peppers. Rice dishes range from long-cooked pork and chestnuts (£6.50); to gong bao chicken with pine nuts (£6.95); and the simpler Szechuan aubergine (£5.50). The side dishes are great fun, with good spare ribs (£3.25); guo tie (£3.95), which are pan-cooked dumplings filled with either vegetables or pork; and onion cakes (£2) – a Beijing street food made from flat, griddled breads laced with spring onions and served with a dipping sauce.

Try the tea here, too. As well as offering Chinese and herbal teas, Jenny Lo has enlisted the help of herbalist Dr Xu who has blended two special therapeutic teas: long-life tea (£1.65), described as "a warming tonic to boost your energy", and cleansing tea (£1.85), "a light tea for strengthening the liver and kidneys". It tastes refreshing and faintly gingery, and is doubtless cleansing, too.

La Poule au Pot

You are in trouble at the Poule au Pot if you don't understand at least some French. It is unreservedly a bastion of France in England, and has been for more than three decades. What's more, several of the staff have worked here for most of that time, and the restaurant itself has hardly changed at all, with huge dried-flower baskets and a comfortable rustic atmosphere. The character of the place, however, is very different at lunch and dinner. The wide windows make it bright at lunch but, by night, candlelight ensures that La Poule is a favourite for romantic assignations.

Cost	£17–£40
Address	231 Ebury St, SW1
T	020 7730 7763
Station	Sloane Square
Open	Daily 12.30–2.30pm & 7–11.15pm (Sun until 10.30pm)
Accepts	All major credit cards

A small dish of crudités in herb vinaigrette is set down as a bonne bouche. Different fresh breads come in huge chunks. The menu is deceptive, as there are usually more additional fresh daily specials than are listed. The patient waiters struggle to remember them all and answer your questions about the dishes. As a starter, the escargots (£7.50) deliver classic French authenticity with plenty of garlic and herbs. The soupe de poisson (£8.25) is not the commonly served thick soup, but a refined clear broth with chunks of sole and scallop, plus prawns and mussels. A main course of bifteck frites (£13.75) brings a perfectly cooked, French-cut steak with red-hot chips. Ask for mustard and you get Dijon. The gigot aux flageolets (£13.50) is pink and tender with beans that are well flavoured and not overcooked. There's calves' liver (£13.25), and carré d'agneau à l'ail (£16)- rack of lamb with garlic. The pudding menu features standards like crème brûlée (£4.50) – huge, served in a rustic dish, and classically good – and banane à sa façon (£4.50), which is lightly cooked with a caramel rum sauce and a scoop of ice cream – very rich. There is also a selection of good pudding wines: a glass of Monbazillac (£2.95) makes an excellent companion to the richness of the desserts.

If you are a Francophile, you'll find all your favourites, from French onion soup to boeuf Bourguignon, from quiche to cassoulet. And, such is the atmosphere of the place that, for a few hours at least, you forget that you are in England, particularly if you take advantage of the prix fixe lunch (£14.50 for two courses and £16 for three).

Quilon

Quilon is about as swish as Indian restaurants get – as you'd expect when you learn that it is owned by the Taj Group, which also runs a dozen of India's most upmarket hotels. This elegant, modern 92-seater opened in September 1999, and anyone who still has a mental block and unfairly pigeonholes all Indian restaurants as cheap and cheerful should

Cost	£27–£55

Address 41 Buckingham Gate, SW1
T 020 7821 1899
Station St James's Park
Open Mon–Fri noon–2.30pm & 6–11pm, Sat 6–11pm
Accepts All major credit cards

INDIAN

pop along for a reality check. Quilon has the appearance of a sophisticated restaurant; you get the service you'd expect in a sophisticated restaurant; you get the quality of cooking you'd expect from a sophisticated restaurant. And, unsurprisingly, you get the size of bill you'd expect from a sophisticated restaurant. Chef Sriram's menu, built around "Coastal Food", showcases the splendid cuisine of Kerala – lots of fish, seafood, fresh peppercorns and coconut. The food is very good indeed.

Start with the Coorg chicken (£5.25) – chunky chicken with rich spicing and a hint of Coorg vinegar. Or pepper shrimps (£6.25) – prawns fried in batter with plenty of chilli and a touch of aniseed. In season there may be partridge masala (£5.25), cooked in really fresh spices. Moving on to the mains, seafood tempters include clams chilli fry (£13.95) and prawns Byadgi (£18.25); the latter are enormous prawns grilled with the specially imported and pleasantly hot Byadgi chillies. Or try Canara lamb curry (£13.25) – very, very rich with a clean and honest heat; or the guinea fowl salan (£13.50), cooked with coconut milk and yoghurt. These are all fairly spicy choices, but there is also gentler fare, with plenty of chicken options, and several duck dishes. All the main courses come with a vegetable of the day, but the vegetable dishes themselves are worthy of note. Standouts include a coconut gravy made tangy by a hint of tamarind, and a spinach poriyal (£7) made with freshly grated coconut, mustard leaves and split Bengal gram.

In the middle of the dining room there is an outpost kitchen where a busy chef works at an array of burners making fresh appams (£1.95), the feathery rice pancakes which are stunning hot and so-so cold. Here, having them cooked in front of you in the dining room, you get to taste them at their very best.

Rhodes in the Square

Get him away from all that television hype, and Gary Rhodes is actually a very good cook. In his restaurants there is a real respect for genuine British ingredients, and the resulting dishes are always good to eat. It's hard to understand why restaurant critics tend to rank his food below that of his more French-inspired peers. Rhodes in the

Cost	£21–£75

Address Dolphin Square, Chichester St, SW1
T 020 7798 6767
Station Pimlico
Open Tues–Fri noon–2.30pm & 7–10pm, Sat 7–10pm
Accepts All major credit cards

Square is the place to make up your mind. It's very swish, the large, plush dining room set off with dark-blue velvet and gleaming metalwork. This is not a cheap restaurant, though you could maybe console yourself by thinking of all the bond dealers tucking in at Gary's City restaurant – they're paying a bit more for the same quality. And, as always seems to be the case, this quality of food is most wallet-friendly at lunch: two courses for £17.80, and three courses for £19.80 is not so bad.

In the evenings, dinner costs £36.50 for three courses, with only a couple of supplements. Starters are simple and stunning: spicy smoked haddock and saffron soup; rillette of braised oxtails with fresh horse-radish cream; pan-fried fillet of red mullet on a light garlic mash; risotto of duck confit with prunes, finished with a sesame oil dressing. But the one starter on the dinner menu that every self-respecting hedonist must try is the lobster omelette thermidor (£2.50 supplement) – presented in its own little pan, this is a melting omelette with a rich sauce and chunks of lobster. Main courses are equally rich and reassuring: steamed whiting on tomato fondue with a fresh crab ravioli; steamed mushroom, onion and marjoram suet pudding with fresh herb-buttered vegetables; two salmons with sorrel flavoured leeks and crème fraîche mashed potatoes. For pudding, you could pass up the famous Rhodes bread and butter pudding – though it is a signature dish – and try the warm chocolate mousse with bitter chocolate sorbet, or the chocolate Grand Marnier pot served with bitter oranges.

Since the opening in 1998, the menu here has become somewhat simpler and, if anything, prices have not increased as rapidly as they have elsewhere. Anything that makes this kind of honest cooking more accessible is to be applauded.

Roussillon

Roussillon is a restaurant that got off to a slow start but has quietly gone on to earn a growing reputation and a cupboard full of awards. The main-spring is a young French chef called Alexis Gauthier who is obsessed with the quality and freshness of his ingredients. His dishes invariably combine strong flavours, and make good use of fine English foods. To see the advantages of being season- and market-driven, try the terrific-value set lunch at Roussillon: £15 for two courses and £18 for three. The main menu runs in at two courses for £29, three for £35, and four for £42. At which point you will probably feel the urge to splash out on one or other of the seven-course showing-off menus – the vegetarian "Garden Menu" (£35) and the "Seasonal Menu" (£50).

Cost	£20–£90
Address	16 St Barnabas St, SW1
T	020 7730 5550
Station	Sloane Square/ Victoria
Open	Mon–Fri noon–2.30pm & 6.30–10.45pm, Sat 6.30–10.45pm
Accepts	All major credit cards except Diners
W	www.roussillon.co.uk

FRENCH

The menu has four sections to it: the classics, the garden, the sea and river, and the land. Overlook the coy names and listen to your taste buds. Open with blue Bembridge lobster salad; or a terrine of duck foie gras with peppered jelly and toasted brioche. Into the garden: Jersey Royal potatoes roasted with mature Cheddar, sour cream and shallots on the side; or girolle risotto, chicken jus. Fish dishes may include fillet of cod cooked in a pot, with tender artichoke, confit tomato and basil; boiled freshwater crayfish, green dandelion and lemon balm; or roast langoustines with a salad of raw purple artichoke and lemon pepper. The land brings beef that is organically raised Aberdeen Angus from Donald Russell, served with larded vegetables and thick French fries; or try the light battered calf's sweetbread with sautéed early-season broad beans. Or there may be an awesome extravaganza for two, like the honey-roasted Barbary duck in three services – the filet comes with glazed long radishes and bitter young turnips; the leg is cooked slowly and served with Kentish leaves; and it is followed by soya duck consommé. This is gastronomic stuff. Onwards to cheese, fruit and chocolate.

At the bottom of the menu is written: "Our home-made breads are all prepared with organic yeast from Gloucestershire, crab apple, grape and white wine." Now, that would be the height of pretension, were it not for the fact that they are very delicious breads indeed.

Tate Britain Restaurant

MODERN BRITISH

In these days of a "sandwich at the desk" office culture, you have to think very long and hard before recommending a restaurant that is only open for lunch, especially when it has the potential to be a pretty wallet-challenging affair. For the foodie, the Tate Britain Restaurant is worth a visit; for the winey it is an essential pilgrimage. This restaurant's love affair with wine began in the

Cost	£25–£100

Address **Tate Britain, Millbank, SW1**
T **020 7887 8877**
Station **Pimlico**
Open **Mon–Sat noon–3pm, Sun noon–4pm**
Accepts **All major credit cards except Diners**

1970s, when the food was dodgy and it seemed as if the only customers were wine merchants marvelling at the impossibly low prices. Today there are fewer florid gents enjoying a three-bottle lunch, but the atmosphere is soothing, the food is good and the wine list is not only fascinating – it's still outstanding value as well.

The menu changes on a monthly basis and offers admirably seasonal dishes. There's also a set lunch with two courses at £16.75, and three at £19.50. Although there is no indication on the menu, dishes are split into two categories: there are things to suit the oenophiles, and dishes for civilian diners. Thus wine folk might choose starters like Cornish crab timbale (£8.75), or sauté of wild mushrooms (£7), while the others can enjoy char-grilled baby squid with sweet chilli sauce (£7.50) – a dish that would make wine matching well nigh impossible. Thus mains swerve from roast rack of lamb (£15.75) to chicken Kiev (£12.75), or from deep-fried courgette flowers with Ricotta, olives and pepper filling (£11.75) to roast sirloin of veal (£14.25). The cooking is good. The food is fresh and unpretentious. There are more than enough tempting puddings to allow you a chunter through the dessert wines.

The wine list is wonderful, and constantly changing as bins run out. It takes the form of a vast book, but do not be intimidated and take your time. The wine waiters are both knowledgeable and helpful. Bottles are served at the right temperature and decanted without fuss when necessary. As a strategy, how about picking a few good half-bottles? For example, a St Romain 1998 Francois d'Allaines (£14.50); Chateuneuf-du-Pape La Crau 1996 (Domaine de Vieux Telegraph £15.50); Chateau Beycheville 1989 St Julien (£22)? This combo makes for a very good lunch.

Waterloo & The South Bank

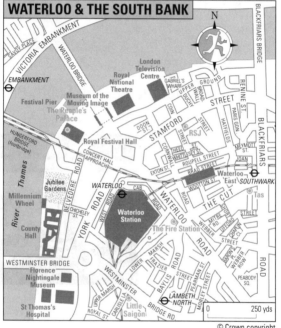

WATERLOO & THE SOUTH BANK

N

BLACKFRIARS BRIDGE

VICTORIA EMBANKMENT

SAVOY PLACE

WATERLOO BRIDGE

EMBANKMENT

London Television Centre

Royal National Theatre

GABRIEL'S WHARF

UPPER GROUND

BROAD WALL

RENNIE ST

STREET

PARIS GDN

Festival Pier

Museum of the Moving Image

The People's Palace

DOON ST

CORNWALL

STAMFORD

DUCHY

STREET

HATFIELDS

BLACKFRIARS

HUNGERFORD BRIDGE (footbridge)

Royal Festival Hall

CONCERT HALL APPROACH

THEED

RSJ

EXTON ST

ROUPELL STREET

MEYMOTT ST

JOAN

Thames

Jubilee Gardens

WATERLOO

CAB

BRAD STREET

Waterloo East

SOUTHWARK

WOOTTON ST

Tas

Millennium Wheel

YORK ROAD

BELVEDERE ROAD

CHICHELEY ST

WEST ROAD

WATERLOO

Waterloo Station

ROAD

THE CUT

STREET

River

County Hall

The Fire Station

MITRE RD

WEBBER

STORD

GRAY

COLON CL

BENNE

ROAD

WESTMINSTER BRIDGE

Florence Nightingale Museum

LOWER MARSH

FRAZIER STREET

BAYLIS ROAD

PEARMAN ST

MORLEY STREET

WEBBER ROW

PEABODY SQ

St Thomas's Hospital

UPPER MARSH

CARLISLE LA

ROYAL ST

WESTMINSTER

Little Saigon

BRIDGE RD

LAMBETH NORTH

0   250 yds

The Fire Station

When you arrive at The Fire Station it's hard to imagine that the food will be of much distinction. This is a big barn of a place with pumping music, and to get to the restaurant at the back you have to fight your way through noisy waves of colourful-drink-swillers. Decoration is scant, consisting mostly of red and cream paint, and blackboards painted with popping champagne corks. At first glance, it looks exactly like a theme hamburger bar. But if you look a little closer you'll see an open-plan kitchen preparing good-looking food, and a lot of happy diners. It's worth persevering.

Cost	£18–£35
Address	150 Waterloo Rd, SE1
T	020 7620 2226
Station	Waterloo
Open	Mon–Sat noon–2.45pm & 5.30–11pm, Sun noon–9.30pm
Accepts	All major credit cards

MODERN BRITISH

The menu offers everything but hamburgers. It changes daily but there are some simple things that often feature – starters like carrot, orange and coriander soup with croutons (£4.25); braised duck leg and couscous salad with hoi-sin dressing (£6); salmon, halibut and asparagus terrine with dill mustard dressing (£6); and grilled quail, bacon and spinach salad with red onion marmalade (£6). Equally appealing are mains such as slow-roasted pork belly with leek mash, red cabbage and red-eye gravy (£11.95); mussels steamed in mustard, celery and leek cream, with fries and aioli (£10.25); or spinach and potato gnocchi with garlic chives, courgette, aubergine, tomato sauce, cheese fondue, rocket and Parmesan (£10.25). Or how about braised shank of lamb, root vegetable puree, curly kale and button mushroom sauce (£12.25)? Or even spiced seared tuna, noodles, stir fried vegetables, cashew nuts and lime chilli sauce (£12.25)? The cooking is sound enough, and the service is friendly. The only problems stem from a tendency towards "sorlin" cooking (it's-all-in) and, though it seems churlish to comment on overgenerosity, the gargantuan portions. Thankfully, puddings are simple, but there are four huge scoops for one helping of caramel ice cream with butterscotch sauce (£3.95). To wash it all down, there's a decent wine list with five reds and whites by the glass as well as a 50cl carafe.

There's a set menu available up to 7pm – two courses for £10.95, three for £13.50 – which makes it a sensible place to drop in to on the way to the Old Vic or the National Theatre. It's a little less frenetic then, as well.

Little Saigon

After ten years running a restaurant in Frith Street, the Long family had had enough. Soho rents were hitting the stratosphere and the lease was up for renewal. So Mr Long and his wife opened Little Saigon, just behind Waterloo Station, a homely restaurant serving good Vietnamese food from a comprehensive menu. Stick to the indigenous dishes, and take the opportunity to get to grips with Vietnamese spring rolls – both the crispy deep-fried kind and the "crystal" variety. The latter are round discs of rice pastry like giant, translucent communion wafers, which you soak in a bowl of hot water until pliable and then roll around a filling made up of fresh salady things, interesting sauces, and slivers of meat grilled on a portable barbecue.

Cost	£15–£35
Address	139 Westminster Bridge Rd, SE1
T	020 7207 9747
Station	Waterloo/Lambeth North
Open	Mon–Fri noon–3pm & 5.30–11.30pm, Sat & Sun 5.30–11.30pm
Accepts	All major credit cards

Run amok with the starters. Sugar-cane prawns (two for £3.20) are large prawn "fish cakes" impaled on a strip of sugar cane and grilled. Vietnamese imperial spring rolls (£2.60) are of the crispy fried variety, but they are served cut into chunks and with lettuce leaves to roll them up in. Also good is the strangely resilient Vietnamese grilled squid cake (£3.50). Topping the bill are special spring rolls (four for £2.60) – delicate pancakes, thin enough to read through, filled with prawns and fresh herbs – which in this case have been "pre-rolled" and are quite delicious. It's as if each of the starters comes with its own special dipping sauce, and the table is soon littered with an array of little saucers – look out for the extra-sweet white plum sauce and the extra-hot brown chilli oil. For mains, ha noi grilled chicken with honey (£5.30), special Saigon prawn curry (£6.40), and the house special, fried crispy noodles (£4.80), can all be recommended.

Do try and master the "specialities". Make an intermediate course of the crystal pancakes and use them to wrap the crunchy salads and the meats barbecued at the table. You have to soak your own pancakes and it is trickier than it looks: soak them too long and they stick to the plate; not long enough, and they won't wrap. Grilled slices of barbecued beef (£12) and grilled slices of pork in garlic sauce (£12) both make splendid fillings.

The People's Palace

When this restaurant first opened, there were tales of diners who had finished their dinner late being locked into the Festival Hall and of others wandering for ages between levels. It is still not the most straightforward venue to find, but it has its own entrance now, opposite Hungerford Bridge. And it's worth seeking out. It's a very large place, run with the high standards you would hope for – considering that it is within the South Bank Centre and many diners are either pre- or post-concert, which makes timing crucial. The food is well presented and accurately cooked; there may not be too many culinary high jinks but the menu is composed of well-balanced, satisfying dishes at reasonable prices. Add the fabulous view overlooking the Thames, the sound service, a child-friendly policy (they're nice to kids, and provide highchairs and children's menus), and it all adds up to an attractive package.

Cost	£16–£35
Address	Level Three, Royal Festival Hall, South Bank, SE1
T	020 7928 9999
Station	Waterloo
Open	Daily noon–3pm & 5.30–11pm
Accepts	All major credit cards
W	www.peoplespalace.co.uk

The bargains at the People's Palace are its fixed-price menus. Lunch menus are available daily at £12.50 for two courses, while the all-day Sunday and pre-theatre menus are £16.50 for two courses. For this, you choose from a good spread of daily selections. On the à la carte you'll find starters like Manouri cheese, chicory and French bean salad with wild thyme and honey dressing (£6.25); squab pigeon and corn cake with piquant dressing (£9.50); Jerusalem artichoke and watercress soup; and poached chicken and oyster (£7). Mains include poached sea trout, fennel and cucumber salad, with curried mussel nage (£14.50); rack of lamb, chorizo Sarladaise, roast tomato and marjoram jus (£17); pan-fried sea bass, oysters, and ginger and mirin broth (£16.50); and roast leg of rabbit, leek farci, prosciutto and mustard cream (£15). Puddings (£5) ring the sweet tooth bell: sticky toffee pudding with vanilla ice cream; pecan and banana pudding with clotted cream and toffee sauce; Sauternes crème brûlée with Armagnac prunes.

It's worth figuring the Festival Hall's concert programme into your plans. On a popular night, you'll need to book for pre- or post-concert sittings. When you call to make a reservation, ask the receptionist, who will know just what's on and when it finishes.

RSJ

Rolled Steel Joist may seem a curious name for a restaurant, but it is appropriate – there is an RSJ holding up the first floor if you really want to see it. What's more interesting about RSJ is that it's owned and run by a man with a passion for the wines of the Loire. Nigel Wilkinson has compiled his list mainly from wines produced in this region and it

Cost	£19–£55

Address 13a Coin St, SE1
T 020 7928 4554
Station Waterloo
Open Mon–Fri noon–2.30pm & 5.30–11pm, Sat 5.30–11pm
Accepts All major credit cards
W www.rsj.uk.com

features dozens of lesser-known Loire reds and whites – wines which clearly deserve a wider following. Notes about recent vintages both interest and educate, and each wine is well described, so that you know what you're going to get.

The menu is based on classical dishes, but with a light touch and some very innovative combinations as well. The starters might include bresaola of wild boar with celeriac and rocket salad (£7.50); grilled marinated vegetables with buffalo Mozzarella (£6.50); or mussel soup with tomatoes and pasta (£6.25). Moving on to the main courses, typical choices might include char-grilled swordfish with aubergine, tomato and black olives (£14.95); pumpkin risotto with Parmesan (£12.95); and fried lamb sweetbread with garlic puree and wild mushrooms (£17.95). The menu also features an above average number of vegetarian options – some of which seem inspired, like fig and chestnut ravioli with buttered cabbage (£5.95/£11.25), or agreeably simple, like polenta with wild mushroom broth (£6.50/£12.95). The puddings can be the kind of serious stuff that you really should save room for – chocolate cheesecake with mint Anglaise (£5.25); warm pear and almond tart with vanilla ice cream (£4.25); or maybe panna cotta with rhubarb compote (£4.95).

Like the Peoples' Palace (see p.163), RSJ is situated close to the South Bank Centre's cinema, concert halls and theatres, and is clearly enjoyed by patrons. It appears to cater for both the hastier pre-theatre crowd and a late crowd who are not rushed in any way – always a good sign. The set meals at £15.95 for two courses and £17.95 for three represent jolly good value. Use the Web site to check out the RSJ Wine Company, whose list is a joy to anyone devoted to the fine wines of the Loire.

Tas

Tas wears its colours on its sleeve. It's a bright and bustling Turkish restaurant where eating is cheap. The menu and the set menus have proliferated until there is an almost baffling choice. There is often live music. All of which explains why the place is heaving with office parties, birthday bashes and hen nights every night of the week. The management is obviously alert to the possibilities of a modern restaurant serving Turkish dishes – the feel of this place is closer to a busy West End brasserie than to your standard street-corner Turkish grills. Expect colourful crockery, plenty of plants and an overdose of noise. If lively is what you like then Tas will do just fine.

Cost	£8–£35

Address 33 The Cut, SE1
☎ 020 7928 1444
Station Southwark
Open Mon–Sat
noon–11.30pm, Sun noon–
10.30pm
Accepts All major credit cards
except Diners

The menu is a monster. Four soups, followed by twelve cold starters, twelve hot starters, ten salads, eight rice dishes, four side orders, six pasta dishes, ten vegetarian dishes, fourteen grills, ten casseroles (including mousakka, which is stretching things a bit), fourteen fish and shellfish dishes, and nine desserts. Overwhelmed? You should be, everyone else is. Which is probably why Tas also offers four set menus starting at three courses for £6.45 and peaking at a combo of six mezze, a grill, dessert and a coffee at £17.95 (for a minimum of two people). Now you can see why the parties flock here. The first thing to say about the food is that it is well presented and tastes wonderfully fresh. From the cold starters, favour the zeytin yagli bakla (£3.25), which is a fine dish of broad beans with yoghurt; the patlican salatasi (£3.25), a rich aubergine puree; and the cacik (£2.75), a simple cucumber and yoghurt dip. The bread is very good. Stars of the hot starter menu are the borek (£3.25), which is filo pastry filled with cheese and deep fried; and the sucuk izgara (£3.25), a Turkish garlicky sausage. Unless you have particular likes or prejudices to pander to, go on to the good, sound grills: bobrek izgara (£5.95) are lambs' kidneys; and tavuk shish (£6.95) is a chicken kebab. The fish dishes are accurately cooked and come in large portions – grilled halibut (£8.95) comes with tomato sauce, while the kalamari (£6.95) brings squid with a walnut sauce.

As the menu announces, "Tas is our traditional Anatolian cooking pot, used to prepare casseroles". So overlook the moussakka and turn instead to the bademi tavuk (£6.45), a casserole of chicken and almonds.

City & East

Brick Lane & Spitalfields

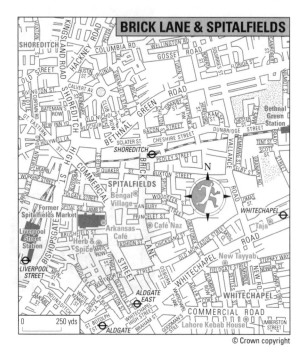

BRICK LANE & SPITALFIELDS

© Crown copyright

Arkansas Café

As you approach the Arkansas Café the glow from its steel-pit barbecue invites you in. Bubba Helberg and his wife Sarah claim that they serve the best barbecue this side of the pond, and they may just be right, for they are regularly in demand as the US Embassy's barbecue experts (they will also open here for evening parties of twelve or more). Their food is fresh and simple, and Bubba only uses the highest–quality ingredients, choosing his own steaks individually from Smithfield market to make sure that the meat is marbled enough for tenderness. The provenance of his lamb and sausages is listed for all to see. He marinates and smokes his own beef brisket and ribs, and his recipe for the latter won him a soul food award back home. His secret home-made barbecue sauce is on every table, but he won't sell the recipe to anyone.

Cost	£9–£18
Address	Unit 12, Old Spitalfields Market, E1
T	020 7377 6999
Station	Liverpool Street
Open	Mon–Fri noon–2.30pm
Accepts	MasterCard, Visa

Decor is spartan – clean-scrubbed tables, canvas chairs and paper plates – but this does not intrude on the quality of the food. There are no starters, so you just get stuck in. Any of the steaks – Irish steak platter (£9), USA steak platter (£12.50) – are good bets, char-grilled with Bubba's special sauce and served with potato salad and a vegetable salad. Note that the price is genuinely market sensitive and can rise and fall. Corn-fed French chicken (£7) is tender and full of flavour; a side order of chilli (50p) provides a spicy sauce-like accompaniment. USA beef brisket sandwich (£7) comes meltingly tender and smoky. Most of the other dishes on the menu are platters or sandwiches, the latter including choices like duck breast sandwich (£6), free-range pork rib sandwich (£5) and, of course, hot dog (£3.50). Puddings (all £2.25) include New York-style lemon cheesecake and New Orleans pecan pie. They are as sweet and as solid as they should be. The wine list is short and to the point, but the beer list is long, with a large selection of serious beers including Budvar and Budweiser (both £3.25), and the American Anchor Steam (£2.50).

Diners at Arkansas usually include expat Americans homesick for authentic barbecue, which has to be a good sign. Eat in and take an extra order home.

Bengal Village

No doubt about it, Brick Lane is becoming more sophisticated. Where once all was BYOB restaurants serving rough-and-ready curries at bargain-basement prices to impoverished punters seeking chilli and all things familiar, you will now find a crop of slick new establishments serving authentic Bangladeshi cooking. The Bengal Village

Cost	£8–£18
Address	75 Brick Lane, E1
T	020 7366 4868
Station	Aldgate East/ Liverpool Street
Open	Daily noon–midnight
Accepts	All major credit cards
W	www.bengalvillage.com

is one such place. There's a blonde wood floor and modernist chairs, but it's about more than just design. The menu touches all the bases; trad curryholics can still plough their way through more than a hundred old-style curries – korma, Madras, vindaloo – but now they can also try some more interesting Bangladeshi dishes, too.

Bucking what seems to be becoming the trend, starters are not the best dishes at the Bengal Village – the onion bhajis (£1.95) are, well, onion bhajis, and the chicken tikka (£2.10) is no more than sound. Move straight along to the Bangla specialities. Bowal mas biran (£5.80) is boal fish that has been deep fried with a rich sauce. There are four shatkora curries – the shatkora being a small green fruit that has a delightful bitter citrus tang and goes very well with rich meats – lamb shatkora (£4.85), for example. Then there are ureebisi dishes, traditionally made with the seeds of a large runner-bean-like plant – in the UK butter beans are often substituted and nobody seems to mind. Try chicken ureebisi (£4.85). There are also some rather splendid vegetarian options: chalkumra (£3.95), subtitled "ash-ground", and supposed to be made with a pumpkin-like gourd, in practice turns out to be slices of marrow in a korma-ish sauce. The marrow kofta is a curry with large and satisfactorily dense vegetable dumplings floating, or rather sinking, in it. There are two thalis available, offering a complete meal (either vegetarian or non-vegetarian) for £6.75 or £9.70.

The wine list comes on a small card which makes splendid reading. "Bolinger Champaign – £39.95"; "Moet and Chandan – £40.95"; "Jacobs Greek (Red Wine) – £8.75". Go for a large Cobra beer (£2.95) or follow the great Brick Lane tradition and take your own refreshment with you in a carrier bag.

Café Naz

Café Naz dominates Brick Lane with its elegant facade, complete with an all-glass staircase and spacious upstairs dining room. "Contemporary Bangladeshi Cuisine" is what it says on the menu and generally speaking that is what you get, though you will find some of the Indian restaurant standards – a list of baltis and, of course, chicken tikka masala. The decor is certainly contemporary: bright colours, modern furniture and a gleaming open kitchen where you can watch the chefs at work. Prices are low – thirty curry restaurants within a stone's throw makes for serious competition – and service is attentive.

Cost	£9–£22
Address	46–48 Brick Lane, E1
T	020 7247 0234
Station	Aldgate East
Open	Mon–Fri noon–midnight, Sat noon–3pm & 6pm–midnight, Sun noon–3pm & 6pm–midnight
Accepts	All major credit cards
W	www.cafenaz.com

Start with the boti kebab (£2.95), either lamb or chicken, cooked in the tandoor and served with a plateful of fresh salad. Or there's adrok chop (£3.95), small pieces of lamb chop which have been marinated in ginger and garlic before getting the treatment in the clay oven. Fish cutlet (£2.95) brings pieces of a Bangladeshi fish called the Ayre, deep-fried and served with fried onions. These could be called goujons if they weren't so big and didn't contain a good many large bones. For main courses, the dhansak (£4.50) comes as either mutton or chicken and is very tasty – it's cooked with lentils and turns out at once hot, sweet and sour. Or how about palak gosht (£4.95), a simple dish of lamb and spinach? Then there's gosht kata masala (£5.95), a splendidly rich lamb curry; or chicken sour masala (£5.95), which is chicken in a very tomatoey tomato sauce sharpened with a little vinegar. Naan bread (£1.35) is freshly cooked, and wiped with butter – delicious. And there are a range of vegetable dishes (all £2.75) – niramish, mutter aloo, bindi, sag aloo, brinjal. Very sound and very good value.

Weekdays, the buffet lunch is an attractive option – a chance to go through the card for £7.95, sampling curries, tandoori chicken, rice dishes and a constant flow of hot naans. If you want to do this justice, pick a day when all is serene – a nap after such a lunch is obligatory.

Herb & Spice

Do not let the tiny, rather gloomy dining room and huge swags of plastic flowers put you off this treasure of a curry house on Whites Row, a small road just off Commercial Street and tucked in behind Spitalfields. A loyal clientele from the City means that to secure one of the 22 seats you'll probably have to book! The menu here includes all the curry classics, plus one or

Cost	£7–£15

Address 11a Whites Row, E1
T 020 7247 4050
Station Aldgate East/
Liverpool Street
Open Mon–Fri 11.30am–
2.30pm & 5.30–11.30pm
Accepts Amex, Diners,
MasterCard, Visa

two dishes you may not have spotted before, but what sets Herb & Spice apart from the pack is that the dishes are freshly cooked and well prepared and yet the prices are still reasonable. When the food arrives it will surprise you: it's on the hot side, with plenty of chilli and bold, fresh flavours.

It's not often that the popadoms (55p) grab your attention. They do here. Fresh, light and crisp, they are accompanied by equally good home-made chutneys – perky chopped cucumber with coriander leaf, and a hot, yellowy-orange, tamarind-soured yoghurt. The kebabs make excellent starters: murgi tikka (£2.75) – chicken, very well cooked; shami kebab (£2.75) – minced meat with fresh herbs; gosht tikka (£2.55) – tender lamb cubes. For a main course you might try the unusual murgi akhani (£6.95), a dish of chicken cooked with saffron rice and served with a good, if rather hot, vegetable curry. Or there's bhuna gosht (£4.95), a model of its type – a rich, well-seasoned lamb curry with whole black peppercorns and shards of cassia bark. Murgi rezalla (£5.95) is chicken tikka in sauce; it's much hotter – and comes with more vegetables – than its cousin, the chicken tikka masala. The breads are good, too: from the decent naan (£1.65) to the shabzi parata (£1.95), a thin, crisp wholemeal paratha stuffed with vegetables.

For a real tongue-trampler, try the dall shamber (£2.75), a dish of lentils and mixed vegetables which is often overlooked in favour of that popular garlicky favourite, tarka dhal. Traditionally served hot, sweet and sour, at Herb & Spice dall shamber comes up hot (very hot, with an almost chemical bite from the large amounts of chilli) and very, very sweet indeed. Not for the faint-hearted.

Lahore Kebab House

For years, the Lahore was something of a cherished secret among curry-lovers – a nondescript, indeed downbeat-looking, kebab house serving excellent and very cheap fare. Recent years, however, have seen a few changes. Gone are the sticky carpet and the bleak Formica table tops; there are no longer sacks of gram flour stacked inside the door; even the theatrical drama of the open kitchen has been tamed. Thankfully, the food is still good and spicy, the prices are still low, and the service brusque enough to disabuse you of any thoughts that the new round marquetry tables and posh shop front have taken the Lahore upmarket. What they do here, they do very well indeed. And if you need any further proof, look at all the other similarly named places which have sprung up all over town.

Cost	£4–£14
Address	2 Umberstone St, E1
T	020 7481 9737
Station	Whitechapel/Aldgate East
Open	Daily noon–midnight
Accepts	Cash or cheque only
W	www.lakoe.com

INDIAN

There is no elegant menu at the Lahore, merely a board on the wall listing half a dozen dishes. Rotis (50p) tend to arrive unordered – the waiter watches how you eat and brings fresh bread as and when he sees fit. For starters, the kebabs are standouts. Seekhe kebab (50p), mutton tikka (£2.50) and chicken tikka (£2.50) are all very fresh, very hot and very good, served with a yoghurt and mint dipping sauce. The meat or chicken biryanis (£6) are also splendid, well spiced and with the rice taking on all the rich flavours. The karahi gosht and karahi chicken (£5.50 for a regular portion or £11 for a huge one) are uncomplicated dishes of tender meat in a rich gravy. The dal tarka (£3.50) is made from whole yellow split peas, while sag aloo (£3.50) brings potatoes in a rich and oily spinach puree. A sad loss from the menu is paya (an awesome dish of long-stewed sheeps' feet, thought by some to be the hallmark of any genuine Pakistani restaurant) – apparently it's impossible to get top-quality sheeps' feet nowadays. Much more palatable, if you want a very Lahore kind of delicacy, is the home-made kheer (£2). This is a special kind of rice pudding with cardamom.

This Lahore is unlicensed but happy for customers to bring their own beer or wine – and there's a nearby off-licence ready to oblige. You will certainly need some complement to the generally hot food – though note that alcohol isn't the best cooling agent. For that, order a lassi.

New Tayyab

🍴 The Tayyab has spread since it first opened in 1974. After the initial café came the sweet shop, and now that the New Tayyab occupies what was once the pub there is an uninterrupted sweep of Tayyab enterprises on the north side of Fieldgate Street. Inside the New Tayyab it looks as if someone has made a determined assault on the record for fitting the

Cost	£3–£10

Address 83 Fieldgate St, E1
T 020 7247 9543
Station Whitechapel/Aldgate East
Open Daily 5pm–midnight
Accepts Cash or cheque only
W www.tayyabs.co.uk

greatest number of chairs in the smallest possible space, while going for double points in the grotesque furniture category. The food is straightforward Pakistani fare: good, freshly cooked, served without pretension, and at prices lower than you would believe possible – something that is much appreciated by the hordes of impoverished students who make up a large proportion of the customers. Booking is essential and service is rough-and-ready. This is not a place to umm and err over the menu.

The simpler dishes are terrific, particularly the five pieces of chicken tikka, served on an iron sizzle dish alongside a small plate of salady things and a medium-fierce, sharp, chilli dipping sauce (£2). They do the same thing with mutton (also £2). Four lamb chops – albeit thin ones – cost £2.80. Sheekh kebab are 70p each; shami kebab, 60p each; and round fluffy naan breads, 60p. The karahi dishes are simple and tasty: karahi chicken (chicken in a rich sauce) costs £3.80 for a normal and £7.40 for a large portion. Karahi batera (quails) are £4 and £8. Karahi aloo gosht (£3) is lamb with potatoes in a rich sauce heavily flavoured with bay leaves. Or there's karahi mixed vegetables (£2.80). There is also a list of interesting daily specials, such as the splendidly named meat pillo (£3.50) served every Wednesday. Chunks of mutton slow-cooked in rice, it's a dish that's rich, satisfying and seeded with whole peppercorns for bite.

The Tayyab is strictly BYOB if you want alcohol; to judge by its own offerings it is something of a shrine to Coca-Cola. But whether you're going for beer or Coke, make sure you try the Tayyab lassi anyway; a yoghurt drink served in a pint glass, it comes sweet or salted (£1.50), and with mango or banana (£2).

Taja

🍴 Taja's exterior of black and white vertical stripes certainly jolts the eye. Venture in and you find a dining area accommodating sixty covers across two floors. The counter is ultra-modern in stainless steel and the seating has recently been upgraded from stools to comfy chairs. On the ground floor, large windows look out onto the hurly-burly of passing traffic just inches away. The food tastes very fresh, and is markedly cheap.

Cost	£5–£12
Address	199a Whitechapel Rd, E1
T	020 7247 3866
Station	Whitechapel
Open	Mon–Wed & Sun 11am–midnight, Thurs–Sat 11am–12.30am
Accepts	All major credit cards
W	www.taja.net

So far so good. By now, those in the know will have recognized that the restaurant in question is a converted toilet in the Whitechapel Road. And, as if that is not novelty enough, Taja is a genuine rarity – a thoroughly modern Bangladeshi restaurant. The menu is both enlightened and lightened, with a host of vegetarian dishes balancing the traditional favourites.

Start with that great test of a tandoor chef, chicken tikka (£1.95). At Taja you get half a dozen sizeable chunks of chicken, cooked perfectly – not a hint of dryness – with the obligatory salad garnish (a waste of time) and a yellowish "mint sauce". Or try chotpoti (£1.95), described on the menu as "green peas and potatoes with spices, served with a tamarind chutney – high in protein". Move on to a biryani – mixed vegetable, lamb, chicken or prawn (all £4.95); a good-sized portion comes with a dish of really splendid vegetable curry by way of added lubrication. There are also a host of curry-house favourites. Chicken bhuna (£4.29) is an outstanding choice, with a really fresh sauce, hot but not too hot, and lots of fresh herbs. Very good indeed. The naan breads – plain, peshwari or keema (£1.50) – are large, thick-rimmed and very fresh, as a naan should be. The Taja got its licence in 1999 but you can still bring your own for a small corkage. Healthier types will enjoy the fresh juices – orange and carrot (£1.95) is especially good.

Taja offers all sorts of set meals and deals. The "fast snack – ready in five to ten minutes" weighs in at £5.50 for veggies, £6.50 for omnivores. Or you could splash out on the "All day and every day buffet eat as much as you like non-vegetarian and vegetarian £5.95 per person" – the "day" in question being restricted to 11am–6pm.

City

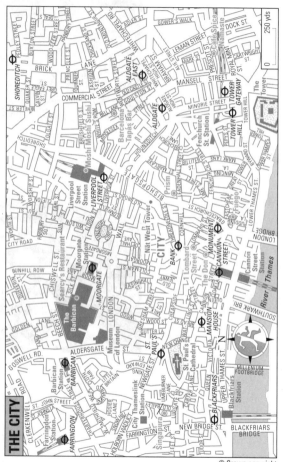

THE CITY

© Crown copyright

1 Lombard Street, The Brasserie

The Brasserie at 1 Lombard Street was formerly a banking hall and the circular bar sits under a suitably imposing glass dome. This is a brasserie in the City, of the City, by the City and for the City. It is connected to Bloomberg – a sort of elitist Ceefax-cum-email system which keeps City traders in touch with each other, rather like passing notes at

Cost	£25–£65
Address	1 Lombard St, EC3
T	020 7929 6611
Station	Bank
Open	Mon–Fri 11.30am–3pm & 6–10pm
Accepts	All major credit cards
W	www.1lombardstreet.com

MODERN FRENCH

school – and messages flash in and out. "Can you confirm your reservation at 1 Lombard Street?"; "Yes. But we'll be ten minutes late." The brasserie menu is a model of its kind, long but straightforward with a spread of dishes that is up to any meal occasion – starters and salads, soups, egg and pasta, caviar, fish, crustacea, meat, puddings. It delivers on pretty much every front, serving satisfying dishes made with good fresh ingredients, and surprisingly it manages to be both stylish and unfussy at the same time. The bar, meanwhile, is like any chic City watering hole – loud, brisk and crowded, with simultaneous conversations in every European language.

The brasserie menu changes every couple of months to satisfy the band of regulars, and there are daily specials in addition. The starters can be ambitious, like red mullet with Provençal vegetables (£8.95), or simple, like carpaccio of salmon (£9.95), while further down the menu there will be some even more comfortable options like a soft-boiled free-range egg (£8.25 or £11.95 main course) served with baked potato, smoked salmon, sour cream and chives. There's enough listed under crustacea to fuel even the wildest celebrations, including seared scallops with a fennel and Pernod velouté (£19.95), and clam stew (£8.50/£12). Then the meat section features a very well-made coq au vin à la Bourguignon (£14.95) plus steaks, sausages, liver and chops. During the season you may also find fricassée of pheasant in puff pastry (£18.95).

There is a smaller, forty-seater room at the back of the bar set aside for fine dining at fancy prices. It's interesting to note, however, that caviar is a brasserie dish – 50g of beluga served with blinis, steamed potatoes and sour cream will set you back £78.

Barcelona Tapas Bar

At the start of the East End, not a hundred yards from the towering buildings of the City, you find yourself among the market stalls of Petticoat Lane and Middlesex Street. On one of the less salubrious corners you'll see a banner bearing the legend "tapas". Note that the arrow points down. As you

Cost	£10–£25
Address	1a Bell Lane, E1
T	020 7247 7014
Station	Aldgate
Open	Mon–Fri 11am–11pm
Accepts	All major credit cards
W	www.barcelona/tapas.com

descend the stairs into a cramped basement which seats about twenty, try to still the thought that this is an inauspicious start to your lunch or evening. Barcelona is, in fact, one of London's best tapas bars. The range of snacks wouldn't be sniffed at in Barcelona or Madrid, and includes a fair few Catalan specialities – including the classic tomato-and-garlic-rubbed bread, a good accompaniment to any tapas session.

You'll find a number of tapas lined up in typical Spanish style along the back half of the bar – these are just a few of the selection on offer. The Barcelona has a vast (in more ways than one) menu written in Spanish and Catalan with English translations. Many are simple, like Serrano ham (£7.50), or queso Manchego (£3.95), or aceitunas (olives, £1.50 to £2.50), and rely on the excellent quality of the raw ingredients. Then there are peasant dishes like fabada Asturiana (£3.25), a stew of white beans with chorizo. More skill is involved in creating the paellas; the paella Valenciana (£10.95 per person) is particularly good. And there is also a chicken brochette (£6.95). But, for those with meetings within 24 hours, avoid anything that advertises its garlic. The Spanish seem blithely unaware of the havoc they wreak with the social lives of unsuspecting diners. And here, as well as being delicious, the gambas al ajillo (£6.95) are pungent enough to give you heartburn and the kind of breath that gets you elbow room in a thronged rush-hour tube.

Unusually for such a small place with such a huge choice, there's no need to worry about freshness. There is a bigger, smarter, newer and less charming Barcelona nearby, and the apparent lull between ordering and receiving your dish may be because the girl is running around the corner to the other kitchen to fetch a portion.

Café Spice Namaste

During the week this restaurant is packed with movers and shakers, all busily moving and shaking. They come in for lunch at 11.59am and they go out again at 12.59pm. Lunchtimes and even weekday evenings the pace is fast and furious, but come Saturday nights you can settle back and really enjoy Cyrus Todiwala's exceptional cooking. What's more, with the City "closed for the weekend", parking is no problem. It is well worth turning out, for this is not your average curry house. The menu, which changes throughout the year, sees Parsee delicacies rubbing shoulders with dishes from Goa, North India, Hyderabad and Kashmir, all of them precisely spiced and well presented. The tandoori specialities, in particular, are awesome – fully flavoured by the cunning marinades but in no way dried out by the heat of the oven.

Cost	£12–£30

Address 16 Prescot St, E1
T 020 7488 9242
Station Aldgate East/
Tower Hill
Open Mon–Fri noon–3pm &
6.15–10.30pm, Sat 6.30–
10.30pm
Accepts All major credit cards
W www.book2eat.com

Start with a voyage around the tandoor; the murg kay tikkay (£3.50/£7) tastes as every chicken tikka should, with yoghurt, ginger, cumin and chillies all playing their part. Or there's venison tikka aflatoon (£4.25/£8.50), which originates in Gwalior and is flavoured with star anise and cinnamon. Also notable is the dahi kachori (£3.85), a Gujarati pastry case filled with moong beans and fried. For a main course, fish-lovers shouldn't stray past the fish cooked ambotik ani xit (£10.25) – hot and sour, with the tang of palm vinegar. Choose meat and you should try the beef xacutti (£10.25 including mushroom pulao rice), a most complex curry containing more than twenty ingredients. Breads are also excellent, while some of the accompaniments and vegetable dishes belie their lowly status at the back of the book-sized menu. French beans jeera (£3.95) are cooked with chopped shallots and roasted cumin seeds – simple and very good. Choney ani oemio chey ussal (£4.25) is a splendid Goan dish of chickpeas and mushrooms with coconut in the masala.

It's a good idea at Café Spice Namaste to do as the in-the-know diners do, and choose from the speciality menu that changes every week.

The Don

George Sandeman first took over these cellars, at 20 St Swithin's Lane, in 1798. And very fine cellars they are too, complete with an ornate, black, iron "Capital Patent Crane" for lowering barrels into the depths. Towards the end of 2000, The Don restaurant and bistro opened for business on the site, taking its name from the trademark portrait of Sandeman port's "Don" which was rehung, with due ceremony, at the gateway to this hidden courtyard. The vaulted brick cellars make a grand backdrop for the bistro, while the lofty room on the ground floor makes a striking restaurant. The restaurant floor is real wood – so real that it squeaks underfoot – and the walls are hung with suitably enigmatic modern art. The whole place reeks of aspiration.

Cost	£25–£65
Address	20 St Swithin's Lane, EC4
T	020 7626 2606
Station	Bank
Open	Mon–Fri noon–3pm & 6–10.30pm
Accepts	All major credit cards

The food in the restaurant is good. It is important to understand that the upstairs restaurant is setting its cap at great things, by aiming directly for the fine dining market. This is a strategy that may well work in the long term as the food is accomplished (if a little over-dressy) and you couldn't ask for a better-heeled catchment area. Starters range from a very well-made ballotine of foie gras, chicken and sweetbreads with a truffled potato salad (£7.95), and a terrine of Scottish salmon, hot-smoked over peat, with grilled artichokes and a whisky dressing (£6.75) – both of which show skill in the charcuterie department – to salade paysanne of boudin noir, pancetta and quails eggs (£6.25). Mains may include fillets of sole with nut butter, fine capers and herbs (£13.95); loin of young New Zealand venison with garlic pommes purees and honey-roast parsnips (£16.50); and a well-judged grilled calf's liver with bacon lardons and roast baby onions (£15.50). The cooking is good but the presentation is ambitious and tends towards old-fashioned "tall food". Puds are comforting: harlequin of black and white chocolate (£5.75); banana tarte Tatin with rum and raisin ice cream (£5.75). And there are savouries, including a delicious French rarebit (£7.75) – Reblochon on toast.

The bistro downstairs offers simpler, cheaper food and there is a grand private room in the next-door cellar.

Fuego

Fuego, a subterranean tapas bar and restaurant, is sited in Pudding Lane, where the first flickerings of the Great Fire of London started out on their path of destruction. A good many contemporary paths to destruction likely set out from these parts too as, unlike many City establishments, Fuego doesn't close mid-evening but braves it out until 2am on weekdays. As a result, and because of its good-value snacks and meals, it's a popular haunt for reckless City folk who don't care what time they go home. Typically, the clientele are suit-clad and arrive in single-sex groups. However, the segregation doesn't last long, as after 8pm, from Tuesday to Friday, Fuego transforms into a disco. For a more sophisticated atmosphere, you could try the lunchtime-only restaurant or come on a Monday night.

Cost	£12–£30

Address 1a Pudding Lane, EC3
T 020 7929 3366
Station Bank/Monument
Open Restaurant Mon–Fri 11.30am–4pm & 5.30–9.30pm
Tapas bar Mon–Fri 11.30am–2am
Accepts All major credit cards
W www.fuego.co.uk

The menu is the same wherever in Fuego you choose to dine: typical tapas fare with hot and cold dishes ranging in price from £3.40 for sopa de pueras (onion and leek soup) to £4.95 for the more expensive meat and seafood dishes. A couple of these and some French fries or, better still, fiery tomato patatas bravas (both £2.40) make a good foundation. The gambas al pil pil (£4.95) – tiger prawns with a garlic, chilli and wine sauce – are particularly good. Or try pulpo a la Gallega (£4.70) – octopus served with paprika, rock salt and olive oil. After a bad day at the office, the albondigas en salsa (£3.40) – meatballs in tomato sauce – make reassuring comfort food. More lively are the chorizo and polenta (£3.60) with red wine sauce, and the rinones a la mostaza (£3.40), kidneys in a grain mustard sauce. And you should always look out for the weekly specials (some are only available in the restaurant), which are often interesting. For the less adventurous, home-made hamburguesas (£5.50 to £5.95) and sizeable toasted sandwiches (£4.75–£5.95) are available with French fries. And if you're not drinking beer or sherry you can fall back on a decent house wine (£9.50).

As if things were not wild enough already, there's a happy hour in the tapas bar (5–7pm), after which intensive preparation the long haul to 2am becomes fairly intimidating.

Moshi Moshi Sushi

Moshi Moshi Sushi serves healthy fast food, Japanese style – its dishes circulate on a *kaiten* or conveyor belt. There are a dozen or so such places in London these days, but this one claims to have been the first. Its location, inside Liverpool Street railway station, meshes perfectly with the concept. With its glass walls and ceiling, and no-smoking policy, it is a great and very wholesome place to eat before setting off on a train journey. It is, however, much more than a refuelling stop for commuters and, reassuringly, you'll find both local office workers and Japanese diners enjoying leisurely meals. Either sit at the bar and watch your dinner circulate, or opt for table service, with some nice views of the old station arches. Set menus range from £6.70 to £11.50.

Cost	£10–£25
Address	Unit 24, Liverpool Street Station, EC2
T	020 7247 3227
Station	Liverpool Street
Open	Mon–Fri 11.30am–9.30pm
Accepts	MasterCard, Visa
W	www.moshimoshi.co.uk

If you opt for a bar seat, the ordering system is child's play – just pluck your chosen dishes from the conveyer belt as they trundle past. You'll be charged according to the pattern on each individual plate you end up with. All the sushi is good and fresh, and there's a decent range of authentics, from the somewhat acquired taste, or texture, of uni (£2.90) – sea urchin – through to flying fish roe (£2.90). There are some delicious California hybrids too, such as avocado and crabstick combined with a sweet, sticky sushi rice rolled with sesame seeds (£2). Regular sushi choices such as negitoro temaki (£2.90) – a seaweed-wrapped roll of tuna and spring onion, or shakemaki (£2) – salmon roll, are done well, too, as is the Nigiri sushi (£1.20 to £2.90). Of the puddings (all £2.50), the custard pancake, or dorayaki, is good, as are the various ice creams. Unless you're a fan, avoid adzuki dishes, no matter how dark, sticky and mysterious they look; they consist of over-sweetened red-bean paste – definitely an acquired taste.

Look out for the cartoons on the laminated cards, which give handy tips spelling out which sushi are best for beginners and which are "challenging". There are also helpful hints on just how to treat the fiery, ground wasabi that will clear your sinuses faster than anything else on the planet.

Prism

The question we should ask ourselves is: where have all the banks gone to? And the answer is probably that they have vanished into cyberspace behind hole-in-the-wall machines, leaving free all these tantalizing banking halls with the kind of lofty ceilings and grandiose pillars that make restaurant designers drool. Prism, part of the Harvey Nichols plan for world domination, is an expensive City restaurant – in fact price rises during 2001 mean that it only just scrapes under our threshold. You have been warned! Eating here is rather like being inside a towering, white-painted cube; very slick, and very much an old banking hall. The food is a well-judged blend of English favourites and modernist influences. There is the obligatory long bar, and the obligatory suave service. As a restaurant it has no pronounced character but rather leaves an impression of modernity – no bad thing in the stuffy old City.

Cost	£35–£110

Address 147 Leadenhall St, EC3
T 020 7256 3888
Station Bank
Open Mon–Fri
11.30am–3.30pm & 6–10pm
Accepts All major credit cards
W www.prismrestaurant.co.uk

Starters are well executed. Parsnip soup (£7) – they must be some parsnips. Caesar salad (£9). King prawn and chorizo risotto (£12.50). Ham hock terrine sauce gribiche (£9). Potted shrimps get accompanied by Poilaine toast and a price tag of £10. When it comes to main courses, the menu splits half fish and half meat. On the fish side there are simple dishes like roast cod with potatoes, Savoy cabbage and bacon, parsley sauce (£17), and more adventurous offerings like monkfish wrapped in Carpegna ham with sauerkraut, chorizo sausage and haricot beans, red wine sauce (£21). The meat side offers braised lamb shanks and minted butter-bean puree, port jus (£17), as well as fillet of Scotch beef and rosti potato, with red wine, Béarnaise or poivre sauce (£21). On a slightly more adventurous note there is sea bass with celeriac puree, and Champagne and caviar sauce (£22) Puddings all cost £7 and include apple tart, crème brulée and chocolate mousse.

Like the pricing, the wine list is for bankers. There are a few bottles to be had for sensible prices but the main thrust is towards whatever the traffic will bear. Which is the best deal: a bottle of Krug for £130 or a magnum of Dom Perignon for £250? Simple – buy both.

CITY & EAST

FRENCH

Searcy's Restaurant

In February 2001, this restaurant, hidden in the depths of the Barbican Centre, was relaunched complete with a newly refurbished dining room and a new chef. But the changes were much more than just skin deep: there is a whole new attitude about the place. It may seem contradictory but the food has sped upmarket while the service and ambience have become less formal. These are both welcome changes. As far as the service goes, Searcy's is now an agreeable place to eat, full of cheery gourmets rather than hushed aesthetes. And the kitchen is really going for it. The dishes are ambitious and well-cooked, carefully plated but with none of that "tall food", over-fussy nonsense. This will be one to watch in the awards stakes.

Cost	£25–£80

Address Level 2, The Barbican Centre, Silk St EC2
T 020 7588 3008
Station Barbican
Open Mon–Fri noon–3pm & 5.30–10.30pm, Sat 5.30–10.30pm, Sun noon–3pm & 5.30–7.30pm
Accepts All major credit cards

The chef manages to combine classic principles with some iconoclastic touches. Everything is well seasoned and technically very good; reductions are rich but not over-gluey. Starters include a terrine of foie gras pressed with gingerbread (£12) – on the face of it, dodgily whimsical, but this is a really well-made terrine and the combination does work. Roast scallops with crispy pork and carrots (£13.50) is outstanding: good scallops, a rich carrot purée with a hint of spice, a thin rasher of belly pork crisped in the pan – great tastes and textures. Mains are also accomplished: there's a braised pig's trotter with black pudding (£18.50) – good trotter, good gravy, good mash. Or casserole of roasted lobster with baby vegetables (£24.50). Or tranche of turbot with moules marinière. Or red wine beef with roasted onion and bone marrow (£16.50) – very good flavours and with the bone marrow turned into little parsleyed dumplings. Desserts are very elegant (all £6.50): star anis bavarois with roasted pineapple; rhubarb tart with marscapone ice cream. Add smiling service and a long wine list and you have a very good restaurant.

There is a bargain table d'hôte menu and, for once, the restricted choice is more than compensated for by the quality of the grub – two courses at £19.50 and three at £22.50.

Singapura

Not only has this large, modern restaurant just off Ludgate Hill won a succession of accolades as "London's most beautiful restaurant", but it is also one of just a handful of places outside Singapore where you can sample Nonya cuisine. Singapore boasts four great culinary traditions: Chinese, Indian, Malay and Nonya. Nonya food, which belongs to the people once known as the "Straits Chinese", is a fusion of the Malayan and Chinese traditions and ingredients. It is generally – but not always – spicy, sweet, and characterized by a good deal of garlic, galangal and lime leaves. At Singapura it's very well done, if at quite a price.

Cost	£25–£50
Address	1–2 Limeburner Lane, EC4
T	020 7329 1133
Station	Blackfriars/St Paul's
Open	Mon–Fri 11.30am–3.30pm & 5.30–10pm
Accepts	All major credit cards
W	www.singapuras.co.uk

In many ways the starters are the stars here, and not just because you hit them with a fresh appetite. Siput (£6.95), described as "mussels stir-fried with lemon grass, lime leaves, chillies and ginger in a sherry sauce", resembles an Oriental moules marinières – small, sweet mussels are cooked in a broth that would make a delightful, if fiery, soup. Chicken satay (£5.75) comes juicy and with an assertive peanut sauce, while the udang somtan (£6.95) is an indulgence – tiger prawns with a green papaya and carrot salad. From the main courses you might try babi chin (£9.50), a Nonya speciality made with pork in a spicy coriander, soya and tamarind sauce. Char kuay teow (£7.50) is Singapore street food – broad rice noodles, stir-fried with fairly pungent chunks of fishcake, egg and prawns. In the vegetable section, choi sum (£4.95) is a supercharged version of the Chinese favourite "greens with oyster sauce" – stronger, fishier, and packed with garlic and ginger. By the time the puddings come around, your tongue is probably only fit for the home-made ice creams, which come in moody varieties like Earl Grey, marmalade parfait and brown bread – two scoops cost £4.50.

Maureen Suan-Neo, master chef of the Singapura restaurants, has introduced a list of speciality dishes with the emphasis on game – five starters and five mains – to titillate Western palates unused to the delights of such exotic ingredients as blachan. Blachan is made from dried, salted shrimps, and smells a bit like rotten fish. Surprisingly enough, it tastes yummy.

Clerkenwell

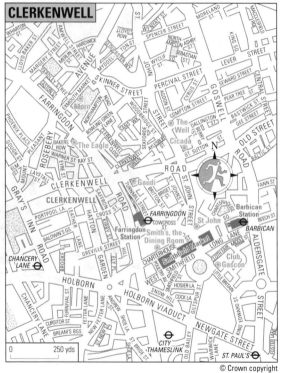

© Crown copyright

Cicada

Once Clerkenwell was where you went for printing and watch repairs. But it's fast becoming London's coolest City-fringe dormitory – a fact that is reflected in its growing choice of restaurants and bars. Cicada is one of a number catering to the growing local population. Part bar, part restaurant, it offers an unusual menu loosely based in Southeast Asia that changes three or four times a year and allows you to mix and match from small, large and side dishes. This suits a lot of modern tastes, as everyone can share dishes and different flavours.

Cost	£17–£37

Address 132 St John St, EC1
T 020 7608 1550
Station Farringdon
Open Mon–Fri noon–11pm, Sat 6–11pm
Accepts All major credit cards

To start, try the ocean trout tartare with sushi rice, avocado and tobiko – a kind of Japanese caviar – (£5). Or try the dashi, soba noodle and shitake soup (£4.50). The rest of the "small dishes" are, as the name implies, more complex than the usual run of starters. Chilli-salt squid comes with adjud sauce (£6), and there is tea smoked quail, mango salad and spicy dressing (£6), and crispy fried fish with chilli, holy basil and lime leaf (£5.50). Moving on to the large dishes, how about a big bowl of pad Thai – vegetable (£7.50) or prawn (£8.25)? Or mixed seafood tempura with mirin dip (£9.50)? Other good choices might be the sweet ginger noodles (£2.50), a tasty bowlful; the rare char-grilled beef salad with pungent nah jhim (£8.50); or chicken teriyaki (£8.50). Puddings include tempting offerings like crispy white-chocolate dumplings (£5.40), steeped fruit plate with coconut sherbet (£5), and a chocolate bento plate (£8 to share). There is a good selection of mid-priced wines and beers, including Tiger beer (£2.80) if you want to go Oriental, and a house Sauvignon from the part of Mexico that is almost southern California – particularly good at a not-too-unreasonable £14.50 a bottle.

Cicada has a friendly bar-like atmosphere, and staff members are young and easy-going. If the weather is good it's a great place to sit outside – it's set back from the main part of the street so the pavement tables give a degree of privacy. All in all, it makes a good bridge between going to a bar for a drink and going to a restaurant for a meal: a sound precursor to the night ahead.

Clerkenwell

Club Gascon

Club Gascon burst onto London's collective palate in 1998. Critics swooned. Reviewers raved. Awards were dispensed. It remains shockingly popular: if you want a booking, they advise calling two or three weeks ahead, though you may strike lucky with a cancellation. Pascal Aussignac is the chef here, and his cooking is that of the southwest of

Cost	£35–£75

Address 57 West Smithfield, EC1
T 020 7796 0600
Station Farringdon
Open Mon–Fri noon–2pm & 7–10pm, Sat 7–10.30pm
Accepts MasterCard, Visa

France, tidied up a little but generally authentic. The menu is set out as six sections and the portions are larger than some starters but smaller than most mains, the idea being that you indulge in your very own dégustation, trying several dishes – not the cheapest way of eating.

The sections are "La route du sel" – cured meats and charcuterie; "Le potager" – vegetables and cheese; "Les foies gras"; "L'océan" – fish and shellfish; "Les pâturages" – mainly duck and cassoulet; "Le marché" – game and offal. There are forty different dishes. It's important to spread your ordering and not just to pick from one section – no matter how good, five consecutive foie gras dishes are bound to pall. Here are a couple of promising combinations: farmhouse jambon du Bearn (£8); black truffled egg, grissin and ard-gasna (£5.80); grilled foie gras of duck with grapes (£10.50); three oysters with grilled chipolata (£5.50); beef fillet a la plancha, Madeira sauce and stuffed pimento (£8.50); roast confit of duck, crème forte (£7). Or maybe marinated fresh salmon, dill and pastis des landes (£5.80); home-made French fries with fleur de sel (£3.80); le spécial Gascon en terrine (£8); grilled fresh scallops, cream of caviar and crispy potato (£12). The problem with eating like this is that you can hit on a dish that is amazing and therefore too small. You must have the time and confidence to order a second or even third serving.

If you feel daunted, try the tasting menu, which changes monthly: five courses for £30 (but everyone at the table must order it). One such menu might lead you from a foie gras dish to grilled oysters, a crisp risotto of Aquitaine smoked eel and a casserole of guinea fowl, culminating in black cherry shortbread and smooth cheese. A pretty good way to shed £30.

The Eagle

The Eagle was for years a run-down pub in an unpromising part of London. Then in 1991 it was taken over by food-minded entrepreneurs who transformed it into a restaurant-pub turning out top-quality dishes. They were pioneers: there should be a blue plaque over the door marking the site as the starting place of the great gastro-pub revolution. In the years since, neither the food nor the decor has changed much, though there is now an interesting gallery

Cost £8–£20

Address 159 Farringdon Rd, EC1
T 020 7837 1353
Station Farringdon
Open Meals served Mon–Fri 12.30–2.30pm & 6.30–10.30pm, Sat 12.30–3.30pm & 6.30–10.30pm, Sun 12.30–3.30pm
Accepts No credit cards

MEDITERRANEAN/PUB

upstairs. The Eagle itself remains a crowded, rather shabby sort of place – and the staff still have attitude. The kitchen is truly open: the chefs work behind the bar, and the menu is chalked up over their heads. It changes daily, or even hourly, as things run out or deliveries come in. The food is broadly Mediterranean in outlook with a Portuguese bias, and you still have to fight your way to the bar to order and pay.

This is a pub with a signature dish. Bife Ana (£8.50) has been on the menu here since the place opened and they have sold tens of thousands of portions. It is a kind of steak sandwich whose marinade has roots in the spicy food of Portugal and Mozambique, and it is delicious. The rest of the menu changes like quicksilver but you may find the likes of the famous caldo verde (£4.50) – the Portuguese chorizo and potato soup which takes its name from the addition of spring greens. There may be a grilled plaice with roast vegetables, and shallots with honey and balsamico (£9.50); or a delicious and simple dish like roast spring chicken with celeriac, celery, cream and bay "al forno"(£9.50); or a shoulder of lamb "en sofrito" with chilli and caraway seeds and couscous with dried fruit and nuts (£9.50). To finish, choose between a fine cheese – perhaps a Sardinian pecorino served with flatbread and marmalade (£6), or the siren charms of those splendid, small, Portuguese, cinnamony custard tarts – pasteis de nata – at £1 a piece.

Even with pavement seating providing extra capacity in decent weather, The Eagle is never less than crowded. The music is always loud and the staff are busy and brusque. A great place nonetheless.

Gaudí

🍴 Gaudí is a restaurant hidden within a nightclub – Turnmills – which in the past has meant it has kept rather strange opening hours. But as the stature of the restaurant has increased, so the opening hours have got less eccentric. They are still closed at weekends but no longer ask everyone to leave in the middle of Friday night. This is a good thing, as chef Nacho Martinez serves

Cost	£32–£68

Address 63 Clerkenwell Rd, EC1
T 020 7608 3220
Station Farringdon
Open Mon–Fri noon–2.30pm & 7–10.30pm
Accepts All major credit cards
W www.turnmills.co.uk

some of the most interesting Spanish food in London. Not the sometimes weary food of the Costas and tapas bars, but high-flown, well-executed Modern Spanish cuisine. This sophistication has been reflected in the prices, which took a hike upwards in 2001. Do not allow the asymmetric, soft-shaped, flowing curves of the Gaudiesque interior put you off, even if you do expect Dr Who to step from behind a plaster-of-Paris boulder at any moment.

Chef Martinez changes his menu in line with the season and, perhaps for some simple linguistic reason, his dish descriptions are both exhaustive and somewhat exhausting. Start with "ensalada de Jamon 'pata negra' con mousse de queso Manchego, membrillo nueces, higos, salsa de Queso y vinaigreta de Jerez Balsamico" (£12) – which stands for a ham salad with cheese mousse and quince. Or there's a millefeuille Spanish omelette with saffron béchamel (£10). Or cocido, a rich Castillian soup with chorizo and black pudding (£10.50). Mains are also imaginative and complex: spider crab soufflé with vegetables and cheese (£16); shoulder of Spanish suckling lamb with sweetbreads (£17); black rice with jumbo king prawns plus baby squid filled with mushrooms, and aioli mousse (£17); wild boar loin with a wild mushroom terrine (£17.25). If all these exotic combinations make you nervous, and sound as if this is a chef who has gone well over the top, take heart. This is good food, and even the wildest flights of fancy tend to work well.

Puddings are all £6 – pastries, deep-fried ice cream, a mousse made from Manchego cheese – imaginative stuff, as you'd expect. And there's a grand and expansive wine list with enough Spanish rarities to please even the most demanding Iberian oenophile.

Moro

In its relatively short life Moro has scooped up a hatful of awards. This modern, rather stark restaurant typifies the new face of Clerkenwell and attracts a clientele to match. In feel it's not so very far away from the better pub-restaurants, although the proprietors have given themselves the luxury of a slightly larger kitchen. This is also a place of pilgrimage for disciples of the wood-fired oven, and as the food here hails mainly from Spain, Portugal and North Africa, it is both Moorish and moreish. There is also good Spanish drink: dry fino and manzanilla for an aperitif or to accompany a meal; sweet Pedro Ximenez to go with the puds. The only problem lies in Moro's popularity. It's consistently booked up, which places a bit of a strain on both kitchen and waiting staff. A relatively new development is the tapas menu which offers a good range of small dishes priced between £2 and £4 – a good way to test things out.

Cost	£18–£48
Address	34–36 Exmouth Market, EC1
T	020 7833 8336
Station	Farringdon/Angel
Open	Mon–Fri 12.30–2.30pm & 7–10.30pm, Sat 7–10.30pm
Accepts	All major credit cards

Soups are among Moro's best starters. How about leek and yoghurt soup with caramelized butter (£4.50)? Depending on the season and the fresh produce in the markets you may also be offered starters such as pan-fried calves' liver with cumin, garlic and yoghurt (£6), scrambled egg with broad beans and jamon (£6), or piquillo peppers stuffed with salt cod and potato (£5.50). Or there's another classic combination of brandada – salt-cod puree with olive oil and potato – with toast made from the superb sourdough bread produced in the wood-fired oven, piquillo peppers and olives (£5). Main courses are simple and are often traditional combinations of taste and textures. As with the starters, it's the accompaniments that tend to change rather than the core ingredients. Look out for wood-roasted duck with pomegranate molasses and winter tabbouleh (£13), or perhaps wood-roasted sea bass with salsa verde and lentils (£14.50). There are usually some other fishy options too, along the lines of charcoal-grilled monkfish with roast beetroot and walnut tarator (£14).

Do not miss the splendid Spanish cheeses (£4) served with membrillo – traditional quince paste. And there's no excuse to avoid the Malaga raisin ice cream (£4).

Clerkenwell

St John

One of the most frequent requests, especially from foreign visitors, is "Where can we get some really English cooking?" Little wonder that the promise of "olde English fare" is the bait in so many London tourist traps. The cooking at St John, however, is genuinely English. It is sometimes old-fashioned and makes inspired use of all those strange and unfashionable cuts of meat which were once commonplace in rural England. Technically the cooking is of a very high standard while the restaurant itself is completely without frills or design pretensions. You'll either love it or hate it. But be forewarned, this is an uncompromising and opinionated kitchen, and no place to take a hard-core vegetarian. In 2001 St John was the Moët & Chandon London Restaurant of the year. Deservedly so.

Cost	£20–£40
Address	26 St John St, EC1
T	020 7251 0848
Station	Farringdon
Open	Mon–Fri noon–3pm & 6–11pm, Sat 6–11pm
Accepts	All major credit cards
W	www.stjohnrestaurant.co.uk

The menu changes every session but the tone does not, and there's always a dish or two to support the slogan "nose to tail eating". Charcuterie, as you'd imagine, is good: a simple terrine (£5.70) will be dense but not dry – well judged. Or, for the committed, what about a starter of roast bone marrow and parsley salad (£5.80)? Truly delicious. Or potted pig's head (£5)? Or lamb, fennel and butterbean broth (£5.20)? Be generous to yourself with the bread, which is outstanding (the bakery is in the bar, and you can purchase a loaf to take home). Main courses may include roast Middlewhite – a rare, traditional breed of pig – with split peas (£14.80), or deep-fried skate with tartare sauce (£11.20). Maybe there will be pigeon and celeriac (£12.50), or a dish of Stinking Bishop – a wonderful, pungent Gloucestershire cheese – with potatoes (£7); perversely, in this den of offal, this is a veggie delight. Puddings are trad and well executed: rice pudding with plums (£5), or a slice of strong Lancashire cheese with an Eccles cake (£5). Joy of joys, sometimes there is even a seriously good Welsh rarebit (£4.50).

St John has forged quite a reputation, and booking is a must. How encouraging to see a party of Japanese businessmen forsaking tourist pap for roast sirloin, dripping toast and horseradish (£16). Whatever your feelings about meat and offal cookery, be assured that St John serves English food at its most genuine.

Smiths, the Dining Room

Calling Smiths of Smithfield an ambitious project is like saying that pyramid building calls for a large work-force. For a similar nest of restaurants: first take a Grade II listed warehouse overlooking Smithfield Market, then gut it. Rebuild the inside in ultra-modern meets Bladerunner style and – hey presto – two restaurants, two bars, private rooms, kitchens and whatever, spread over four floors. On the ground floor there's a bar and café serving an ocean of drink and good, sensible food from breakfast to bedtime. At the top is the "rooftop restaurant", a 70-seater which pays particular attention to quality meat with good provenance. Sandwiched in between is the 130-seater "Dining Room". The culinary mainspring is John Torode, who should be congratulated on his enlightened buying policy – quality, quality, quality.

Cost	£18–£50

Address 67–77 Charterhouse St, EC1
T 020 7236 6666
Station Farringdon
Open Café Mon–Fri 7am–5pm, Sat & Sun 10.30am–5pm; Restaurants Mon–Fri 11am–3pm & 6–11pm, Sat 6–11pm
Accepts All major credit cards
W www.smithsofsmithfield .co.uk

MODERN BRITISH

The Dining Room is a large space around a central hole which looks down onto the smart bar area. Eating here is rather like sitting at the centre of a deactivated factory – a tangle of exposed pipes and girders. The menu is divided into Larder (which means starters), Soups, Mains, Grills, Daily Market Specials, Sides, and Sweet Tooth. The way the prices are expressed, however, is coy and irritating – Larder "all at 4_ Pounds"; "Sides 2_ Pounds". Bah humbug. But the starters are simple and good: cured Cumbrian ham and celeriac salad, soft boiled egg (£4.75); potato gnocchi with Gorgonzola and rocket (£4.75); Smiths of Smithfield salad with Parmesan and croutons (£4.75). Main courses show off the careful buying policy: crisp belly of pork with mashed potato and green sauce (£9.50); marinated venison haunch with kale, Savoy cabbage and bacon (£9.50); roast skate and champ potato (£9.50). The lunch specials are from the comfort-eating school, and feature such delights as shepherds' pie (£9.50). Puds are good. Try hot cinnamon waffles and maple-syrup ice cream (£4).

There's a decent breakfast on offer in the café-bar-pub downstairs, with porridge (£2) or bacon, egg, beans, sausage, mushrooms, black pudding, tomatoes, bubble and toast (£6). And it is available all day, so Dr Johnson would have been happy.

Clerkenwell

The Well

🍴 Taking its name from the well that served the clerken hereabouts and so inspired the name of the area, The Well is a buzzy bar-cum-gastropub where the diners, staff and owner Tom Martin all appear to be friends having a good time. Scrubbed tables and old church chairs give a fresh, accessible feel to this corner venue which is open as a bar throughout the day and as a restaurant during

Cost	£30–£70
Address	180 St John St, EC1
☎	020 7251 9363
Station	Angel/Farringdon
Open	Mon–Wed noon–3pm & 6–10pm, Thurs–Fri noon–3pm & 6–10.30pm, Sat noon– 10.30pm, Sun noon–10pm
Accepts	All major credit cards

kitchen hours (listed above). Daily specials on a blackboard complement the modern mixed menu, which appears to be geared to everyone's favourite dishes rather than any particular cuisine. The wine list runs from a respectable Italian house red or white at £9.95 to a Dom Perignon 1992 champagne at £140 – and a Chateau Petrus 1992 at £350 for the Clerkenwell-heeled.

Starters include French onion soup (£4.25); "pint o' prawns" with mayonnaise (£5.50); chicken liver terrine with brandy, blueberries and leaves (£5.25); and smoked duck with celeriac remoulade and sweet chilli oil (£5.95). The chicken liver terrine is rich but light, with the tang of blueberries, and comes on a chunk of grilled brioche. The duck is rare and smoky, the flavours lifted by the finely shredded celeriac and home-made mayonnaise. Main courses are equally accomplished. Home-made chilli con carne with crème fraîche, grated cheese and bread (£7.95) is hot and highly flavoured with cumin; the home-made is gratuitous, as everything at The Well is home-made. Rabbit with borlotti beans, Savoy cabbage and grain mustard jus (£10.95) is served in a deep dish, the rabbit meltingly tender, the cabbage still crisp, the sauce rich enough to need extra bread to sop it up. Other mains include paella Valencia (£10.95); Toulouse sausages with garlic mash and onion gravy (£9.95); and chump of lamb with rosemary jus and gratin Dauphinois (£11.95). For dessert, the chocolate marquise (£3.95) contains about half a pound of chocolate in a smooth, unctuously melting slab; this is almost a doggy-bag dessert.

The Well attracts an unusually varied crowd from the surrounding dot-com millionaire loft roosts and council estates; but they all seem to enjoy its lively atmosphere and good value.

Docklands

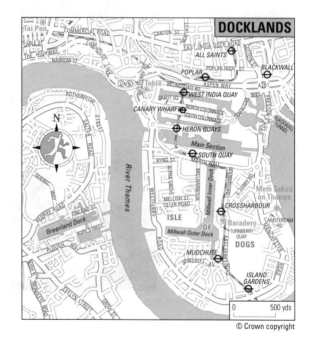

© Crown copyright

Baradero

Baradero is modern, light, tiled and airy. And, as far as the view of Millwall dock and proximity to the London Arena will permit, you could almost think yourself in Spain. Essentially a tapas bar, it offers main courses too, and both are of restaurant quality. Take a seat at the bar or at one of the well-spaced tables, order yourself a bottle of Estrella beer or

Cost	£15–£30
Address	Turberry Quay, off Pepper St, E14
T	020 7537 1666
Station	DLR Crossharbour
Open	Mon–Fri noon–11pm, Sat 6–10.45pm
Accepts	All major credit cards

SPANISH

a glass of fino sherry, and set about the tapas. There is even a floor-show of sorts in the form of the balletic automatic orange juicer, called a Zumm, which seems to wave the whole oranges about for inspection before squashing them for juice.

Start with an order of pan con aioli (95p) – good bread with a pot of fearsome but seductive garlic mayonnaise. Or pan con tomate (£1.45) – Catalan-style toast drizzled with olive oil and rubbed with garlic and tomato. Add some boquerones (£3.25) – classic white anchovies sharp with vinegar and garnished with raw garlic slices, and jamon serrano (£5.50) – a large portion of dark, richly flavoured, dry-cured ham. Then follow up with hot tapas such as croquetas de pollo (£3.95). Whoever would have thought that croquettes could taste so good? Or pulpo a la Gallega (£5.25) – octopus boiled and seasoned in Galician style. Or the particularly delicious fabada Asturiana (£4.95) – an Asturian bean stew loaded with chunks of sausage, black pudding and ham hock. Also lurking on the tapas menu is paella Valenciana (£17.50). This is the real thing, with chicken and shellfish, and it feeds two. If you can restrain your ordering and don't end up crammed full of tapas, move on to the list of main courses, which changes weekly. Try chuletas de cordero al romero (£12.50) – charcoal-grilled lamb cutlets, which are simple and good. Or maybe lubina al horno (£13.50) – baked sea bass with salted "Canary" potatoes and a Mediterranean salad. There is also a convenient special offer – prix fixe hot and cold tapas (from £19.50 per person) – which runs all day.

As well as adding new tapas and main courses each week to keep regulars from getting bored, the proprietors of Baradero organize food festivals, during which visiting Spanish chefs prepare serious regional food – small lambs, suckling pigs, all manner of delights.

Docklands

Mem Saheb on Thames

Mem Saheb on Thames has certainly got an evocative address. "Amsterdam Road" conjures up pictures of old-fashioned docks and wharves, rolling fog banks and cheery East Enders. In practice this bit of Docklands is a lot like Milton Keynes: Amsterdam Road (along with nearby Rotterdam Drive and Rembrandt Court) are all new. Not brand spanking new, but new enough for you to notice that some of the paintwork is starting to get chipped. The redeeming factor is the river – as the Thames sweeps round in a majestic arc, the restaurant has a superb view across the water to the Millennium Dome. Mem Saheb is certainly "on-Thames". As a result there's a good deal of squabbling for the middle table in the non-smoking section (pole position as far as the view is concerned) – ultimately, however, the lucky winner must balance the delights of the twinkling lights of the Millennium folly with the piped-music speaker that hovers directly above the table.

Start by sharing a tandoori khazana (£8.95), which is a platter of mixed kebabs from the tandoor, including good chicken tikka. Or perhaps salmon samosas (£2.50)? Also tasty is the kabuli salad (£2.95), a winning combination of chickpeas and hard-boiled egg in a sharp tamarind dressing. Of the main courses, boal dopiaza (£6.95) teams meaty steaks of boal fish from Bangladesh with an onion-based sauce; chicken bemisal (£6.95) is sweet and sour with a welcome belt of green chilli; while prawn and pumpkin (£6.95) balances hot and sweet, although is rather let down by the small and undistinguished prawns. The breads and vegetable dishes are good, particularly the aloo chana (£4.50) – a simple dish of potatoes and chickpeas. The chef is to be commended for avoiding artificial additives and colourings.

The spicy dhal (£2.50/£4.50) is made with yellow split peas and small, red, dried chillies. The chilli flavour infuses the dhal and this is a very successful dish … until the moment when the unwary diner bites into one of these little red booby traps. The ensuing pain is enough to banish any calm induced by the restful river view.

Cost	£12–£28
Address	65–67 Amsterdam Rd, E14
T	020 7538 3008
Station	DLR Crossharbour
Open	Mon–Fri noon–2.30pm & 6–11.30pm, Sat & Sun 6–11.30pm
Accepts	All major credit cards

Tabla

Paradoxically, for a restaurant within a lunchtime's stroll from the ants' nest that is Canary Wharf, one of the salient features of this slick new Indian restaurant is its sixteen-space car park. Tabla is located in the Dockmaster's House at what was once the gate to the West India Dock but is now the hub of its own network of mini-motorways, flats and multiplex cinema – in

Cost   £20–£50

Address The Dockmaster's
House, Hertsmere Rd, E14
T 020 7345 0345
Station DLR West India Quay
Open Mon–Fri noon–3pm &
6–11pm, Sat 6–11pm
Accepts All major credit cards
W info@tablarestaurant.com

INDIAN

such a location, a car park is handy. The food is good, modern and authentic, which might seem to be something of a contradiction but works well. Take hot and sour haddock curry as an example: the restaurant is barely a quarter-mile from Billingsgate and the chef has taken the sensible decision to use fresh British fish rather than frozen Indian ones. Thus haddock supplants kingfish in this South Indian favourite, resulting in an accomplished dish that is wonderfully fresh.

The menu is written in English – no transliterated words here – with a short list of starters including mussels with coriander and mild spices (£4.50), lentil soup with rice flour dumplings (£3.95), chicken tikka (£4.95) and crab cakes with coconut and chilli (£4.95). Then there's a selection of tandoori dishes – tandoor work being a speciality of the chef here – as well as classics like lamb chops (£5.95/£10.95) and tiger prawns (£7.60/£14.95). Main courses are original and well-spiced. There's the above-mentioned haddock in a hot and sour sauce (£11.50), chicken tikka in a tomato and fenugreek sauce (£9.50) – which is reassuringly close to chicken tikka masala – lamb shank on the bone (£9.50), the admirably succinct hot South Indian chicken curry (£8.95), and tiger prawns with saffron sauce (£12.95). The vegetable side dishes are also simple and delicious: green beans with coconut (£3.95) and black lentils slow-cooked with cream, also known as dal Bukhara (£3.50). The breads are all good.

Good curry, Italian furniture, linen tablecloths, a demystified menu – all elements that will fill Tabla with lunchers cast adrift in the desert of Canary Wharf. In the evenings, however, the prospect of a place to park is what will really pack them in. You'd better book.

Tai Pan

As anyone who has followed the adventures of Sherlock Holmes will know, Limehouse was London's first Chinatown, complete with murky opium dens. So, despite the well-intentioned efforts of the Docklands Development Board to promote the area, today's Limehouse seems pretty tame in comparison. It can, however, boast about the Tai Pan. This restaurant is very much a family affair – the ebullient Winnie Wan is front of house, running the light, bright dining room, while Mr Tsen commands the kitchen. He organizes a constant stream of well-cooked, mainly Cantonese dishes, and slaves over the intricately carved vegetables which lift their presentation. He's a good cook, and as well as all the old favourites the menu hides one or two surprises.

Cost	£15–£30

Address 665 Commercial Rd, E14
T 020 7791 0118 or 0119
Station DLR Limehouse
Open Mon–Thurs & Sun noon–11.15pm, Fri & Sat 6–11.45pm
Accepts All major credit cards

After the complimentary prawn cracker and seriously delicious hot-pickled shredded cabbage, start with deep-fried crispy squid with Szechuan peppercorn salt (£6.80), or fried Peking dumplings with a vinegar dipping sauce (£4.30) – both are delicious. Or try one of the spare-rib dishes (£5.60), or the soft-shell crabs (£4.30 each), or the nicely done, crispy, fragrant aromatic duck with pancakes and the accoutrements (£15.50 for a half). Otherwise, relax and order the Imperial mixed hors d'oeuvres (£4.40 per person, for a minimum of two), which offers a sampler of ribs, spring rolls, seaweed, and prawn and sesame toast, with a carrot sculpture as centrepiece. When ordering main dishes, old favourites like deep-fried shredded beef with chilli (£5.80), and fried chicken in lemon sauce (£5.30) are just as you'd expect. Fried seasonal greens in oyster sauce (£4.30) is made with choi sum and delicious, while the fried vermicelli Singapore style (£5.20) will suit anyone who prefers their Singapore noodle pepped up with curry powder rather than fresh chillies.

Sometimes there are "specials" which don't feature on the main menu. They're generally worth trying. Hun tsui kau (£2.90) – green banana or plantain encased in minced prawn and deep-fried – is particularly popular. There are also some bargains to be had among the special lunch deals. Asking Winnie to recommend something is always a good idea. Sinking your teeth into the carved vegetables is not.

Hackney & Dalston

HACKNEY & DALSTON

© Crown copyright

500 yds

Anatolya

This small – five-table – diner has no menu other than the neon list, all in Turkish, above the counter. There are scores of such places in Hackney and on nearby Green Lanes, and there's not much, at first glance, to distinguish this from countless others. But, as the regulars know, the Anatolya stands out for its unbeatable combination of consistently good and absurdly cheap food, and extraordinarily friendly service. Waiters put everyone at their ease, patiently describing for non-Turkish speakers each dish on the mangal (grill). Anatolya takes the Turkish tradition of hospitality seriously and, depending on the whim of the waiter, you may well find yourself plied with a sticky baklava, or a complimentary tea served in a delicate, tulip-shaped glass.

Cost	£3–£10
Address	263a Mare St, E8
T	020 8986 2223
Station	BR London Fields/ Bethnal Green
Open	Daily 6am–midnight
Accepts	Cash or cheque only

Dishes change daily, but you can usually depend upon the lhamacun (£1.20) – spicy minced lamb on feather-light charred flatbread enlivened with buttery juices, red peppers and herbs. For mains it's best to stick with the lamb, which comes in a variety of guises: et sote (£3.80), fried with chilli sauce, is a little rich, but the skewered minced lamb, charred to perfection on the grill is flawless, the red peppers and flat-leaf parsley rounding off a good, robust flavour. It costs £4.40 before 3pm and £5.50 thereafter. Or try the barbecued chicken (£4/£5.50) – eight crisp-skinned wings piled onto a plate with bulghur and fresh salad. There are usually a couple of casseroles bubbling away, too; the sulu yemekler (literally "watery meal") can take a number of forms, usually entailing chunks of meat with soft-cooked carrots, potatoes and courgettes (£3.50). Side dishes (all £2) include the usual hummus and taramasalata, along with a punchy haydari, a kind of rough garlic paste with chopped parsley, and a creamy cacik, whose cool combination of cucumber, garlic and yoghurt makes a perfect accompaniment to the spicy grilled meats.

Even counting the three stools over the mangal, and the tiny bar at the back, Anatolya is often crowded, especially on weekend evenings, so it can be a good idea to book a table.

Centuria

Centuria is a "new pub". It looks like a place that's had the windows reglazed, the floors stripped, the clientele changed and a back-room restaurant added. And so it has, and is all the better for it. Where once a few glasses of stout and pork scratchings changed hands, now a lively Italian restaurant flourishes. The menu, chalked on huge boards, changes throughout the evening as ingredients run out – a sign of freshness and quality, and also good entertainment, as the cooking is done behind an open counter. Modern as this Italo-gastro-pub might be, the giant pepper mill is alive and well at Centuria, and portions are reassuringly huge.

Cost	£10–£30
Address	100 St Paul's Rd, N1
T	020 7704 2345
Station	BR Canonbury or Highbury & Islington
Open	Mon–Fri 6–11pm, Sat 12.30–11pm, Sun 12.30–10.30pm
Accepts	MasterCard, Visa, Switch

Starters include traditional favourites like insalata tricolore (£4.50), funghi al aglio (£4.25), and calamari alla griglia (£5.50), but there are some more adventurous offerings. Try Mediterranean merguez (£5.25) – spicy sausages on a bed of rocket and served with toasted Tuscan bread and hummus; or the fegato di pollo con spinaci (£5.25) – chicken livers fried with goats' cheese and spinach. Very rich. There are five pastas on offer – among them fusilli al salmone (£7.50), penne Centuria (£6.50) with sun-dried tomatoes and broccoli, and tagliatelle al funghi (£6.50) – and twelve main courses. Grilled lamb steak with beans, ginger and mint sauce (£9.50) is very good; merluzza al forno (£9.50) is baked cod on a mussel risotto; and tonno alla Siciliana (£9.50) is served just-cooked, with couscous and peperonata. A side order of bruschetta (£2.85) comes heaped with grilled vegetables and pesto. Puddings include the ubiquitous tiramisù (£3.25), banoffee pie (£3.25), and cheesecake (£3.25), and there's a rich bitter-chocolate tart served with mascarpone (£3.25), which is everything that it promises and more. Wines are reasonably priced, with a very crisp Sauvignon Blanc Gato Negro going for £13.50.

Centuria, situated at a small road junction, is also the only pub in the immediate area. Both of which make it a focal point with a nice villagey feeling. It's a pleasant venue for young Islingtonians, making it a busy place, and if you drop in for a beer and hope to get a table in the restaurant you should make your play early. Better to book.

Faulkner's

Faulkner's is a clear highlight among the kebab shops and chippies that line the rather scruffy Kingsland Road: a spotless fish-and-chip restaurant, with a takeaway section next door. It is reassuringly old-fashioned with its lace curtains, fish tank, uniformed waitresses and cool yellow walls lined with sepia-tinted piscine scenes, and it holds few surprises – which is probably what makes it such a hit. Usually Faulkner's is full of local families and large parties, all ploughing through colossal fish dinners while chatting across tables. It also goes out of its way to be child-friendly, with highchairs leaned against the wall, and a children's menu priced at £3.95.

Cost	£6–£20
Address	424 Kingsland Rd, E8
T	020 7254 6152
Station	Liverpool Street
Open	Mon–Thurs noon–2pm & 5–10pm, Fri noon–2pm & 4.15–10pm, Sat noon–10pm, Sun noon–9pm
Accepts	Cash or cheque only

House speciality among the starters is the fish cake (£1.55), a plump ball made with fluffy, herby potato. Or there's smoked salmon (£4.20), which comes in two satisfying wads, or prawn cocktail (£3.50). If you fancy soup, you've got tomato (£1.05) or a more exotic French fish variety, peppery and dark (£2.15). For main courses, the regular menu features all the British fish favourites, served fried or poached and with chips, while daily specials are chalked up on the blackboard. Cod (£7.60) and haddock (£8.75, £8.95 on the bone) retain their fresh, firm flesh beneath the dark, crunchy batter, while the subtler, classier sole – Dover (£13.50) or lemon (£10.95) – is best served delicately poached. The mushy peas (90p) are just right, lurid and lumpy like God intended, but the test of any good chippy is always its chips, and here they are humdingers – fat, firm and golden, with a wicked layer of crispy little salty bits at the bottom. Stuffed in a soft doughy roll, they make the perfect chip butty. Most people wet their whistles with a mug of strong tea (55p), but there are a few bottles of wine on offer, including a Merlot (£7.95) and a Chablis (£17.25).

Though always lively, Faulkner's is particularly fun at Saturday lunchtime, when traders and shoppers take time out from the local market to catch up, gossip, and joke with the waitresses.

Huong Viet

Huong Viet is the canteen of the Vietnamese Cultural Centre, which occupies a rather four-square and solid-looking building that was once one of Hackney's numerous public bath houses. It has long had a reputation for really good, really cheap food, and the regulars were understandably nervous when a refurbishment was announced at the beginning of 2000. Would the Huong Viet

Cost	£7–£22

Address An Viet House, 12–14 Englefield Rd, N1
T 020 7249 0877
Station BR Dalston Kingsland
Open Mon–Fri noon–3.30pm & 5.30–11pm, Sat noon–4pm & 5.30–11pm
Accepts MasterCard, Visa

end up all bleached wood and modern art? Would it be transformed into Dalston's answer to Mezzo? Everyone can breathe a sigh of relief, as the new Huong Viet is pretty much like the old Huong Viet in every important respect. The food is still fresh, unpretentious, delicious and cheap, although prices are creeping upwards. The service is still friendly and informal. And the building still looks a lot like an ex-council bath house.

Start with the spring rolls (£3.90) – small, crisp and delicious. Or the fresh rolls (£3.50), which resemble small, carefully rolled-up table napkins. The outside is soft, white and delicate-tasting, while the inside teams cooked vermicelli with prawns and fresh herbs – a great combination of textures. Ordering the prawn and green leaf soup (£3.50) brings a bowl of delicate broth with greens and shards of tofu. Pho is the most famous Vietnamese soup, but calling this meal-in-a-bowl soup seems to be selling it short. The pho here is formidable, especially the Saigon white noodle soup, filled with pork and prawn (£3.90). Hot, rich, full of bits and pieces, it comes with a plate of herbs, crispy beansprouts and aromatics that you must add yourself at the last moment so none of the aroma is lost. The other dishes are excellent too. Look out for mixed seafood with pickled veg and dill (£6.50) – this works exceptionally well. You should also run amok with the noodle dishes – choose from the stir-fried soft egg noodle dishes, or the crispy fried egg noodles (various £5 to £5.70).

All the food tastes fresh – it has obviously been freshly cooked and the chef has used spankingly fresh ingredients. There is a set lunch (£6) which comprises a starter and a main course, accompanied by jasmine tea, mineral water or sweet home-made lemonade.

Little Georgia

You could be forgiven for thinking that the Little Georgia was just another pub which had been converted into a trendy restaurant. It is certainly bare. The tables and chairs are certainly resolutely ordinary. But then you clock the blackboards with their unpronounceable specials, and the greeting of the somewhat harassed maitre d' who

Cost	£14–£34
Address	2 Broadway Market, E8
T	020 7249 9070
Station	Bethnal Green
Open	Tues–Sat 6.30pm–midnight, Sun 1–4pm
Accepts	All major credit cards

approaches with a beaming smile. Even if you are not intimately familiar with Georgian and Russian food, spotting a genuine welcome is easy enough, and you'll find one here. You'll also find an interesting list of essentially peasant dishes. From the menu it would seem that Georgians live on walnuts, pomegranate and beetroot, and that in order to make something of such basics they are not averse to adding the occasional handful of spice.

The starters fall into two categories – cold (£4.10) and hot (£4.30). Among the colds there are some exciting dips, or phkalis, which are a kind of pounded mixture: choose beetroot and walnuts, or the one predominantly made of leeks, or the one made from spinach and walnuts. They are good, with strong flavours and interesting textures. Then there is the Russian salad. Even if youthful encounters with the tinned, mass-produced variety have left you scarred for life, do try this, as it is terrific. The soups here are also very fine: there is usually a soup of the day, which could well be something imaginative like wild mushroom with red basil and red wine – a surprisingly successful meeting of flavours. Main courses veer from things you will have heard of, like shashlik (£9.50) and beef stroganoff (£9), to more obscure ethnic dishes like khingarli (£9). Order the latter and the front of house will gently enquire whether you have had them before. "They are", he will explain, "very … Georgian". When they arrive, khingarlis turn out to be large, solid dumplings stuffed with spicy minced meat and naked save for a knob of butter. Very tasty and very, very filling. There is also plenty of choice for vegetarians, and the puddings do not disappoint.

Finally, you should make a point of trying the Georgian red wines: unsubtle, tannic, rich, fruity, almost musty – and cheap!

CITY & EAST

FRENCH

Soulard

Squeezed improbably into the front room of a converted house on a residential street, Soulard pays homage to all those wonderful meals remembered from holidays in provincial France, and whisks you out of this Hackney/Islington no-man's-land – the oddly named

Cost	£20–£34
Address	113 Mortimer Rd, N1
T	020 7254 1314
Station	BR Dalston Junction
Open	Tues–Sat 7–10.30pm
Accepts	MasterCard, Visa

enclave of De Beauvoir Town – to Provence or the Dordogne. Looking for all the world like some regional French country-hotel restaurant, with the dining room centred on a large brick chimney, Soulard is a great find, serving sound food at practical prices. Everyone's in a good mood here, from the solicitous patron, who will greet you and ask after your welfare throughout the night, to the well-dressed, special-occasion clientele.

The proprietors at Soulard are eager to keep things as simple as possible. Meals are prix fixe: three courses will cost you £19.95 (excluding wine), while two go for £16.95. The small, fine-tuned menu is supplemented by blackboard specials; all are written in French, but there's always someone hovering to translate. As you would hope, there's a considered wine list, including a classy selection of dessert wines. Of the starters, escargots come in a whimsical puff-pastry snail, which trails a creamy, garlicky sauce and is packed with nicely cooked molluscs; quail are boned out and served roast with lentils and a port sauce; and there are old-time classics like prawns flamed in cognac with a white wine sauce. Specials may include grilled calamari salad, all primary colours, fragrant oil dressing and the tenderest charred squid. Main courses are rich; meat-lovers will favour the traditional duck confit with garlic potatoes. Various fresh fish dishes are also listed on the blackboard, and precisely cooked, be it in a creamy mushroom sauce or in a sea-salty broth.

Although soulard is French for "drunkard", you should try and stay sober for the desserts, which are Gallic to the hilt. Don't try to resist the bavarois aux framboises, light and delicate, or the inspired black-and-white chocolate mousse, the bitter chocolate top layer contrasting beautifully with the sweet-as-spun-sugar base.

Hoxton & Shoreditch

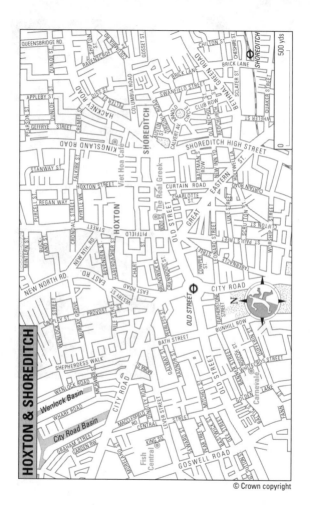

HOXTON & SHOREDITCH

© Crown copyright

500 yds

Carnevale

This rather strange little restaurant is tucked into an ordinary shop-like space halfway along a scruffy street which is all street market by day and dingy grubbiness by night. Inside is a clean, light, but cramped space, full of blond wood tables and chairs, with carefully selected (if not particularly original) prints on the walls and a faux garden to the rear. The interior has not so much been designed to the hilt, as is the current fashion, but rather put together in workable form to meet the needs of the customers. Mercifully, the enduring tendency of vegetarian restaurants to litter the premises with hippie references has been brought under control.

Cost	£12–£20

Address 135 Whitecross St, EC1
T 020 7250 3452
Station Old Street
Open Mon–Fri noon–3pm & 5.30–10.30pm, Sat 5.30–10.30pm
Accepts Cash, cheque or Switch
W www.carnevale restaurant.co.uk

Instead, close attention seems to have been paid to the food, which is cooked with care. Take your time over some very good marinated Greek olives (£1.50) and bread dipped in nutty olive oil while you decide what you'll eat. The menu, which changes every couple of months, is not over-long – ten dishes in all – but is as varied as you could wish for, with starters ranging from potato, chilli and herb frittata with tomato chilli jam and rocket salad (£4.50); through home-made papardelle with artichokes, sun-dried tomato paste, herbs and Parmesan (£4 starter, £7 main); to a salad of marinated beetroot, French beans and new potatoes with skordalia (£4.50). They are good enough to be served in many grander establishments. Main courses are equally eclectic: felaffel with spicy roasted Mediterranean vegetables and lemon tahini sauce (£8.50); Glamorgan sausages with garlic mash and Puy lentils in red wine sauce (£9); baked corn pepper stuffed with spicy vegetable couscous with garlic roast potatoes and basil and almond dressing (£9). There is a plentiful list of side orders, though given the size of the portions it is unlikely that you'll need any. If your stamina is up to them, puddings (£4.25) are good too: try the rhubarb and elder-flower jelly with dairy-free vanilla cream, or Pavlova with chocolate mousse, passionfruit and caramelized banana.

Service is relaxed, coffee is good and there are a number of alternative drinks on offer. But if you are a wine drinker take care with the short list, and aim above the house selection (£9.75), which is unforgiving.

Fish Central

The Barbican may appear to be the back of beyond – a black hole in the heart of the City – but perfectly ordinary people do live and work around here. Apart from the theatres and concert hall and the proximity to the financial district, one of the main attractions of the place is Fish Central, which holds its own with the finest fish-and-chip shops in town. Fish Central is also to be commended for its pricing policy. As each issue of this guide comes out prices move inexorably upwards, but the latest price rises here only apply to a handful of dishes and tend to be kept within bounds. If only this were the case everywhere.

Cost	£7–£18

Address 151 King's Square, Central St, EC1
T 020 7253 4970
Station Barbican
Open Mon–Sat 11am–2.30pm & 4.45–10.30pm
Accepts All major credit cards

Though at first sight Fish Central appears just like any other chippy – a takeaway service one side and an eat-in restaurant next door – a glance at its menu lets you know that this is something out of the ordinary. All the finny favourites are here, from cod to rock salmon (both £4), but there's a wholesome choice of alternatives, including grilled Dover sole (£9.90) and roast cod (£7.50) with rosemary and Mediterranean vegetables. Many of these dishes would not be out of place in much grander establishments. You can eat decently even if you are not in the mood for fish. Try the Cumberland sausages (£3.95) with onions and gravy, or the chicken breast (£4.95). If you think your appetite is up to starters, try the prawn cocktail (£2.85) – the normal naked pink prawns in pink sauce, but genuinely fresh – or the seafood terrine (£3.45), which puts all of those run-of-the-mill Italian restaurants to shame. Chips (£1.30) come as a side order, so those who prefer can order a jacket potato (£1.50) or creamed potatoes (£1.30). Mushy peas (£1.30) are … mushy and Wallies (40p) – pickled gherkins to you – come sliced and prettily served in the shape of a flower.

Fish Central certainly pulls in a crowd of devoted regulars. On any given night, half the customers seem to know each other. Unusually for a chippy, it has an alcohol licence, which means there's a palatable dry Garrogny house white (£7.90) or, at a modest splash, champagne (£19.95) – the perfect partner for mushy peas.

The Real Greek

This particular Real Greek is called Theodore Kyriakou, the able chef who launched the original Livebait behind Waterloo. Traditionally, Greek food has had a pretty rough deal in Britain. Sure, there are quantities of restaurants which call themselves "Greek", but they are usually run by Greek Cypriots with a menu that concentrates on Cypriot food. Thus, for generations of Brits, Greek food has meant greasy, lukewarm moussaka, lurid-pink cod's roe gloop, and pine-flavoured wine. Real Greek food is nothing like that, and showing off the authentic dishes of his homeland is the difficult mission Kyriakou has embarked upon.

Cost £16–£40

Address 15 Hoxton Market, N1
T 020 7739 8212
Station Old Street/Shoreditch
Open Mon–Sat noon–3pm & 5.30–10.30pm
Accepts Amex, MasterCard, Visa
W www.therealgreek.co.uk

GREEK

The restaurant is small and comfortable, with the kitchen centre stage. The menu changes with the seasons and comes as a shock: the first section is mezedes and it explains that in Greece you would have small portions of a wide range of dishes. Here each platter has three or four components – cold stuffed leg of lamb accompanies dolmades, cured grey mullet roe, and a yoghurt, cucumber and garlic dip (all for £7.65), while cured, sliced fillet of beef comes with chopped peppers and Feta cheese, and preserved chicken with walnuts (£8.45). Or try Kalamata olives, yellow split-pea puree, a coarse salami from Levkas, warm salad of seasonal leaves, and pan fried Kefalotiri cheese (£8). On to the small dishes, which could be either starters or sides: crevette filo pie with turnip and carrot salad (£8), or cannellini bean soup served with a cheese soufflé (£7.20). Main courses are a revelation: hot-pot of kid served with green dandelion and leek fricassée (£16.70); fish soup served with fish terrine (£15.20); roast rack of pork served with hilopites – a Greek noodle – cooked with wild mushrooms and dressed with grated Kaseri cheese (£15). Then there is a whole range of Greek cheeses and desserts – the honey doughnuts (£4.90) and the revani, a rich syrup-soaked cake (£4.90), are outstanding.

There is a genuine bargain set lunch and "early doors" dinner (5.30–7pm) which costs just £14.50 for two courses. The Real Greek has another surprise for you – the list of stunning wines at reasonable prices. Look out for the pudding wines and the sophisticated reds.

Viet Hoa Café

The Viet Hoa dining room is large, clean, light and airy, with an impressive golden parquet floor. The café part of the name is borne out by the bottles of red and brown sauce which take pride of place on each table. The brown goop turns out to be hoisin sauce and the red stuff a simple chilli one, but they have both been put into recycled plastic bottles on which the only recognizable words are "Sriracha extra hot chilli sauce – Flying Goose Brand". Apparently this has made all but the regulars strangely wary of hoisin sauce.

Cost	£8–£18

Address 72 Kingsland Rd, E2
T 020 7729 8293
Station Old Street
Open Daily noon–4pm &
5.30–11.30pm
Accepts All major credit cards
except Amex

As befits a café, there are a good many splendid "meals in a bowl" – soups and noodle dishes with everything from spring rolls to tofu. For diners wanting to go as a group and share, an appetizer called salted prawn in garlic dressing (£4.60) is outstanding – large prawns are marinated and fried with chilli and garlic. From the list of fifteen soups, pho (£3.10 or £4.15) is compulsory. This dish is a Vietnamese staple eaten at any and every meal – including breakfast. Ribbon noodles and beef, chicken or tofu are added to a delicate broth. It comes with a plate of mint leaves, Thai basil and chillies, your job being to add the fresh aromatics to the hot soup – resulting in astonishingly vivid flavours. Main courses include shaking beef (£6.60) – cubes of beef with a tangy salad; and drunken fish (£6.50) – fish cooked with wine and cloud-ear mushrooms. Both live up to the promise of their exotic names. Bun bi (£4.15) is a splendid one-pot dish – noodles with shredded pork and moreish spring rolls, plus a side dish of "fish sauce" – light, chilli-hot, sharp, sweet and fishy all at once. Also in one-pot-with-vermicelli territory you'll find bun nem nuong (£5) which features grilled minced pork, and that old favourite, Singapore noodles (£4.25).

This is a good restaurant in which to make a first foray into Vietnamese food. It is very much a family-run place, with the grandparents sitting at a table dextrously rolling spring rolls and the younger generations waiting the tables. They're very helpful to novices.

Further East

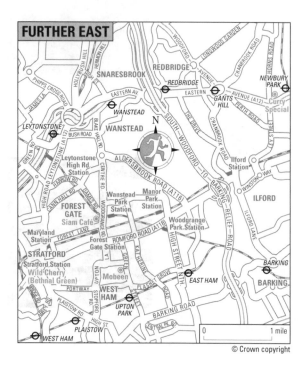

FURTHER EAST

SNARESBROOK

REDBRIDGE

REDBRIDGE

NEWBURY PARK

Curry Special

PHIPPS CROSS ROAD

HOLLYBUSH HILL

WOODFORD AVENUE

LONGWOOD GARDEN

CRANBROOK ROAD

HORNS ROAD

JAMES LA

EASTERN AV

EASTERN

GANTS HILL

AVENUE (A12)

PERTH ROAD

LEY STREET

WANSTEAD

WANSTEAD

LEYTONSTONE

GREEN RD

HIGH ROAD LEYTONSTONE (A12)

BUSH ROAD

BLAKE HALL RD

CENTRE RD

N

THE DRIVE

SOUTH-WOODFORD-TO-BARKING-RELIEF-ROAD

CRANBROOK ROAD

Ilford Station

Leytonstone High Rd. Station

ALDERSBROOK ROAD (A116)

ILFORD

HARROW RD

CANN HALL RD

JAMES RD

Wanstead Park Station

Manor Park Station

Woodgrange Park Station

WINSTON WAY

ILFORD LANE

FOREST GATE

Siam Café

WOODGRANGE RD

Maryland Station

FOREST LANE

ROMFORD ROAD (A118)

HIGH STREET NTH

STRATFORD

Forest Gate Station

KATHERINE

Stratford Station

Wild Cherry (Bethnal Green)

GREEN ST

PLASHET GROVE

BARKING

BARKING

Mobeen

EAST HAM

EAST HAM

PORTWAY

WEST HAM

STOPFORD RD

UPTON PARK

PLASHET ROAD

BARKING ROAD

PLAISTOW RD

HIGH ST

CENTRAL PK R

PLAISTOW

WEST HAM

| 0 | | 1 mile |

© Crown copyright

Curry Special

The remote branches of the Anand family (see The Brilliant, p.477) stretch far and wide, and the restaurants all serve a particular kind of Punjabi-meets-Kenyan food. Curry Special is the Eastern outpost in far-off Essex – when interrogated about why they picked Newbury Park when deciding to open a restaurant in 1982, the proprietors talk about "having friends and family in the area". Suffice to say they have had things pretty much to themselves and this restaurant has become a magnet for anyone out east who wants something a bit more interesting than the standard curry-house menu. Rich flavours are achieved by long, slow cooking and carefully chosen spices; there are no instant fixes, no cream, no yoghurt, no handfuls of nuts. Spring 2001 saw a major refurb disarmingly described as "Essex posh"!

Cost	£5–£28

Address 2 Greengate Parade, Horns Rd, Newbury Park, Essex
T 020 8518 3005
Station Newbury Park
Open Tues–Sat 12.30–2pm & 6–11.30pm, Sun 6–11.30pm
Accepts All major credit cards

Great pickles. Pause amongst the poppadoms to enjoy the carrot pickle, a genuinely Punjabi-hot super-crunch. Then go on to try the butter-fried chicken (half a chicken £6.50; whole £12), which is suitably, uncannily buttery, and something of a signature dish – as you'd expect, considering dynastic links with The Brilliant. There's also jeera (cumin) chicken, at the same price, and chilli chicken (half £7; whole £13) – very tasty. The specials board is worth investigating: pili pili bogo (£3) is a dish of mixed vegetable pieces dusted in spiced flour and deep-fried. The curries are simple and rich: try methi chicken (for one £6.50; half-chicken £16; whole £30), or the delicious palak lamb (£5). From the vegetables section, choose the tinda masala (£3). You will be asked – rather disconcertingly, as how hot is how? – whether you want your curry mild, medium or hot. Perhaps the spicy Punjabi grub has shocked some previous Essex punters, but whatever the reason, medium here is pretty tame, and you may want to go for hot. Bread-wise, indulge yourself with a hot bhatura (£1.50), which could be subtitled "fried bread meets doughnut".

For all its suburban location opposite B&Q, and its strangely dated name, Curry Special is busy enough to make booking advisable even early in the week. Essex folk seem to know what they like.

Mobeen

If you have never been to West Ham, the whole of Green Street is likely to come as a surprise. It has the feel of Brick Lane and Southall, but everything is much, much cheaper – in the market here you can buy a whole goat for the price of a dozen lamb chops in the West End. Mobeen itself seems to operate at "factory gate" prices, offering a kind of 1950s Asian works-canteen ethos – with appropriate decor – and it is a strategy that has been so successful that there is now a chain of these strictly halal Pakistani caffs. As you go in, the kitchen lies behind a glazed wooden partition to your left, while to your right are café tables and chairs. The clientele hits this place like a breaking wave – it can be impressively busy at 11.50am.

Cost	£4–£16
Address	222–224 Green St, E7
T	020 8470 2419
Station	Upton Park
Open	Daily 11am–10pm
Accepts	Cash only

The dishes and prices are listed above the servery hatches and the food is displayed below. You go up to the hatch, wait your turn and then order up a trayful, which will be reanimated in the microwave. Then it's off to another hatch for fizzy soft drinks and to yet another port of call to pick up cutlery and glasses. This is workmanlike food in large portions at basic prices, and most things are available in two sizes. Chicken tikka (£2.50/£3.40) is red and hot, very hot. Sheekh kebabs are spicy and piping hot (thanks to the microwave). Meat samosas are just 50p each. Masala fish (£3.30) is rich and good. The biryani (£3/£4) is commendably ungreasy and may actually have benefited from being cooked and reheated. There's also spinach and meat curry (£2.70/£3.50), a meat curry (£2.70/£3.50), and a bhuna meat curry (£2/£3). The breads are serviceable, and there is a notable kind of very thick, fried, stuffed paratha (£1), that will tip you over your cholesterol allowance for about a fortnight. This establishment is just up the road from West Ham's home ground – you have to wonder what Alf Garnett would have made of it all.

Mobeen is unlicensed and bringing your own is not allowed, but among the soft drinks and juices are some novelty items: for 50p you can try a fizzy mango juice in a lurid can. Just the thing to tempt a jaded palate.

Siam Café

There is an inordinate number of outré hairdressing salons where Woodgrange Road turns the bend before the railway bridge, but it is still a mainish sort of main road, with shops and pubs interspersed with cafés. One of these is the Siam Café, cast very much in the mould of the late lamented Pie Crust Café. By day the Siam is a greasy spoon serving trad English greasy stuff, and by night it transforms into a family-run Thai eatery. This is one of the few restaurants in London where, after a solicitous enquiry as to whether this is your first visit, you may be treated to a short speech of welcome. The decor is fairly rugged and the lighting is neon – this is not one of your ultra-cool West End establishments – but the welcome is a warm one and the food carefully made, workmanlike, and cheap.

Cost	£6–£14

Address 103 Woodgrange Rd, E7
T 020 8536 1870
Station BR Wanstead Park
Open Mon–Sat 7–10pm
Accepts MasterCard, Visa

Starters here tend to hail from the fryer, and that includes the chicken satay (£4.50). Best of all are the crispy wonton (£3) and the steamed dumplings – a mix of prawn and pork (£3.80). The squid rings are crisp (£3.20). The rest of the menu falls into a series of categories – soups, red curries, green curries, stir-fries and noodles – and all these dishes offer simple home cooking of a high standard. Spicing is accurate, everything tastes fresh and the sauces are good and clean-tasting. Soups are good value: try the tom yum kai – chicken soup (£3.25). The stir-fries include chicken ginger (£4.60) and prawns with chilli and basil leaves (£5.75). The classic noodle dish, pud Thai, comes with chicken (£5.50) or king prawns (£6.50) among the stir-fried noodles with egg, ground peanut, spring onion, dried shrimp, dried turnip and cabbage. It lives up to its billing on the menu – "very tasty indeed".

You may bring your own drinks to the Siam Café, which is probably a very good thing as the jasmine tea (the high point of the drinks list) is redolent of neither jasmine nor tea, though it does come in a nice mug from that rustic collection given away by a leading petrol station.

Wild Cherry

Wild Cherry is a vegetarian restaurant that, as the mission statement by the door proclaims, "exists firstly to provide fresh home-cooked vegetarian meals for the local community". It's part of the London Buddhist Centre around the corner and was once a soup kitchen for workers and devotees.

Cost	£5–£20

Address 241 Globe Rd, E2
T 020 8980 6678
Station Bethnal Green
Open Mon 11am–3pm,
Tues–Fri 11am–7pm
Accepts All major credit cards except Diners

It's a bright, clean, self-service venue with modern wooden tables and Arno Jacobsen chairs. A blackboard lists the daily menu and you choose from selections like cauliflower and almond cheese pie with one salad (£4.50); spaghetti with creamy pea, mushroom and fresh mint sauce (£4.25); hot quiche of the day with two salads (£4.25); and polenta pie with roasted vegetables and one salad (£4.50). There's a choice of three different salads every day, and there's always a soup and a quiche and two hot dishes. Baked potatoes include a choice of comforting fillings like humous (£2.40); grated cheddar (£2.80); and tzatsiki (£2.80). Salads (large mixed £3.50; regular mixed £2.40; single scoop £1.20) include choices like arame rice; ruby chard, cherry tomato and fresh chive; mixed leaf; Moroccan chickpea with rocket; and coleslaw with vegan mayonnaise. Puddings include chocolate and beetroot cake (£1.40); prune and honey cake (£1.25); and banoffee pie (£2.25). There's no liquor licence, but you can bring your own for £1 corkage. There are, however, fourteen different teas (80p or 90p), ten of them herbal, plus free-trade coffee (£1.10 per mug; £1.80 per cafetiere), and a choice of soya or cows' milk. Daily choices often include wheat-free and sugar-free dishes and some are vegan. The portions are huge, it all tastes wholesome and it's amazing value. The resto is relaxed and you can have anything from a full meal to a refreshing cup of camomile tea.

Reading the full mission statement is a must. You learn that "We promote vegetarianism by making it both available and, hopefully, irresistible". You read on and discover that Wild Cherry is run by seven Buddhist women whose "working practices are based on the Buddhist principles of non-violence, honesty and generosity." Surely worthwhile aims in any restaurant kitchen?

North

Camden Town & Primrose Hill

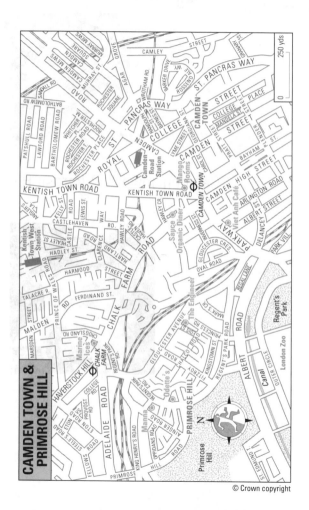

CAMDEN TOWN & PRIMROSE HILL

© Crown copyright

The Engineer

The Engineer is one of that burgeoning roster of gastro-pubs whose food side has grown and grown – it now has tables in the bar, a more formal restaurant, tables in the garden (for those occasional summer days), and a salle privée on the first floor. Wherever you end up sitting, you'll get offered the same menu (which changes every two weeks) and you'll pay the same price. The cooking is accomplished, with good strong combinations of flavours, and a cheerful, iconoclastic approach to what is fundamentally Mediterranean food. The latest development is that they open for breakfast seven days a week. When do they sleep?

Cost	£10–£35

Address 65 Gloucester Ave, NW1
T 020 7722 0950
Station Chalk Farm
Open Mon–Fri 9–11.30am, noon–3pm & 7–11pm, Sat 9am–noon, 12.30–3.30pm & 7–11pm, Sun 9am–noon, 12.30–3.30pm & 7–10.30pm
Accepts MasterCard, Switch, Visa
W www.the-engineer.com

MEDITERRANEAN/PUB

Your hackles may rise at £1.75 for home-made bread and butter, but the bread is warm from the oven, with a good crust, and the butter is beurre d'Isigny and, as they refill the basket after you've scoffed the lot, you end up feeling happier about paying. Starters are simple and good. There's soup (£3.75). There may be a summery salad such as Feta cheese, dandelion leaf, watermelon and mint with an orange dressing (£5.95), or crab coriander and spring onion fritters with herb salad and sweet chilli jam (£5.30). At lunchtime the mains will probably be quite light – eggs Benedict, eggs Florentine, a pan-fried organic beef burger. For dinner, expect dishes like char-grilled loin of swordfish with a salad of mango, cucumber, mint and chilli sauce (£11.75), or a risotto cake with butternut squash, rocket leaves, Mediterranean vegetables and pesto sauce (£9.85). There's often a new twist put on familiar ingredients, so shredded spiced duck-leg salad is served with a tossed salad of mouli, mint, coriander and red chilli with frisée and lemon and lime dressing (£9.25). A complex blend of textures. Do not miss out on a side order of baker chips (£2.25) – thick wedges of baked potato fried until crispy. Thanks to The Engineer's pub status, there is always a decent pint of beer to be had and the coffee is excellent, too. All in all, plenty of reasons why it's so busy, and plenty of reasons why you should book.

At the bottom of the menu it says proudly, "Please note that all our meat is free range and organic". Hurrah! They deserve your support.

Mango Rooms

🍴 Mango Rooms is an engaging place, although it does make you wonder why everyone in this part of London is striving so hard to be laid-back. Hereabouts the coolness seems a little forced, and the casualness somehow elaborate. No matter. This restaurant describes itself as offering "traditional and modern Caribbean cuisine". The walls are bright and shabby, the staff gentle and the cooking reliable.

Cost	£10–£35
Address	10 Kentish Town Rd, NW1
T	020 7482 5065
Station	Camden Town
Open	Mon 6pm–midnight Tues–Sun noon–3pm & 6pm–midnight
Accepts	MasterCard, Visa
W	www.mangorooms.co.uk

If there is a fault to be found, it would be that the spicing and seasoning is somewhat tame, as if the act has been cleaned up a little. Perhaps Camden's restaurateurs simply have an unusually good grasp of what their customers like? Mango Room is certainly very full, and everyone seems to be having a great time, in a laid-back, Camden-cool kind of way.

Traditional starters are the most successful, like the salt cod fritters with apple chutney (£3.80), or crab and potato balls (£3.70) – the exception to the under-spiced rule. Ebony wings, marinated in chilli pepper, garlic and soya with a hot and sweet dipping sauce (£3.70) is a nice dish but not a hot one. For a main course, "Camden's famous curry goat with hot pepper, scallions, garlic, pimento and spices" (£8) is subtitled "A hot, spicy, traditional dish", which it isn't. But it is very tasty: well presented and with plenty of lean meat. For fish-eaters there is Creole snapper with mango and green peppercorn sauce (£9). The side dishes are excellent – plantain (£1.70), rice and peas (£1.70), white and sweet potato mash (£2.50), and a very good, dry and dusty roti (£2.50). The cooking is consistent and the kitchen makes a real effort with the presentation. If you like your Caribbean food on the sweet side and without the fierce burn of lantern chillies or pepper sauce, you will have a great time here.

Puddings are good – the mango and banana brûlée (£3.50) sports an exemplary hard top – and the Mango Rooms' special rum punch (£4.50) is sweet enough for most people to class it as a dessert. The bar here is lively and seems to be ever-expanding.

Manna

If your new film – the one where a beautiful American business-woman meets a tongue-tied but cute Brit aristo, you know the kind of thing – needed an authentic 1970s veggie restaurant for a crucial hand-holding scene, the decor at Manna would fit the bill perfectly. In this world of chic modern restos and chic modern restaurant designers, it is increasingly hard for anywhere to look old-fashioned and casual without being sneered at. Manna don't care! This stubborn gentleness sometimes extends to the service, so don't pitch up here in a hurry, or without a serious appetite – there is no whimsy about the portions here. The cooking is very sound, and if there is such a thing as a peculiarly "veggie" charm, this place has it.

Cost	£15–£45
Address	4 Erskine Rd, NW1
T	020 7722 8028
Station	Chalk Farm
Open	Mon–Fri 6.30–11pm, Sat & Sun 12.30–3pm & 6.30–11pm
Accepts	MasterCard, Visa
W	www.manna-veg.com

VEGETARIAN

The menu devolves into five sections: starters, salads, mains, sides and desserts. You can also order a selection of any three salads or starters as the "Manna meze" (£12.95). Soup of the day is a sound option, as it comes with the solid but satisfying home-made bread. The menu changes regularly but may include starters like cucumber jade pillars (£5.50) – the cucumber is filled with smoked tofu and leek and comes with a Thai basil dipping sauce. Or how about polenta-crusted stuffed chillies (£6.50), filled with "coriander and spring onion cream cheese on salsa verde, sales roja and chocolate mole"? Mains are an eclectic bunch: a steamed pudding (£11.50) is veg-packed and boosted with truffle oil; there's a Mexican tortilla galette (£11.25); there's iman bayaldi (£10.95), rich with aubergine, onion and oil; and a green coconut laksa (£10.25), which is suitably soupy and nourishing. Puds are mainstream: mocha torte (£5.75); Manna organic fruit crumble (£4.25). For the early diner there's an early-evening menu that offers two courses for £11.95 and sets out a variety of options drawn from the main menu.

The menu here is decodable. (v) Stands for vegan dishes; (vo) means vegan option and adds "please ask"; (org) means an organic dish; and (g) means gluten free. All of which is very helpful. Whether committed vegetarians or not, we should all take more interest in just what it is that we are eating.

Marine Ices

Marine Ices is a family restaurant from a bygone era. In 1947, Aldo Mansi rebuilt the family shop along nautical lines, kitting it out with wood and portholes (hence the name). In the half-century since, while the family ice cream business has grown and grown, the restaurant and gelateria has just pottered along. All for the good. That means old-fashioned service and home-style, old-fashioned Italian food. It also means that Marine Ices is a great hit with children, for, in addition to the good Italian food, there is a marathon list of stunning sundaes, coupes, ice creams and sorbets.

Cost	£8–£25
Address	8 Haverstock Hill, NW3
T	020 7482 9003
Station	Chalk Farm
Open	Restaurant Mon–Fri noon–3pm & 6–11pm, Sat noon–11pm, Sun noon–10pm; Gelateria Mon–Sat 10.30am–11pm, Sun 11am–10pm
Accepts	MasterCard, Switch, Visa

The menu is long: antipasti, salads, pastas and sauces, specialities and pizzas. Of the starters, you could try selezioni di bruschetta (£3.80), which combines one each of three well-made and fresh bruschetta – roast vegetables, sardines and tomatoes. Or go for the chef's salad (£3.95), a rocket salad with pancetta and splendid croutons made from eggy bread. Pasta dishes are home-made: casarecce Aldo (£6.80), from the specials list, has a tasty sauce of spring onions, spinach and ricotta – simple, and very good. Main courses range from pollo valdostana (£7.40) to scalloppa Milanese (£8.60) and fegato alla Veneziana (£8.90). Pizzas are immense, freshly made and very tasty, in whichever of their many guises you choose (£5.20 to £6.50). And where others may be set on saving Venice, at Marine they support the Rebuild the Roundhouse fund; for every Roundhouse pizza sold – cheese, tomato, ham, mushroom and fresh chilli (all £6.50) – they donate 50p.

When you've had your meal, take a breath and ask for the gelateria menu. There are sundaes from peach Melba (£2.40) to Knickerbocker Glory (£3.65). There are coppe, including Stefania (£4.40) – one scoop each of chocolate and hazelnut ice cream, covered in nuts and hot fudge sauce. There are bombe, cassate, and best of all, affogati (£4.20) – three scoops of ice cream topped with Marsala or – even nicer – espresso coffee. Or create your own combo from fourteen ice creams and eight sorbets. They're £1.25 a scoop.

Odette's

Odette's is a charming, picturesque restaurant, ideally set in pretty Primrose Hill. The walls are crammed with gilded mirrors and hanging plants, there's a pleasant conservatory at the back (with a skylight open in warm weather) and candles flicker in the evenings. Add well-judged modern British food, the odd local celeb, and staff who always try to make you feel special, and you have all the ingredients for a very successful local restaurant. In summer, try to get one of the tables that spill out onto the villagey street.

Cost	£20–£40
Address	130 Regent's Park Rd, NW1
T	020 7586 5486
Station	Chalk Farm
Open	Mon–Fri 12.30–2.30pm & 7–11pm, Sat 7–11pm
Accepts	All major credit cards

MODERN BRITISH

The food makes commendable use of seasonal produce, so do not expect to find all the dishes listed every time you visit. However, the olive and walnut bread is a constant – warm and delicious. Starters, if you strike lucky, might include cream of Jerusalem artichoke soup (£4.50), or an asparagus salad with poached egg on toast and Hollandaise sauce (£7.50). When in season, the Irish oysters (£8) are a good choice, and arrive well-presented, with grilled spicy sausages and Cabernet Sauvignon vinegar on the side. Mains generally include at least one choice each of fish, meat, game and chicken. Salmon baked with leeks, salsify and Noilly Prat (£13) – delicious. Cumin roast neck of new-season lamb, soft polenta and spring greens (£13) is another good choice, as is the roasted blackleg chicken with watercress and a fried herb risotto (£14). Roast monkfish is teamed with black olive and langoustine toast, confit of potatoes and tomatoes and bouillabaisse sauce (£15), while veggies might go for home-made linguine, roasted garlic and aubergine puree with marinated peppers (£10.50). Puddings (all £5) are wonderfully indulgent, and include chocolate espresso tart with crème fraîche, lemon curd parfait with strawberries, and an outstanding mango and stem ginger sorbet. The set lunch (Mon–Fri, £10) is worth noting.

Odette's has a very long wine list, with something to suit all tastes and purses. It's also nice to get such a large choice of wines by the glass and half-bottle. Try a glass of South African Chardonnay for £3.15, or a half bottle of Sauvignon de Touraine for £8.25.

Camden Town & Primrose Hill

Sauce Organic Diner

If organic is the new rock'n'roll then Sauce is another band on the scene. Associated with the well-known Camden Brasserie (upstairs), Sauce (downstairs) is dedicated to wholesome, tasty plates of organic food, served all day. Sauce claims 95 percent of the ingredients are free from chemicals, pesticides and preservatives, and produced by farmers who care for the environment. Sauce also provides a juice and cocktail bar, with juices and smoothies like carrot,

Cost	£15–£30

Address 214 Camden High St, NW1
T 020 7482 0777
Station Camden Town
Open Mon–Thurs noon–10.30pm, Fri & Sat noon–11pm, Sun noon–4.30pm
Accepts Delta, MasterCard, Switch, Visa

apple and ginger (£3.10) – very perky it is, too – and cocktails like Margaritas (£4.25 glass, £15 pitcher). Newspapers and flyers for worthy causes provide food for the mind as well, and it's fine just to drop by for a beer or a coffee.

Start with corn fritter with roast vegetables and tomato salsa (£4.75) and you get a solid, almost meaty, fritter; or soup of the day (£3.50), perhaps red pepper; or crab cakes with sweet chilli sauce (£4.95) – very moreish. Main courses include an obligatory veggie burger with nuts, seeds, tomato relish and fat fries (£6.50) – crisp and tasty; and a beef burger with tomato relish and fat fries (£7.50) – as good a burger as you'll eat anywhere. Or try saffron lamb slow-cooked with red peppers over herbed polenta (£9.95). There are also fine sandwiches and wraps – try the spicy black beans, rice, pepper and melted cheese in a tortilla wrap (£5.95), and, if you're hungry, add shredded chicken for an extra £1. Puddings include chocolate nut brownie with caramel sauce (£3.50); fresh fruit of the day over waffles with maple syrup (£3.25); and baked banana with caramel sauce and vanilla ice cream (£3.25). There are organic teas, coffees and fruit tisanes, and you can choose dairy or soya cream – it must be said that, from a taste perspective, cows beat beans hands down when it comes to turning out cream. If you fancy something stronger, there's Freedom lager and a host of organic wines.

Sauce provides the security of well-chosen organic ingredients served in a chic environment. If you want to eat this way (and you know it makes sense), then this place is a godsend.

Viet-Anh Cafe

Authentic, it says on the card, and authentic it tastes on the plate. Viet-Anh is a bright, cheerful café with oil-cloth covered tables run by a young Vietnamese couple who cook and give service that's beyond helpful. In complete contrast to the occasionally intimidating feel of some of the more obscure Chinese restaurants, this is a friendly and welcoming place. If there is anything puzzling or unfamiliar they'll tell you what and show you how. It's the sort of place where single diners feel quite at home.

Cost	£15–£40

Address 41 Parkway, NW1
T 020 7284 4082
Station Camden Town
Open Daily noon–4pm & 5.30–11pm
Accepts MasterCard, Visa

VIETNAMESE

Vietnamese vegetarian spring rolls (£2.95) and Vietnamese meat pancake (£4.95) are classic starters. The former are crisp, well-seasoned, and flavoured with fresh coriander; the latter are a delight – two large, paper-thin, eggy pancakes stuffed with vegetables and chicken, and served with large lettuce leaves. You hold these in the palm of your hand and manipulate a slice of the pancake onto the leaf, roll it up together, dip in the pungent lemony sauce and eat. Hot and cold, crisp and soft, savoury and lemony – all in one. Beef sugar-cane stick (£4.95) is dry minced beef wrapped around a cane stick. Bite off the beef in chunks and chew into the cane. Savoury and sweet in one mouthful. Pho chicken soup, accurately described as the House Special (£3.95), is made with slices of chicken and vegetables plus flat rice stick noodles in broth. Slurp the noodles and lift the bowl to drink the soup. Lemongrass chicken on boiled rice (£4.50) is a more fiery dish – you can have it medium hot or very hot, just ask. There are over a hundred dishes on the menu, ranging from £1 to £12 and most are complete one-plate meals. Wines come in at around the £15 mark, or there is sake (300ml for £8) as well as various Far East beers. Try the Shui Sen tea (£1.20) – it's more fragrant than jasmine tea, and just as refreshing.

To complete the café feel, huge (1lb 12oz) plastic bottles of sauce with squeezy tops adorn the tables. They are labelled "Sriracha HOT chilli sauce", and the label is as much a warning as an inducement. If you like your food as spicy as the Vietnamese customers do, you're only a squeeze away.

Hampstead & Golders Green

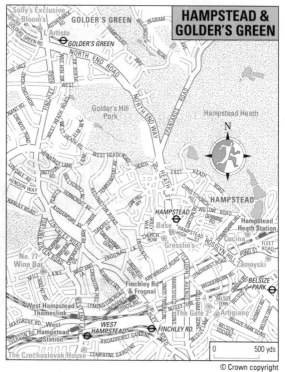

HAMPSTEAD & GOLDER'S GREEN

Solly's Exclusive
Bloom's
GOLDER'S GREEN
L'Artista
ROTHERWICK RD
GOLDER'S GREEN
GOLDERS GREEN RD
NORTH END ROAD
INGRAM
HAMPSTEAD WAY
WILDWOOD
ROAD
THE VALE
FINCHLEY ROAD
WEST HEATH ROAD
NANT RD
BROOKS RD
WEST HEATH ROAD
Golder's Hill Park
NORTH END WAY
SANDARS ROAD
Hampstead Heath
N
HERMITAGE LANE
WEST HEATH ROAD
HEATH RD
EAST HEATH ROAD
HEATH ST
CHRISTCHURCH
HAMPSTEAD
LYNDALE AV
PLATTS RD
HENDON WAY
REDINGTON ROAD
TEMPLEWOOD
OAK WK
WILLOW ROAD
DENNING RD
Hampstead Heath Station
RANULF ROAD
FORTUNE GREEN ROAD
FINCHLEY ROAD
FERNCROFT AV
KIDDERPORE AV
DROVE
DAKGILL AV
GREENAWAY GDNS
HOLLY WK
HAMPSTEAD HIGH ST
CHURCH ROW
FROGNAL
HAMPSTEAD
Base
Cucina
ROSSLYN HILL
FLEET ROAD
Gresslin's
POND ST
Zamoyski
No. 77
Wine Bar
MILL LANE
WEST END LA
CRICKLEWOOD LANE
WEST END LA
FROGNAL
LYMINGTON RD
FINCHLEY HILL
PARK WRIGHT RD
LINDEN GDNS
MARESFIELD GDNS
ST JOHN'S AVENUE
LYNDHURST ROAD
WEDDERBURN RD
BELSIZE PARK
Finchley Rd
& Frognal
West Hampstead
Thameslink
MAYGROVE RD
West Hampstead Station
IVERSON RD
WEST HAMPSTEAD
FINCHLEY RD.
The Gate 2
Artigiano
NUTLEY TERR.
BELSIZE TERR.
BELSIZE SQUARE
BELSIZE PARK GDNS
BROADHURST GARDENS
COMPAYNE GARDENS
The Czechoslovak House

0   500 yds

© Crown copyright

Artigiano

This is one of London's more diffi-cult-to-find restaurants, situated halfway up a dead-end street in the rabbit warren of Belsize Park. Never-theless, tracking it down is well worth the effort. When you do find it, you will be confronted with a bright, airy restaurant, glass-fronted and with generous sky-lights. There's more chance of seeing a traffic warden than a passing car and the only disturbance from outside is the rustle of leaves. For such an out-of-the-way place the restaurant is sur-prisingly big, with more than a hundred covers. It's remarkably busy, too, full of thirty-something professionals who've sought it out for the same reasons you have – good food and service, convivial atmosphere, and an escape from the rat race.

Cost	£15–£24

Address 12 Belsize Terrace, NW3
T 020 7794 4288
Station Belsize Park
Open Mon–Sat noon–3pm & 6.45–11pm, Sun noon–3pm & 6.45–10pm
Accepts All major credit cards
W www.etruscagroup.com

ITALIAN

The menu is longer than you'd expect in such a restaurant, with eight first courses and eight pastas followed by as many main courses, but it seems that the kitchen can cope. There is an admirable tendency to use spanking fresh ingredients and to let them be themselves. Antipasti might include insalata mista con erbe fresche e vinaigrette all'Aceto Bal-samico (£5.25) – the Italian for mixed leaves! Or prosciutto made from wild boar and served with rocket, orange and walnuts (£8.50), or a good beef carpaccio with a mustardy dressing (£8.50). Pastas are home-made and innovative. Casoncelli (£7) are small pasta parcels stuffed with duck and pistachios; stracci di pasta al pesto di carciofi e granchio reale (£8.50) is a mixture of strips of pasta with fresh crab and a basil and artichoke pesto. The "pesce" list also offers a good choice: gilt head bream pan-fried with a saffron sauce (£13.50); or seared tuna steak (£14.50). Meat eaters will turn to the ossobuco in gremolata (£13.50), which is served with a timbale of saffron rice, or the grilled wild boar cutlet (£15), which comes with a potato tartlet. The chocolate sorbet (£4) is seductive and the strawberries (£4.50) are marinated in spumante and balsamic vinegar.

Having weathered the first few years, Artigiano looks set fair. If you are able to make it at lunchtime, go for the set menu – £12.50 for two courses, £14 for three.

ITALIAN/PIZZA

L'Artista

Situated opposite the entrance to Golders Green tube, and occupying an arch under the railway lines, L'Artista is hard to miss. With its pavement terrace, abundant greenery and umbrellas, this is a lively, vibrant restaurant and pizzeria that exercises an almost magnetic appeal to the young and not so young of Golders Green.

Cost	£15–£24
Address	917 Finchley Rd, NW11
T	020 8731 7501
Station	Golders Green
Open	Daily noon–midnight
Accepts	MasterCard, Visa

At the weekend it is literally full to bursting and tables spill onto the terrace – a perfect spot to eat alfresco, providing the traffic isn't too heavy on the Finchley Road. Inside, the plain decor is enhanced by celebrity photographs; the waiters are a bit cagey if asked just how many of them have actually eaten here, but the proximity of the tables ensures that you get to rub shoulders with whoever happens to be around you, famous or otherwise.

The menu offers a range of Italian food with a good selection of main courses such as fegato Veneziana (£7.10), a rich dish of calves' liver with onion and white wine. The trota del pescatore (£6.90) is also good, a simple but effective trout with garlic. But L'Artista's pizzas are its forte. They are superb. As well as traditional thin-crust capricciosa (£5.90) – with anchovies, eggs and ham – or quattro formaggi (£5.60), there are more unusual varieties such as mascarpone e rucola (£5.10), a plain pizza topped with Mascarpone cheese and heaps of crisp rocket, which is actually very good. The calzone (£5.70) – a cushion-sized rolled pizza stuffed with ham, cheese and sausage and topped with Napoli sauce – is wonderful. Pastas are varied and, for a change, the penne alla vodka (£5.40), made with vodka, prawns and cream, is well worth a try. For something lighter, try the excellent insalata dell'Artista (£4.80), a generous mix of tuna, olives and fennel, with an order of equally good garlic pizza bread (£2.50).

L'Artista tries hard to bring something of the atmosphere of Naples to Golders Green. By a happy accident this ambience is enhanced by the Vesuvian tremors which occur whenever a Northern-line train rumbles ominously overhead.

Base

Pierre Khodja's restaurant has undergone several changes since the last edition. He's given Hampstead diners the choice of a mezze menu, and also given them a separate café, finally settling on what people seem to prefer – a single venue that offers a café-restaurant by day and a more formal atmosphere in the evenings. So while

Cost	£15–£50
Address 71 Hampstead High St, NW3	
T 020 7431 2224	
Station Hampstead	
Open Mon–Sat noon–3pm & 7–11pm, Sun noon–3pm	
Accepts All major credit cards	

there's a full menu at lunch, you can also enjoy a coffee or a light snack. And in the evenings the tables are relaid to give a more genteel feel.

The menu blends North African with Middle Eastern influences, adds a leavening of modern British and ends up with light and intensely flavoured dishes that are unusual, yet familiar. Start with lentils and beetroot salad with balsamic dressing and garlic croutons (£3.95); tabouleh salad with halloumi fritter and lemon (£3.95); or roasted peppers and artichoke salad with caper berries (£4.50). The lentil and beetroot salad is sweet and crunchy, the tabouleh salad is crisp, salty and fresh, and the roasted peppers and artichoke salad is rich with concentrated flavour. Share them between you, mezze style, so that everyone can have a taste. Main courses are equally interesting. Try mechoui of lamb with herbs and harissa on white bean ragout (£11.50) – the lamb steak hot and spicy on the melting beans; or duck bastilla with mango chutney (£11.50) – slow-cooked duck baked in filo pastry, a rich, melting texture. Fish dishes include fresh tuna with roasted peppers, tomato casserole and olive tapenade (£10.50); baked whole sea bass, lemon, chillies and tahini (£13.00); and Base's own bouillabaisse (£14.00), complete with rouille. Side orders are equally exotic (all £3.00): lime-pickled roast potatoes; garlic beans; steamed carrots with cumin and lemon. Puddings (all £4.50) include prune tart and cinnamon ice cream with crème fraîche; coconut rice pudding, quince and star anise; and grapefruit sorbet with orange and mint salad. The latter tastes refreshing and ultra clean.

It is something of a puzzle that the "pied noire" food from French North Africa hasn't taken the world by storm. This accomplished and unusual cooking deserves a wider audience. Perhaps Hampstead will be the springboard for world domination!

Bloom's

Bloom's goes way back to 1920, when Rebecca and Morris Bloom first produced their great discovery – the original Veal Vienna. Since then "Bloom's of the East End" has carried the proud tag as "the most famous kosher restaurant in the world". Setting aside the indignant claims of several outraged New York delis for the moment, given its history it's a shame that the East End Bloom's was forced to shut, and that they had to retrench to this, their Golders Green stronghold, in 1965. Nonetheless, it's a glorious period piece. Rows of sausages hang over the takeaway counter, there are huge mirrors and chrome tables, and you can expect inimitable service from battle-hardened waiters.

Cost	£12–£30

Address 130 Golders Green Rd, NW11

T 020 8455 1338

Station Golders Green

Open Mon–Thurs & Sun noon–11pm, Fri 10am–2pm/3pm (winter/summer)

Accepts All major credit cards except Diners

W www.blooms-restaurant.co.uk

So, the waiter looks you in the eye as you ask for a beer. "Heineken schmeineken," he says derisively. At which point you opt for Maccabee, an Israeli beer (£1.90), and regain a little ground. Start with some new green cucumbers (90p) – fresh, crisp, tangy, delicious – and maybe a portion of chopped liver and egg and onions (£4.20), which comes with world-class rye bread. Or go for soup, which comes in bowls so full they slop over the edge: beetroot borscht and potato (£2.90), very sweet and very red; lockshen, the renowned noodle soup (£2.90); or kreplach, full of dumplings (£3.50). Go on to main courses. The salt beef is as good as you might expect (£13.50). And there are solid and worthy options like liver and onions (£9.20). In 2000 Bloom's – now run by Jonathan Tapper, one of the fourth generation of the Bloom family – was "refurbished" once again but the inimitable ambience remains intact and you can still order extra side dishes – those legendary dishes that have made the reputation of Jewish food.

Whatever else you try, don't leave without sampling the latkes (£1.90) – enormously solid and uncompromising potato pancakes. And the tzimmas (£1.90) – honeyed carrots so cloyingly sweet that they could claim a spot on the dessert menu. It's filling, wholesome, comforting food. Enjoy!

Cucina

This single-fronted restaurant, next to a bakery near South End Green, looks like the archetypal traiteur, or smart food shop. And that is what it is, at least downstairs, where the Hampstead literati feast upon a range of rather good meals to go. But if you enter and turn right up the stairs you come to a large, brightly painted, wooden-floored, roof-lit dining room. Very modern, very fashionable, very chic. At lunch, all is relatively quiet and talk at the scattered tables is generally of business. Things hot up in the evening, however, when the à la carte menu takes over. This menu changes every two weeks or so and darts about between cuisines and continents, but wherever you alight you can be sure of well-presented dishes and service that is friendly and efficient.

Cost	£18–£40
Address	45a South End Rd, NW3
T	020 7435 7814
Station	Belsize Park
Open	Mon–Thurs noon–2.30pm & 7–10.30pm, Fri & Sat noon–2.30pm & 7–11pm, Sun noon–3pm
Accepts	All major credit cards except Diners

Dinner-time starters may include deep-fried quail in a chickpea batter with chermoula and red cabbage (£5.75); roast new potatoes, crispy fried pancetta and Taleggio sauce (£5.75); wok fried squid with roasted seaweed noodles, chilli and soy (£5.95); or, if that isn't spooky enough for you, Szechuan seared kangaroo, shitake, lotus root and mizuna salad with mirin dressing (£6.25). Among the main courses there is always a fish of the day, often something interesting like mahi-mahi. Other fish dishes feature, too, such as salmon poached in coconut milk with sticky black crab rice (£12.50). Or how about pan-fried lamb's kidneys, porcini and basil sauce, truffle oil mash (£11.95)? Or char-grilled butternut squash, mustard potato curry, yoghurt and poppadom (£10.50)? Or confit of duck with sesame fried courgette noodles, plum and ginger chutney (£13.50)? For the more traditional diner there is always a very sound char-grilled rib of beef (for two) with frites (£26.95).

All the puds are £5 and two of them – steamed banana pudding with maple sauce and sugared pecans; and bitter chocolate rocky road mousse cake have a little star beside them which leads to the rather helpful comment "Too full! Why not get a pudding to take home?" Taken home they cost £3.

The Czechoslovak House

With its low prices and bafflingly retro decor – the kind of ambience where Harry Lime would feel right at home – The Czechoslovak House is always filled with a happy mix of students and locals. It is situated in the old, established Czechoslovak National House (too good an institution to be sundered – or even to adapt its name), and its dining room is a class act. Genuine flock wallpaper gives a unique backdrop for some striking portraits: among them Václav Havel, Winston Churchill, and a very young-looking Queen Elizabeth II with her crown and regalia picked out in glitter powder.

Cost	£12–£26
Address	74 West End Lane, NW6
T	020 7372 5251
Station	West Hampstead
Open	Tues–Fri 6–10pm, Sat & Sun noon–3pm & 6–10pm
Accepts	Cash or cheque only

Menu-writers across London should be forced to study here – it is hard to improve on the concision of "meat soup" (£2.50). Passing that dish by, try starting with tlacenka (£2.50), which is home-made brawn with onions. Or Russian egg (£4) – egg mayonnaise with salad, ham and onions. Or the rather good rollmops (£2.20), again with onions. (You need to like raw onions to do well at the starters.) Main courses deliver serious amounts of home-made, tasty food. Beef goulash with dumplings (£7.70) is red with sweet paprika, and cooked long and slow until the meat is meltingly tender. Order smoked boiled pork knuckle, sauerkraut and dumplings (£8.70), and you will be served a vast and tasty ham hock, good (if rather sweet) sauerkraut and dumplings, plus a small jug of wildly rich pork gravy. If you don't fancy dumplings, the roast veal comes with creamed spinach and superb fried potatoes (£8.40). For drink, set your sights on beer – Gambrinus on draught is £2.20 a pint and there are a number of other bottled Czech beers, including one whose label is fetchingly decorated with a motorcycle and sidecar. There is a story behind this graphic, which the amiable bartender will explain – not that you will be able to remember the tale after drinking the stuff.

There is one pudding that will have any cholesterol-wary diner clutching at their pacemaker. Apricot dumpling (£3.50) is a cricket-ball-sized lump of dough with an apricot inside. It comes under a coat of sour cream, and sits in a sea of melted butter. The only concession to modern fresh-food fads is the garnish of three grapes. It is awesome.

The Gate 2

There are vegetarian restaurants and there are restaurants that happen not to use meat or fish in the cooking. The Gate 2 in Belsize Park, sister to The Gate in Hammersmith (see p.438), is one of the latter, serving excellent and original dishes with intense and satisfying tastes and textures. Even the dedicated carnivore won't miss anything.

Cost	£25–£50

Address 72 Belsize Lane NW3
T 020 7435 7733
Station Belsize Park
Open Mon–Sat noon–3pm & 6–11pm, Sun noon–5pm
Accepts All major credit cards
W www.gateveg.co.uk

Starters include green banana fritters (£5.75), herb-crusted goat's cheese (£5.75), risotto with spaghetti squash, sage, Parmesan and truffle oil (£5.75), and futo maki (£5.00) – vegetable and seaweed rolls with miso and peanut sauce. The fritters arrive as balls of plantain and banana, seasoned with ginger, shallots and coriander, plus a fresh coconut and lime chutney; the risotto is sweet and nutty with flaked rather than grated Parmesan; the goat's cheese is melty inside and crispy on the outside, with intense herb flavours and a fresh, home-made chutney alongside. The futo maki, with a finely shredded salad filling, wouldn't disgrace a sushi bar anywhere. Main courses are equally accomplished. Buffalo Mozzarella terrine (£10.50) is a tower of aubergine, pimentos and basil, with Mozzarella and a sharp sauce vierge. Tarragon gnocchi (£10.50) is well-herbed and served with roasted mushrooms, artichoke hearts and a rich sorrel velouté sauce. Linguine with garlic leaves, pesto, roasted red peppers and sunflower seeds (£7.50) – the menu's pasta of the day – is intensely flavoured and satisfyingly al dente. Breads come in five varieties. For pudding, try lemon and fig galette (£5.00) – a pyramid of caramelized fresh figs, lemon curd and shortbread, the sharpness of the lemon balancing the rich, sweet biscuit and the figs. Otherwise, try the mille feuille (£5.50) – poached apples, dates and roasted pecans on a crisp filo case, with an orange and red-wine syrup. Wines are well-priced, with a house wine at £10.50 and a flinty Sauvignon de St. Bris 1998 at £14.50.

Decor is modern and minimalist, presentation is decorative but not over fussy and the kitchen downstairs is open to view – always a good sign. If you think vegetarian food is only for the devoted, The Gate 2 might well change your mind.

MODERN EUROPEAN

Gresslin's

Michael Gresslin's, a small, rather humble-looking restaurant on Hampstead's busy Heath Street, has stayed the course since opening in 1996. It has had a recent facelift – all glass, stainless steel and leather – but the menu follows the same star as before, and the cuisine is still Modern European. Here you'll find a succession of dishes all given an imaginative twist – very much in the modern idiom, where Mediterranean flavours meet Oriental flourishes – and presentation on the plate is taken very seriously. This combination has secured Gresslin's a considerable and devoted following.

Cost	£12–£38
Address	13 Heath St, NW3
T	020 7794 8386
Station	Hampstead
Open	Mon 7–10.30pm, Tues–Sat noon–2.30pm & 7–10.30pm, Sun noon–2.30pm
Accepts	All major credit cards except Diners

The efficient French waiters are knowledgeable about the food and happy to recommend something they think you'll like, but it is hard in any case to go far wrong. The seasonal menu is short and well thought out, underpinned by quality, fresh ingredients, and with a good balance of fish, meat and vegetarian options. Starters might include spa risotto of woodland mushrooms (£6), or hoisin chicken and pickled vegetable salad (£4.50), or a red lentil soup with cumin and mint (£3), or even a twice-baked cheese soufflé (£5.50), which comes with baby spinach salad, caramelized apples and pecan nuts. Everything is precisely cooked. For mains, you get a choice of around ten dishes. Potato-crusted fish cakes, stir fried Swiss chard, fresh tomato sauce (£11) appeals, as does the roast cod with butternut squash and Savoy cabbage, bubble and squeak, green pea sauce (£11.50). Or perhaps Thai duck curry with steamed rice (£12)? Desserts are good, too. Try the chocolate pecan brownies with hot chocolate fudge sauce and vanilla ice cream (£3.50), or the grilled pineapple, mango and pink peppercorn sorbet (£3).

It's unlikely you'd visit Hampstead just to go to Gresslin's, but it's a real asset when you're there. Look out for the set menus, all of which offer a choice: dinner, served Monday to Thursday, is £14.95 for two courses and £17.95 for three. Sunday lunch gives you a choice of four starters, five mains and four desserts – £14.95 for two courses and £17.95 for three.

No.77 Wine Bar

2000 was the year when No.77 went down the smart food route, and although the refurbished kitchen turned out some pretty good stuff it never won the hearts and minds of the regulars. They pined for the serious hamburger which used to be listed on the menu as "the fat bastard". Good news for the locals, just in time to celebrate No. 77's twentieth birthday in 2002: the smart stuff

Cost	£16–£38
Address	77 Mill Lane, NW6
T	020 7435 7787
Station	West Hampstead
Open	Mon & Tues noon–11pm, Wed–Fri noon–midnight, Sat 1pm–midnight, Sun 1–10.30pm
Accepts	MasterCard, Visa

has been consigned to the dustbin of gastro-history and the burger is back. Despite the return to casual dining and a more eclectic, less classical menu, the wine list is long, informed and offers good value.

Starters range from smoked haddock, pea and saffron risotto cake with tomato confit (£4.55); to hoisin spare ribs with crispy noodles (£4.95); or char-grilled aubergines, goat's cheese and beef tomato stock with pesto (£4.50). The soupe de jour has come down to earth as "soup of today" (£3.95), while for main course, also in keeping with the old spirit, there is a pasta dish of the day (£7.95). But what about the roasted tandoori salmon with warm vegetable salad noodles and mango (£9.75)? Or sirloin steak with Portobello mushrooms, baked sweet potatoes and jus (£12.50)? Or there's confit duck leg with bubble and squeak (£9.65). Vegetarians might opt for the fresh winter-vegetable stew served with herb and cheese dumplings (£7.95). The new polite name for the triumphantly returning Fat Bastard is "No 77 beefburger topped with smoked Cheddar and served with braised capsicum onions, potato fries and salad" (£8.75). Welcome back. The pud list is littered with familiar faces such as tiramisù with whipped cream (£4.50) and panna cotta with berry compote (£4.50). Lemon brulée with meringue and berries (£4.50) is a hair's breadth from lemon meringue pie.

Like the menu, the wine list changes as whim and stocks dictate, but look out for delights such as La Grange Neuve de Figeac 1994 (£37.95) or Three Choirs Estate Reserve, lightly oaked, 1997 (£13.95). Anyone visiting Mill Lane for the first time should bear in mind that in this part of North London the busiest night of the week is Thursday, which is when the wine bar will be at its liveliest. They certainly know how to party in these parts.

Solly's Exclusive

What makes Solly's Exclusive so exclusive is that it is upstairs. Downstairs is Solly's Restaurant, which is less exclusive – a small, packed, noisy place specializing in epic falafel, those crispy balls of minced chickpeas that are deep-fried and served with all manner of salads. You'll find Solly's Exclusive by coming out of Solly's Restaurant, turning left, and left again around the side of the building, and then proceeding through an unmarked black door. Upstairs, a huge, bustling dining room accommodates 180 customers, while a back room provides another 100 seats which lie in wait for functions, bar mitzvahs and so forth. The decor is interesting – tented fabric on the ceiling, multi-coloured glass, brass light fittings – while waitresses, all of them with Solly's Exclusive emblazoned across the back of their waistcoats, maintain a brisk approach to the niceties of service.

Cost	£16–£35

Address 146–150 Golders Green Rd, NW11
T 020 8455 2121
Station Golders Green
Open Mon–Thurs 6.30–10.30pm, Sat (winter only) 8pm–1am, Sun 12.30–10.30pm
Accepts All major credit cards except Diners

The food is tasty and workmanlike. Start with the dish that pays homage to the chickpea – hoummus with falafel (£4.25) – three crispy depth charges and some well-made dip. Even the very best falafel in the world cannot overcome the inherent problems of eating chickpeas – their thunderous indigestibility – but as falafel go Solly's are pretty good. Otherwise, you could try Solly's special aubergine dip (£3.25), or the Moroccan cigars (£5), made from minced lamb wrapped in filo pastry and deep-fried. Solly's pitta (£1.25) – a fluffy, fourteen-inch disc of freshly baked bread – has more in common with a perfect naan than Greek-restaurant bread. Pittas to pine for. For a main course, the lamb shawarma (£9.75) is very good, nicely seasoned and spiced, and served with excellent chips and a good, sharp-tasting mound of shredded cabbage salad. The barbecue roast chicken with the same accompaniments (£9.50) is also good. Steer clear of the Israeli salad (£2.75), however, unless you relish the idea of a large bowl of chopped watery tomatoes and chopped watery cucumber.

Solly's Exclusive is kosher and under the supervision of the London Beth Din, so naturally its opening days and hours don't follow the same rules as non-Jewish establishments. If you're not fully conversant with the Jewish calendar, check before setting out.

Zamoyski

Zamoyski is a small, friendly place with a long menu, supplemented by various specials written on a mobile blackboard, and a list of vodkas that is longer still. Downstairs there's room for twenty in the bar, and upstairs there's a larger dining room. The staff are cheerful and prices are low – a combination which

Cost	£12–£30

Address 85 Fleet Rd, NW3
T 020 7794 4792
Station Belsize Park
Open Tues–Sat 5.30–11pm,
Sun 12.30–11pm
Accepts All major credit cards

POLISH

pulls in a broad spectrum of customers from middle-aged couples taking dinner à deux, and people enjoying an early-evening drink with a starter or two, to large parties (often from the nearby Royal Free Hospital) intent on laying into the vodka. The watershed here is about nine o'clock, by which point you'll need to start viewing the place through the bottom of a shot glass.

This is one of those Slavic/Polish restaurants where the starters have a distinct edge on the main courses; ordering three starters per person and sharing is a very attractive strategy. The management have spotted this trend and offer a "9 course Polskie Mezze" for £6.95, an outrageously low price (sadly, it is not available after 7pm on Friday or Saturday). One daily special always worth including in your raft of starters is the soup (£2.20), which could be anything from sorrel to beetroot. Then try some herring: sledz wedzony (£4.75), smoked herring with horseradish cream, or sledz w oleju (£4.75), the sweeter matjes fillet, both come with an accompanying shot of vodka. You might move on to placki losos (£4.50), little potato and walnut pancakes topped with smoked salmon. Among the main-course specials you might find kaszanka, which is home-made black pudding with mash (£8), or zywiecka, a tasty smoked garlic sausage (£8). And don't miss out on the pierogi rozne (£4) – small dumplings stuffed with potato and cheese, or mushrooms, or meat. Regular main courses are made of sterner stuff, their mission to be more filling than fanciful: kotlet cielecy (£9.50) is a veal escalope; kaczka z jabikami (£9.50) is a frazzled half-duck; and schab ze sliwkami (£8) is a tenderloin of pork stuffed with prunes.

Take a look at the barrels on the bar: they are full of bisongrass vodka. Feeling nervous? You should. Anywhere that serves vodka by the barrel deserves respect!

Highgate & Crouch End

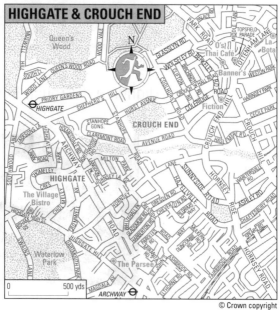

HIGHGATE & CROUCH END

Queen's Wood

CROUCH END

HIGHGATE

The Village Bistro

Waterlow Park

The Parsee

0   500 yds

ARCHWAY

© Crown copyright

Banner's

The 1960s are alive and well at Banner's. This is a characterful restaurant and cocktail bar with a real community feel. Noticeboards proclaim events and accommodation, kids draw using crayons kept in little red wellies, World music plays ... It's a welcoming kind of place if this slant on life matches velocities with your own.

Cost	£10–£30

Address 21 Park Rd, N8
T 020 8348 2930
Station Highgate
Open Mon–Thurs 9am–11.30pm, Fri 9am–midnight, Sat 10am–midnight, Sun 10am–11pm
Accepts MasterCard, Visa

CARIBBEAN/MODERN BRITISH

With all-day breakfasts, small meals, big meals, kids' meals, sandwiches and no-meat sections, Banner's menu pleases all tastes. Small meals include salt-fish cake with fresh tomato, chilli and lime salsa (£4.85); char-grilled minced lamb kebabs with harissa (£3.95); and gado gado salad – Indonesian salad with noodles, bean shoots and a spicy peanut dressing (£4.95). They're tasty, good and large enough for a light meal. Big meals include rib-eye steak, grilled with goat's cheese and pine nuts, with chips (£10.75); Jamaican jerk chicken with fried plantain or rice'n'peas and peanut sauce (£9.50); grilled fresh tuna loin with coconut rice and lime butter (£10.65); and Yorkshire sausages and mashed potatoes with cider onion gravy (£7.95). A generous plateful, tasty and satisfying. Side dishes include bubble and squeak (£2.75); cornmeal, sweetcorn and jalapeno spoon bread (£2.75); sweet-potato fries (£2.50); and garlic chips (£2.50) – for the certified lover of the bulb. Desserts include fried plantain with cinnamon, rum butter sauce and ice cream (£4.25); and hot dark-chocolate and walnut brownie, with ice cream (£4.50). Ices are from Marine. But the all-day-breakfast menu is the star, with choices like two Manx kippers with brown or white toast (£5.25); bubble and squeak with two fried eggs (£4.50); salt-fish Creole with onions, peppers and tomatoes, with flat fry bread (£8.95); and a proper fry-up with everything, including toast (£6.50).

The "world" feel extends to beers from Lapland and Argentina, exotic cocktails by the glass (£4.95) or jug (£20), cigarettes from the US, and postcards from Crouch End. And, to the relief of other diners, parents are warned, for safety reasons, not to let kids rush around on their own. Easy-going and family-oriented by day, Banner's livens up in the evening to become very busy with a lively, cocktail-drinking crowd; booking is advised.

SPANISH

La Bota

This bustling tapas bar and restaurant enjoys a good evening trade – and with good reason. It's a Galician (northwest Spanish) place, and that's always a good sign, particularly for seafood. The best of its tapas fall into two categories: there are the "raw" ones like Serrano ham, which simply need careful buying and good bread as accompaniment, and there are the stews which have been made in the morning and reheated as necessary – thankfully, most of the rich, unfussy dishes of

Cost	£10–£25

Address 31 Broadway Parade, Tottenham Lane, N8
T 020 8340 3082
Station Finsbury Park/ Turnpike Lane
Open Mon–Fri noon–3pm & 6–11.30pm, Sat noon–3.30pm & 6–11.30pm, Sun noon–11pm
Accepts Amex, MasterCard, Visa

Galicia lend themselves well to this treatment. Your first decision is a crucial one: do you go all out for tapas (there are 21 on the menu, plus 15 vegetarian ones, plus another 18 or so daily specials chalked on a blackboard)? Or do you choose one of the main courses – Spanish omelette, paellas, steaks, chicken, fish and so forth? Perhaps the best option is to play to La Bota's strengths and order a few tapas, then a few more, until you have subdued your appetite and there's no longer a decision to make. In the meantime enjoy the air conditioning – and the house wine at a very reasonable £7.60.

Start with simple things. Boquerones en vinagre (£3) brings a plate of broad white anchovies with a pleasant vinegar tang. Jamón serrano (£4.20) is thinly sliced, ruby red and strongly flavoured – perfect with the basket of warm French bread that is on every table. Then move on to hot tapas: mejillones pescador (£3.40) is a good-sized plate of mussels in a tomato and garlic sauce; chistorra a la sidra (£3) a mild sausage cooked in cider; rinones al Jerez (£3) is a portion of kidneys in a sherry sauce, rich and good. Alas de pollo barbacoa (£3) is an Iberian take on chicken wings. Then there's arroz al campo (£3) – rice cooked with saffron and vegetables; rabbit cazuela (£3.25); chicken Riojana (£3.25); and patatas bravas (£2), the tasty dish of potatoes in a mildly spicy tomato sauce. Just keep them coming…

If you like squid, and don't mind looking at a whole one, opt for chipirones a la plancha (£3.85) – four squidlets grilled to tender perfection.

Fiction

Opposite a hairdresser called Pulp sits the restaurant named Fiction. Fact. But the restaurant was there first, and it was named after the bookshop whose premises it took over – the hairdressers are the film buffs and named their place accordingly. And there's no gore in the tale, as Fiction is strictly vegetarian, although not in the missionary hair-shirt and holier-than-thou style. Rather, the idea is to rediscover the use of indigenous herbs, and to cook, with plenty of wine, dishes that were popular in the days when people ate a lot less meat than they do now. All dishes and wines are marked as vegetarian, vegan and organic, where relevant.

Cost	£20–£40

Address 60 Crouch End Hill, N8
T 020 8340 3403
Station Finsbury Park/ Highgate
Open Wed–Sat 6.30–10.30pm, Sun 12.30–4pm & 6.30–10.30pm
Accepts MasterCard, Visa
W www.fiction-restaurant .co.uk

While Fiction's menu changes every six to seven weeks, there are a few signature dishes: black truffle pâté (£4.95), served with lemon olives and three-seed crostini, is one of them. It's very rich and very tasty. Or try herby onion polenta cake with a cream and sage sauce (£4.95), or cheesy sweetcorn and coriander fritters served with salad garnish and a delicious sweet chilli sauce (£3.95) – a bit like Thai crab cakes without the crab. The signature main courses are wood-roasted butternut squash (£9.65), and "The Good Gamekeeper's Pie" (£9.85); the former is described fulsomely as "a succulent 'steak' of squash filled with lemon-garlic mushrooms", the latter as "chestnuts, wild mushrooms, 'mock duck', leek, carrot and broccoli, prepared in an old English marinade of red wines, and baked in a puff pastry pie". Both are very nicely flavoured. There's also a take on the Indonesian favourite, gado gado (£8.95) – peanuts, tomatoes, noodles. Side dishes include roast garlic mash with olive oil (£2.70), roast seasonal vegetables in butter and marjoram (£2.95), and the mini power plate – a salad of mixed leaves and organic freshly-sprouted legumes and alfalfa (£3.95). The signature pudding is triple chocolate terrine with fresh berry coulis (£3.95) – just one taste will tell you why it stays on the menu.

The large outdoor area, with its beautifully planted gardens, helps make Fiction a summer favourite but it is essential to book, whatever the season may be.

O's Thai Café

O's Thai Café is young, happy and fresh – just like O himself. With his economics, advertising and fashion-design background, and a staff who seem to be having fun, O brings a youthful zip to Thai cuisine. His café is fast and noisy, and the music is played at high volume. But that's not to say the food is anything less than excellent, and very good value too. Order from the comprehensive and well-explained menu or from the blackboard of specials which runs down an entire wall.

Cost	£10–£25

Address 10 Topsfield Parade, N8
T 020 8348 6898
Station Finsbury Park
Open Mon 6.30–11pm, Tues–Sat noon–3pm & 6.30–11pm, Sun noon–3pm & 6.30–10.30pm
Accepts MasterCard, Visa
W www.oscafeandbars.co.uk

Of the many starters you can do no better than order the special (£7.95 for two), which gives you a taster of almost everything. Satay are tasty, prawn toasts and spring rolls are as crisp as they should be, and paper-wrapped thin dumplings really do melt in the mouth. Tom ka chicken soup (£3.75) is hot and sharp, with lime leaf and lemongrass. Main courses include Thai red and green curries – the gaeng kiew, a spicy, soupy green curry of chicken and coconut cream (£5.50), is pungently moreish – as well as an interesting selection of specials such as yamneau, aka weeping tiger (£9.50) – sliced, spiced, grilled steak served on salad with a pungent Thai dressing. If you like noodles, order a pad mee si iew (£5.50), a stir-fry of vermicelli with vegetables, soy sauce, peanuts and the main ingredient of your choice: chicken, beef, pork, king prawn or bean curd. Puddings include khow tom mud – banana with sticky rice wrapped in banana leaf (£1.95), Thai ice cream (£2.50), and fruit fritters served with golden syrup and ice cream (£2.50). There is a wide and varied wine list, with Budweiser, Budvar, Gambrinus and Leffe beers on draught. O's does takeaway too.

If you're new to Thai food, O's is a good place to learn, as the staff are happy to explain how it all works and you can specify how hot you like your food. Most main courses are around £6, which makes for very good value, and all of them are served with a delightfully moulded mountain of rice which is included in the price. They also offer a discount if you eat early and vacate your table by 8.30pm.

The Parsee

London has had an aclaimed Parsee chef for some years now. His name is Cyrus Todiwalha and his main restaurant is Café Spice Namaste (see p.183). Since 2001, however, London has also had what may be the world's best Parsee restaurant (there have been murmurings about the other one in Bombay). Parsees are Zoroastrians who originally came to India from Persia, and in Indian society they seem to have specialized as surgeons and politicians. They are also renowned for their love of food – and for being the most demanding of customers. They start from the admirable standpoint that nothing beats home cooking and complain vehemently if everything is not exactly to their liking. They will be at home in this part of North London, and happy at Cyrus Todiwalah's new restaurant.

Cost	£15–£40
Address	34 Highgate Hill, N19
T	020 7272 9091
Station	Archway
Open	Daily noon–3pm & 6–11pm
Accepts	All major credit cards
W	www.theparsee.co.uk

The food here is very good. Honest, strong flavours; rich and satisfying. Start with the admirable home-style akoori on toast (£3.75) – splendid, spiced, scrambled egg; or the tarka na bhajia (£3.25) – light and delicious vegetable fritters; or maybe the lamb chops from the grill, laal masala na champ (£6.50/£13.95) – juicy and spicy. Main courses include that most famous of Parsee dishes, the dhansak (£10.95), a rich dish of lamb and lentils served with a pulao flavoured with star anise and little crisp meatballs. Then there's the patra ni machchi (£9.25), for which a whole pomfret fish is marinated in green spice paste and steamed in a banana leaf; or the murgh ni curry nay chawal (£10.25), which is a richer-than-rich Parsee chicken curry made with roasted chickpeas, peanuts, cashew nuts and sesame seeds. The breads – rotli (£1.25 for two) – are very good: nutty and moreish. The vegetable dishes are good too: khattu mitthu stew (£3.75/£7.25) seems to contain an entire market garden, and is a popular dish at Parsee weddings. Save room for the toffee apricot ice cream (£3.75), rich with concentrated Hunza apricots.

This is a friendly, small, "family" restaurant serving delicious and unfamiliar Indian food. An adventure well worth having.

The Village Bistro

FRENCH

Having served French food of varying fashionability for decades, The Village Bistro is something of an institution in Highgate. You can almost forget you're in London here; all is quaint and countrified in this narrow Georgian house approached by a corridor off Highgate's main road. Inside can be a bit of a squeeze, and the decor is all chintzy curtains and crooked paintings, but any sense that you're sitting in an old aunt's living room is swept away by the food, which is Modern French. Presumably this combination of ancient and modern is exactly what hits the spot in Highgate, as this restaurant is, and has been, consistently successful. Downstairs, the windows peek out onto the hilly High Street, while a spindly, winding staircase leads upstairs to the smokers' floor.

Cost	£20–£42

Address 38 Highgate High St, N6
T 020 8340 5165
Station Highgate/Archway
Open Mon–Sat noon–3pm & 6–11pm
Accepts All major credit cards

Come here hungry: sauces can be rich and dishes very filling. The menu, which changes every few months, includes a range of old stalwarts along with a sprinkling of more contemporary creations. A really tasty starter is deep-fried goat's cheese with dried tomatoes, rocket and green olive dressing (£6.25). Also good is the Parma ham with French beans, pear, soft-boiled egg and walnuts (£6.95). Traditionalists might opt for the fine French onion soup with cheese croutons (£3.95), or, in season, asparagus with Hollandaise sauce (£6.50). There's a good choice of main dishes, and always two specials – dishes like a panaché of seafood with Parmesan, lemon and olive oil (£13.50). For a well-judged mix of flavours and textures, go for the veal fillet with Madeira, wild mushrooms and parsnip puree (£14.50). Or you might try sauté of monkfish and king prawns in garlic butter on a crab and herb tartlette (£15.95), or maybe sirloin steak glazed with Stilton and green peppercorn sauce (£14.95).

Desserts (all £4.50) can be solid and formidable. The white chocolate parfait with dark chocolate truffle is not for anyone wearing tight clothing. The classic crème brûlée, and crêpe filled with vanilla ice cream and hot raspberry sauce, are wiser choices, although still satisfactorily self-indulgent. From Monday to Saturday there is a set lunch at £13.50 for two courses; on Sunday it's £14.95 for three.

Holloway & Highbury

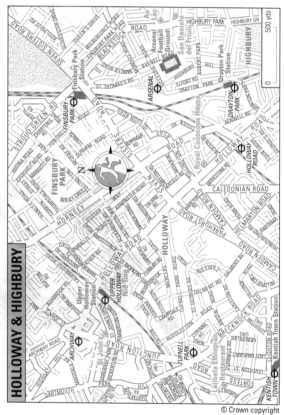

HOLLOWAY & HIGHBURY

© Crown copyright

Au Lac

Vietnamese restaurants in London tend to divide into two camps. On the one hand there is the spartan canteen – no frills, no nonsense and no concessions to non-Vietnamese speakers. And on the other there is a sprinkling of glossy, West End establishments that charge big bucks and would be puzzled if you wanted authenticity. Au Lac doesn't fall into either of these categories. For a start, it is hidden away in Highbury and, what is more, it is a genuinely family-run restaurant – the dining room is comfortable in an informal, shabby sort of way, there are knick-knacks on the walls, and the family cover all the bases from the kitchen to the front of house.

Cost	£8–£25
Address	82 Highbury Park, N5
T	020 7704 9187
Station	Arsenal
Open	Mon–Fri noon–2.30pm & 5.30–11pm, Sat & Sun 5.30–11pm
Accepts	MasterCard, Visa

VIETNAMESE

Start with goi cuon (two for £2.20). These are soft rice-flour pancakes wrapped around crunchy veg and large grilled prawns. Fresh and light. Then there's goi tom (£6) – you get large steamed prawns, a small pot of hot and spicy sauce, and several large iceberg lettuce leaves. Take a leaf, add sauce and prawn, wrap, eat, enjoy. The deep-fried squid with chilli (£5.50) is very good. There are good soups, too. The noodle soups – pho, bun bo and tom hue – come in large portions. They are cheap and tasty, good for eating when alone. For a more sociable, sharing meal, try the sea-spiced chicken (£4.80) – this is a well-spiced stir fry of chicken with bamboo shoots and black mushrooms. The noodles are also very good – pho xao do bien (£5) is a grand dish of stir-fried rice noodles with fresh herbs and seafood, providing a good combination of flavours and textures. Another very impressive dish is the "minced pork with dried fish and aubergine in hot pot" (£6). Ordering this brings a small casserole whose contents appear almost black. Very dark, very rich, very tasty.

Lurking in the drinks section is "Vietnamese sake". This potion was the one thing from his homeland that the head of the household (now banished to the kitchen) pined for. So the family made it for him. This clear hooch is served warm, and tastes like dry cleaning fluid. To enjoy it you would have to be very homesick indeed.

Lalibela Ethiopian Restaurant

The real Lalibela is a twelfth-century Ethiopian church carved in the shape of a cross from a huge outcrop of solid rock. Its namesake in Tufnell Park is remarkable for serving uncomp-romisingly authentic Ethiopian food and for its genuine understanding of hospitality. It has a slightly harassed, but still laid-back, feel that is a great comfort to the diner. And, however ignorant of Ethiopian cuisine and customs you may be, pure ungild&d hospitality shines through. Upstairs, you will be seated on low, carved, wooden seats around traditional low tables (so that you can eat with your hands). If your knee joints won't take that kind of punishment, ask for a table downstairs and resign yourself to dripping sauce down your front.

Cost	£10–£30

Address 137 Fortess Rd, NW5
T 020 7284 0600
Station Tufnell Park
Open Mon–Thurs 6pm–midnight, Fri–Sun 6–11pm
Accepts All major credit cards except Diners

Starters are few, but they banish any inkling you may have about being in an odd kind of curry house. The lamb samosas (£3.25) have very dry, papery pastry and a savoury, spicy filling – delicious. The Lalibela salad (£3.25) is potatoes and beetroot fried together with a spicy sauce and served hot. Main courses are served traditionally, that is to say as pools of sauce set out on a two-foot-diameter injera bread. Injera is cold, made from fermented sourdough, and thin. You tear off a piece and use it to pick up something tasty. Portions are small, which makes prices seem high. But flavours are intense. If you prefer, you can have the dishes with rice or mashed potato. What goes on the injera? Wot, that's what … doro wot (£6) – a piece of chicken and a hard-boiled egg in a rich sauce; or begh wot (£5.85) – lamb with a bit more chilli. Lalibela ketfo (£7.50) is savoury mince and amazing, highly spiced, cottage cheese – delicious. King prawn special (£6.50) is prawns in a tomato, onion and chilli sauce.

Do try the Ethiopian traditional coffee (£5), which is not only delicious, but also something of a feast for the eyes. After parading a small wok full of smoking coffee beans through the restaurant, the staff bring it to you in a round-bottomed coffeepot on a plaited quoit.

Nid Ting

What are restaurants for? Some pundits would have you believe that restaurants are for posing in; some that their mission is to entertain. Nid Ting is a place that feeds people. Lots of them. And it feeds people well, serving good, unfussy Thai food. The dishes here have not been tamed to suit effete Western palates, and you'll get plenty of chilli heat and pungent fish sauce. You'll also get good value and brisk service – both of which obviously appeal, as the place is usually packed. This is a genuine neighbourhood restaurant at ease with its surroundings.

Cost	£8–£20

Address 533 Holloway Rd, N19
T 020 7263 0506
Station Archway
Open Mon–Sat 6–11.15pm, Sun 6–10.15pm
Accepts All major credit cards

The starters are neat platefuls of mainly fried food: chicken satay (£3.95) is sound, although the sauce is a bland one; a much better bet is the "pork on toasted" (£3.95) – this is a smear of rich, meaty paste on a disc of fried bread. The prawns tempura (£4.95) are large and crisp, and the peek ka yas sai (£3.95) is very successful – stuffed chicken wings are battered and deep fried. The menu then darts off into numerous sections: there are hot and sour soups; clear soups; salads; curries; stir fries; seafood; rice; noodle dishes; and a long, long list of vegetarian dishes – all before you get to the chef's specials. From those specials, try the lamb Mussaman curry (£8.75), which is rich and good, made with green chillies and coconut milk. From the noodles, try pad see ew (£5.50), a rich dish made with thick ribbon noodles and your choice of chicken, beef or pork. As a side order, try the som tum (£4.50), which is a pleasingly astringent green papaya salad. Also worth noting is the pla muk kaprow (£6.95), a dish of squid with chilli, garlic and Thai basil; and the koong kra prow (£6.95), which is a dish of prawns that have been given the same treatment.

One of the commonest criticisms of Thai food is that it can be insubstantial, and that dishes can start out looking cheap but end up as pretty bad value when portion size is taken into account. This is not the case at Nid Ting. Here, the cooking is accomplished, and dishes arrive both immaculately presented and in man-sized helpings.

Royal Couscous House

Karim Menhal, the diffident young man dressed in immaculate whites, is billed as head chef here. He also manages to do the bills, run the bar, wait on tables and hold open the front door. Described as "handsome" in one of the many admiring restaurant review clippings that adorn the front window, he certainly has a way about him. His restaurant is long, and the tables are topped with oilcloth. The walls are lined with Moroccan tourist posters, cheap carpets (you have to hope they are cheap, as they've been nailed to the decorative wood cladding) and pretend firearms. The food is very fresh, very tasty and very good value, and Mr Menhal keeps the service well up to scratch.

Cost	£11–£26
Address	316 Holloway Rd, N7
T	020 7700 2188
Station	Holloway Road
Open	Tues–Sun 5–11pm
Accepts	MasterCard, Visa

Begin with an array of starters and hot bread. The bread is particularly tasty. The aubergine dip (£2.20) is amazing, with chopped aubergines that have been cooked and cooked to concentrate the flavour. Smoked pepper (£2) is made with strips of roasted green peppers. Even the spicy olives (£1) are worthy of note – black and green olives with chunks of red chilli. Then there's the merguez salad (£3.95) – a few links of the small and spicy lamb sausages with a terrific tomatoey sauce and some salad. Main courses split into couscous and tagines. The laksour couscous (£8.95) is a combination of lamb, merguez and mixed vegetables, with light and nicely cooked couscous. Royal tagine (£7.95) is a classic Moroccan dish of lamb with prunes, sesame seeds and slices of boiled egg – sweet and rich. Tafraout tagine (£6.95) is made from chicken with olives and those wholly delicious brine-preserved Moroccan lemons. For pudding, try the seffae (£2.50) – a mound of couscous cooked in butter, sugar, cinnamon and almonds. Finish with mint tea (£1.20) or Moroccan coffee (£1.20) – a kind of heavily spiced cappuccino.

You can BYOB and incur a corkage of just £1 per person, but the Moroccan wine list features eight honest wines (all reasonably priced at £8.99 to £13.99) – a far cry from the days when proudly producing a bottle of Moroccan red was enough to strike fear into the heart of any dinner party guest.

St John's

Archway's unprepossessing Junction Road is an unlikely setting for this fine gastro-pub, where the emphasis is firmly on the gastro rather than on the pub. The food is broadly Mediterranean, with a passion for all things rich, earthy and flavoursome, and there's a real joie de vivre in the combinations of tastes, textures and colours. Not only that, the dining room, which lies beyond the pub itself, looks fabulous – all louche, junk-store glamour with its high, gold-painted ceiling, low chandeliers and plush banquettes. There's an open kitchen at one end of the room, while at the other a giant blackboard displays the long menu. You get lots of food here, so be sure to arrive hungry.

Cost	£12–£35
Address	91 Junction Rd, N19
T	020 7272 1587
Station	Archway
Open	Mon 6.30–11pm, Tues–Sat noon–4pm & 6.30–11pm, Sun noon–4pm & 6.30–10.30pm
Accepts	All major credit cards except Amex

MEDITERRANEAN/PUB

As an opening move, friendly staff bring fresh white bread and bottles of virgin olive oil and balsamic vinegar. The menu changes day by day but you might find starters like smoked halibut, white and green bean and rocket salad with tarragon dressing (£5.50). The food is robust and piled high on the plate: how about a warm salad of pigeon breast, black pudding, pancetta, quails' eggs and beetroot with mustard dressing (£5.75)? Or, on a simpler note, pea, ham and parsley soup with Parmesan croutons (£4)? Main courses range from the traditional – char-grilled rib-eye steak with roast tomatoes, chips, watercress and green peppercorn sauce (£13) – to the adventurous – seared swordfish, chermoula spices, roast red pepper and herb couscous (£12). The fish is invariably good: perhaps roast dorade, sauté potatoes, spinach, caper, almond and parsley butter (£11). You'll need to take a breather before venturing into pud territory (all £4.25). The rhubarb and raspberry crumble with ginger ice cream is good, but the star turn must be the blissful strawberry and clotted cream fool with shortbread. The intelligent wine list includes a dozen by the glass, with a Cava at £5.

St John's gets more crowded and more convivial as the night goes on, but it is possible to have a dîner à deux; just make sure you're ready to be romantic by 7.30pm, when you've a chance of getting a table. You should book, whatever time you come.

San Daniele del Friuli

Highbury Park is a strange place to find a football club. Lots of grand, renovated houses, wide streets, trees and, just a stroll around the corner, there's the Arsenal. Don't attempt to go to San Daniele on match days, when it will be full of happy, very respectable, middle-class footie fans loading up on Italian grub before braving the bitter wind to watch the Gunners. San Daniele opened in the summer of 1996, with a

Cost	£27–£50

Address 72 Highbury Park, N5
T 020 7226 1609
Station Arsenal
Open Mon 8.30–10.45pm, Tues–Fri noon–2.30pm & 8.30–10.45pm, Sat 8.30–10.45pm
Accepts MasterCard, Visa

chef from Friuli – that bit of Italy in the extreme northeast around Trieste. The dining room is large and airy, and manages to combine echoes of the old, giant-pepperpot-style Italian restaurants with the more spartan modern look. The service is family-style, both attentive and informal, and the dishes lean that way as well, being substantial and unfussy. The menu is a long one. So unless nostalgia gets the upper hand and you are swept away on a wave of desire for whitebait or insalata tricolore, pay special attention to the "altri Friuliani" (regional delicacies) and to the chef's specials.

The cooking here scales no modern gastronomic heights, and it is not cheap, but portions are large and the hospitality wholehearted. Simple things are well presented, like the vegetali grigliati (£4.50) – grilled vegetables with olive oil; the insalata di mare misto (£6) – a seafood salad; or the excellent prosciutto di San Daniele (£6.50), served plain or with melon. Or there's the pasticcio alla Friulana (£6.50), a lasagne made with speck and Asagio cheese. There are also risotto and pasta dishes, from an imaginative daily specials board. For a main course you can choose between a dozen different Neapolitan pizzas, fresh fish dishes and lots of old favourites – the huge calves' liver (£11) comes in a classic butter and sage sauce and is accurately cooked to order. Scallopine di vitello (£7.50) is trad veal escalope and there are several options by way of sauce including the classic Marsala and black peppers.

For pudding there is an old-fashioned tiramisù (£4), rich with alcohol and mascarpone – delightfully different from the fluffy, faffy fakes that are all the rage in the W-fronted postcodes.

Islington

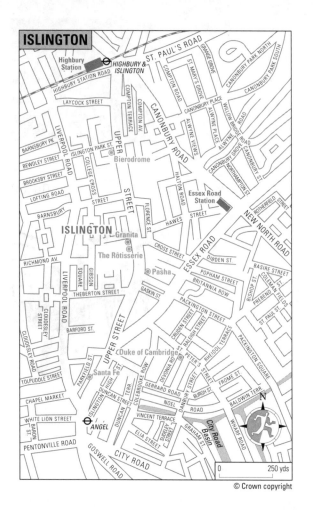

ISLINGTON

Highbury Station
HIGHBURY & ISLINGTON

HIGHBURY STATION ROAD

ST. PAUL'S ROAD

LAYCOCK STREET

BARNSBURY PK.

BEWDLEY STREET

BROOKSBY STREET

LOFTING ROAD

BARNSBURY

RICHMOND AV.

CLOUDESLEY STREET

CLOUDESLEY ROAD

TOLPUDDLE STREET

CHAPEL MARKET

WHITE LION STREET

BARON ST.

PENTONVILLE ROAD

LIVERPOOL ROAD

ISLINGTON PARK ST.

COLLEGE CROSS

UPPER STREET

Bierodrome

ISLINGTON

Granita

The Rôtisserie

GIBSON SQUARE

Pasha

THEBERTON STREET

GASKIN ST.

BARFORD ST.

LIVERPOOL ROAD

UPPER STREET

PARKFIELD ST.

Duke of Cambridge

Santa Fe

ISLINGTON HIGH ST.

DUNCAN TERR.

DUNCAN STREET

COLEBROOKE ROW

VINCENT TERRACE

ELIA STREET

ANGEL

CITY ROAD

GOSWELL ROAD

COMPTON TERRACE

COMPTON AV.

CANONBURY ROAD

HALTON ROAD

FLORENCE ST.

CROSS STREET

HAWES STREET

COMPTON ROAD

ST. MARY'S GROVE

GRANGE GROVE

CANONBURY PLACE

CANONBURY GROVE

ALWYNE VILLAS

ALWYNE PLACE

ALWYNE ROAD

CANONBURY PARK NORTH

CANONBURY PARK SOUTH

WILLOW BRIDGE ROAD

ALWYNE ROAD

CANONBURY NORTHAMPTON ST.

CANONBURY RD.

Essex Road Station

ESSEX ROAD

DIBDEN ST.

POPHAM STREET

BRITANNIA ROW

PACKINGTON STREET

CRUDEN STREET

RALEIGH STREET

ST. PETER'S STREET

RHEIDOL TERRACE

GERRARD ROAD

DANBURY STREET

NOEL ROAD

BURGH ST.

SURLEY STREET

DANBURY ST.

GRAHAM ST.

City Road Basin

NEW NORTH ROAD

ROTHERFIELD STREET

BASIRE STREET

COLEMAN FIELDS

BISHOP

PREBEND STREET

ST. PAUL ST.

PACKINGTON SQUARE

FROME ST.

BALDWIN TERR.

WHARF ROAD

N

0   250 yds

© Crown copyright

Bierodrome

Bierodrome is part of the Belgo empire (see p.32), and shares their emphasis on modernist and iconoclastic architecture. The long, low bar is a temple to beer, and with that beer you can eat if you wish. The menu introduces a change of pace from the other branches – yes, there is life after mussels! Here there are "tartines", or smart snacks, along with steaks, lobsters, croquettes and frites. Surprisingly enough, the beeriness runs amok in the dessert section, where, as well as a sorbet made from cherry beer, there is an ice cream made with Leffe blond beer. There's another Bierodrome in South London, at 40–44 Clapham High St (☎020 7720 1118).

Cost	£7–£55

Address 173–174 Upper St, N1
T 020 7226 5835
Station Highbury & Islington
Open Daily noon–11pm
Accepts All major credit cards
W www.belgo.restaurants .com

It is no surprise that when the Bierodrome first opened they found that the customers were walking off with the beer and wine list. It makes stunning reading, with more than seventy beers to pore over and ultimately pour out. At random, consider: a banana beer – Chapeau Tropical 25cl (£2.55); a very strong beer – Kasteel bier Ingelmunster 11% 75cl (£11.75); and a very expensive beer – La Gauloise Brune 75cl (£124!). As you work your way through your delicious malty glassful, what you will need is some food. Croquettes make good starters: try the Trappist cheese with piccalilli (£4.50). Salads are tasty: Liègeoise (£4.50) teams bacon, tomatoes, French beans, onions, boiled egg and new potatoes. Then there are the famous Belgo mussel pots: a kilo pot costs £9.95 and can be had marinière, Provençale, Dijon or even Congo – the latter cooked with creamed coconut and lemongrass. Or there's half a spit-roast chicken with frites (£7.50). Steaks include a 6oz sirloin with frites, salad, tomatoes and garlic butter (£10.95). There are lunch bargains – tarte à l'onion followed by half a chicken followed by chocolate mocha costs £5.

The atmosphere in this place is much as you'd expect with a raft of strong beers on offer. And the huge Nebuchadnezzars containing fifteen litres of La Veille Bon Secours, at a thought-provoking £635 a pop? They do not sell those quite so quickly as the others!

Duke of Cambridge

In the canon of organic, things don't get much holier than this, the first gastro-pub to be certified by the Soil Association. Game and fish are either wild or caught from sustainable resources, and the forty-strong wine list is ninety-five percent organic. There's a small bookable restaurant at the back, but most diners prefer to share the tables in the noisy front bar – the Duke is for the gregarious as well as the organic battal-

Cost	£15–£35
Address	30 St Peter's St, N1
T	020 7359 3066
Station	Angel
Open	Mon–Fri 12.30–3pm & 6.30–10.30pm, Sat 12.30–3.30pm & 6.30–10.30pm, Sun 12.30–3.30pm & 6.30–10pm
Accepts	All major credit cards
W	www.singhboulton.co.uk

ions. And it now has a sibling, The Crown Organic Pub in Victoria Park (020 8981 9998).

The blackboard menu changes twice daily and is commendably short; you order from the bar. Robust bread with good olive oil and grey sea salt is served while you wait. Starters may include white bean and chilli soup with greens (£4) or chicken liver pâté with pickles, relish and toast (£5). Main courses are an eclectic bunch: a char-grilled whole grey mullet may be partnered with sweetened red cabbage and couscous (£9), while seared scallops come with sautéed potatoes, bacon and spinach (£10.50) – tasty and fulfilling. Roast loin of lamb is stuffed with tapenade and served with pepperonata and polenta chips (£14). Portions are serious, a million miles away from bar snacks. There are vegetarian choices too, such as a potato and mushroom pie with mixed leaves (£7.50). Puddings include plum and apple crumble – with custard, of course (£5); and a chocolate, prune and praline cake with crème fraîche (£5). The wines are well-chosen and varied, with a Greek Domaine Spiropoulos Porfyros at £16, and a New Zealand Te Aria Malbec at £21.

There are also many unusual bottled beers and non-alcoholic drinks, all organic. Connoisseurs will seek out the deliciously light and refreshing Eco Warrior ale, or the Freedom Brewery's organic Pilsener. But the zenith of the beer list must be Singhboulton ale. The Pitfield Brewery brews this rich, organic beer exclusively for the Duke of Cambridge, and it is named after the owners, Geetie Singh and Esther Boulton.

Granita

Architecturally minimalist, modern and very Islington, Granita is stark when empty at 7.30pm, but comes to life from 9pm when it fills with locals who look upon it as their local. Run by Vicky Leffman, front of house, and Ahmed Kharshoum, in the kitchen, it offers some interesting modern ideas with influences from the Mediterranean and beyond. The menu is short, with around six starters and five main courses, and changes weekly as, according to Vicky, Granita's customers visit often and seek variety.

Cost	£17–£45

Address 127 Upper St, N1
T 020 7226 3222
Station Highbury & Islington/Angel
Open Tues 6.30–10.30pm, Wed–Sat 12.30–2.30pm & 6.30–10.30pm, Sun 12.30–3pm & 6.30–10pm
Accepts MasterCard, Visa

A typical starter at Granita is grilled squid with marinated red chicory and chilli oil (£7.50); or real buffalo Mozzarella in crème fraîche with red pepper, olives and toast (£6.50) – both determinedly Mediterranean flavours. Or you might find lentils with lemon, olive oil, cumin, yoghurt and flat bread (£5.95) – equally simple. For the main course, new season's chump of lamb, char-grilled, with a butter bean, rosemary, lemon and olive oil stew and a spinach salad (£14.95); or char-grilled sea bass with aubergine and tomato pillaf, sweet onion and rocket (£14.95). The menu may also include a plain dish like Welsh rib of beef, braised green beans and chips (£14.50), which simply demonstrates Granita's versatility. There are no side dishes on offer, so whatever you order comes as complete as the descriptions promise. Puddings may feature a hot parkin pudding with butterscotch and cream (£4.95), and other satisfyingly, tooth-cringeingly sweet offerings like caramel ice cream with fudge sauce (£4.95). There is an excellent selection of sweet wines too, including Elysium black muscat (£3.95) from the US, which is almost sherry-like in its density, and a luxurious Tokaji Aszu 5 put-tonus – the sweetest of Hungary's Tokajis (£4.95). The wine list is equally cosmopolitan, though with more choices from the New World than the Old.

Tony Blair was a famed Granita habitué, prior to his ascension, and the place is still a favourite with North London's social intelligentsia. Set lunches of two (£13.50) and three (£15.50) courses are good value. It's advisable to book, whatever time you plan to eat.

TURKISH

Pasha

If you picture Turkish food as heavy and oil-slicked, think again. Pasha is dedicated to producing fresh, light, authentic Turkish food that's more suited to modern tastes. Dishes are made with virgin olive oil, fresh herbs, strained yoghurts and fresh ingredients prepared daily. It doesn't look like a traditional Turkish restaurant either, being open and airy with only the odd brass pot for deco-

Cost	£15–£30

Address 301 Upper St, N1
T 020 7226 1454
Station Angel
Open Mon–Fri noon–3pm & 6–11.30pm, Sat & Sun noon–midnight
Accepts All major cards except Switch

ration. The management describe it as "Modern Ottoman". It has clearly adapted well to its Upper Street location – so well, in fact, that the wine list offers spritzer for £2.95.

For anyone new to Turkish cooking the menu is a delight. Dishes are clearly described so that you can try them on a no-risk basis. Staff are helpful and will encourage you to eat in Turkish style with lots of small "meze" dishes. There are set menus (minimum two people) of £10.95 for thirteen meze and £17.95 for a Pasha Feast, which gives diners ten meze plus main courses, dessert and coffee. Meze may include hummus, tarama, cacik, kisir – a splendid bulghur wheat concoction – falafel, courgette fritters, meatballs and a host of others. Other noteworthy starters include Albanian liver (£3.95), which is lamb's liver served with finely chopped onions and sumac. Main courses are more familiar – a selection of kebabs and the like – but again there is a better than usual choice. Try kilic baligi (£10.95) – fillet of swordfish marinated in lime, bay leaf and herbs and served with rice; Pasha kofte (£7.50) – the standard minced lamb kebab, but well-seasoned and well-presented; or istim kebab (£8.95) – roasted aubergine filled with cubes of lamb, green peppers and tomatoes with rice; or yogurtlu iskender (£8.45) – a trio of shish, kofte and chicken on pitta bread soaked in fresh tomato sauce with fresh herbs and topped with yoghurt. Though meat undeniably dominates the menu, there are five vegetarian and three fish selections. Puddings include the usual Turkish stickies but once again are light and freshly made.

Wines are priced fairly, there is Efes beer from Turkey (£2.50), and that powerful spirit raki (£2.95) for a tongue-numbing blast of the real Middle East.

The Rôtisserie

The Rôtisserie is buzzing, brightly painted and unpretentious, with a commitment to quality underlying both food and service. Its South African owner makes regular trips to Scotland to lean on the farm gate and make small talk about Aberdeen Angus steers (which, if they did but know it, will soon be visiting his grill), and his menu's claim, "Famous for our steaks", seems well earned. The kitchen also frets about the quality of their chips, which is no bad thing, as the classic

Cost   £15–£30

Address 134 Upper St, N1
T 020 7226 0122
Station Highbury & Islington/
Angel
Open Mon & Tues 6–11pm,
Wed–Fri noon–3pm &
6–11pm, Sat noon–11pm,
Sun noon–10pm
Accepts All major credit cards
W www.rotisserie.co.uk

combination of a well-grilled steak with decent frites and Béarnaise sauce is one of life's little luxuries. The restaurant's success is shared by two other branches, offering much the same menu, at 56 Uxbridge Rd, Shepherd's Bush, W12 (☎020 8743 3028) and 316 Uxbridge Rd, Hatch End, Middlesex (☎020 8421 2878).

Rôtisserie starters are sensibly simple: a good Caesar salad (£3.95), tiger prawns peri peri (£4.95), char-grilled vegetable salad with balsamic (£4.25). Having brushed aside these preliminaries, on to the steaks, all Scottish Aberdeen Angus; 225g rib-eye (£12.95); 300g sirloin (£14.95); 200g fillet (£14.95) – carefully chosen, carefully hung, carefully cooked. All of them (and all other main courses) come with a good-sized bowl of frites. Since the vanquishing of the fatuous beef-on-the-bone ban there is now a 400g T-bone (£15.95). If you don't want steak, try one of the other rôtisserie items, such as the French, corn-fed chicken leg and thigh (£5.95); or the wonderful spit-roasted Barbary duck – half a duck with fruit chutney (£12.95). The rest of the menu covers the bases for non-meat eaters. There's a grilled fish of the day (£11.95), or vegetable brochettes with spiced rice (£7.95). Puddings are sound, and range from apple and cinnamon cake with hot caramel (£3.50) to home-made ice cream (£3.50).

The South African influence is a constant lurking presence behind these chunks of grilled meat, so expect "monkey gland" sauce – rich and dark, made to a secret recipe rumoured to include both Coca-Cola and Mrs Ball's Chutney.

SOUTHWEST AMERICAN

Santa Fe

Two words are banned at Santa Fe. They are Tex and Mex. The chef (one Rocky Durham – a name which sounds so appropriate that it must be his own) would like the cuisine at Santa Fe to be described as "American Mexican", presumably to distance his creations from the T and M words, and from the strange southwestern dishes that feature on some London menus. The restaurant is quiet at lunchtimes but gets very busy in the evenings and at week-ends. Symbols are used to classify dishes as hot, healthy low-fat, and vegetarian.

Cost	£20–£45

Address 75 Upper St, N1
T 020 7288 2288
Station Angel
Open Mon–Fri noon–
10.30pm, Sat noon–11pm,
Sun noon–10pm
Accepts All major credit cards
except Diners

Lovers of the margarita (£4.15 to £20) will be able to indulge, as there are eleven different versions on offer, together with nineteen classic cocktails (£4.15 to £6.25) and beers like Negra Modelo (£2.95). You are encouraged to plan your meal over drinks and tortilla chips with salsa (£2.95). Start with a flauta – a warm, crisp tortilla – filled with roast chicken, Jack cheese and pico de gallo salsa (£3.95); or shrimp ceviche (£3.95) – tiger prawns marinated in a zesty vegetable relish, with lime and chilli. Or try five different starters in a Santa Fe sampler (£9.95). Tastes are fresh and clean, but dishes are hot unless you specify otherwise. For mains, try Santa Fe steak and fries (£12.95), or rack of lamb adovado (£12.95). The steak is spice-rubbed and served with fresh salsa and chilli-dusted chips; the lamb is chilli-marinated, grilled and served with chilli mashed potatoes and dried fruit chutney. The different chillies bring out the flavours well and make dishes very moreish. It is possible to escape the chilli, but this isn't the place for anyone who likes bland food. There's also a southwest Caesar salad (£4.00/£5.75) with tortilla chips and, yes you guessed it, a chilli-spiked dressing. Puddings include Santa Fe cheesecake (£3.50), which comes with cinnamon-spiced whipped cream, and brownie with canela ice cream (£3.65), which is very rich, and doubly warm combined with the cinnamon ice cream. There are separate lunch and dinner menus, lunch featuring some lighter and more wrap-based dishes.

Santa Fe is a great venue for groups who prefer cocktails and beer to wine, and who like their food chilli-spicy. Quiet and mild it isn't.

Maida Vale & Kilburn

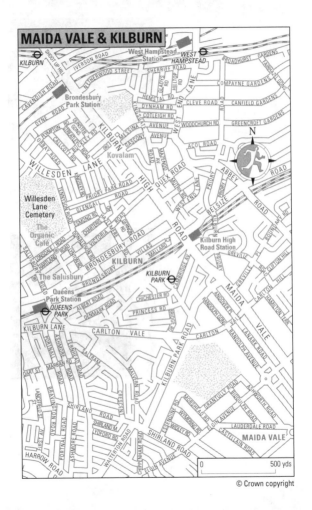

MAIDA VALE & KILBURN

© Crown copyright

Kovalam

In the 1960s and 1970s, Willesden Lane was something of a magnet for curry lovers, as it boasted a couple of London's first authentic South Indian vegetarian establishments. These places shocked diners, who at that time were "curry and chips at closing time" sort of folk, by serving cheap and honest veggie food that included such exotica as dosas. Over the years, other parts of town have caught up, and Willesden Lane is no longer the cutting edge of curry, but that

Cost	£10–£25

Address 12 Willesden Lane, NW6

T 020 7625 4761

Station BR West Hampstead/ Brondesbury Park

Open Sun–Thurs noon– 2.30pm & 6–11.15pm, Fri & Sat noon–2.30pm & 6–11.45pm

Accepts MasterCard, Visa

did not dissuade some South Indian entrepreneurs from taking over the curry house at number 12, at the begining of 2001, and relaunching it as "Kovalam – South Indian cuisine". As is the current vogue, Kovalam offers racey fish, seafood and meat dishes, as well as vegetarian favourites.

Kovalam is a brightly lit if traditionally decorated restaurant, where the best dishes are the specials, rather than the curry-house staples that creep onto the list, So think authentic and order accordingly. Start with the ghee-roast masala dosa (£4.95), which is large, crisp and buttery … and has a suitably chilli-hot potato heart. Ordering the cashewnut pakoda (£2.95) brings a good, big helping of the deep-fried nuts. The paripu vada with chutney (£1.90) are very good – crisp lentil cakes with good, coconutty chutney. For your main courses, look closely at the vegetable dishes and the specials: aviyal (£4.25) is creamy with coconut; and there is kaya thoran (£2.50) – green bananas with grated coconut, shallots and mustard. The koonthal masala (£5.25) is a "worth trying" – it's squid in a very rich sauce that has been sharpened with tamarind; the sauce may be a bit too creamy and korma-like for some, but it's very good. Also try the aaterechi fry (£4.95) – dry-fried cubes of lamb with onion, curry leaves and black pepper – very tender and very tasty. Or perhaps the kadachachka kootan (£3.90) – a dish of curried breadfruit, heavy with coconut? The breads are good, as are the scented plain rices – lemon (£1.95) and coconut (£1.95).

Do not be fooled by the terminology of the menu. Aaterechi Madras sounds authentic, but *aaterechi* is just a South Indian word for lamb, and this is our old friend, meat Madras, in disguise. In fact, the menu includes a good many curry house dishes masquerading under new, "authentic" names.

The Organic Café

The Organic Café is a real treat. Even for those whose heart sinks when confronted with such an obviously worthy establishment, this is a genuine neighbourhood gem in a quiet, semi-private road. When it is too cold to enjoy one of the pavement tables, enter instead the largish blue-painted dining room, decorated with branches of twisted fig and reclaimed chicken-wire light fittings, and relax. Though many Londoners still find the idea of a restaurant that serves wholly organic food a bit suspect, there is nothing alternative about the quality of the cooking here.

Cost	£17–£35

Address 21–25 Lonsdale Rd, NW6
T 020 7372 1232
Station Queens Park
Open Mon noon–5pm, Tues–Sun 9.30am–5pm & 7–10.30pm
Accepts MasterCard, Visa
W www.organiccafe.co.uk

The menu changes sporadically and is divided traditionally into starters, mains and puds, with the addition of one-course dishes consisting of salads and pastas. But you can mix and match as you wish. Vegetarian choices are exceptionally good, but there is plenty for meat eaters as well. The cooking is reasonably classical and well grounded, with little that is unnecessarily fancy. Expect a couple of soups – pumpkin and coconut (£4.50), perhaps, or an antipasto platter (£4.90). Or confit of duck leg with braised Puy lentils and red wine jus (£6.50). Thereafter there are four main sections – veggie mains; fish mains; meat mains and steaks. So … seared, marinated tofu with wok-fried egg noodles and sweet soy dressing (£10.80) vies for attention with grilled salmon fillet with roasted fennel and an orange butter sauce (£13.20); while braised lamb shank with vegetable couscous and harissa dressing (£11.50) competes with the stunning steaks – organic Welsh beef sirloin with frites and Béarnaise sauce (£16.80). Puddings (£4.80) are on the heavy side – chocolate and marquise with apple and lemon sauce, say, or sweet potato and coconut terrine. The organic drinks list is short, but there is a range of wines, beers, spirits and juices.

Most of the customers (many of whom are families) are regulars. There is no music to disturb animated conversations – except for jazz on Sunday nights – and service is informal but efficient. Lunchtime is brunchtime.

The Salusbury

On the surface, the Salusbury is a straightforward pub in the middle of a parade of shops. It's fun and friendly and clearly a home from home for a table-hopping crowd who all seem to know one another. To get to the restaurant, you shoulder your way through the packed bar to find a quieter room filled with the kind of tables your mum had in her living room, stripped and scrubbed, with a display of eclectic art lining the walls.

Cost	£16–£35

Address 50–52 Salusbury Rd, NW6
T 020 7328 3286
Station Queens Park
Open Mon 7–10.30pm, Tues–Sat 12.30–3.30pm & 7–10.30pm, Sun 12.30–3.30pm & 7–10pm
Accepts MasterCard, Visa

The excellent and varied menu follows a mainly modern Italian theme rather than the more predictable Modern British bias of so many gastropubs. Starters (and a raft of dishes that could be starters or mains) may include sautéed prawns with chilli and garlic (£7/£10.50); chickpea soup with rosemary (£4); pan-fried squid with chilli and rocket (£6.50/£9); beetroot papardelle with goat's cheese and mint (£7.50); or prawn and radicchio risotto (£7/£9.50). There's a practical emphasis on pasta and risotto. More mainstream main courses range from lobster and seafood stew with tomato (£15), and cartoccio of sea bass fillets with mushrooms and radicchio (£13), to pan-fried calf's liver (£10) and grilled rib-eye steak with chips (£12.50). Moving on to pud territory, Amaretto, ricotta and almond pudding (£3.95) vies with sgroppina (£3.95) – a soft lemon sorbet doused in grappa – and pure chocolate tart (£3.95). The wine list is not large, but it is well chosen. There is a very good French Pinot Noir for £20 that tastes like it ought to cost a lot more. Bread and olive oil are served while you wait, and most of the starters can be had as main courses though, with portions sized the way they are, you would be unlikely to miss the extra.

The Salusbury serves a highly critical crowd with excellent food in stimulating surroundings. If there's one niggle, it's that portion sizes can be daunting. In Yorkshire they call it being "over-faced", but if sound Italian-accented cooking coupled with excellent value is what rings your bell, you'll like the Salusbury a lot.

St John's Wood & Swiss Cottage

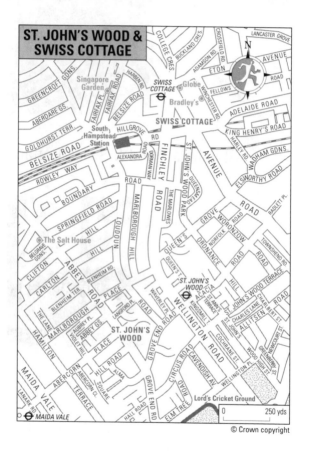

© Crown copyright

Bradley's

🍴 Bradley's, tucked away in a side street behind Swiss Cottage, is hard to find – and you get the impression that the regular clientele would prefer to keep the secret to themselves. The food here is pretty impressive, but that's not all. The atmosphere is warm and inviting, the menu covers and (metal) plates are probably the heaviest in London, and the loos are definitely a must-visit. All of

Cost	£15–£40

Address 25 Winchester Rd, NW3
T 020 7722 3457
Station Swiss Cottage
Open Mon–Fri & Sun noon–3pm & 6–11pm, Sat 6–11pm
Accepts All major credit cards

which forms a good backdrop for chef/proprietor Simon Bradley's cooking and presentation. Dishes revolve around a combination of fresh ingredients and are served with a view to making the most of the visual appeal. They can look terrific.

In 2001 the eponymous Mr Bradley changed the way the menu works and instituted a prix fixe, so now lunch costs £10 for two courses and £15 for three (rising to £15/£18 on Sunday); dinner costs £22/£27, all mercifully few supplements. Starters range from char-grilled squid with warm potato salad and caper vinaigrette; and pan-fried ox tongue with roasted Jerusalem artichoke and beetroot; to Ricotta and lemon ravioli with leek and sage butter; or a classic Mediterranean fish soup with aioli and croutons. Mains appeal along straightforward lines: lemon sole fillets with braised leeks, mushroom duxelles and potato gallette; pan-fried scallops with crab risotto; vegetable pot au feu with basil tortellini; venison haunch with braised red cabbage and mustard spatzle; roasted monkfish with braised split yellow peas and crispy pancetta; confit leg and pan-fried loin of rabbit with prunes and potato dumplings. These are enlightened dishes that mix tried and tested combinations of ingredients with flair. Puddings continue the theme: there's a fine apple tart with baked apple ice cream; a blood orange and Campari sorbet with chocolate tuille; and sticky date and ginger pudding with vanilla ice cream.

Bradley's extensive wine list includes some unusual and higher-priced New World wines that can be hard to find. A lively, but full-flavoured, biscuity Veuve Delaroy champagne at £29.95 is good value, too, making Bradley's a fine venue for a celebration dinner.

Globe

The bright, blue-and-yellow splash of colour tucked away behind Swiss Cottage underground station has a story attached to it. Quite simply, Neil Armishaw, owner and manager of Globe, brought back some unique hand-made blue and yellow plates from the US and decorated the restaurant to match them. However idiosyncratic, the locals have taken to this friendly, buzzy place, where the food – an accomplished meld of modern and traditional – is in keeping with the decor.

Cost	£15–£30

Address 100 Avenue Rd, NW3
T 020 7722 7200
Station Swiss Cottage
Open Mon & Sat 6–11pm,
Tues–Fri noon–2.30pm &
6–11pm, Sun noon–3pm &
7–10pm
Accepts Amex, MasterCard,
Visa
W www.globerestaurant.co.uk

Among the starters you may find warm duck confit salad with hoi sin dressing (£5.50); tomato, Feta and black olive stack with basil oil (£4.50); something simple like a chicken Caesar salad with crispy bacon; or something colourful like terrine of tuna with sweet, white and purple potatoes and saffron piccalilli (£4.50). Main courses may include fillet of Scottish beef with Pont Neuf potatoes, pea puree and fried quail's egg (£14.95); pan-fried sea bass with sage tagliatelle and vanilla sauce (£13.95); roast cod on Savoy cabbage with red wine, baby onion and bacon sauce (£12.95); or pan-fried duck breast with Dauphinoise potatoes, thyme jus and crispy leeks (£12.95).Vegetarians are pretty well treated here – perhaps a tomato and Mozzarella risotto with green herb pesto and Parmesan wafer (£5.95/£11.95), or toasted bruschetta with char-grilled Mediterranean vegetables (£10.95)? Puddings include the ubiquitous crème brûlée, here with chocolate-dipped banana (£4.50), and a mango sorbet with black pepper tuille (£4.50). But the star of the show must be the warm vanilla risotto with sable biscuits and gooseberries (£4.50).

Globe is built like a conservatory, with a glass roof and sliding doors that pull open, and an open-front courtyard for alfresco dining. The lunch menu follows closely on the heels of the dinner menu with many overlapping dishes and a few extra, simpler, platefuls. Overall the lunch menu prices are a pound or so cheaper than in the evening.

The Salt House

The Salt House combines corner pub, bar, restaurant and flower stall. There is a paved area set back from the road with benches and tables for the few alfresco dining days, the restaurant is reached through a large pub-style bar, and the whole has a relaxed friendliness where women on their own can feel quite at home. In 1999 The Salt House was bought by Adam Robinson, proprietor of

Cost	£22–£50

Address 63 Abbey Rd, NW8
T 020 7328 6626
Station St John's Wood
Open Mon–Fri noon–3pm & 6.30–10.30pm, Sat & Sun noon–4pm & 7–10.30pm
Accepts All major credit cards except Diners

The Chiswick (see p.436); now Andrew Green, the chef here, follows the style that's found such favour with Chiswickians. The cuisine is based on what's fresh and in season, prepared simply and with a supporting cast designed to bring out the best in the main players. It is no surprise, therefore, that the menu changes daily according to what is best at the markets.

The food is all carefully cooked, well presented and unfussy. Starters may include the simple – French onion soup (£4) – as well as more complex offerings like deep-fried sole with black bean dressing and coriander (£5.50); or a straightforward salad of chicory, walnuts, apple and Cashel blue (£5.50) that contrasts with a technically difficult rabbit and foie gras terrine served with toast and chutney (£6.75). Main courses also appeal – Spanish fish stew comes with saffron potatoes (£10.75); calf's liver with semolina gnocchi and sage (£10). Or there may be roast wood pigeon with caramelized baby onion tart and truffle oil (£10.50). There's also a super trad option for two: rib of beef, chips and field mushrooms (£28) – how very appealing. Puddings include blood-orange jelly with clotted cream (£3.95); rhubarb fool and shortbread (£3.75) – pleasantly tart and creamy at the same time; and, for the unreconstructed sweet tooth, a chocolate and almond torte (£3.95).

The food here is that superb combination of simple and stylish, the service is attentive and friendly, and there's a well-chosen wine list with a welcome absence of extravagant prices. But the real stars at the Salt House are the customers. Everyone seems to be enjoying themselves, and the mood is infectious.

Singapore Garden

Singapore Garden is a busy restaurant – don't even think of turning up without a reservation – and performs a cunning dual function. Half the cavernous dining room is filled with well-heeled, often elderly family groups from Swiss Cottage and St John's Wood, treating the restaurant as their local Chinese and consuming crispy duck in pancakes, money-bag chicken and butterfly prawns. The other customers, drawn from London's Singaporean and Malaysian communities, are tucking into the squid blachan and the Teochew braised pig's trotters. So there are cocktails with parasols and there is Tiger beer. But it's always busy, and the food is interesting and good.

Cost	£15–£35
Address	83a Fairfax Rd, NW6
T	020 7328 5314
Station	Swiss Cottage/ Finchley Road
Open	Daily noon–2.45pm & 6–10.45pm
Accepts	All major credit cards
W	www.singaporegarden.com

Start with a fresh crab fried in its shell (£12.75). It's a trade-off, to be honest, as frying (rather than baking) means that the leg and claw meat can be on the dry side, but also ensures that there are sublime crispy bits encrusting the brown meat. It comes with ginger and spring onions, Singapore chilli sauce or black pepper and butter. If you're feeling adventurous, follow with a real Singapore special – the Teochew braised pig's trotter (£10), which brings half a pig's worth of trotters slow-cooked in a luxurious, black, heart-stoppingly rich gravy. Or try the claypot prawns and scallops (£12), which delivers good, large, crunchy prawns and a fair portion of scallops, stewed with lemongrass and fresh ginger on glass noodles. Very good indeed. From the Malaysian list you might pick a daging curry (£6) – coconutty, rich and not especially hot. You must also try the mee goreng (£5), because this is how this noodle dish should be – a meal in itself.

At the bottom of the menu you'll find the "healthy alternative" known as Steamboat (£31.50 per person, for a minimum of two). This is a kind of party game. Eager participants drop tasty pieces of fresh meat and seafood into a cauldron of broth, which bubbles away at the table, then experience agonies of frustration when they find that they haven't the dexterity to fish them out with chopsticks.

Stoke Newington

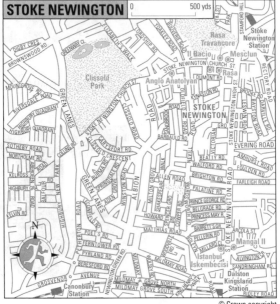

STOKE NEWINGTON

© Crown copyright

Anglo Anatolyan

The food is sound at the Anglo Anatolyan, the bills are small, and the tables so crowded that you get to meet all the other diners. But the most intriguing feature of the restaurant is the large and impressive royal crest which is engraved in the glass of the front door: under it, an inscription reads, "By Appointment to Her Majesty Queen Elizabeth II, Motor Car Manufacturers". Why? Do the Windsors slip up to Stoke Newington when they feel a new Daimler coming on? Predictably, asking the waiters for provenance doesn't help much: they look at you seriously and confide that they "got the door secondhand".

Cost	£8–£20

Address 123 Stoke
Newington Church St, N16
T 020 7923 4349
Station BR Stoke Newington
Open Mon–Fri 5pm–midnight,
Sat & Sun 1pm–midnight
Accepts MasterCard, Visa

TURKISH

Royal warrants aside, the food at the Anglo Anatolyan is usually pretty decent. The bread in particular is amazing. Large, round flat loaves about two inches deep, cut into chunks, soft in the middle and crisp on the outside; it is baked at home by a local Turkish woman and is a far cry from the flat, hard, mass-produced pitta pockets of the supermarkets. To accompany it, start with ispanak tarator (£2.95), spinach in yoghurt with garlic. And a tremendous, coarse tarama (£2.45). And sigara borek (£2.95), crisp filo pastry filled with cheese and served hot. And arnavut cigeri (£2.95), cubes of fried lamb's liver. Dine mob-handed so that you can try more starters. The main courses are more easily summarized: sixteen ways with lamb, one with quails, two with chicken, one with prawn, and two vegetarian dishes. Kaburga tarak (£6.25) is crisp, tasty lamb "spare-ribs"; iskander kebab (£6.75) is fresh doner on a bed of cubed bread and topped with yoghurt and tomato sauce; kasarli beyti (£6.75) is minced lamb made into a patty with cheese and grilled. They are all pretty good.

Like all the Turkish restaurants in this end of town, this is a very laissez-faire kind of place and standards can vary from visit to visit, but when you've eventually had your fill you'll be presented with a handwritten bill, at the bottom of which is printed "Another cheap night out". This, for once, is simply the truth.

Il Bacio

Opened in 1995 by Sardinian childhood sweethearts Luigi and Michela, Il Bacio has justly become one of the most popular fixtures on Stoke Newington's "restaurant row". The decor is upbeat – sunshine-yellow walls are lined with splashy modern canvases – and each (smallish) table has a vase of fresh flowers. Potted palms screen off a couple of tables for privacy, but, although *bacio* means "kiss", don't plan a romantic dinner here. This is a noisy place, loud with laughter and birthday parties.

Cost	£6–£20

Address 61 Stoke Newington Church St, N16
T 020 7249 3833
Station BR Stoke Newington
Open Mon–Fri 6–11pm, Sat & Sun 12.20–11.15pm
Accepts MasterCard, Visa

If you feel you'll have room for a starter, try the insalata di mare (£5.50), packed with fresh clams, calamari and prawns, or the ultra trad Mozzarella tricolore (£4.95) – Mozzarella, tomato and avocado, a welcome blast from the Seventies. The garlic bread (£2.65) is good, though if you're having pizza as a main course bear in mind that this is simply a base without the topping. Perfectly judged main course pastas include gnocchi di patate (£6.50), in a confident tomato and basil sauce, and velvety penne al salmone (£6.95). But it's the colossal pizzas that keep Il Bacio full every night: spilling off the plate, they never fail to produce a shriek of amazement from first-timers. Bases are paper-thin, cooked expertly in a wood-burning oven, so there's none of the unpleasant greasy oozing prevalent in lesser pizzas. There are twenty-three in all, ranging from classics like margherita (£4.75) and quattro stagioni (£6.95) to more ambitious combos. All except for the pescatora (£6.95) – seafood, capers, parsley – are built on a sauce of tomato and Mozzarella. The Sardegna (£6.50), with its aubergines and onion, and the Bacio (£7.50), topped with frankfurters and olives, both add a twist. Of the home-made desserts, the tiramisu (£3.50), a luscious, sozzled brick of sponge, cream and liquor, wins star prize.

In summer, French windows open out onto the pavement. It's a great place to survey the street life, but be warned that Il Bacio is opposite the local fire station. Sudden ear-shattering siren wails can send even the juiciest Mozzarella morsel shooting down the wrong way.

Istanbul Iskembecisi

The Istanbul Iskembecisi is just across the road from Mangal II (see p.294), and at heart they are singing off the same sheet. Despite being named after its signature dish – Iskembe is a limpid tripe soup – the Istanbul is a grill house. Admittedly it is a grill house with chandeliers, smart tables and upscale service, but it is still a grill house. And because it stays open until late in the morning it is much beloved by clubbers and chefs – they are just about ready to go out and eat when everyone else has had enough and set off home. The grilled meat may be better over at Mangal II, but the atmosphere of raffish elegance at the Istanbul has real charm.

Cost £8–£25

Address 9 Stoke Newington Rd, N16
T 020 7254 7291
Station BR Dalston Kingsland
Open Daily noon–5am
Accepts Cash and cheques only
W www.londraturk.com/istanbuliskembecisi

TURKISH

The iskembe (£2.50) – tripe soup – has its following. Large parties of Turks from the snooker hall just behind the restaurant insist on it, and you'll see the odd regular downing two bowlfuls of the stuff. For most people, however, it's bland at best, and even the large array of additives (salt, pepper, chilli – this is a dish that you must season to your personal taste at the table) cannot make it palatable. A much better bet is to start with the mixed meze (£4.50) – a good hummus and tarama, a superb dolma, and the rest drawn from the usual suspects. Then on to the grills, which are presented with more panache than usual. Pirzola (£6.50) brings three lamb chops; sis kebab (£5.75) is good and fresh; karisik agara (£8.50) is a mixed grill by any other name. For the brave there's a whole section of offal dishes, among them kokorec (£5) – lamb's intestines, and arvnavaut cigeri-sicak (£4.50) – liver Albanian style. Doubtless somebody somewhere is mourning two casualties of what will probably be seen as the "food scares era" – there is no more kelle sogus (roasted head of lamb) or beyin salata (boiled brain with salad).

Just when you think you're on safe ground with the desserts, the menu is still able to spring one last surprise – kazandibi (£2.50) which is a "Turkish type crème caramel, milk based sweet with finely dashed chicken breast". When compared with a chicken pudding served as dessert, boiled brain has much to commend it.

Mangal II

The first thing to hit you at Mangal II is the smell: the fragrance of spicy, sizzling char-grilled meat is unmistakably, authentically Turkish. This, combined with the relaxing pastel decor, puts you in holiday mood before you've even sat down. The ambience is laid-back, too. At slack moments, the staff shoot the breeze around the ocakbasi, and service comes with an ear-to-ear grin. All you have to do is sit back, sink an Efes Pilsener (£1.50) and peruse the encyclopedic menu.

Cost	£6–£25
Address	4 Stoke Newington Rd, N16
T	020 7254 7888
Station	BR Dalston Kingsland
Open	Daily noon–1am
Accepts	MasterCard, Visa

Prices are low and portions enormous. Baskets of fresh bread are endlessly replenished, so it's just as well to go easy on the appetizers. With a vast range of tempting mezeler (starters), however, resistance is well-nigh impossible. The 25 options include simple hummus (£2.50) and dolma (£2.50); imam bayildi (£3) – aubergines stuffed with onion, tomato and green pepper; thin lahmacun (£1.75) – meaty Turkish pizza; and karisik meze (£4) – a large plate of mixed dishes that's rather heavy on the yoghurt. There's a fair spread of salads (£2.50 to £3) as well, though you get so much greenery with the main dishes that it's a wasted choice here. The main dishes (kebablar) themselves are sumptuous, big on lamb and chicken, but with limited fish and vegetarian alternatives. The patlican kebab (£8) is outstanding – melt-in-the-mouth grilled minced lamb with sliced aubergines, served with a green salad of which the star turn is an olive-stuffed tomato shaped like a basket. The kebabs are also superb, particularly the house special, ezmeli kebab (£7.50), which comes doused in Mangal's special sauce. Or, if you don't fancy a grill, there's also a choice of three freshly made and hearty "daily stews" (£3.50 to £5).

After swallowing that lot, dessert might not be feasible, but after a long break – there's no pressure to vacate your table – you might just be tempted by a slab of tooth-achingly sweet baclava (£2). Alternatively, round off the evening with a punch-packing raki (£3) or a slap-in-the-face Turkish coffee, which will often be on the house, courtesy of the genial proprietor, Okkes Torbas. And, for a final blast of Ottoman atmosphere, pay a visit to the bathroom – the no-frills facilities are a real taste of old Istanbul.

Mesclun

Mesclun looks like a special-occasion kind of place, its stylish decor a tad incongruous on this careworn parade of cheap-and-cheerful ethnic restaurants. Small and elegant, with linen tablecloths, pine floor and simple, dark-wood furniture, it seats about forty people. Most of them are relaxed thirty-something locals, quietly complacent that they're onto a good thing. For, despite all appearances, Mesclun is a bargain, serving assured and astonishingly good-value Modern European food.

Cost	£12–£35

Address 24 Stoke Newington Church St, N16
T 020 7249 5029
Station BR Stoke Newington
Open Mon–Sat noon–3pm & 6–11pm, Sun noon–10pm
Accepts MasterCard, Visa

MODERN EUROPEAN

Meals start with complimentary bread and a tapenade of rough-chopped olives, sun-dried tomatoes and capers. Irresistibly moreish, but take it easy – the portions coming are large. This is especially true of the starters, most of which could pass as main courses – like smoked haddock and salmon fishcake with Greek yoghurt sauce (£4.50), or caramelized onion, goat's cheese and olive tart (£5). There are simpler choices, however, such as soup of the day (£3.25). For a main course, consider the superb daily fish specials (prices vary). Choices may include roast cod with basil dressing or char-grilled tuna, depending on what's good at the market. Otherwise there's a judicious balance between meat (free-range/organic) and vegetarian options. The pan-fried calves' liver with smoked bacon, spinach and dolcelatte sauce (£10.95) is meltingly good, or there's a Stilton, courgette and spinach risotto (£7.50). All come with side veg: perhaps a satisfying trio of celeriac Dauphinoise, herby ratatouille and buttery beans. Desserts (all £3.75), are upper-crust comfort food: raspberry crème brulée; bittersweet chocolate tart with vanilla ice cream; sticky toffee pudding with toffee sauce and hazelnut ice cream. The ice creams come from the estimable Marine Ices (see p.234).

Service at Mesclun is patient, attentive and humorous and while there can be long pauses between courses it's simply too pleasurable an experience for anyone to mind much. This place has certainly got a large local following – they sent in enough votes to see Mesclun win the "Evening Standard Londoner's award" at the 2001 Moët and Chandon gong-giving.

Rasa

Rasa has built up a formidable reputation for outstanding South Indian vegetarian cooking. In fact, when diners stop arguing as to whether Rasa is the best Indian vegetarian restaurant in London, they usually go on to discuss whether it is the best vegetarian restaurant full stop. As well as great food, the staff are friendly and helpful and the atmosphere is uplifting. Inside, everything is pink (napkins, tablecloths, walls), gold ornaments dangle from the ceiling, and a colourful statue of Krishna playing the flute greets you at the entrance. Rasa's proprietor and the majority of the kitchen staff come from Cochin in South India. As you'd expect, booking is essential.

Cost	£12–£27
Address	55 Stoke Newington Church St, N16
T	020 7249 0344
Station	BR Stoke Newington
Open	Mon–Fri 6–11pm, Sat & Sun noon–2.30pm & 6pm–midnight
Accepts	All major credit cards
W	www.rasarestaurants.com

This is one occasion when the set meal – or "feast" – (£15) may be the best, as well as the easiest, option. The staff take charge and select what seems like an endless succession of dishes for you. But, however you approach a Rasa meal, everything is a taste sensation. Even the pappadoms are a surprise: try the selection of the crispy things served with six home-made chutneys (£3) – quite simply, a revelation. If you're going your own way, there are lots of starters to choose from. Mysore bonda (£2.50) is delicious, shaped like a meatball but made of potato spiced with ginger, coriander and mustard seeds. Kathrikka (£2.50) is slices of aubergine served with fresh tomato chutney. The main dishes are just as imaginative. Beet cheera pachadi (£3.75) is a colourful beetroot curry, zingy and tasty with yoghurt and coconut; moru kachiathu (£3.85) combines mangoes and green bananas with chilli and ginger. Or go for a dosa – paper-thin crisp pancakes folded in half and packed full with a variety of goodies; masala dosa (£4.75) is filled with potatoes and comes with lentil sauce and coconut chutney. Puddings sound hefty but arrive in mercifully small portions; the payasam (£2.25), a "temple feast", blends dhal with jaggery (raw sugar) and coconut milk – a fine end to a meal.

The word rasa has many meanings in Sanskrit: "flavour", "desire", "beauty", "elegance". It can also mean "affection" – something that the whole of northeast London feels for this wonderful restaurant.

Rasa Travancore

Rasa Travancore is painted glow-in-the-dark Rasa pink, just like the original Rasa (see opposite) which faces it across the roadway. It shows a certain amount of chutzpah on the part of any restaurateur to open a new branch opposite head office, but Das Sreedharan has never been shy. Rasa Travancore moves the spotlight onto a particular facet of Keralan cuisine, Syrian Christian cooking, and a very welcome move it is too. All the South Indian flavour notes are there – coconut, curry leaves, ginger, chillies, mustard seeds, tamarind – but as well as veggie specialities, Syrian Christian dishes feature fish, seafood, mutton, chicken and duck.

Cost	£15–£35

Address 56 Stoke Newington Church St, N16
T 020 7249 1340
Station BR Stoke Newington
Open Daily 6–11pm
Accepts All major credit cards
W www.rasarestaurants.com

The menu is a long one and great pains have been taken to explain every dish, although the language can get a bit flowery. Apparently the king prawns in konjufry (£4.95) have been marinated in "refreshing spices" – whatever. But the prawns are very good – plump and with a rich flavour. Or there's Kerala fish fry (£3.95), a large steak of firm-fleshed kingfish dusted with spice and pan fried. Very delicious. Travancore kozhukkatta (£3.75) is a sort of ninth cousin to those large, doughy Chinese dumplings – steamed rice outside with spiced minced lamb inside. The main course dishes are fascinating and richly-flavoured. Kozhy olthu curry (£5.25) – billed as "a famous recipe from Sebastian's mum"! – is a rich, dryish, oniony chicken curry. Lamb stew (£5.95) is a simple and charming lamb curry. Duck fry (£6.95) is dry-fried chunks of duck with curry leaves and onion. Kappayyum meenum vevichathu (£7.95) is a triumph – a soupy fish curry, delicately flavoured and served with floury chunks of boiled tapioca root dusted with coconut. Very moreish. The veg curries are also good: try the Travancore kayi curry (£3.90), "chef Narayanan's signature dish", which is a splendidly richly-sauced, coconutty mixed vegetable dish.

Excellent accompaniments are the tamarind rice (£2.50), which has an amazing depth of flavour, and the flaky, buttery Malabar paratha (£2).

Wembley

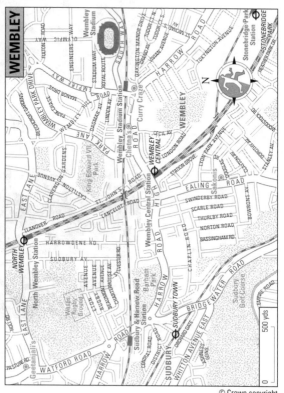

WEMBLEY

© Crown copyright

Chetna's

Chetna's is a remarkable Indian restaurant – busy enough to need a queuing system. You register your interest at the counter and get given a cloakroom ticket, and when your table is ready your number is called. The restaurant has smart wood tables and chairs, ceiling fans and some seriously ornate brass chandeliers, but despite these trappings it is still awesomely cheap. The food is very good indeed and the menu is

Cost	£4–£10

Address 420 High Rd, Wembley
T 020 8900 1466
Station Wembley Central
Open Tues–Fri noon–3pm & 6–10.30pm, Sat & Sun 1–10.30pm
Accepts MasterCard, Switch, Visa

INDIAN/VEGETARIAN

a bit of a surprise, opening with a section headed "seaside savouries" – an odd claim in a vegetarian establishment – and moving through to Chetna's Pizza Corner, confirming once again that when Asians go out to dinner they often want a change from the usual fare. The concept of a large "special vegetable hot pizza" (£5.50) cooked by an Indian chef and made with pure vegetarian cheese, onions, and special Chetna sauce – green pepper, corn and hot green chillies – has undeniable charm.

Start with a truly amazing mouthful – Chetna's masala golgapa (£2.10); these are small, crisp golgapas filled with potatoes, onions, moong, chana, green chutney, sweet and sour chutney, and topped with sev. You load them into your mouth and as you chew different tastes and textures take over. It's an astonishing sensation. Order more portions than you think you'll need. Also try the kachori (£2.10) – a crisp coat encases a well-spiced ball of green peas. Then there are the karela, bhindi and tindora curries (£3). The karela dish, made from bitter melons, is genuinely bitter – very interesting and, word has it, very good for the blood. Or there's Chetna's crispy bhajia (£2.90) – slices of potatoes crisp on the outside with a batter containing bits of chilli, and perfectly cooked. The most visually striking dish must be the paper dosa (£3.50), a giant chewy cone of nutty-tasting pancake with a vegetable sambhar and coconut chutney for dipping.

The award for most comprehensive dish must go to the Delhi Darbar thali (£6.50), which is served with one sweet, one farsan, three vegetables, chutney, vegetable biryani, dhal, raita, papadum and paratha. There's a minimum charge of £3.50 per person at Chetna's – presumably to stop a large family sharing one Delhi Darbar thali for dinner.

INDIAN

Curry Craze

On the face of it, the demise of Wembley Stadium and its attendant crowds of curryholics should have hit Curry Craze badly, but the Malhotras who run the place are made of sterner stuff. Their friendly, genuine, family-run resto has a large and loyal enough following to continue filling the place, particularly at the weekends. Despite its unfortunate 1970s name, Curry Craze is a very good Indian restaurant – an unpretentious

Cost	£8–£15

Address 8–9 The Triangle, Wembley Hill Rd
T 020 8902 9720
Station Wembley Central
Open Mon 6–10.30pm, Wed–Fri 12.30–2.30pm & 6–10.30pm, Sat 6–11pm
Accepts All major credit cards except Diners

establishment that serves predominantly Punjabi food with a smattering of East African Asian dishes. And if some items on the menu have a familiar ring to them, that is because the Malhotras are related to the Anands – the dynasty responsible for the famed Brilliant and Madhu's Brilliant in Southall (see p.477 & p.479).

As at the Brilliants, you could do worse than start with a share of butter chicken, or any of its variants – jeera, methi or chilli chicken (£6.50 for a half chicken). Or the sheekh kebab (four pieces for £4.95) served as a sizzler on an iron dish, and very tasty. Or chilli corn (£2.95) – corn on the cob given the hot sauce treatment. Main courses range from karahai dishes to old favourites like chicken tikka masala (£6.25), biryanis and pure veg dishes. Karahi prawns (£7.95) come in a good rich sauce. Tinda lamb (£5.95) is a delightful dry curry of lamb and tinda – a Punjabi vegetable which is a member of the squash family, something like what you'd expect of a tomato merged with a potato. Punjabi bhartha oro (£4) is a prince among side dishes, a roasted aubergine mashed and cooked with onions and peas. Pakorian raita (£2.45) is very odd indeed, but provides a perfect change of texture – pea-sized balls of gram flour cooked and served cold in a tangy yoghurt sauce. To dip into all these dishes, there are bhaturas (£1) – deep-fried breads like puffy savoury doughnuts and not for dieters – and very delicious peshwari (£2.25) or plain (£1.20) naans.

One house speciality well worth trying is Mrs Malhotra's dall makhani (£4), a rich black lentil and kidney-bean dhal. It is made by combining the dhal with a tarka containing onions, ginger and tomatoes cooked in ghee.

Geetanjali's

There are a good many Indian restaurants in Wembley, and it would be easy to write off Geetanjali's as just one more of the same. On the face of it, for sure, the menu is pretty straightforward, with a good many old, tired dishes lined up in their usual serried ranks – chicken tikka masala, rogan josh and so on and so forth. But Geetanjali's has a secret weapon, a dish that brings customers from far and wide. Word on the street is that this place serves the best tandoori lamb chops in North London. And when you've tasted them you'll agree.

Cost	£12–£26

Address 16 Court Parade, Watford Rd
T 020 8904 5353
Station Wembley Central
Open Daily noon–3pm & 6–11.30pm
Accepts All major credit cards
W www.geetanjali-restaurant.com

INDIAN

This chop lover's haven has a large, roomy dining room, and the service is attentive, if a little resigned when you pitch up and order a raft of beers and a few portions of chops – or, as the menu would have it, lamb chopp (£4.50). Of course, the chops are good. Very good. Thick-cut, exceedingly tender and very nicely spiced. Accompany them with a luccha paratha (£2.50), warm and flaky and presented in the shape of a flower with a knob of butter melting into its heart. The alternative is the intriguingly named bullet nan (£2.50), which promises to be hot and spicy, and delivers in good measure. You have been warned. Even if you're not a complete chopaholic you can also do well here. Go for starters such as the good chicken tikka haryali (£4.50) – chicken breast marinated in green herbs like coriander and mint before being cooked in the tandoor. Rashmi kebab (£3.90) is also good, made from minced chicken and spices. Main courses include mathi gosht (£6.90), which is lamb with fenugreek, lamb bhuna (£6.50), and lamb badam pasanda (£6.90). And should this emphasis on bread and meat leave you craving some of the green stuff, there's sag aloo (£4.50) or karahi corn masala (£4.50).

This is not the cheapest Indian restaurant in Wembley, but it does have a certain style, even extending to the sophisticated peppermint fondant mints that accompany your bill. And it goes without saying it's worth travelling for the best tandoori chops in North London.

Sakonis

Sakonis is a top-notch vegetarian food factory. Crowded with Asian families, it is overseen by waiters and staff in baseball caps, and there's even a holding pen where you can check out the latest videos and sounds while waiting your turn. From a decor point of view, the dining area is somewhat clinical: a huge square yardage of white tiling – easy to hose down. Nobody minds; the predominantly Asian clientele is too busy eating.

Cost	£4–£10

Address 127–129 Ealing Rd, Alperton
T 020 8903 9601
Station Alpertón
Open Mon–Thurs & Sun 11am–11pm, Fri & Sat 11am–midnight
Accepts MasterCard, Switch, Visa

The Indian vegetarian food here is terrific, but it's old hat to many of the Asian customers who dive straight into what is, for them, the most exciting section of the Sakonis menu – the Chinese dishes. These tend to be old favourites like chow mein and chop suey cooked by Indian chefs and with a distinctly Indian spicing. Unless curiosity overwhelms you, stick to the splendid South Indian dishes. There are three branches: 6–8 Dominion Parade, Station Rd, Harrow (T020 8863 3399); 116 Station Rd, Edgware (T020 8951 0058); and 180–186 Upper Tooting Rd, SW17 (T020 8772 4774).

Sakonis is renowned for its dosas. Effectively these are pancakes, so crisp that they are almost chewy, and delightfully nutty. They come with two small bowls of sauce and a filling of rich, fried potato spiced with curry leaves; choose from plain dosa (£3.50), masala dosa (£4.50), and chutney dosa (£4.60) – which has spices and chilli swirled into the dosa batter. Try the farari cutlets (£3.50); not cutlets at all, in fact, but very nice, well-flavoured dollops of sweet potato mash, deep-fried so that they have a crisp exterior. In fact, all the deep-fried items are perfectly cooked – very dry, with a very crisp shell, but still cooked through. A difficult feat to achieve. Also worth trying are the bhel puri (£3.30), the pani puri (£2.50), and the sev puri (£3.30) – amazingly crisp little taste bombs. Pop them in whole and the flavour explodes in your mouth.

Some say that the juices at Sakonis are the best in London, and while that may be hyperbole they certainly are very good indeed. Try madaf (£2.50), made from fresh coconut; melon juice (£2.25), which is only available in season; or the orange and carrot mix (£2.50), which is subtitled "health drink".

Further North

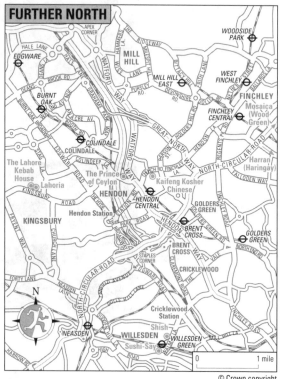

FURTHER NORTH

APEX CORNER

WOODSIDE PARK

HALE LANE

EDGWARE

RIDGEWAY

HAMMERS LA.

MILL HILL

WEST FINCHLEY

BROOK RD.

BURNT OAK

WATFORD WAY

MILL HILL EAST

BALLARDS LA.

FINCHLEY

HILL LANE

DEANS

LONG LANE

BURNT OAK

GRAHAME PARK WAY

EVERSLEY RD

DEVONSHIRE RD

FRITH LANE

FINCHLEY CENTRAL

Mosaica (Wood Green)

ACRE AV.

GREAT NORTH WAY

COLINDALE

COLINDALE

WATFORD WAY

HOLDERS HILL RD

NORTH CIRCULAR ROAD

Harran (Haringay)

The Lahore Kebab House

Lahoria

COLINDEEP

FINCHLEY RD

The Prince of Ceylon

Kaifeng Kosher Chinese

REGENTS PARK RD

FALLODEN WAY

KINGSBURY ROAD

HENDON

HENDON CENTRAL

GOLDERS GREEN

KINGSBURY

Hendon Station

HENDON WAY

BRENT CROSS

GOLDERS GREEN

CHURCH LANE

PARK ROAD

BRENT CROSS

NORTH END RD

GOLDERS GREEN RD

FORTY LANE

STAPLES CORNER

BRENT ST

CRICKLEWOOD

FRYENT WAY

NORTH CIRCULAR ROAD

NEASDEN LANE

EDGWARE ROAD

CLAREMONT RD

N

Cricklewood Station

Shish

FINCHLEY ROAD

NEASDEN

HIGH ROAD

WILLESDEN

Sushi-Say

WILLESDEN GREEN

MILL HILL LA.

HARROW RD

0   1 mile

© Crown copyright

Harran

For a small Turkish restaurant in Haringey, Harran certainly has an impressive waterfall. The back wall of the dining room is given over to a chunky rock face overflowing with water, topped with a clock surmounted by an eagle with wings akimbo. It all has a certain style, as

Cost	£8–£14
Address	399 Green Lanes, N4
T	020 8348 5434
Station	Manor House
Open	Daily 24hr
Accepts	Cash only

does the large wood-fired oven, which is immensely solid, brick-built and looks just like a small cottage. You can only wonder why there are gutters at the bottom of the impeccably tiled roof. Though this establishment has been trading 24 hours a day since it opened in 1997, skirmishes with antiquated British licensing laws mean that the drinks licence may come and go (and on some occasions they cannot even allow BYO). So there may or may not be drinks on offer and, as a consequence, there may or may not even be a printed menu (in which event dishes will be listed on a board over the counter). In a street lined with Turkish restaurants, Harran stands out because of the freshness of the food, the splendid baking and sensibly modest prices.

Start with hunks of hot, fresh bread, lightly dusted with sesame seeds (50p). Perfect with the gloopy salads (all 50p), all of which make great starters – yoghurt and cucumber, yoghurt and salad, and a splendid "chilli" salad (a kind of super salsa). The grills are terrific, and very fresh indeed. Sis kebab (£6), adana kebab (£5.50), and iskender kebab (£7) all arrive with rice and salad. Then there are the Turkish equivalents of pizza: lahmacun (£1.50) and pide – sucuklu pide (£6) comes with sausage and egg. And four soups every day (all £2.50). Puddings are something of a challenge. Keskul (£2), described as "rice pudding without the rice", comes as a small foil takeaway tray full of strange, very sweet, ground-rice pudding topped with walnuts; it has a strangely resilient and pliable skin.

Should you be in Harran at about 10pm, you'll see the baker going into overdrive, plunging tray after tray of delightful little cheesy pastries into the little brick hut. He is gearing up for the rush. Between 1am and 6am, the restaurant offers a running buffet of salads, dips, grills and freshly baked pastries – both savoury and sweet. This is amazingly popular at the weekend, which isn't surprising – it costs just £4 per person.

Kaifeng Kosher Chinese

The Kaifeng Kosher Chinese restaurant is a one-off, an opulent Chinese restaurant that claims to be (and doubtless is) the only kosher Oriental establishment in Britain. According to the family tree on the wall, the most important family of Kaifeng's former Jewish community is named Chao Lunang-Ching. The inscription adds, rather enigmatically, that "Ezekiel is probably Chao Lunang-Ching Gwlyn Gym". So now you know. The long, narrow dining room is filled with affluent locals, happy to pay smart North London prices which have more in common with the West End than the suburbs. But you get a decent deal, friendly and excellent service that almost justifies the fifteen percent surcharge, and fresh, well-cooked (if a trifle under-seasoned) dishes. If you're Orthodox Jewish, Kaifeng must make a welcome change; if you're not, then seeing how favourite dishes like sweet and sour pork, prawns kung po and so forth turn out kosher-style is a lot of fun.

Cost	£25–£50

Address 51 Church Rd, NW4
T 020 8203 7888
Station Hendon Central
Open Mon–Thurs & Sun
12.30–2.30pm & 6–11pm, Sat
1hr after sunset to 11pm
(Sept–April only)
Accepts All major credit cards
W www.kaifeng.co.uk

Start with the spare ribs (£7.50), which are absolutely delicious, made from lamb instead of pork and arguably even better for it. Hunan chicken with lettuce wrap (£12.50) is also fresh and good, while the usual prawn and sesame seed toast becomes sesame chicken (£7.50). Of the main courses, the sweet and sour lamb (£12.95) is slightly less successful – a good, sharp sauce still makes no impression on fairly tough chunks of lamb. But there are some interesting and unfamiliar dishes like beef and straw mushrooms (£12.95), smoked shredded chicken (£12.50) and eggplant in garlic sauce (£6.50). Shellfish dishes, meanwhile, turn into fish, usually sole, which is served in a variety of familiar styles including steamed with ginger and spring onion (£17.95) and drunken (£17.95), which means sliced and served in kosher rice wine.

Given its unique status, the Kaifeng is a pretty popular place and even early in the week it tends to fill quickly. So take the precaution of booking if you're travelling out here specially.

The Lahore Kebab House

This grill house was once a branch of the famous Lahore Kebab House in East London. Then, in 1994, Mr Hameed bought the business, and with it the right to use the name "Lahore Kebab House of East London" anywhere within a five-mile radius of Kingsbury. Although completely independent of the Umber-

Cost	£6–£12
Address	248 Kingsbury Rd, NW9
T	020 8905 0930
Station	Kingsbury
Open	Daily 1pm–midnight
Accepts	Cash or cheque only

stone Street establishment (see p.175), this bare and basic restaurant remains faithful to the spirit of the original. Kebabs are cheap, freshly cooked and spicy, while the karahi dishes are also worth delving into. Recently the Lahore has gained the advantage of a drinks licence, so you can now purchase Tusker and Kingfisher beers without having to pop out to one of the neighbouring off-licences.

There's not much point in coming to the Lahore unless you're after some kind of kebab. If you just want a starter bite, there's seekh kebab (75p each). Or, for more serious eating, there's a list of kebabs all with five pieces per skewer: mutton tikka (£2.20); chicken tikka (£3); jeera chicken (£4.20); chicken wings (£4.20); lamb chops (£5). Everyone is very helpful here, and they are happy to make you up a platter – with three pieces of each kebab, for example – and charge pro rata. Unusually, for such a stronghold of the carnivore, there's also a long list of vege-tarian dishes, all served in the karahi. Include a couple with your order – perhaps karrai dhal (£3.50), or karrai sag aloo (£3.50), which is particu-larly rich and tasty. Back with the meats, karrai ghost (£4.70) is a rich lamb curry, while the "chef's special" (£6), a hand-chopped keema made with both chicken and lamb, is a revelation – very tasty, with recognisable, finely chopped meat, and a far cry from the anonymous mince that forms the backbone of keema dishes in so many curry houses. It is thoroughly recommended. As are the breads – tandoori nan (90p) and tandoori roti (60p) – which are fresh and good.

The Lahore's weekend specials all appeal: karrai nehari (£7), slow-cooked lamb shanks; karrai bhindi (£4), or okra; and karrai karela (£4), made from bitter melons.

Lahoria

This guide used to go on a bit about the shabby, somewhat neglected decor of this Kingsbury stalwart. Then it was refurbished in pink. And now green. But even taking into account the refurbs, it's still true that nobody comes here for the ambience. There's plenty of competition – half a dozen other Indian restaurants clustered on this stretch of road. No matter, this small place is still busy, particularly at the weekend. What makes the Lahoria stand out, what has kept it going from strength to strength, is the sheer quality of the food, which combines two admirable attributes – simple and good.

Cost	£10–£24

Address 274 Kingsbury Rd, NW9
T 020 8206 1129
Station Kingsbury
Open Tues–Thurs 6–11.30pm, Fri & Sat 5.30pm–midnight, Sun 3pm–midnight
Accepts MasterCard, Visa

So, the food: it's fresh, not painfully hot (unless you want it to be) and well balanced. There are a lot of East African Asian specialities, and dishes come by either the plate or the karai. Start with a plate of jeera aloo (£4.50), tasty, rich, soft, fried potatoes with cumin – a sort of Indian pommes Lyonnaises. Or have a plate of masala fish (£4.50), two fat fillets of tilapia cooked in a fresh green masala. You must try the chilli chicken (£5.95), nine chicken wings in a dark green, almost black, sludge that is rich with ginger, chillies, coriander and just a hint of tamarind sourness – triumphant but not so hot that it hurts. You can also try this sauce with potatoes (£4.50). Then there are the tandoori chops (£4.50), which are very good indeed. Also look for the mari chicken (£5.95), which is chicken marinated in cracked black pepper. For a main course it is hard to give high enough praise to the karai spring lamb (£5.75), served on the bone. It is deliciously rich. Or try a simple classic like karai methi gosh (£5.75). The karai red kidney beans (£4.25) and karai bangan ka bartha (£4.95), based on aubergines and onions, are also good bets.

On Friday, Saturday and Sunday, Lahoria offers two notable specials – karai goat (on the bone, £5.95) and karai undhiu (£4.95), which is a dish of mixed vegetables. They also have a magnificent chiller full of bottled beers, including Beck's, Holsten, Carlsberg and Budweiser and – best of all – Tusker from Kenya.

Mosaica

Up in the high pastures of Wood Green there is a large and hideous concrete "Shopping City" whose main claim to fame seems to be "secure parking". Around the corner is a straggle of large, run-down buildings called the Chocolate Factory that has been colonized by artists, potters, designers and anyone arty needing cheap, no-frills space. Mosaica opened in October 2000, in the middle of Building C, and it is an amazing place – spacious, stylish and comfortable. There is a long bar made up of cinder blocks, topped with a twenty-foot sheet of glass. There's a terrace outside in the light well, which will be amazing should we ever get good weather. There's a huge open kitchen. And there are mismatched but comfortable straight-backed chairs. The atmosphere is dead right – stylish but informal, neighbourhood but sharp. The food is a complete surprise. It's terrific.

Cost	£6–£35
Address	Building C, The Chocolate Factory, Clarendon Rd, Off Coburg Rd, N22
T	020 8889 2400
Station	BR Wood Green/ Alexander Park
Open	Tues–Fri 11am–10pm, Sat 6–10pm, Sun & Mon 11am–4pm
Accepts	All major credit cards

The two chef-proprietors, John Mountain and David Orlowski, have done time in various West End establishments, but here, in N22, they are cooking with real passion. Genuine, unpretentious plating, fresh ingredients well handled, and accurate cooking. This is the difficult kind of simple stuff that looks simple until you try to do it. The menu at Mosaica is short and changes daily – at lunch the blackboard includes a cheap pasta dish for starving artists. In the evening, starters range from a well-made roasted tomato and garlic soup (£3.95), to grilled polenta with Serrano ham and oven-dried tomatoes (£5.75), or an old-fashioned, freshly made chicken liver pate with toast and cornichons (£4.95) – very good indeed. The home-made bread comes thick-sliced and char-grilled. It too is very good. Mains range from monkfish with charred radicchio and charlotte potatoes (£12.95), to rare rib-eye steak with garlic mash and spinach (£10.95) – the rib-eye sliced and meltingly tender, the mash rich and not over-gluey. Then there may be an epic dish of slow-roast pork belly, with root vegetables and applesauce (£9.95). Puds are notable. How about a perfect chocolate crème brûlée (£4), or a cinnamon, orange and walnut ice cream (£3.25)?

The wine list is short and the service more enthusiastic than polished. But the food is great and the prices forgiving. Time to look up N22.

The Prince of Ceylon

The Prince of Ceylon has been a mainstay of London's Sri Lankan community for the past twenty years, its quality and rarity (even now there are only a dozen Sri Lankan places in London) transcending its location. Watford Way, reminiscent of a Grand Prix pit lane, at least offers parking spaces. And once inside the restaurant, it's very welcoming,

Cost	£8–£15

Address 39 Watford Way, NW4
T 020 8203 8002
Station Hendon Central
Open Mon 6–11.30pm, Tues–Sun noon– 11.30pm
Accepts All major credit cards

especially during the popular all-afternoon Sunday buffet. Eating Sri Lankan food, which is quite distinct from that served at most Indian places, is an interesting experience. Whereas in an Indian curry house there's a tendency to choose a dish, and then some bread or rice to go with it, Sri Lanka turns this principle on its head. Breads, rices and staples are strange and delightful, forcing the curries, sambals, devilled meats and seafood into a supporting role.

Starters are deceptively named. Mutton rolls (£1.95) are delicious crispy spring rolls filled with spicy lamb and potatoes and served with a chilli-tangy tomato ketchup. The same sauce appears with the fish cutlets (£1.95) – spherical, lemony fish cakes. Or there's rasam (£1.50), a spicy, thin, almost gritty soup with aromatic spices and a wicked chilli kick. Moving on to the main courses, start by picking your staple. Hoppers (75p) are a must: thin, crispy, bowl-shaped breads. Or there are string hoppers (£2.75), cakes of vermicelli that come into their own when dowsed with a bowl of kiri hodi – coconut milk curry. The kiri hodi also accompanies pittu (£3), a plain white cylinder that looks like a narrow roll of kitchen towel; it is made in a special steamer by packing the funnel with a mix of grated coconut and rice flour. Highlight among the breads is coconut roti (£2.25), a crisper, thinner kind of paratha. To lubricate these delights, pick from a range of curries and devilled dishes. The mutton curry (£4.95) is a good meat-and-gravy dish, while the unassumingly named "fried mutton onion" (£4.95) is even better. Good devilled dishes include the devilled prawns (£4.95) – chilli-hot and piquant.

Whatever you order, be sure to get a side dish of seeni sambal (£2.25), a spicy onion jam that adds flavour and texture. And leave room for a pud, either wattalappan (£1.95) – Sri Lanka's second cousin to crème caramel, made with palm syrup – or (buffalo) curd and syrup (£3).

Shish

This is the first Shish, and it opened in March 2001. Shish is pretty slick – a large, curved-glass pavement frontage displays a sinuous bar counter that snakes around the dining room, leaving grills, fridges and chefs' stations in the centre. Diners simply take a stool at the counter, for all the world like being at a modernist sushi bar. All is modern, just as current resto-design fashion dictates, with rough concrete here, polished concrete there, stainless steel... Towards the rear are a couple of further kitchens: one primarily for baking fresh flat breads, and the other for frying, preparation and so forth. This place owes a debt to Israeli roadside eateries, with its falafel and shish kebabs, but the "concept" (all fast food missions have to have a suitable "concept") is much more inclusive. As proclaimed at the top of the menu, the inspiration for Shish is the food of the Silk Road.

Cost	£10–£24
Address	2–6 Station Parade, NW2
T	020 8208 9290
Station	Willesden Green
Open	Daily 11am–11pm
Accepts	All major credit cards except Diners

Starters are divided into lots of cold mezze and a shorter list of hot mezze. The tabbouleh (£1.95) needs a bit more of the green bits – coriander and parsley. The cucumber wasabi (£1.95) is pleasant pickled cucumber. The red and green falafel (£2.25) are well made – and the red variety is engagingly spicy. The hot bread is as delicious as only good hot bread can be. Kebabs are served in two different ways: either plated with rice, couscous or French fries; or in a wrap. The shish kebabs are really rather good. Mediterranean lamb (£5.25) comes up very tender; apricot and ginger (£5.75) teams chicken with good tangy apricot flavour; the Persian chicken (£6.25) is flavoured with saffron, turmeric and citrus fruits. The portions all seem decent sized and there are a number of fish and vegetarian options. Die-hard kebabbers can even insist on a satisfactorily fierce squelch of chilli sauce. This food benefits from being freshly cooked and eaten hot from the grill. It's relatively cheap, too. What's more, Shish is licensed, so there's a cold beer (£1.50) or a glass of wine (£2.50) to turn a quick feed into an enjoyable meal.

Expect Shish to roll out fairly quickly – sites in W1 and somewhere south of the Thames are already on the drawing board. If this is the new face of fast food we should all be jolly grateful.

JAPANESE

Sushi-Say

Yuko Shimizu and her husband Katsuharu run this small but excellent Japanese restaurant and sushi bar. It has a very personal feel, with just ten seats at the bar and twenty in the restaurant, plus a private booth for five or six. Shimizu means pure water and the cooking is pure delight. It's a tribute to how sophisticated our palates have become that a restaurant like this can do well so far out of town. The menu offers a full classical Japanese selection, making it a difficult choice whether to limit yourself to sushi or go for the cooked dishes. Perhaps adapting the European style, and having sushi or sashimi as a starter and then main courses with rice, brings you the best of both worlds, and will give you scope to enjoy this small establishment.

Sitting at the sushi bar allows you to watch Katsuharu at work. With a sumo-like stature and the widest grin this side of Cheshire, his fingers magic nigiri sushi of exquisite proportions onto your plate. It's an accomplished show and the sleight of hand will not fail to impress. In the lower price brackets you'll find omelette, mackerel, squid and octopus (£2.40). At the top end there's sea urchin, fatty tuna and yellow tail (£3.40). In between there is a wide enough range to delight even the experts. Nigiri yoku (£16.50) brings you eleven pieces of nigiri and seaweed-rolled sushi and it's a bargain, heavy on the fish and light on the rice. Cooked dishes do not disappoint. Ebi tempura (£11.30) brings you crispy battered king prawns – the batter so light it's almost effervescent – and menchi katsu (£7) delivers a deep-fried oval shaped from minced beef and salad. There are set dinners for all tastes, priced from £18.50 to £28.50, and mixed sashimi for £16.50. It's worth trying the home-made puddings, such as Goma (sesame) ice cream (£2.60). There's also a selection of special sakes, which are served chilled, and even a half-frozen sake (Akita Onigoroshi) at £6. Less a slush puppy than a slush mastiff.

The menu is in English and the staff are very helpful, so dining at Sushi-Say gives you a good chance to develop your knowledge of Japanese food by trying something new.

Cost

Address 33b Walm Lane, NW2
T 020 8459 2971
Station Willesden Green
Open Tues–Fri 6.30–10.30pm, Sat & Sun noon–2.30pm & 6.30–10.30pm
Accepts All major credit cards except Diners

South

Battersea

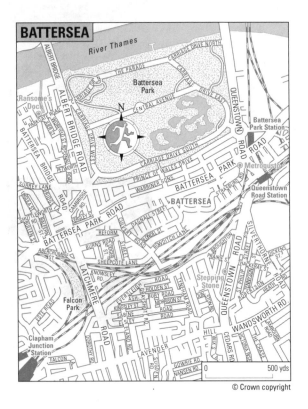

BATTERSEA

River Thames

Battersea Park

Ransome's Dock

ALBERT BRIDGE ROAD

BRIDGE RD

THE PARADE

CARRIAGE DRIVE NORTH

CARRIAGE DRIVE EAST

Central Avenue

N

CARRIAGE DRIVE WEST

PARKGATE RD

ROSSITER RD

PETWORTH ST

SURREY LANE

SHUTTLEWORTH RD

BATTERSEA BRIDGE ROAD

CAMBRIDGE RD

JERSEY ST

BATTERSEA PARK ROAD

REFORM

BURNS ROAD

DAGNALL STREET

BORDER ST

BOWDITCH LANE

ABERCROMBIE ST

SHEEPCOTE LANE

KNOWSLEY RD

LATCHMERE ROAD

ROAD

EVERSLEIGH

ASH

KINGSLEY ST

SABINE

ELSEY ST

HOLDEN ST

BURY ROAD

MORRISON ST

ROAD

ROAD

ESTE ROAD

DOROTHY RD

Falcon Park

Clapham Junction Station

FALCON

TALCON

LAVENDER

GOWRIE RD

NANSEN RD

CARRIAGE DRIVE SOUTH

PRINCE OF WALES DRIVE

WARRINER GDNS

BATTERSEA PARK

BATTERSEA

QUEENSTOWN ROAD

Battersea Park Station

Metro bus stop

Queenstown Road Station

STRASBURG RD

BROUGHTON

PRAIRIE ST

Stepping Stone

ST PHILIP ST

ROBERTSON ST

QUEENSTOWN ROAD

SILVERTHORNE ROAD

DICKENS ST

THACKERAY ST

HACKETT RD

HEATH RD

WANDSWORTH RD

CEDARS RD

VICTORIA RD

HILL

0   500 yds

© Crown copyright

Metrogusto

Arriving at Metrogusto is not inspiring. But, once inside, there are high ceilings, lots of natural light, and a partial view of the kitchen. Wooden tables and chairs lend the room an air of informality, while the modern art on the walls and around the room adds interest. The Metrogusto formula is one of "Italy meets the world" and it is certainly successful, as the opening of a second branch in 2000 – Metrogusto, 11 Theberton St, N1 (℡020 7226 9400) – confirmed.

Cost	£15–£35

Address 50 Battersea Park Rd, SW8
T 020 7720 0204
Station BR Battersea Park
Open Mon–Fri noon–3pm & 6.30–10.45pm, Sat noon–3.30pm & 6.30–10.45pm
Accepts MasterCard, Switch, Visa

ITALIAN

The menu, which changes every month or so, is written in a wonderful mix that could only be called Italglish. You'll find gems like tagliatelle al finochietto with Italian bacon and spinach (£7) and guinea fowl al gusto di honey ginger and broccoli (£13.50). It's a sub-editor's nightmare and refuses to stick to any rules. The philosophy of the kitchen, however, is clearly entirely Italian. Starters include zuppa di ceci (£5) – chickpea soup, and salad of avocado and Mozzarella (£6.50). Pastas come as starters or main courses; there are four or five main dishes, with specials chalked up on a blackboard above the kitchen. The cooking is competent and the portions large. A main course of gnoccheti Sarda alla matrice (£8.50) produces a bowl of accurately cooked, well-sauced pasta big enough to feed four. Or how about lamb al rosmarino with lentil raviolo (£14.50)? Puddings are on the heavy side, but charming nevertheless – witness "A Cuppa choccolate" (£4) – and the ice cream, such as gelato di mela con Calvados sauce (£4), is good. Gratifyingly, ordering cheese (£5.50) brings a selection of British cheeses from Neal's Yard rather than anything from Italy. The all-Italian wine list is long and well chosen, but with no explanations. Thankfully, the managers know it inside out and will advise something sensible.

Metrogusto has a relaxed, friendly atmosphere. The food is good, the pricing fair and the customers – a mixture of locals going out for a bite to eat, families celebrating and clubbers preparing for a night on the tiles. All look happy. No wonder.

Battersea

Ransome's Dock

Ransome's Dock is the kind of restaurant you would like to have at the bottom of your street. It is formal enough for those little celebrations or occasions with friends, and informal enough to pop into for a single dish at the bar. The food is good, seasonal and made with carefully sourced ingredients. Dishes are well-cooked and satisfying, not fussy, the wine list is encyclopedic, and service is friendly and efficient. All in

Cost	£17–£40
Address	35–37 Parkgate Rd, SW11
T	020 7223 1611
Station	BR Battersea Park
Open	Mon–Fri 11.30am–11pm, Sat 11.30am–midnight, Sun 11.30am–3.30pm
Accepts	All major credit cards
W	www.ransomesdock.co.uk

all, Martin Lam and his team have got it just right. Everything stems from the raw ingredients: they use a supplier in East Anglia for the smoked eels; they dicker with the Montgomerys over prime Cheddars. The menu changes monthly, but the philosophy behind it does not. Look out for the weekday set lunch – two courses at £13.50.

Before rampaging off through the main menu, make a pit stop at the daily specials; if nothing tempts you, turn to the seven or eight starters. If it's on, make a beeline for the Norfolk smoked eel with warm buckwheat pancakes and crème fraîche (£8.50). Very rich, very good, and very large. Or there may be a baked Perroche goat's cheese with lettuce and herb salad (£6). Or Morecambe Bay potted shrimps with wholemeal toast (£7.25). Main courses are well-balanced: Dutch calves' liver (£13.95) may come with bubble and squeak, and red wine and pancetta sauce – delicious stuff. Perhaps Elizabeth David's spinach and Ricotta gnocchi with salad leaves (£10) tempts? Or there may be a "shorthorn" sirloin steak (£18.25) with Béarnaise sauce and chips – not just any old steak, but one from a well-hung, Shorthorn steer. Puddings run from the complicated – a hot prune and Armagnac soufflé with Armagnac custard (£6) – to the simple – Greek yoghurt with honey and toasted pistachio nuts (£4.25).

The wine list makes awesome reading. Long, complex, arcane – full of producers and regions you have never heard of – with fair prices. Advice is both freely available and helpful.

Stepping Stone

Although outwardly insignificant among the trendy shops in this recently fashionable part of Battersea, Stepping Stone seems to have engendered a fierce loyalty in its clientele. As you enter, there's little to distract the eye. The walls of the rather plain dining room are jollied up by block painting in lime and brick red, and there's a small bar at one end. Otherwise the restaurant is refreshingly unadorned. There's no question – you're here to eat. Thankfully, there's a chef who likes food and knows how to cook, and a host who intends that his guests enjoy themselves. A better formula for running a successful and ultimately satisfying restaurant has yet to be devised, and the restaurant deserves its strong local following.

Cost	£15–£40
Address	123 Queenstown Rd, SW8
T	020 7622 0555
Station	Clapham Common/ BR Queenstown Road
Open	Mon–Fri noon–2.30pm & 7–11pm, Sat 7–11pm, Sun 12.30–3pm
Accepts	All major credit cards

The menu changes every service, allowing the kitchen the opportunity to be truly market led. Though reasonably fashionable, the cooking stays well within the kitchen's capabilities. There are likely to be a few classics, such as Serrano ham with figs (£6), and prawn and avocado salad (£6.75) – good examples of their type – but the menu ranges further for the more adventurous. A ham hock, foie gras and lentil terrine (£6.25) matches the softness and richness of the foie gras with robust, meaty ham; and scallops with pepperonata (£6.75) is a delicate juxtaposition of just-cooked shellfish with a punchy, powerful accompaniment. Main courses may include the likes of roast saddle of lamb with beetroot (£13.75), or rare grilled tuna with wok fried vegetables (£12.50). You can expect dishes to be generous, cooked with care and served with a friendly smile. Puddings – pear and almond tart (£4.50), or hot chocolate pudding with chocolate ice cream (£5) – are hearty rather than works of art. Commendably, the well-priced, well-planned and mostly European wine list features precious little over £20.

Stepping Stone has taken the admirable decision to oppose the two sittings per table per night trend. This means that it's essential to book, especially at weekends. The weekday set lunch is a bargain at £12.50 for two courses, and Sunday lunch is still good value at £17.50 for three courses.

Brixton

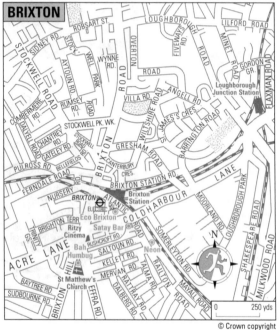

© Crown copyright

Bah Humbug

Bah Humbug lurks in the crypt of a converted church. Hardened Presbyterians may feel a little peculiar eating, drinking and making merry in such circumstances, but the less puritanical may even enjoy the thought that it's a short step to the Bug Bar, the trendy club-bar in the neighbouring crypt, and scarcely any further to the nightclub upstairs. The restaurant's subterranean location makes it naturally atmospheric, and the large space, divided by low vaults, feels remarkably intimate. There are comfortable sofas and chairs at the entrance, with a selection of newspapers to choose from, and the dining area is given a distinctly Gothic feel by velvet and tapestry. But there are no Goths here, just friendly, laid-back staff and people out to enjoy themselves.

Cost	£15–£25
Address	The Crypt, St Matthews Church, Brixton Hill, SW2
T	020 7738 3184
Station	Brixton
Open	Mon–Sat 5pm–midnight, Sun 11am–11.30pm
Accepts	MasterCard, Switch, Visa
W	www.bahhumbug.co.uk

The menu is mostly vegetarian, with a fish dish here and there. Diehard carnivores will be disappointed, but the choice is innovative and interesting enough to satisfy everyone else. You could start with pumpkin and almond roulade with fresh basil pesto and cream cheese filling (£3.80), or perhaps deep-fried Brie wrapped in smoked salmon with lime mayonnaise and red chard (£3.90). Or how about corn pancakes of roast peppers and red onion with coriander salsa and chilli aioli (£3.50)? Main courses run from a Wellington en croute made from cashews, brazils, almonds and mushroom duxelles with a red wine and shallot gravy and a 20-minute wait (£9.20); to spiced yoghurt marinated swordfish with roast squash, Jerusalem artichoke, grape and shallot compote (£11.90); or seared mackerel on crushed rosemary and garlic potatoes with gazpacho sauce (£12.70). Puds are simple but good, leading with a baked chocolate pudding with white chocolate Amaretto sauce (£4.50), and finishing at moody ice creams and sorbets (£2.20 to £3.60).

For the discerning drinker wishing to stray from the wine list, Bah Humbug offers some interesting variations – how about "Hot Shock-o-late" (£3)? Get your sugar high with a mixture of chocolate, whipped milk, cream plus a shot of Drambuie; or Cointreau; or Amaretto. You can even choose to have it made with soya milk – at last, a health drink that's bad for you!

Eco Brixton

PIZZA

If you're in Brixton around noon, Eco is a must for your lunch break. Make your way to Brixton Market – London's first market with electric light – and don't be put off by the smell from the fishmonger's shop opposite. Once inside Eco, the whiff soon gives way to more appetizing wafts of cooked cheese and coffee from your neighbour's table. Peruse the menu while you queue among the trailing shoppers, be prepared to share your table, then sit down to perhaps the best pizza in South London. Pizzeria Franco, now technically Eco Brixton, has the same menu as its sister, Eco on Clapham High Street, but the Brixton branch closes at 5pm. It's small and popular, so things can get hectic. Still, the service is friendly, the pizzas crisp and the salads mountainous. Plus there is an identically priced takeaway menu.

Cost	£8–£20

Address 4 Market Row, Brixton Market, Electric Row, SW9
T 020 7738 3021
Station Brixton
Open Mon, Tues & Thurs–Sat 8am–5pm, Wed 8am–4pm
Accepts MasterCard, Visa
W www.ecorestaurant.com

All the famous pizzas are here: pleasingly pungent Napolitana (£5.50) with the sacred trio of anchovies, olives and capers, and quattro stagioni (£6.50), packed full of goodies. But why not try something less familiar, such as coriander-topped roasted red pepper and aubergine (£6.30)? Or enjoy la dolce vita (£6.50), where rocket, mushrooms and dolcelatte all vie for attention? Or even the amore (£6.30), with its French beans, artichoke, pepper and aubergine? Or one of the calzone (all £6.70)? It's a difficult choice. For a lighter meal – lighter only because of the absence of carbohydrate – try a salad. Tricolore (£5.90) is made with baby Mozzarella, beef tomato, avocado and olives, while antipasto pancetta (£7.80) includes avocado, prawns, chicken, buffalo Mozzarella, pancetta and artichoke. Side orders like the melted cheese bread (£3.10) and mushroom bread (£3.50) are highly recommended. For sandwiches, Eco also impresses: focaccia are stuffed with delights like Parma ham and rocket (£5.90) or chicken and barbecue ham (£5.50).

You could also go for starters, but at lunch they seem a little surplus to requirements. There are just eight options, ranging from avocado vinaigrette (£3.60) to seafood salad (£4.90). Puddings are even scarcer: pecan pie (£3.20), tiramisù (£3.50) and profiteroles (£3.20).

Neon

It took most of the first year to organize, but Neon now has an eponymous light outside as a beacon to passing diners. In a city where more and more restaurateurs are turning to bar trade as a way of making up for the fickle nature of punters, Neon is making progress against the flow, and during 2000 the bar element declined and the restaurant side took over. Wander up

Cost	£10–£30
Address	71 Atlantic Rd, SW9
T	020 7738 6576
Station	Brixton
Open	Mon–Fri 6pm–midnight, Sat 11.30am–3pm & 6pm–midnight, Sun 6–11pm
Accepts	MasterCard, Switch, Visa

Atlantic Road, past the debris left after the day's trading at Brixton Market, and look out for Neon on your left. Despite the fashionably deep-red reception area and the minimalist dining space – all black and white, with a huge monochrome painting on one wall – this is a friendly and laid-back place which has obviously struck a chord with trendy Brixtonians – perhaps they like sitting on black lacquer benches and eating at black lacquer tables.

The food is authentically Italian and the menu broadly seasonal, leading the hungry from breads through pizzas and pastas, then on to some grander main courses, sides and salads, and so to desserts. The "breads" section is interesting: what about focaccia Abruzzese con sfrigole (£4.20), helpfully subtitled fried pork scratchings! Pizzas are bold and good – pizza salsiccia (£7.40) is a successful marriage of Italian sausage with turnip greens and Mozzarella. As you read down the list of pasta dishes, and just as you get past orecchiette alla Pugliese (£4.80/£7.40) there's a shock, cotechino con lenticchie (£5.50/£7.90) – sausage and lentil soup – has been slipped in. What a grand choice! Mains range from classics like porchetta (£9.90) – here it's a slab of belly pork rather than a whole piglet; and baccala e pepperoni (£11.50) – a dish of grilled salt cod; to spiedini di calamari e gamberi (£11.50) – grilled skewers of squid and king prawns. The salads also have lurking wild cards like arancini di riso (£5.40), which are deep fried balls of rice with melting Mozzarella centres. Puds are predictable.

The wine list also underwent a rethink in 2000. It is short and carefully chosen, perfectly attuned to the new menu. There's a decent Soave (£11.40), and a splendid Cannonau (£13.40).

Satay Bar

The Satay Bar, part of the regener-ation of the heart of Brixton, is tucked away behind the Ritzy cinema. First impression of this lively restaurant and bar is one of fun, pure and simple; the term "laid-back" could have been invented for it. The interior is dark and warm, and the non-stop party atmos-phere is bolstered by the thumping beat of the background music. Settle in, relax and take a look at the art. If you happen to like one of the many paintings adorning the walls, buy it – the restaurant doubles as a gallery.

Cost	£14–£27

Address 450 Coldharbour Lane, SW9
T 020 7326 5001
Station Brixton
Open Mon–Thurs noon–3pm & 6–11.30pm, Fri & Sat noon–2am, Sun 1pm–midnight
Accepts All major credit cards
W www.sataybar.co.uk

Dishes are Indonesian with the chilli factor toned down (for the most part) to accommodate European taste buds. The menu is a testing one – at least when it comes to pronouncing the names of the dishes – but the food is well cooked, service is friendly and efficient, and the prices are reasonable. Your waiter will smile benignly at your attempt to say udang goreng tepung (£6.15) – a starter of lightly battered, deep-fried king prawns served with a sweet chilli sauce. Obvious choices, such as the chicken or prawn satay (£5.50), are rated by some as the best in London. Otherwise try the chicken wings with garlic and green chilli (£4.75) – no less appealing. The hottest dishes are to be found in the curry section. The medium kari ikan (£5.50), a salmon-based, Javanese fish curry, packs a punch even though styled "medium", while the ren-dang ayam (£5.95), a spicy chicken dish, is only cooled by the addition of a coconut sauce. For something lighter, the mee goreng (£4.75) is a satisfying dish of spicy egg noodles fried with seafood and vegetables; or there's gado-gado (£4.50), a side dish of bean curd and vegetables with spicy peanut sauce, which is almost a meal in itself.

If terminal indecision sets in and you find yourself pinned by the menu like a rabbit in the headlights, try the rijstafel (£13.95 per person, minimum order for two), a combination of six specially selected dishes. This also has a vegetarian option.

Clapham & Wandsworth

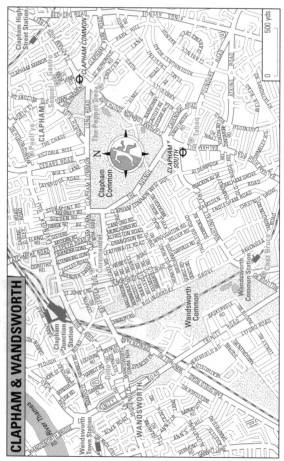

CLAPHAM & WANDSWORTH

© Crown copyright

0   500 yds

Chez Bruce

Bruce Poole's comfortable little restaurant has weathered the storm attendant on gaining a Michelin star with admirable aplomb. All the major pitfalls have been avoided. The regulars may have been nervous, expecting radical change – amuse whatevers; architecturally tall dishes; prissy service – the down side of star chasing. Good news. Chez Bruce is still delivering honest, unfussy, earthy, richly flavoured food. It is old-fashioned food which avoids the latest gastro-trend and often features the likes of pig's trotters, and rabbit, and mackerel. It is also a real bargain. The star has made one difference, however: the wine list has been extended and refined and is now winning prizes of its own. Prix fixe three-course menus offer lunch for £21.50 (Sun £25), and dinner for £27.50.

Cost	£25–£40
Address	2 Bellevue Rd, SW17
T	020 8672 0114
Station	BR Wandsworth Common
Open	Mon–Thurs noon–2pm & 7–10.15pm, Fri & Sat 12.30–2.30pm & 6.30–10.30pm, Sun 12.30–3pm
Accepts	All major credit cards

The menu changes from season to season and day to day. Generally, the lunch menu is a shortened version of the dinner menu. The kind of starters you can expect are cream of asparagus soup, foie gras and chicken liver parfait with toasted brioche, and terrine of smoked and cured fish with beetroot and horseradish. Or there might be a classic lurking, perhaps vitello tonnato. Main course dishes are deeply satisfying. You could well find rump of lamb with galette Sarladaise, ratatouille and aioli, or roast cod with olive oil mashed potatoes, or roast belly of pork with crackling, lentils, girolles and salsa verde, or roast pigeon with fondant potato, mushroom duxelle and Madeira sauce. This is one of those places where everything on the menu tempts, it's also one of the last strongholds of offal (perhaps the reason why this restaurant is the favourite haunt of so many off-duty chefs?). Look out for sweetbreads, or perhaps calves' liver served with spinach and Ricotta ravioli, sage beurre noisette and Madeira jus.

The sweets here are well-executed classics: proper crème brûlée; clafoutis of plums with clotted cream; tarte Tatin aux poires. No wonder Chez Bruce is booked every evening well in advance. Go for lunch instead – it'll make your day.

Coromandel

The Coromandel Coast (bottom of India, on the right) has lost out in the publicity war with the Malabar Coast (bottom of India, on the left). London has a good many Keralan restaurants (Malabar) and a good many Goan restaurants (Malabar-ish), but Tamil Nadu (Coromandel) isn't so readily front of mind. This restaurant hedges its bets quite suc-

Cost	£17–£50
Address	2 Battersea Rise, SW11
T	020 7738 0038
Station	BR Wandsworth Town
Open	Daily 11am–3pm & 6.30–11pm
Accepts	All major credit cards

cessfully, proclaiming itself a "Southern Indian" restaurant and offering a menu that runs all the way from South Indian vegetarian dishes – dosas and so forth – to Keralan dishes, chilli rich Chettinad dishes from Tamil Nadu, and Sri Lankan specialities. Spread over two floors, the dining room is brightly painted, modern and busy. Prices are at about the same level as most of the other restaurants hereabouts, which ends up being somewhat higher than you'd expect in a run-of-the-mill curry house. Which is fair enough, as Coromandel is not run-of-the-mill.

On the menu you will find a small letter "s" beside some dishes, this means that they are only available on selected days. So, on one day starters might include fish cutlets (£4.95), which are a kind of Sri Lankan fish rissole, and on another occasion there may be devilled chicken (£4.95) – a chilli-hot Sri Lankan stir fry. Try the pakodas (£3.45), which are small vegetable fritters, like chunky, spicy, tempura. Or consider starting in the tandoor section with the fish tikka (£4.95), which is a well-marinated kingfish, and very tasty indeed. Main course stars include the famous Chettinad chicken (£6.95), rich with small, infamous, dried, red chillies. Or there's mutton poriyal (£7.95), which is a splendid, dry, almost musty curry. From the fish section try the fish kuzambu (£7.95) – kingfish again in subtle spicy gravy. The vegetable dishes are good – cadju curry (£6.95) is made with cashews and is rather surprising, if only because the nuts have been cooked until quite soft. Coromandel's breads are also worth investigating, as is their lemon rice (£2.50).

The service is solicitous here, but the staff are clearly concerned lest the food prove too hot for you. So remember to insist that your wonderful chicken Chettinad is authentically, painfully, blisteringly hot.

Ditto

Ditto is split down the middle: half is bar, half is restaurant. You are in Wandsworth, on the borders of Clapham, and this is a neighbourhood restaurant with a local clientele. Hold those two images in your mind and you'll have a very clear idea of what this place is like. The bar is busy and loud, the restaurant is busy and loud. Don't even consider popping in at peak time without a booking. Most nights, at just after eight, a trampling herd of affluent nearly-forty-somethings leave their au pairs watching over the infants and arrive for nosebag. The service is adroit, the menu is mainly French or Modern British and the food is good but not great. Thankfully the pricing keeps in perfect step with all of the above and delivers pretty good value.

Cost	£10–£40

Address 55–57 East Hill, SW18
T 020 8877 0110
Station BR Wandsworth Town
Open Mon–Thurs noon–3pm & 6–11pm, Fri noon–3pm & 6–11.30pm, Sat 10.30am–4.30pm & 6–11.30pm, Sun 10.30am–10pm
Accepts All major credit cards
W www.doditto.co.uk

MODERN BRITISH

The menu changes weekly and you can approach it two different ways. There's a set menu offering two courses for £14.50 and three courses for £18.50. There's a choice of three, three, and three and they are not "second best" dishes. Starters might include new potatoes topped with black pudding and a soft poached egg, while mains range from roast darne of salmon to twice-cooked shank of lamb on basil mash. There is also an à la carte. From the starters, a smoked haddock fishcake on chive butter sauce (£4.95) is large and spherical; there's a woodland mushroom and spinach risotto (£5.50) – an interesting dish in which a creamy risotto is topped with a layer of spinach leaves, then some sautéed mushrooms and finally a Parmesan crisp. Mains range from pan-roast tranche of skate with capers and winkles (£12.75), to pork cutlet with grain mustard mash and prune sauce (£9.95). Thankfully, the wine list won't make you dive for your wallet – it stretches across continents and from £11.50 to £30 a bottle.

Lunch is an excellent deal – on weekdays three courses with a glass of wine costs £10. Think about "Goat's cheese, sun-dried tomato crostini; cod fillet pan-roasted on clam Provençale; and sticky toffee pudding". Worth skiving for.

Gastro

You're not allowed to book at this attractive little bistro off Clapham Common and, somewhat annoyingly, they restrict the tables at the front to parties of four and regulars. So if there are just two of you, you are likely to be shown through to the corridor-like room on the side or to places at the communal table at the back. Cheer up, though, the big table is a jolly affair. You'll be able to see what everybody else orders, which always helps when trying to make up your own mind, and you'll have a perfect view of the kitchen, a room so small that the mind boggles at the thought of producing dinner for eight in there, let alone for a restaurantful.

Cost	£14–£22
Address	67 Venn St, SW4
T	020 7627 0222
Station	Clapham Common
Open	Daily 8am–midnight
Accepts	Cash or cheque only

The staff is French and the menu lists all the Gallic favourites, which are inexpensive and generously portioned. Think yourself back to your last French holiday and enjoy. Under hors d'oeuvre you'll find a pukka soupe de poisson (£3.95) with the classic trimmings. Ordering seafood is straightforward: oysters are sold in sixes (£6.95), mussels arrive à la marinière (£5.95); and crabe mayonnaise (£7.95) is exactly that – a whole crab and mayonnaise. No arguments there! A pissaladière (£3.95), the traditional southern tart of onions, olives and anchovies, comes with crumbly, perfectly cooked pastry that looks and tastes as though they make it themselves. The mains will also cosset any Francophile tendencies you may have: lapin aux poivrons (£10.75) – rabbit stew with peppers; filet de Bar grillée au cidre (£14.95) – described as a grilled sea bass fillet with cider sauce; there is even andouillette grillée à la moutarde (£7.45) – the ripely scented tripe sausage that is somewhat "experts only". Perhaps a plain entrecôte (£11.65) tempts? Or half a lobster (£16.95)? And there is always boudin noir pommes puree (£7.25) – black pudding, apples and mash - which is as good and as simple as it sounds. For puds think patisserie, and good patisserie at that.

House wine is served by the glass, carafe and bottle. The red is better than the white, but not by much. If funds are sufficient, delve further into the short list, or do the sensible thing and order a bottle of top-class French cider (£6.25).

Paell'Ya

🍴 Brits on holiday in Spain eat a lot of paella. Those large flat dishes with a gentle mound of rice, made golden by saffron and slow cooking… The combinations of meat and shellfish may puzzle, and the absence of green vegetables, but what the hell – we're on holiday! Paell'Ya has "this is the first of a chain" written all over it, but given the abysmal failure of most chains to provide anything halfway decent to eat we should wish them luck. The food is good here.

Cost	£15–£35

Address 811–813 Wandsworth Rd, SW8
T 020 7627 5151
Station BR Wandsworth Road
Open Daily noon–11pm
Accepts All major credit cards except Amex and Diners
W www.paellya.co.uk

SPANISH

One might question the wisdom of launching a paella establishment on the London restaurant scene. Paellas take at least thirty minutes to cook – at today's frantic pace, will customers wait that long for their main course? They should. It is worth it. While away the time with some tapas: pan Catalan (£2.95) is fine – toast with tomato, garlic and oil; the gambas a la plancha are large, precisely cooked prawns; the patatas bravas (£3.75) are suitably spicy. Then the menu detours through salads before hitting the high spots – the paellas. These are prepared for two, four or eight people and are priced per person. The paella mariscos (£11.95) is delicious. Lots of monkfish, langoustines, prawns and mussels, with a good saffrony base and plenty of those areas where the rice has just caught on the bottom of the pan, giving those splendid crispy bits. Paella campesina (£9.95) is another star turn – rabbit, chicken, snails, green beans and butter beans – hearty, full flavoured and well seasoned. There's also paella vasca (£8.95), made with salt cod and spinach. Or there's the paella bogavante (£17.95), which features a whole roast lobster. Puds are a bit pedestrian – plump for the ice cream with Pedro Ximenez sherry (£4.75).

Beware cheery waitresses bearing a glass flask that looks like a cross between a glass watering can and something from Dr Jekyll's lab. You're supposed to pour white wine from a great height into your open mouth without drowning. Prepare for a trip to the dry cleaners.

The Pepper Tree

Situated on the seemingly endless south side of the Common, just a stone's throw from the tube station, this open-fronted Thai eatery serves no-nonsense, short-order dishes. This kind of spicy Thai food is perfectly in tune with the clientele, which is predominantly made up of twenty-somethings, as will be instantly apparent from both the crowds and the hubbub. Thankfully, the food is well cooked in a pleasantly straightforward sort of way and prices are competitive. Look out for the weekly "chef's special" (£5.50) which depends on a telling combination of the chef's mood and just what ingredients are good each particular week.

Cost	£12–£25

Address 19 Clapham Common South Side, SW4
T 020 7622 1758
Station Clapham Common
Open Mon noon–3pm & 6–10.30pm, Tues–Sat noon–3pm & 6–11pm, Sun noon–10.30pm
Accepts MasterCard, Visa

You can build your meal in stages, rather like you would a Greek meze. Vegetable rolls (£2.25) are made with vermicelli noodles, shaved carrots and Chinese mushrooms wrapped in filo pastry. Egg-fried rice (£1.75), is just that; or there's a stir-fry of mixed seafood (£4.50), which is tossed with fresh chillies, garlic and sweet basil. Green prawn curry (£3.95) is simmered in coconut milk with Thai aubergines, lime leaves and sweet basil, and comes medium-hot. Big tum chicken noodles (£4.75) are thick, yellow and fried with chillies and sweet basil. Among the salads, the Pepper Tree (£3.95) combines marinated grilled slices of beef with lemon juice, coriander, spring onions and chilli. Many dishes use the same ingredients but ring the changes in terms of balance and preparation techniques. Sweet things include stem ginger ice cream (£1.95) and bananas in coconut milk (£2.50) sprinkled with sesame seeds. Sticky rice with mango (£2.50) is described on the menu as mango with sticky rice, which seems a model of accuracy.

The Pepper Tree churns out simple spicy food, which is distributed by cheerful staff and sold at affordable prices. Even the drinks are reasonable – you can get a mug of tea for under a quid and there are bottles of house reds and whites at £7.95. There's also Argentine Norton Merlot (£11.95), which is a real bargain.

Sequel

Venn Street seems to have turned itself into something of a gastronomic Mecca in Clapham, and Sequel, one of the latest to join the ranks, is already proving to be a hit with the pilgrims. If you arrive for an early dinner you'll find the place a little quiet, but it hots up as the evening moves on. There's a pleasant bar at the front of the premises, but for dinner you should make your way to the back, where you'll find a small mezzanine restaurant area.

Cost	£20–£50

Address 4 Venn St, SW4
T 020 7622 4222
Station Clapham Common
Open Mon–Fri 5pm–midnight,
Sat 10.30am–midnight, Sun
11am–midnight
Accepts All major credit cards

FUSION

The food is of the modern eclectic variety, with plenty of lateral thinking and fusion ideas. Fusion food may have fallen from the very pinnacle of fashion, but it can still prove interesting. In 2001 the menu here reverted to the ordinary way of doing things and now there are starters and mains rather than a single list of dishes arranged by price. The starters lead from the relatively straightforward – chilli beef and tamarind soup (£5.50); through "fusions" like sweet potato, mint, salted cashews, dahlmooth (£4.50); to the outer fringes of credibility – kangaroo tartare, shitake salad, quail's egg (£6). There is little familiar or comfortable among the mains either – try choosing between Cape Malay lamb shank, plantain tatale, scotch bonnet pepper jelly (£12), and paperbark-roasted wild boar, smoked aubergine mash, goats cheese, red onion marmelade (£14). It makes crusted chicken breast, Bombay potato, cucumber and pickled ginger raita (£10.50) sound tame. When successful these dishes are exciting – full of passion and new ideas. But whether they work for you will depend upon how adventurous you are and the kind of taste combinations you like.

There are only about thirty seats in the restaurant so you'd be wise to book. Should you arrive before your companions (or become bored with them) there are classic movies to watch – think Life is Beautiful or Rear Window – with the sound turned down.

Clapham & Wandsworth

Tabaq

The owners of Tabaq used to drive up from the suburbs to work in a smart West End restaurant, and on the way they would travel up Balham Hill and past Clapham Common. They had set their sights on having a restaurant of their own, smarter than the usual curry house, somewhere they would serve traditional Pakistani specialities. So when signs went up outside 47 Balham Hill they took the plunge. They named their restaurant after the tabaq – a large serving dish – and set about dishing up authentic Lahori fare. Plaudits soon arrived: in 1998 and 1999 they won the Best Pakistani Restaurant in the UK and National Curry Chef awards.

Cost	£14–£24
Address	47 Balham Hill, SW12
T	020 8673 7820
Station	Clapham South
Open	Mon–Sat noon–2.45pm & 6pm–midnight
Accepts	All major credit cards
W	www.tabaq.co.uk

The menu comes with a multitude of sections – starters, grills, seafood, chicken curries, specialities, rice, breads, natural vegetables. To start go straight for the tandoor and grill section, which features some of the best dishes on the menu, and most commendably carries the boast "we do not add colour to our food". Seek kabab Lahori (£6.25) is made from well-seasoned minced lamb, and shish kabab lamb (£6.25) is delicious. Or try the masala machli Lahori (£6.25) – fish in a light and spicy batter. As an accompaniment order raita (£1.95) – yoghurt with cucumber, herbs and spices, and maybe a naan-e-Punjabi (£2.50) – heavy, butter-rich bread from the tandoor – with kachomer (£1.95), a kind of coarse-cut Asian salsa. At this stage of your meal you may well be tempted to choose simply from the salan or chicken curries. There's murgh taway ka makhani (£8.50) - this sauce is thought to be a buttery ancestor of chicken tikka masala – or murgh palak (£7.25), chicken and spinach served in a handi. Maybe you'd like to try one of the dishes that won the Tabaq chef one of his many awards? Zaikadaar haandi gosht (£8.50) is a rich dish of lamb marinated in yoghurt and cooked in a traditional cooking pot. And there are good biryanis.

Desserts include one item you do not immediately associate with Pakistani cuisine – baked Alaska (£12), which serves two and must be ordered in advance.

Greenwich & Blackheath

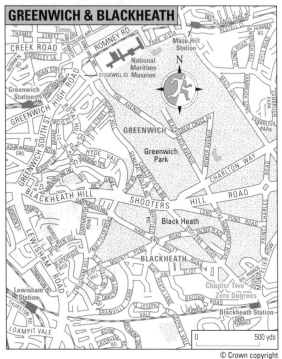

GREENWICH & BLACKHEATH

© Crown copyright

Chapter Two

Occupying a bright, sunny position (weather permitting) in a small smart parade of shops just off the heath, Chapter Two seems to promise good things even from the outside. Its clean, half-clear, half-frosted glass frontage allows you to glimpse the band of well-dressed diners enjoying themselves within. And when you enter you'll find yourself in a sleek, modern space, with light wood and metal complemented by richly coloured walls, all coming together to set off crisp linen and sparkling glassware. The whole place has a professionally-run air, exuding comfort and confidence.

Cost	£15–£40

Address 43–45 Montpelier Vale, Blackheath, SE3
T 020 8333 2666
Station BR Blackheath
Open Mon–Thurs noon–2.30pm & 6–10pm, Fri & Sat noon–2.30pm & 6–11pm, Sun noon–3.30pm & 7–9.30pm
Accepts All major credit cards

This feeling of competence also embraces the menu. Dinner is a set price affair: £16.50 for two courses; £19.50 for three, from Sunday to Thursday, going up to £22.50 on Friday and Saturday evenings. There's nothing particularly unusual or showy on offer, but there's plenty of choice among the reasonably classic, well-thought out dishes that use decent ingredients to good advantage. Among the first courses you'll find pumpkin soup with coriander gnocchi and cardamom; a classic chicken liver and foie gras parfait served with bacon bread; and the increasingly fashionable soused herring with a potato and watercress salad. Main courses include the likes of delicate, pan-fried Jersey plaice with aioli potatoes; or a daube of beef with horseradish, parsley dumplings and root vegetables for the heartier appetite. Portions are generous and presentation is top class. Someone in the kitchen obviously fancies him or herself as a bit of an artist, and when it comes to puds it seems they've been given a free rein. It has resulted in some quite architectural fancies. Thankfully, the substance of the puds – chocolate and orange ganache with shortbread; banana tarte Tatin with chocolate sauce and vanilla ice cream – is perfectly sound.

Chapter Two is a decent local restaurant, special enough for annual occasions but not so expensive as to prohibit more regular visits. Service is efficient and professional rather than pally, and someone has obviously given the wine list some thought: there's a wide range of wines from around the world, available at ungreedy prices, including a fair choice by the glass. If you've a nose for a bargain, visit for lunch, when the menu is much the same as the evening but prices fall to £14.50 for two courses and £18.50 for three (Sunday lunch, £13/£16).

Time

FUSION

A boatswain's hail from the Cutty Sark (and anywhere in Dome-land) is not promising territory for a food lover. This is tourist terrain, where the restaurants don't need to work very hard to pull in the punters. Thankfully, Time is an exception. First impressions are no great shakes, mind you. Beyond the impressive doorway, entrance is gained up a flight of insignificant stairs to the right, and when you reach the first level you'll be confronted with a noisy bar with little sign of dining. But simply glance onwards and upwards towards the dining room above, work your way to the back of the bar and up another set of stairs, and you'll suddenly feel very comfortable. Here is a small (just 35 or so seats), appealing dining room, with roomy tables and an elegant clientele overlooking the merry mayhem below.

Cost	£22–£50

Address 7a College Approach, SE10
T 020 8305 9767
Station Cutty Sark Gardens
Open Tues–Sat 6.30–10.30pm, Sun noon–7pm
Accepts All major credit cards except Diners
W www.timerestaurant.co.uk

The menu is not a long one, with just six starters and six main courses, but it offers plenty of choice, changing regularly to reflect what the markets have to offer and celebrating flavours borrowed from around the world. First courses vary from roast chorizo salad with soft poached egg and fig (£5.95) to an interesting guineafowl and oyster-mushroom terrine with dressed French beans (£7.95). On the way you might find marinated char-grilled king prawns with roast beetroot and mango salsa (£8.95). Main courses range from roast salmon with red onion marmalade, char-grilled polenta and grapefruit salsa (£12.95) to char-grilled calves liver with pancetta, mash and onion gravy (£12.95), and pan-fried swordfish with potato tartar and pak choi (£12.95). Vegetarians are well served, with dishes like basil and hazelnut risotto with rocket salad and Parmesan snap (£10.95). Portions are generous but not oppressively so. Desserts are substantial rather than froufrou.

Visit midweek and you'll probably be entertained by some light jazz, but whether there is music playing or not you'll find the place both friendly and lively, and the service agreeable. Booking is essential.

Zerodegrees

0° – as the logotype, napkins, menus and so forth would have it – is a lively fun factory in the heart of sedate and respectable Blackheath. The proprietors have taken the microbrewery, a formula that has been honed to perfection in the West End, and put together a lively venue. It's a grand looking space, all aluminium cladding and stainless steel brewing equipment, with a large bar which dominates and a small area for seating and eating by the open kitchen.

| Cost | £8–£20 |

Address 29–31 Montpelier Vale, Blackheath SE3
T 020 8852 5619
Station BR Blackheath
Open Daily noon–11.30pm
Accepts All major credit cards except Diners
W www.zerodegrees-microbrewery.co.uk

ITALIAN/PIZZA

The menu is an obvious one. Other beer places do wood-fired pizzas – so does Zerodegrees. Other beer places do special sausages – so does Zerodegrees. Other beer places do mussels … you've guessed it, so does Zerodegrees. It's an engagingly simple idea, and given that this is a loud, happy place full of people keen to get blatted by some pretty decent beers, the food admirably fulfils its role as a solid counterweight. If you want starters, it's best to keep it simple – garlic bread (£1.95); or there's a sound if uninspired Caesar salad (£6.50) – pity there are no anchovies. Sausages come with mash (£6.95), mussels come in a kilo pot with frites and mayo (£10.95) and there are eighteen different pizzas all tasting suitably smoky (£4.25 to £6.75).

Five different beers are brewed on the premises: a pilsner; a good, hoppy-tasting pale ale; a brown ale; a wheat ale; and a "special" which changes regularly to stop you getting bored. The pricing is simple: halves (£1.10); pints (£2.20); four-pint jugs (£8); and, at happy hour – in force from 4–7pm Monday to Friday – all pints are £1.50. Beer and loud music – everything you need to get happy, and then a pepperoni pizza to follow. It may not be original, and it's certainly not for the middle aged, but it works.

Kennington & Vauxhall

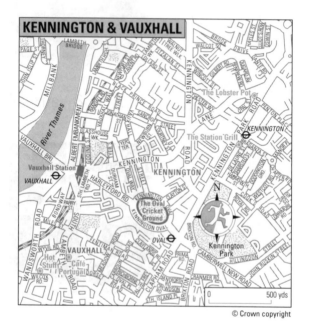

© Crown copyright

Café Portugal

When setting up a bar, café or restaurant, the first item on any proud new Portuguese owner's shopping list must be the telly. All the televisions in South Lambeth Road seem to be turned up loud, and the one in the bar of Café Portugal is no exception (thankfully the one in the restaurant half of the operation is not always switched on). Portuguese restaurateurs have all mastered the trick of integrating their establishments with the community and Café Portugal is a laid-back, easy-paced kind of eatery with distinctly dodgy mud-orange decor. The food is workmanlike and appears authentically Portuguese, as do some of the television programmes.

Cost	£10–£25

Address Victoria House, South Lambeth Rd, SW8

T 020 7587 1962

Station Vauxhall

Open Daily 8am–11pm

Accepts All major credit cards except Diners

PORTUGUESE

To start with you can veer towards the tapas menu which runs from the steady – calamares (£3.50), fried squid, and sopado dia (£2.10), the soup of the day – to the more evocative orelha de porco (£2.50), billed as "pork's ear, garnished". Otherwise aim for the starters proper, which include dishes like ameijoas a Café Portugal (£3.60) – clams – and that trusty old Portuguese special, avocado with prawns (£3.10). Scouring the tapas list may well be the more rewarding option. The menu goes on to list a dozen fish options: salmon, sea bass, Dover sole, three monkfish dishes and three ways with salt cod. Of the latter, the most adventurous sounding, bacalhau à Gomes de Sá (£8) turns out to be a stunning and gloriously simple dish of salt cod cooked in the oven with potatoes, onions, and chunks of hard boiled egg. For the meat eater there's carne de porco à Alentejana (£8), another all-in-one, home-cooked kind of meal. Small chunks of pork are served with some clams, chorizo, and chopped pickled vegetables, then small cubes of crisp-fried potato are scattered over the top. The resulting dish is a grand blend of tastes and textures. At Café Portugal, puddings are largely pastries and you are doomed if you don't like eggy confections.

The wine list here is a Portuguese affair, and reasonably priced, so look out for interesting little numbers from the Dão and the Douro. Café Portugal caters to its knowledgeable, mainly Portuguese, clientele.

Hot Stuff

This tiny restaurant, run by the Dawood family in south Lambeth, is something of an institution. It has only a few seats and offers simple and startlingly cheap food to an enthusiastic local following. The food is just what you would expect to get at home – assuming you are part of Nairobi's Asian community. Trade is good and has been the catalyst for a refurb – the place is elegant in soft blues and greens.

INDIAN

Cost	£10–£20

Address 19 Wilcox Rd, SW8
T 020 7720 1480
Station Vauxhall/Stockwell
Open Mon–Fri noon–10pm,
Sat 4–10pm
Accepts All major credit cards
W www.eathotstuff.com

The starters are sound rather than glorious, so it's best to dive straight into the curries. The list grew in 2001 and now there are over a dozen chicken curries and a similar number of lamb dishes, all priced at between £3 and £5. The most expensive is the king prawn biryani, which costs £6.50, not much more than you would pay for a curried potato in the West End. And it is hard to find any fault with a curry that costs just £3! The portions aren't monster-sized, and the spicing isn't subtle, but the welcome is genuine and the bill is tiny. Arrive before 9.30pm and you can sample the delights of the stuffed paratha (£1.30) – light and crispy with potato in the middle, they taste seriously delicious. Chickpea curry (£2.30), daal (£2.20) and mixed vegetable curry (£2) all hit the spot with vegetarians. For meat-eaters, the chicken Madras (£3.15) is hot and workmanlike, while the chicken bhuna (£3.15) is rich and very good. However, the jewel in the crown of the Hot Stuff menu is masala fish (£3.50), which is only available from Wednesdays to Saturdays. Thick chunks of tilapia are marinated for 24 hours in salt and lemon juice before being cooked in a rich sauce with coriander, cumin and ginger.

Hot Stuff closes prudently before the local pubs turn out, and part of the fun here is to watch latecomers – say a party of three arriving at 9.50pm – negotiating with the indomitable chef and matriarch, Beley Dawood. Promising to eat very quickly may do the trick, as this restaurant is driven by the principles of hospitality and puts many more pretentious establishments to shame.

The Lobster Pot

You have to feel for Nathalie Régent. What must it be like to be married to – and working alongside – a man whose love of the bizarre verges on the obsessional? Britain is famed for breeding dangerously potty chefs, but The Lobster Pot's chef-patron, Hervé Régent, originally from Vannes in Brittany, is well ahead of the field. Walk down Kennington Lane towards the restaurant and it's even money as to whether you are struck first by the life-size painted plywood cutout of Hervé dressed in oilskins, or the speakers relaying a soundtrack of seagulls and melancholy Breton foghorns. Inside, portholes allow you a glimpse of swimming fish, while in the upstairs bar there's a ship's wheel to play with while you await your table.

Cost	£10–£35
Address	3 Kennington Lane, SE11
T	020 7582 5556
Station	Kennington
Open	Tues–Sat noon–2.30pm & 7–11pm
Accepts	All major credit cards

VERY FRENCH/FISH

These clues all point towards fish, and doubtless Hervé will appear to greet you in nautical garb, moustache bristling, and guide you towards his good catches of the day. The fish here is pricey but it is very fresh and very well chosen. Starters range from well-made, very thick, traditional fish soup (£6.50) to a really proper plateau de fruits de mer (small £11.50, large £22.50). The main course specials sometimes feature strange fish that Hervé has discovered on his early-morning wanderings at Billingsgate. There are good spicy dishes too, such as fillet de thon a la Creole (£14.50), tuna with a perky tomato sauce, and monkfish with Cajun spices and white butter sauce (£15.50). Simpler, and as good in its way, is la sélection de la mer à l'ail (£14.50), which is a range of fishy bits – some monkfish tail, an oyster, a bit of sole, tiny squid, and so on – all grilled and slathered in garlic butter. The accompanying bread is notable, a soft, doughy "pain rustique", and for once le plateau de fromage "à la Française" (£6) doesn't disappoint.

The Lobster Pot's weekday set lunch (£13.50) – which could get you moules gratinées à l'ail followed by filet de merlan sauce créole and crêpe sauce à la mangue – makes lots of sense. And for a serious beano there is an eight-course surprise menu (three fish, one meat and so on, for £39.50 per person). In any case, whatever you plan on eating, do not venture here without your sense of humour.

The Station Grill

FRENCH

In 1962 the Station Grill, a steak house, opened for business, and proceeded over the next 37 years to build up a steady trade. Then, in December 1999, the proprietor's son, Erkin Mehmet, took up the baton. All change at the Station. In came a new dining room, a new kitchen and new

Cost	£18–£32

Address 2 Braganza St, SE17
T 020 7735 4769
Station Kennington
Open Tues–Sat 6–10pm, Sun 12.30–2.30pm
Accepts MasterCard, Visa

chefs. Mehmet switched from the kitchen to front of house and the Station Grill greeted 2000 as a surprisingly good French restaurant. Erkin's new chefs spent their formative years in the kitchens of the Roux Brothers catering division, and now the Station's menu (which changes regularly) offers tasty, well-presented, "bourgeois" French food that combines two blissful attributes: good cooking and low prices.

The menu is broadly seasonal and very ambitious. It costs £19.95 for two courses, £24.95 for three, and there's a thought-provoking four courser at £29.95. Astonishingly, whatever the kitchen tries seems to come off in some style. Starters range from a hot lobster soufflé with a coriander and capsicum sauce to a salad of veal sweetbreads sautéed in sage butter with lardons and croutons. Consommé of game comes with venison ravioli; the warm terrine of confit chicken is served with wild mushrooms and Savoy cabbage. Main courses are also comfortingly attractive: braised wild boar served with grelot onion, globe artichoke and pan fried mustard seed dumpling; grilled fillet of black bream with haricot vert, celery, new potatoes and a saffron and lemon dressing; rib-eye of beef topped with mushroom duxelles, watercress and a green peppercorn crust. Puddings are top-notch, too. Anyone for a hot chocolate soufflé with hot chocolate sauce? Or a rhubarb bread and butter pudding served with a warm vanilla Anglaise?

Very good stuff. And even when under pressure the service never loses its smile. The people working here care. In 2001 a rethink saw the demise of the steakhouse wine list and the introduction of a more contemporary selection at mercifully sensible prices. What would the old-time customers have made of a glass of Andrew Quady's black muscat dessert wine Elysium for £6?

Putney

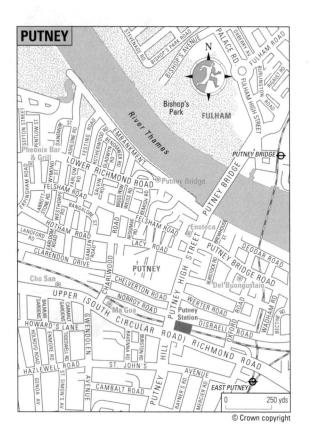

PUTNEY

N

River Thames

Bishop's Park

FULHAM

PUTNEY BRIDGE

Phoenix Bar & Grill

SEFTON STREET
BRENTLOW STREET
DANEHER ST
ASHLONE RD
FESTING ROAD
ROTHERWOOD RD
BENTHAM RD
GLADWIN RD
EMBANKMENT
BISHOP'S PARK ROAD
STEVENAGE RD
BISHOP'S AVENUE
PALACE RD
OXBERRY AV
FULHAM ROAD
BURLINGTON ROAD
NIGAULT RD
FULHAM HIGH STREET

Putney Bridge

LOWER RICHMOND ROAD
TARLOW RD
SALVIN RD
BRIGGS ROW
WEISS RD
BEMISH RD
FELSHAM ROAD
Enoteca
BREWHOUSE ST

FELSHAM ROAD
LACY ROAD
ROAD
REDGRAVE RD

WYMOND ST
WESTHORPE RD
ABBOTT STONE RD
BANGALORE ST
HOTHAM ROAD
PUTNEY HIGH STREET
PUTNEY BRIDGE ROAD
DEODAR ROAD

FINHAM ROAD
LANDFORD RD
EARLSDOM ROAD
CLARENDON DRIVE
GAMLEN ROAD
CHARLWOOD
PUTNEY
CHELVERTON ROAD
BURSTOCK RD

Cho San

Del Buongustaio

UPPER (SOUTH
BALMAR GARDENS
CARMALT GARDENS
NORROY ROAD
WERTER ROAD
WADHAM RD
BECTIVE RD

HOWARD'S LANE
ENMORE RD
TIDESWELL RD
Ma Goa
CIRCULAR ROAD)
Putney Station
DISRAELI ROAD
OXFORD ROAD

HOLROYD ROAD
GWENDOLEN
BURSTON RD
RAVENNA RD
RICHMOND ROAD

HAZLEWELL ROAD
GENOA AV
ST SIMON'S AV
ROAD
AVENUE
ST. JOHN'S
PUTNEY HILL
AVENUE
EAST PUTNEY

CAMBALT ROAD
RAYNER'S RD
MERCIER RD

0   250 yds

Del Buongustaio

On the first day of each month it's all change at Del Buongustaio as they unleash a new menu on the appreciative residents of Putney. The menu here features well-cooked, authentic food, with a sprinkling of less familiar dishes from Cinderella regions like Puglia and Piedmont, as well as some painstakingly researched gems that once graced tables in Renaissance Italy. The dining room is light, airy and pleasantly informal. The cooking is good too, with authentic dishes and friendly service. Take time to study the wine list, which is particularly strong on classy bottles from the less well-known provinces.

Cost	£19–£45

Address 283 Putney Bridge Rd, SW15
T 020 8780 9361
Station East Putney
Open Mon–Sat noon–3pm & 6.30–11pm
Accepts Amex, MasterCard, Visa
W www.theitalian restaurant.net

ITALIAN

Who knows what the next menu will bring? But you can hazard a guess that there will be interesting pasta dishes such as a splendid spaghetti con melanzane e Ricotta (£5.90 starter, £8.40 main) – spaghetti with cherry tomato, aubergine and Ricotta. Or perhaps garganelli al sugo d'anatra (£6.45) – pasta quills served with a ragout of duck. Thoroughly delicious. The piatto pizzicarello (£7.50), described with disarming modesty as a "plate of savouries", is a regular starter option. And then there is the torta rinascimentale di fave, Ricotta e prosciutto (£6.25) – an amazing multi-layered cake of broad beans, prosciutto, Ricotta and Fontina cheese that comes with a rocket and egg sauce. Main course dishes may include lamb, sea bass, veal, pork, chicken, guinea fowl, cod or perhaps a Swiss chard and Ricotta pudding. In season there may be a pastello di cacciagione (£15.50) which is a kind of medieval game pie containing a bit of everything. Look out for the rustic "dal campo" side dishes, particularly spinaci al burro e aglio (£2.95), spinach with butter and garlic!

It's worth saving space for a dessert if only for the eight splendid pudding wines, served by the glass, including Vin Santo (£3.80), the befuddlingly alcoholic Aleatico di Puglia (£3.80) and a 1995 Recioto della Valpolicella (£4.50). There is also a huge selection of merciless grappas…

Cho-San

JAPANESE

🍴 Too many Japanese restaurants use extremely high prices and ultra-swish West End premises to keep themselves to themselves. As a European adventurer basking in the impeccably polite and attentive service, it's hard not to feel a little anxious. What should you order? How do you eat it? Will it taste nice? How much does it cost? If you have ever been assailed by

Cost	£8–£35
Address	292 Upper Richmond Rd, SW15
☎	020 8788 9626
Station	BR Putney
Open	Tues–Fri 6.30–10.30pm, Sat & Sun noon–2.30pm & 6.30–10.30pm
Accepts	All major credit cards

these worries you should pop along to Cho-San in Putney. This small, unpretentious, family-run restaurant opened in 1998 and has gradually built up a mixed trade. As well as a host of knowledgeable Japanese drawn by the good fresh food and sensible prices there are interested Londoners tucking into sushi with gusto – on one occasion these devotees included a twelve-year-old girl, who, judging by her uniform, had dropped in for dinner on the way home from school.

The menu is a book. And one worth reading. This is your chance to try all those dishes you have never had, without wounding your pocket. The sushi is good. The sashimi is good. And a giant boat of assorted sushi and sashimi, with miso soup and dessert costs £15.90. But why not try some more obscure sushi? The prices of the fancy ones range from £2.60 to £5 for two pieces. Or, if you prefer your fish cooked, choose the perfect cuttlefish (£5.60) – a stunning achievement, its batter light enough to levitate. And then there's always the kushiage – dishes where something is put onto a skewer, gets an egg and breadcrumb jacket and is treated to a turn around the deep-fryer. Ordering tori kushiage (£3.90) gets you two skewers, each of which holds two large lumps of chicken and a chunk of sweet onion. Delicious. Or opt for tempura seafood and vegetable (£8.60), tempura king prawn (£8.60) or vegetable pancakes (£5.60). Then there are the meat dishes, the fish dishes, the rice dishes, the soba noodles, the udon noodles … and the hot sakes, cold sakes, and beers. You could eat your way to a good understanding of Japanese food here. Ask the charming, helpful staff and get stuck in.

If Japanese food isn't your special subject, take the easy option: there is a profusion of seven-course set meals costing between £15.80 and £16.80.

Enoteca

If you like your Italian food a little more adventurous than the usual, then it is worth making the journey to Putney and Giuseppe Turi's newly refurbished restaurant. Enoteca has been in the forefront of modern Italian cooking for some years now, and always has interesting new twists on traditional favourites. Everything is based on fresh

Cost	£25–£60
Address	28 Putney High St, SW15
T	020 8785 4449
Station	Putney Bridge
Open	Mon–Fri 12.30–2.30pm & 7–11pm, Sat 7–11pm
Accepts	All major credit cards

ITALIAN

ingredients and, like some other notable venues, Enoteca offers a very personal version of good Italian regional cooking – Turi himself hails from Apulia, and many dishes are based on recipes from this area. Enoteca takes its name from the Italian term for a smart wine shop, so it's hardly surprising that wines are a prominent feature. There's a monumental list of more than ninety specialist Italian wines and a separate by-the-glass menu offering eleven Italian regional wines – an excellent way to educate the palate. Exploring the Italian wine regions is something of a hobby for Turi; he has bought widely and wisely and laid them down for future drinking.

As for the food, you'd do well to start with the sgombro con insalata di verdura e giardiniera (£6.90) – confit mackerel; or on a simpler note, bresaola con insalata di spinaci (£7.90). Pasta choices may include ravioli con funghi di bosco (£9.50) and tagliolini al frutti di mare (£11.50), fine black and white pasta with a tasty mix of seafood. Main courses may include petto di faraona ripieno di Ricotta, spinaci e menta (£12.90) – guineafowl stuffed with Ricotta, spinach and mint (£12.90). There is always a fresh fish of the day and a dish of the day. Desserts will test your mettle – go for the torta di cioccolata con nocciole (£4.95), a blockbusting chocolate and hazelnut cake, or perhaps the particularly good, authentic tiramisù (£4.75).

Though there are many good restaurants in this area, Enoteca has a loyal following and, except for Monday and Tuesday nights, it is essential to book. If you're more of a wine bluff than a wine buff you'll be grateful for the discreet numbers printed beside each dish on the menu – they represent the recommended wines, all of which are available by the glass.

Putney

Ma Goa

Despite the stylish ochre interior complete with fans and blond wooden floor, despite the café-style chairs and tables, and the computer system to handle bills and orders, the overwhelming impression you are left with when you visit Ma Goa is of eating in somebody's home. It's the inspired home cooking that does it. And it helps that all the staff are related. This place is as far as you can possibly get from the chuck-it-in-a-frying-pan-and-heat-it-through school of curry cookery. The food is deceptively simple, slow-cooked and awesomely tasty. And it is authentically Goan into the bargain.

Cost	£14–£28

Address 244 Upper Richmond Rd, SW15
T 020 8780 1767
Station BR Putney/ East Putney
Open Tues–Sat 6.30–11pm, Sun 6–10pm
Accepts All major credit cards
W www.magoa.co.uk

The menu is fairly compact: half a dozen starters are followed by a dozen mains, while a blackboard adds a couple of dishes of the day. Shrimp balchao is a starter made from shrimps cooked in pickling spices and curry leaves (£4). Sorpotel (£4) is made from lamb's liver, kidney and pork in a sauce rich with roast spices, lime and coriander. The Goan sausage is, well, a sausage; it's rich too, with palm vinegar, cinnamon and green chillies (£4). Main courses are amazing. The spices are properly cooked out by slow cooking, which makes lifting the lids of the heavy clay serving pots a voyage of discovery. Porco vindaloo (£8.75), sharp with palm vinegar, is enriched with lumps of pork complete with rind. At the other end of the heat spectrum is gallina kodi (£8) which is a gentle guineafowl curry made with rose water. Ma's fish caldin (£8.75) is kind of fish stew with large chunks of fish in a coconut-based sauce. Or there's kata masala (£8.95), a chicken dish served on the bone (hooray) and heavy with cinnamon, black pepper, ginger and lime. Vegetarians are equally well served. Bund gobi (£3.50/£6.50) is stir-fried, shredded cabbage with carrots, ginger and cumin, while tauri (£3.50/£6.50) is courgettes with tomatoes and mustard seed. The rice here is excellent.

On the specials board you might be lucky enough to find lamb kodi (£8), described as "lamb with cloves, garlic and chilli". On the electronic message winging its way to the kitchen this is shortened to "Bella's lamb" – dishes here really are made from family recipes.

Phoenix Bar and Grill

This restaurant is a member of London's leading family of neighbourhood restaurants, and is related both to Sonny's (see p.397) and the Parade (see p.417). Anyone fancying their chances in what is a deadly, cut-throat marketplace would do well to study these establishments. They are all just trendy enough, the service is just slick enough and the cooking is marginally better than you would expect, with competitive pricing. And as a direct result they are wildly popular – it isn't only West End eateries where you have to book weeks in advance. The Phoenix has a large, white-painted room inside and a large, white-painted courtyard out front where you can eat alfresco (weather permitting – usually about three days each year).

Cost £15–£45

Address 162–164 Lower Richmond Rd, SW15
T 020 8780 3131
Station BR Putney
Open Mon–Thurs 12.30–2.30pm & 7–11pm, Fri & Sat 12.30–2.30pm & 7–11.30pm, Sun 12.30–3pm & 7–10pm
Accepts All major credit cards

The menu is commendably short and commendably seasonal. The service may be a tad too brusque for some, but this is an efficient, friendly place where the food comes flying out of the kitchen without delay, and the lack of pretension is to be admired. Starters range from the polished – a foie gras terrine, onion confit and toasted brioche (£8.50); to the more elegant – smoked eel with choucroute, bacon and butter sauce (£6); and the downright filling – wild rabbit papardelle, mushrooms and pancetta (£7). Mains could include a dish of smoked haddock, mash, black pudding and asparagus (£12.50) – a good chunk of peerless smoked haddock, firm and flaky. Or a duck breast with rosti and a chicory and orange salad (£13.50). Or seared tuna, spinach, soy, wasabi and ginger (£14.50). Or roast skate wing with anchovy butter (£12). This is a place that is perfectly in tune with its customers, even when it comes to puddings. There's treacle tart with clotted cream (£5); white- and dark-chocolate truffle cake (£5.50); and three English cheeses in good condition (£5.50).

The set lunch and "early bird" dinner (order by 7.45pm and go home by 8.45pm) are grand value at £12 for two courses and £15 for three. Try cream of garlic soup with poached egg, then grilled salmon, broccoli and butter sauce, culminating in chocolate brownie with vanilla ice cream. This is good value, worthy of the attentions of any early bird.

Putney Bridge

Putney Bridge occupies a purpose-built modern building that has deservedly won plaudits from the great and the good in the world of architecture. The chef, Anthony Demetre, favours a full-on approach: amuse-gueules and pre-desserts, accomplished presentation and a wine list that leads you gently through the expensive classics. And it is an approach that has already found favour with Mr Michelin and his band of inspectors. The food is good. Flavours are well balanced, everything looks attractive and there is plenty of inspiration. Then you pay, and this is not a bargain bite – unless, of course, you are very well heeled. Entry level is a three course set lunch at £18.50, thereafter the price increases to £42.50 for three courses (with occasional swingeing supplements) and £79.50 for a ten-course Menu Dégustation.

Cost	£25–£85
Address	The Embankment, SW15
T	020 8780 1811
Station	Putney Bridge
Open	Tues–Sat noon–2.30pm & 7–10.30pm, Sun 12.30–3pm
Accepts	All major credit cards
W	www.putneybridge restaurant.com

The menus change to reflect what produce is available. A typical set lunch might start with a light soup of chick peas and chorizo, a crisp samosa, then a piece of Charolais beef with a red wine and parsley sauce followed by an almond milk sorbet with caramelized Italian meringue. Very nice too. Venturing on to the à la Carte (at £42.50) you might start with red mullet "bécasse de mer" salad of cauliflower, broccoli, courgettes and tomatoes – this is challenging stuff. Or tortellini of duck confit and foie gras, vegetable and shimeji mushroom bouillon. Or roast young squid, marinated seafood and red pepper puree. For mains there are four fish and four meat, all elegant. What about a tournedos of monkfish, with roast vegetables flavoured with rosemary, caper beignets and a shrimp and parsley jus? Or roast squab pigeon with dolmades of liver, the juice scented with coffee and cardamom? All ingredients are top-quality and the sauces very well made. The wine list must be taken seriously by both you and your wallet.

Even if you can avoid the allure of a very good French cheeseboard (supplement £3), you won't be able to dodge the baked meringue and rhubarb "Alaska" or the zingy blood-orange sorbet.

Tower Bridge & Bermondsey

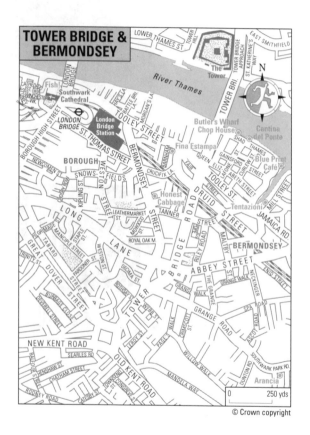

TOWER BRIDGE & BERMONDSEY

LOWER THAMES ST
TOWER HILL
EAST SMITHFIELD
TOWER BRIDGE APPROACH
ST. KATHERINE'S WAY
The Tower

River Thames

N

CATHEDRAL ST
Fish!
WINCHESTER WK
LONDON BRIDGE
Southwark Cathedral
LONDON BRIDGE
London Bridge Station
TOOLEY STREET
BATTLE BRI
DUKE ST
LA ST
MORGAN'S LA
ST. THOMAS STREET
BERMONDSEY
Butler's Wharf
Chop House
SHAD THAMES
Cantina del Ponte
TOWER BRI

BOROUGH HIGH STREET
NEWCOMEN ST
BOROUGH
ST. THOMAS STREET
WESTON ST
CRUCIFIX LA
GAINSFORD
Fina Estampa
QUEEN ELIZABETH ST
ELLIOTS ROW
CURLEW ST
Blue Print Café

REDCROSS WAY
SNOW'S FIELDS
KIPLING ST
Honest Cabbage
TANNER STREET
DRUID STREET
MILL STREET
Tentazioni
JAMAICA RD

LONG LANE
PILGRIMAGE ST
MANCIPLE STREET
STAPLE ST
LEATHERMARKET ST
MAROCCO ST
WESTON ST
ROYAL OAK M.
DECIMA ST
BRIDGE ROAD
RILEY ROAD
MALTBY
BERMONDSEY
ABBEY STREET
NECKINGER
ENID STREET

GREAT DOVER STREET
TRINITY ST
TABARD ST
HANOVER ST
BOURNE'S RD
WEBB ST
TOWER BRIDGE ROAD
PAGE'S WALK
WILSON
GRANGE WALK
THE GRANGE
GRANGE WALK
SPA ROAD

NEW KENT ROAD
BURRAGE STREET
MITCHELL STREET
LEROY'S ST
GRANGE ROAD
SOUTHWARK PARK RD
ASCOT RD
DUNTON RD
Arancia

SEARLES RD
HENSHAW ST
CHATHAM STREET
OLD KENT ROAD
TOWNSEND ST
THURLOW ST
WILLOW WALK
MANDELA WAY
BALFOUR ST
RODNEY ROAD
CATESBY ST

0   250 yds

© Crown copyright

Arancia

ITALIAN

Gentrification is spreading through this part of town, where the neat rows of rather nice old terraced houses have been spotted by people toiling in the City of London. Arancia is a product of these changing times; ten years ago this patch was all pie and mash and car chases. Now sensible and authentic Italian food is quite acceptable – and the proprietors of Arancia are to be congrat-

Cost	£10–£20
Address	52 Southwark Park Rd, SE16
T	020 7394 1751
Station	BR Bermondsey
Open	Mon & Tues 7–11pm, Wed–Sun 12.30–2.30pm & 7–11pm
Accepts	MasterCard, Visa

ulated on keeping the food cheap enough to attract the long-term residents, while at the same time good enough to ensnare newcomers. Success on all fronts. This is an old-fashioned, regularly changing, seasonally inspired menu. At Arancia they manage to offer a two-course set meal for £7.50, and three courses for £10.50 – a bargain whether you are bourgeois or Bermondsey.

Starters might include zuppa di peperoni (£3), a soup made from roast red peppers and served with crème fraîche and bruschetta. Or you might have a big helping of gnocchi di semolina (£4). Tortine di granchio (£4.50) is a home-made crab tartlet spiked with dill and olive oil. For main course there may be risotto al frutti di mare (£9.30) a seafood risotto made with sun-dried tomatoes and served with a red chard salad. You can also bank on pork somewhere on the menu, perhaps scaloppe di maiale (£8.90) – classical pork escalopes served with lemon. Or there may be pollo al prosciutto (£9), which is a poached fillet of chicken that has been wrapped in Parma ham and served with a sauce enriched with porcini mushrooms. The puddings are adventurous: perhaps a rather good chocolate semifreddo (£3), or dried date and almond tart (£3.40), or that quintessentially Italian pud, ice cream terrine (£3.70)?

The pursuit of bargain prices is also the theme when you look at the all Italian wine list. There are certainly inexpensive wines, they are all drinkable, but if you're after something really splendid you'll be out of luck. The proprietors of Arancia also run an outside catering business. With food as simple and as good as this, it should be worth investigating.

Tower Bridge & Bermondsey

Blue Print Café

On the first floor of the Design Museum you'll find the Blue Print Café, the oldest of Sir Terence Conran's gastrodome restaurants. It has since acquired his Pont de la Tour, Butler's Wharf Chop House (see opposite) and Cantina del Ponte (see p.364) as neighbours, but the Blue Print has an identity that borrows from no one. It can turn out pricier than you might expect from a cursory look at the menu, and the service can be a bit uptight, but the cooking is honourable, and the dishes imaginative, and the setting and views are as good as London offers.

Cost	£20–£45

Address Design Museum, Shad Thames, SE1
T 020 7378 7031
Station Tower Hill/London Bridge
Open Mon–Sat noon–2.45pm & 6–10.45pm, Sun noon–2.45pm
Accepts All major credit cards
W www.conran.com

Starters manage to sound both simple and interesting. You might find pickled herrings, potato and cucumber salads (£6), or salt duck, watercress and redcurrant jelly (£7.50), or a dish of pappardelle with chicken livers (£7,50), but they will have one thing in common – top-quality ingredients, strong flavours and pleasing combinations of textures. Mains also aim for simplicity, like the pork belly, mustard and red cabbage (£14); or a bourride of red mullet (£15); the saddle of rabbit with butternut squash puree (£16); or sea bass with mushrooms, celeriac and fennel puree (£16.50). These are all dishes that appeal to diners who know their food. As are the puddings, which include favourites like crème brûlée (£5.50) – thinly crusted with slightly soft crème brûlée, just as it should be – or vanilla petit pot (£6); a pear and hazelnut tart (£6.50) or even chocolate brownie with fudge sauce and vanilla cream (£6.50). The eclectic wine list has many unusual offerings as well as particularly good house champagne (£35) – and the Blue Print is a fine place to celebrate.

The Blue Print has superb river views and, as evening falls, the lights of Tower Bridge and the skyline opposite make the City look almost beautiful. Book in advance and ask for a table near a terrace window – or, when it's open (and they are reluctant on all but midsummer days and nights for fear of filling the indoor tables and having nowhere to move you to if it rains), out on the terrace itself.

Butler's Wharf Chop House

Butler's Wharf Chop House – another Conran creation – really deserves everyone's support. For this is a restaurant that makes a genuine attempt to showcase the best of British produce. There's superb British meat, splendid fish, and simply epic British and Irish cheeses. What's more, the Chop House wisely caters for all, whether you want a simple dish at the bar, a well-priced set lunch or an extravagant dinner. The dining room is spacious and bright and the view of Tower Bridge a delight, especially from a terrace table on a warm summer's evening.

Cost	£15–£40

Address 36e Shad Thames, SE1
T 020 7403 3403
Station Tower Hill/London Bridge
Open Restaurant Mon–Fri & Sun noon–3pm & 6–11pm, Sat 6–11pm; Bar Mon–Sat noon–3pm & 6–11pm, Sun noon–3pm
Accepts All major credit cards
W www.conran.com

Lunch in the restaurant is priced at £19.75 for two courses and £23.75 for three. The menu changes regularly but tends to feature starters such as Jerusalem artichoke soup with smoked sausage; or Loch Fyne smoked salmon; or chicken livers on toast. Mains will include dishes like pan-fried skate wing with green sauce, as well as the house speciality of spit roasts and grills. They do a flawless roast rib of beef with Yorkshire pudding and gravy, and excellent braised lamb shank with mashed potato and red wine. After that you just might be able to find room for a pud like rhubarb crumble tart with vanilla ice cream. Dinner follows the same principles but is priced à la Carte and adds a few more complex dishes to the choice. Thus, there may be starters like venison and wild boar faggot served with black pudding and sage (£7.50), or a wild duck and smoked goose salad served with brandied cherries (£7.75). Mains may include steak, kidney and oyster pudding (£15.50) or grilled pork chop and crackling (£15). There's also steak and chips, priced by size – from £16.50 for an 8oz sirloin to £25 for a 12oz fillet.

The bar menu is appealing – two courses for £8, three for £10. You might choose crab soup, roast lamb and lemon tart: a pretty good tenner's worth.

Cantina del Ponte

Jostling for attention with its more renowned and considerably pricier Conran neighbour, the Pont de la Tour, the Cantina del Ponte does not try to keep up, but instead offers a different package. Here you are greeted with the best earthy Italian fare, presented in smart Conran style. The floors are warm terracotta, the food is strong on flavour and colour, the service is refined, and the views are superior London dockside. There are many Italian restaurants around town within the same price range, but this one is competitive – not least because of the setting, which rivals a fair few Italian cities. Book ahead and bag a table by the window or, better still, brave the elements in summer and sit under the canopy watching the boats go by. Inside is OK but less memorable, and the low ceilings are a bit claustrophobic if you're seated at the back.

ITALIAN

Cost	£10–£35
Address	Butler's Wharf, Shad Thames, SE1
T	020 7403 5403
Station	Tower Hill/London Bridge
Open	Mon–Sat noon–3pm & 6–11pm, Sun noon–3pm & 6–10pm
Accepts	All major credit cards
W	www.conran.com

The seasonal menu is a meander through all things good, Italian-style, with a tempting array of first courses, and mains that include pizzas, pasta and risotto, not to mention the side orders, puddings and cheeses. Simple, classic combos like roast vine tomato and buffalo Mozzarella bruschetta and fresh anchovies (£6.50) always appeal. Veggie dishes like baked Ricotta cannelloni, creamed pumpkin and basil oil (£8.95) are good, or how about wild mushroom and Jerusalem artichoke risotto with white truffle oil (£10.95)? Pizzas are equally filling, and feature imaginative toppings such as spiced chorizo sausage with caramelized onion and fontina (£6.95). Main courses range from whole roasted sea bass, fresh herbs and lemon olive oil (£14.75) to pan-fried sirloin of beef with Lyonnaise potatoes (£14.50), and grilled best end of pork with bean cassoulet and Toulouse sausage (£13.25). Puds veer from tiramisù through torta di cioccolata to roast peach and marscapone tart (all £5.95).

Cantina does a mean line in takeaway pizzas – always presuming that you live near enough to fetch it yourself, or perhaps that you like a serious snack when you get home after dinner out.

Fina Estampa

PERUVIAN

While London is awash with ethnic eateries, Fina Estampa's proud boast is that it is the capital's only Peruvian restaurant. Gastronomy may not be the first thing that springs to mind when one thinks of Peru, but the husband-and-wife team running the place certainly tries hard to enlighten their customers and bring a little downtown Lima to London Bridge. With its fresh bright-yellow interior and throbbing rhythms (live music on Friday and Saturday nights), Fina Estampa has a warm and bright ambience, and the attentive, friendly staff add greatly to the upbeat feel.

Cost	£5–£15

Address 150 Tooley St, SE1
T 020 7403 1342
Station London Bridge
Open Mon–Fri noon–2.30pm
& 6.30–10.30pm, Sat
6.30–10.30pm
Accepts All major credit cards

The menu is traditional Peruvian, which means there's a great emphasis placed upon seafood. This is reflected in the starters, with such offerings as chupe de camarones (£6.95), a succulent shrimp-based soup; cebiche (£5.95), a dish of marinated white fish served with sweet potatoes; and jalea (£9.50), a vast plate of fried seafood. Ask for the salsa criolla – its hot oiliness is a perfect accompaniment. There is also causa rellena (£4.95), described as a "potato surprise" and exactly that: layers of cold mashed potato, avocado and tuna fish served with salsa – the surprise being how straightforward can taste so good. Main courses – the fragrant chicken seco (£10.95), chicken cooked in a coriander sauce; or the superb lomo saltado (£12.95), tender strips of rump steak stir-fried with red onions and tomatoes – are worthy ambassadors for this simple yet distinctive cuisine. Perhaps most distinctive of all is the carapulcra (£10.95), a spicy dish made of dried potatoes, pork, chicken and cassava – top choice for anyone seeking a new culinary adventure.

One particularly fine, and decidedly Peruvian, speciality is the unfortunately named Pisco sour (£3.50). Pisco is a white grape spirit and the Peruvian national drink, not dissimilar in taste and effect to tequila. Here they mix Pisco with lemon, lime and cinnamon, then sweeten it with honey, add egg white, and whip it into a frothy white cocktail, which is really rather good.

Fish!

You feel like a fish at Fish! The restaurant's huge windows and glass ceiling contribute to a tank-like feeling. They also contribute to high noise levels and a general party ambience. The restaurant is large and there's a courtyard for alfresco eating, plus bar seating for armchair chefs who like to watch the real ones at work.

Cost	£20–£50
Address	Cathedral St, SE1
T	020 7234 3333
Station	London Bridge
Open	Mon–Sat 11.30am–11pm, Sun noon–4pm
Accepts	All major credit cards
W	www.fishdiner.co.uk

The menu is place-mat style, so you get sat down and start reading. On one side there are Fish! homilies that explain the restaurant's ethic – kids' menus and games, highchairs, GM-free fish(!), takeaway, a Web site, a nutrition section – so much, in fact, that as a good read the B-side almost eclipses the real menu on the reverse, which is certainly innovative. On the one card is a smallish selection of dishes, wines and accompaniments, but the main justification for Fish! is the self-selection menu. From a printed list of twenty-two contenders there is a daily choice of nine kinds of fresh fish, depending on what the market has come up with. You select your favourite, choose whether you want it steamed or grilled, and then choose salsa, Hollandaise, herb butter, olive oil dressing or red-wine fish gravy to go with it. Create your own combo. Prices range from £8.50 for mullet to £15.95 for Dover sole. Portions are huge and the fish is as good and fresh as you'd expect. The traditional menu offers starters like prawn cocktail (£6.95), unreconstructed and with a properly pink, ketchupy sauce. Main dishes include fish cake (£7.80), made with salmon and smoked haddock; spaghetti tuna Bolognaise (£8.50), with fresh tomatoes and minced tuna; or fish and chips with mushy peas (£11.80). And for poor lost carnivores who have rather missed the point there is even a grilled free-range chicken breast (£11.50). If you like a traditional approach to fish, Fish! won't disappoint. Puddings include stalwarts like lemon sponge pudding and custard (£3.95), and bread and butter pudding (£3.95), the latter rich with double cream. The house white, a Sauvignon de Touraine (£9.90), is light, crisp and a bargain.

Fish!'s menu adds interest to eating, with information that makes sense. There's also a Fish! shop next door for wet fish and sauces and a touch-screen recipe machine.

Honest Cabbage

The Honest Cabbage is heralded by a beguiling picture of a cabbage crowned with a halo, which sticks out into Bermondsey Street like an inn sign. Without the sign, the restaurant would be difficult to spot, as the Cabbage, for all its honesty, seems to lurk shyly away from the limelight. Once found, the place is a welcome lesson in simplicity – dark wooden tables and chairs are dotted around a medium-sized, plain room. At the far end is a small bar and counter, but the whole of the shopfront is sheet glass, giving a spacious and well-lit feel. Decoration is provided by glass jars of pulses along the windowsills.

Cost	£12–£35

Address 99 Bermondsey St, SE1
T 020 7234 0080
Station London Bridge
Open Mon–Wed noon–3pm & 6.30–10.30pm, Thurs–Sat noon–3pm & 6.30–11pm, Sun noon–4pm
Accepts MasterCard, Visa
W www.thehonest cabbage.co.uk

MODERN BRITISH

The menu is chalked up on a blackboard, though if you can't quite see it they have a printed version as well. There is a choice of ten or eleven dishes, with no division between first and main courses. It follows a simple formula of a soup, a sandwich, a salad, a pasta, a pie, a pot, a vegetarian dish, and so forth. The menu changes every day broadly in line with the seasons and what the markets have to offer. So you might choose red kidney bean soup with guacamole (£4) or a BLT (£5), either of which would make a satisfying light lunch. Or the pot might be braised oxtail (£12); the pasta garganelli, cockles and saffron cream (£4/£7). And then there are the fresh meat and fresh fish options (these cost £12), which might be a large portion of calves' liver with sage butter, spinach and caramelized onions plus mash or chips. Or a whole grilled sea bass, with orange and ginger Hollandaise. Puddings are straightforward – like a good lemon meringue pie (£4).

A short but considered drinks list not only provides a couple of organic wines but also a succession of bottled and draught beers. The Cabbage's strengths lie in its attitude and pricing, so, as you would expect, it is consistently busy. There's a serious brunch on Sunday morning.

Tentazioni

This small, busy and rather good Italian restaurant has crept up behind Sir Terence Conran's Thameside flotilla of eateries and is giving them a good run for their money. The food is high-quality peasant Italian, with strong, rich flavours and simple quality. The pasta dishes are good here, as are the stews, and the wine list is interesting. They also offer a "Menu Degustazione", which gets you five courses for £36. This serious little Italian restaurant now has a sibling on the other side of town: the notable Riso, in Turnham Green – 76 South Parade, W4 (☎020 8742 2121).

Cost	£10–£20

Address 2 Mill St, SE1
T 020 7237 1100
Station Bermondsey/
Tower Hill
Open Mon–Fri noon–2.30pm
& 7–10.45pm, Sat 7–10.45pm
Accepts All major credit cards
W www.tentazioni.co.uk

The starters here are all priced at £7 or £8, unless you choose to have one of them as a main course, in which case the price goes up to £9. The menu changes to reflect the seasons and the markets, so you may find choices such as tagliolini neri freddi con vongole e broccoli, an unusual dish of black tagliolini served cold with clams and broccoli; or the tasty pappardelle quaglie e piselli, which is pappardelle with quails and peas; or Mozzarella di bufala con caponata di verdure – buffalo Mozzarella with vegetable caponata. In season there is a good deal of game on the menu, and often a particularly good traditional pasta with a richer-than-rich sauce made with hare or the like. Main courses offer hammer blows of flavour – bocconcini di coniglio impanati con car-cofini (£15), which is described as a breaded navarin of rabbit with artichokes; or triglie con cicoria, fave e Pecorino (£14.50) – pan-fried red mullet with chicory, broad beans and Pecorino. Or an unusual dish like filetto di manzo al vapore con verdurine, salsa verde e mostarda (£16.50), which is steamed fillet of beef given vibrant colour from the salsa verde and a hit of flavour from the mustard-pickled fruits. For pudding it is hard to better the torta alle prugne e pere con gelato alla vaniglia (£6), a delicious plum and pear tart with vanilla ice cream.

The "Degustazione" provides an interesting and very tempting option. How does this sound? First, vitello tonnato, then agnolotti di patate e menta con peperoni, then the red mullet mentioned above, then a rabbit dish, and finally panna cotta alla grappa con arance caramellate. Pretty convincing.

Wimbledon & Southfields

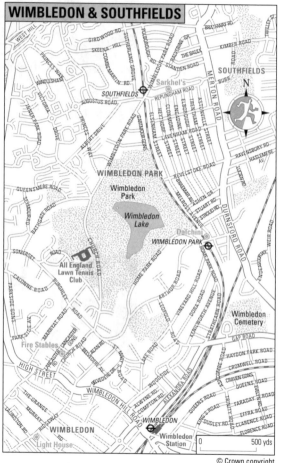

WIMBLEDON & SOUTHFIELDS

WEST HILL
GIRDWOOD RD.
SUTHERLAND GROVE
SKEENA HILL
BRATHWAY RD.
KIMBER ROAD
TWILLEY
PRINCE'S WAY
WIMBLESHAM RD.
COMBEMARTIN RD.
WIMBLEDON PARK ROAD
RAVENSBURY GR.
THE BAULY
STANDEN ROAD

SOUTHFIELDS
MERTON ROAD
BURR

Sarkhel's
REPLINGHAM ROAD
SOUTHFIELDS

VICTORIA
DRIVE
AUGUSTUS ROAD
ASTONVILLE STREET
N

INNER PARK ROAD
PRINCE'S WAY
ALBERT DRIVE
REVELSTOKE ROAD
ELSENHAM STREET
CLONMORE STREET
CLONMEL STREET
ELBOROUGH STREET
ELLORA RD.
LAVENHAM ROAD
RAVENSBURY RD.
HASLEMERE AV.

QUEENSMERE ROAD
WIMBLEDON PARK
REVELSTOKE ROAD
Wimbledon
Park
BARHAM RD.
ASHEN GR.
MELROSE RD.
STUART RD.
STOKOPD RD.

SCHOMBURG
BATHGATE ROAD
Wimbledon
Lake

SOMERSET ROAD
CHURCH ROAD
Dalchini
WIMBLEDON PARK
DURNSFORD ROAD
WEIR ROAD

All England
Lawn Tennis
Club
BURGHLEY ROAD
HOME PARK ROAD

PARKSIDE GDNS.
CALONNE ROAD
ARTHUR ROAD
DORA ROAD

PARK SIDE
MARRYAT ROAD
LANCASTER RD.
LANCASTER GDNS.
BELVEDERE DR.
BELVEDERE AV.
WOODSIDE
VINEYARD HILL ROAD
LEOPOLD ROAD
REVELL ROAD
EDGE HILL ROAD
STRATHEARN AVENUE
Wimbledon
Cemetery

Fire Stables
CHURCH RD.
GAP ROAD
HAYDON PARK ROAD
CROMWELL ROAD

HIGH STREET
WIMBLEDON HILL ROAD
ALWYNE RD.
COMPTON RD.
LAKE ROAD
ALEXANDRA ROAD
CRAVEN GDNS.
QUEENS ROAD
GLADSTONE ROAD
FARADAY ROAD
EFFRA ROAD

THE GRANGE
MURRAY RD.
RIDGEWAY
WIMBLEDON
QUEENS ROAD
KING'S ROAD
DUDLEY RD.
CLARENCE ROAD
FLORENCE ROAD

LAURISTON RD.
Light House
WIMBLEDON
Wimbledon
Station

0   500 yds

© Crown copyright

Dalchini

Dalchini is an Indian word for the cinnamon-like spice cassia, made by combining the words dal, meaning bark, and chini, meaning China. Which makes it a jolly appropriate name for this small and friendly family restaurant, as Dalchini serves the kind of Chinese food that has emigrated to Bombay! This is Chinese food with a pronounced Indian accent – lots of spice and a good deal of chilli. The restaurant was opened in early 2001 by Udit Sarkhel's (see p.374) wife Veronica, who is Hakka Chinese and comes from a long line of Chinese restaurateurs based in Bombay.

Cost	£12–£30

Address 147 Arthur Rd, Wimbledon Park, SW19
T 020 8947 5966
Station Wimbledon Park
Open Tues–Thurs & Sun noon–2.30pm & 6–10.30pm, Fri & Sat noon–2.30pm & 6–11pm
Accepts Amex, MasterCard, Visa

INDIAN-CHINESE

Upstairs, Dalchini is a coffee bar and deli, serving everything from coffee, cakes and pastries to lunchboxes and Indian dishes. Downstairs, the restaurant is pleasantly unpretentious. Toy with a few starters and then turn to the specials list for the classic Indo-Chinese dishes. Start with the onion pancake (£2.95), a Chinese street-food favourite, stuffed with chopped spring onions and packing an extra kick of spice and chilli. Team these with the vegetables pickled in sweet vinegar (£1.50). Five spice chicken wings (£3.75) is a rich, sweet and sticky dish. The tofu pepper and salt (£3.75) is a revelation – fingers of tofu are cooked in the lightest possible batter and served with chilli and spring onion. It's amazingly delicious, a vegetarian option that excels. The Dalchini special main courses are great fun. There is chilli chicken (£6), a big seller in Bombay, sweet and chilli hot; or "American chicken chop suey" (£6) – the story goes that chop suey was a dish first devised by Chinese coolies working on the American railroads. The standing pomfret (£9.95) is a cunningly de-boned, fried pomfret that is presented upright as if swimming. As an accompaniment to all this, Hakka noodles fit the bill.

You also deserve to try the star dish: belly pork with preserved vegetable (£6). This is a slow-braised dish of pork cooked slowly on a pile of cabbage. It is very rich, and comes with a stellar gravy.

The Fire Stables

The Fire Stables is very much a 2001 affair, and as soon as the doors opened this place started to rake in complimentary reviews. One notable award's short-listing was in the gastro-pub category, but there must be a problem deciding just what the Fire Stables represents. It certainly has a busy bar, and there is bar food available, but there is a formal restaurant as well. But, by any measure, the "gastro" side has the pub on the back foot; as modern restaurants go, this is a pretty good example. The chairs are comfortable and the tables big enough, the high ceiling and large windows give a spacious feel, the floor is made of painted floorboards, and the music will be familiar to forty- and fifty-somethings, as Brubeck's "Take Five" segues into The Average White Band.

Cost	£12–£40

Address 27–29 Church Rd, SW19
T 020 8946 3197
Station Wimbledon
Open Daily noon–3pm & 5.30–10.30pm
Accepts All major credit cards

The menu changes daily and the food is well-presented and reasonably priced. Starters range from fennel soup (£4.50) to a sound ham-hock terrine w parsley and celeriac remoulade (£5). You may already have spotted the typographical idiosyncrasy, which wears pretty thin pretty quickly: they don't write "with" at the Fire Stables, what they put is w. So you get gravadlax w mustard dressing (£6) – this could get irritating by the time you get to cheese w Bath Olivers. The gravadlax is good – full flavoured and rich – but the mustard dressing is a little bland. A starter of Portobello mushrooms w slow roasted tomatoes and Mozzarella on bruschetta (£6) is much more successful – good mushies, very tasty. Main courses include a crowd-pleasing sirloin steak w Caesar salad and big chips (£12); sea bass w bok choi and teriyaki sauce (£12.50); and pan-fried calves' liver w bacon, mash and balsamic jus (£12) – the latter wholly satisfactory, a large portion of precisely grilled liver and decent bacon, atop real mashed spuds. Fire Stables chicken tagine w couscous is another sound dish, if a tad under-seasoned.

Puds are reliable numbers like panettone bread and butter pudding, and chocolate tart w pistachio ice cream (all £5).

Light House

Light House is a strange restaurant to find marooned in leafy suburbia – you would think that its modern, very eclectic menu and clean style would be more at home in a city centre than in a smart, quiet, respectable neighbourhood. Nevertheless it seems to be doing well. The restaurant, which opened in late 1999, has found its feet and the local clientele quite obviously enjoy it and keep coming back for more. First impressions always count and a light, bright interior – cream walls and blond wood – plus genuinely friendly staff make arriving at Light House a pleasure.

Cost	£20–£50

Address 75–77 The Ridgway, SW19

T 020 8944 6388

Station Wimbledon

Open Mon–Sat noon–2.45pm & 6–10.30pm, Sun 12.30–3.15pm & 6.30–9.30pm

Accepts All major credit cards except Diners

MODERN EUROPEAN

At first glance the menu is set out conventionally enough in the Italian style: antipasti, primi, secondi, contorni and dolci. But that's as far as the Italian formality goes – the influences on the kitchen here are truly global. Starters may range from a celeriac-stuffed courgette flower, pistachio and rocket salad with tahini dressing (£5.20), to Egyptian aubergine and tomato soup with tahini (£4.50), or deep-fried prawn ravioli on sautéed porcini and oyster mushrooms with grilled nori (£7.20). It would be very easy to get this sort of cooking wrong, but in fact Light House does remarkably well. Among the "secondi", dishes like braised lamb shank on sautéed spinach, marinated carrots and scotch broth with salsa verde (£14) jostle with seriously fusion combinations like pan-fried red tilapia on braised red cabbage, ratte potatoes and piquillo pepper relish (£13.50), or Caribbean roti wrap with re-fried black beans, spicy field mushrooms and crème fraîche (£9.70). Perhaps the cooking is a little overcomplicated, but it's well executed and certainly intriguing. Puddings take us back towards Italy (ish!) with dishes like green tea semifreddo with mango salad and shaved coconut (£4.75).

Someone has had a lot of fun choosing the wine list – a selection of about twenty each of whites and reds which crosses as many frontiers as possible. If you want a bargain, go for lunch – a steal at £12.50 for two courses.

Sarkhel's

Before opening his own place in SW18, Udit Sarkhel was heading the kitchens of the famous Bombay Brasserie in the West End, where he had all the latest kit and a large brigade of chefs. Moving to Sarkhel's in Southfields must have been like resigning as conductor of an orchestra and setting up a one-man band, but it is certainly a huge asset to South London. And South London has certainly responded – the dining room seems to be enlarged at

Cost	£11–£30
Address	199 Replingham Rd, Southfields, SW18
T	020 8870 1483
Station	Southfields
Open	Tues–Thurs 6–10.30pm, Fri & Sat 6–11pm, Sun noon–2.30pm
Accepts	Amex, MasterCard, Visa
W	www.sarkhels.com

least once a year. Today Sarkhel's is a large, elegant restaurant, serving well-spiced food with a number of adventurous dishes scattered through the menu – the hot, fresh Chettinad dishes are particularly fine. Moreover, it's a pleasant, friendly, family-run place offering good cooking at prices, which, though not cheap, certainly represent good value (particularly on Friday, Saturday and Sunday lunchtimes, when you can get a bargain set lunch for £9.95). Booking is recommended.

Start by asking Udit or his wife if there are any "specials" on. These are dishes which change according to what is available at the markets. You might be offered a starter of macchli Koliwada (£4.25) – fish cooked in a spicy batter, a famous Bombay dish. Or a shrimp balchao (£5.95), chilli-hot and served with mini popadoms. The achari chicken tikka (£6.50) is as good as you'll find anywhere. For main-course dishes, check the specials again – it might be something wonderful like a kolmi nu Patia (£8.50), a spicy Parsee prawn dish. On the main menu, try the chicken korma narangi (£6.50), rich and citrussy, made with orange juice and preserved orange peel; or the achar gosht (£6.50), which is lamb cooked slowly in a sealed pot "dum phukt" style; or perhaps the jardaloo ma gosht (£6.50), a sweet and sour lamb dish made with apricots. All are delicious, without even a hint of surface oil slick.

Be sure to add some vegetable dishes. The bhindi Jaipuri (£5.50), a small haystack of slivered okra and onions deep fried until crisp then served dusted with mango powder, is addictively good.

Further South

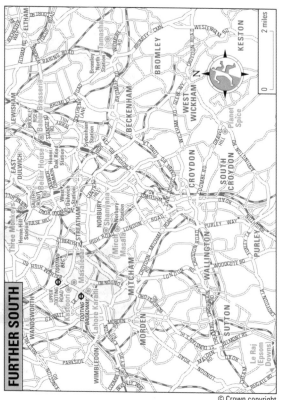

FURTHER SOUTH

© Crown copyright

Babur Brasserie

The Babur Brasserie is a stylish and friendly restaurant serving elaborate and interesting dishes which bear no resemblance to run-of-the-mill curry house fare – an unexpected find in SE23. The food is both subtle and elegantly presented and, while it does cost a touch more than most suburban Indian restaurants, you are still paying a great deal less than you would in a French or Italian place of similar quality. There is a buffet lunch on Sunday (£8.95) at which children eat free if they are less than seven years old...

Cost	£10–£25

Address 119 Brockley Rise, SE23
T 020 8291 2400
Station BR Honor Oak Park
Open Daily noon–2.30pm & 6–11.30pm
Accepts All major credit cards
W www.babur-brasserie.com

How nice to be faced with a list of appetizers and see so few familiar dishes. Patra (£3.25) is a Catherine wheel sliced off the end of a roll of avial leaves that have been glued together with chickpea paste and deep-fried. The result is crispy and very tasty. Ragda pattice (£3.75) is a grown-up potato croquette with a dried pea curry. Calamari balchao (£3.95) is a Goan-style squid dish, agreeably hot, while harrey murgh tikka (£3.95) gets you a plate of chunks of chicken which have been marinated in green spices, then cooked in a tandoor – delightfully juicy inside. Main courses are just as good. Try jalfrezi (£7.25) – lamb with onions, ginger and capsicums. Or the green fish curry from Goa (£8.95) – salmon in a typical Goan hot and sour sauce. Guinea fowl Darjeeling (£7.95) is a spicy dish with a hint of orange zest, while duck xacutti (£8.75) is a complex curry made from a smoked duck breast and an awesomely long list of spices. Then there are ten fresh vegetable dishes – vegetarians will applaud the thali option of picking three from the list with raita, rice and a naan bread for an inclusive price of just £11.75. On the subject of bread, try the lacha parata (£1.95) – a flaky paratha made with ghee. The dessert menu is more extensive and more elaborate than usual, too, running the gamut from rasmalai with summer berries (£3.75) to kulfi (£3.75), that dense and tasty Indian ice cream.

Hing, or asafoetida, is a spice that has not only a distinctive flavour but also a rude name. In oonbhariu (£4.95) – a dish from the vegetables section – it is blended with lovage and cumin to accompany bananas, sweet potato, baby aubergines and shallots. Particularly delicious, and not stinky at all.

Belair House

(🍴) Belair House is a large, pale Georgian establishment, standing alone in Belair Park. A Grade Two listed building, it was sensitively and painstakingly restored in 1998 by the actor Gary Cady and his wife Jayne. In summer the two terraces do sterling service, one filled with diners and the other with drinkers. This establishment is already justly popular with locals, and Sunday lunch in particular is booked up well ahead. With

Cost	£18–£65

Address Gallery Rd, Dulwich Village, SE21
T 020 8299 9788
Station BR West Dulwich
Open Mon–Sat noon–2.30pm & 7–10.30pm, Sun noon–2.30pm
Accepts All major credit cards
W www.belairhouse.co.uk

its head start of tall, well-proportioned rooms and a sweeping staircase, the decor is both elegant and surprisingly bright – research shows that, when built, the interior of the building would have been painted in the lurid colours fashionable at the time. In 2001 a new chef took over the kitchens and the restaurant abandoned à la Carte in favour of prix fixe arrangements. The kitchen makes use of whatever is best from the markets to produce a regularly changing seasonal menu.

The deals work like this: Monday to Saturday the set lunch costs £17.95 for two courses and £21.95 for three; on Sunday the three-course set lunch costs £25.95. The three-course dinner is priced at £29.95, while the six-course dégustation menu will set you back £45. The cooking is ambitious and eclectic with starters like cep bavarois – snails, garlic and cep cream; tea-smoked quail salad, foie gras and sauternes jelly; tartar of red tuna with bergamot and pickled cucumber; or minestrone of langoustine, butternut squash and pine nuts. By now you will have gathered that the menu steers very close to the demarcation line that marks out "fusion food". Mains like lobster pot au feu, Pithivier of oxtail and morels, and Pecorino tart with confit of vine tomatoes are equally intriguing; chicken tagine with saffron sounds relatively sedate. Puddings are a more sober and self-indulgent affair – pear tarte Tatin comes with vanilla ice cream; chestnut and raspberry pancake gets chestnut ice cream; and marscapone tartlet is served with a balsamic sorbet.

Look carefully in the toilets downstairs and you will spot vestiges of a former incarnation of Belair House – it used to act as a changing room for teams using the surrounding playing fields.

Kastoori

Anyone who is genuinely puzzled that people can cope on – and indeed enjoy – a diet of vegetables alone should try eating at Kastoori. Located in a rather unpromising-looking bit of Balham, Kastoori is a Gujarati "Pure Vegetarian Restaurant". The food they serve is leavened with East African influences, and so delicious that you could invite even the most hardened carnivore and

INDIAN

Cost	£12–£20
Address	188 Upper Tooting Rd, SW17
T	020 8767 7027
Station	Tooting Broadway
Open	Mon & Tues 6–10.30pm, Wed–Sun 12.30–2.30pm & 6–10.30pm
Accepts	MasterCard, Visa

be pretty sure that they would be as entranced as everybody else. The large and cavernous restaurant is run by the admirably helpful Thanki family – do be sure to ask their advice, and act on it. Kastoori's most recent facelift has changed the decor from pink to blue and yellow, but thankfully the quality of the food has stayed the same.

First onto the waiter's pad (and indeed first into the mouth, as they go soggy and collapse if made to wait) must be dahi puri (£2.75) – tiny crispy flying saucers filled with a sweet/sour yoghurty sauce, and potatoes, onions, chickpeas and so forth. You pop them in whole; the marriage of taste and texture is a revelation. Samosas (three for £1.95) are excellent, but also in the revelation category are the onion bhajis (five for £2.10) – bite-sized and delicious, a far cry from the ball-of-knitting variety served in most high-street curry emporia. Then make sure that someone orders the vegetable curry of the day (£4.50), and others the outstanding cauliflower with cream curry (£4.50) and special tomato curry (£4.50) – a hot and spicy classic from Katia Wahd. Leave room for the chilli banana (£4.75), bananas stuffed with mild chillies – an East African recipe – and mop everything up with generous helpings of puris and chapatis (both at £1.30 for two).

The smart move is to ask what's in season, as the menu is littered with oddities which come and go. For example, you might find rotlo – millet loaf (£2.50, served only on Sunday), or the dish called, rather enigmatically, "beans of the day" (£4.25). Another interesting and esoteric dish is drumstick curry (£4.50). Drumsticks are thin, green, Asian vegetables about eighteen inches long and twice as thick as a pencil. You chew the flesh from the stalk. This is a place where it pays to experiment.

INDIAN

Lahore Karahi

Though the bright neon spilling onto the pavement beckons you from Tooting High Street, spiritually speaking, the Lahore Karahi is in the curry gulch of Upper Tooting Road. It's a busy place, which has increased the number of seats to cope with the ever-growing swell of customers, and now

Cost	£9–£22
Address	1 Tooting High St, SW17
T	020 8767 2477
Station	Tooting Broadway
Open	Daily noon–midnight
Accepts	Cash or cheque only

even boasts air conditioning. Behind a counter equipped with numerous bains-marie stand rows of cooks, distinguishable by their natty Lahore Karahi baseball caps, turning out a daily twelve-hour marathon of dishes. Prices are low, food is chilli-hot, service is speedy. Don't be intimidated: simply seat yourself in a Habitat chair, don't worry if you have to share a table, and start ordering. Regulars bring their own drinks or stick to the exotic fruit juices – mango, guava or passion, all at just £1.

Unusually for what is, at bottom, an unreconstructed grill house, there is a wide range of vegetarian dishes "prepared under strict precautions". Karahi karela (£2.95) is a curry of bitter gourds; karahi saag paneer (£3.50) teams spinach and cheese; and karahi methi aloo (£2.95) brings potatoes flavoured with fenugreek. Meat-eaters can plunge in joyfully – the chicken tikka (£2.25), seekh kabab (£1.20 for two), and tandoori chicken (£1.75) are all good and all spicy-hot, the only fault being a good deal of artificial red colouring. There are also a dozen chicken curries and a dozen lamb curries (from £3.95 to £4.25), along with a dozen specialities (from £3.95 to £7.50 for king prawn karahi). Those with a strong constitution can try the dishes of the day, like nihari (£4.95), which is lamb shank on the bone in an incendiary broth, or paya (£3.95), which is sheep's feet cooked until gluey. Breads are good here: try the jeera nan (70p) or the tandoori roti (60p).

The Lahore Karahi comes into its own as a takeaway, and there's usually a queue at the counter as people collect their considerable banquets – not just chicken tikka in a naan, or portions of curry, but large and elaborate biryanis as well – meat (£3.25), chicken (£3.25), prawn (£4.95), or vegetable (£2.95). For wholesome, fast-ish food, the cooking and the prices here are hard to beat.

Masaledar

What can you say about a place that has two huge standard lamps, each made from an upturned, highly ornate Victorian drainpipe, topped with a large karahi? When it comes to interior design, Masaledar provides plenty of surprises – and a feeling of spaciousness that's the very opposite of most of the bustling Indian restaurants in Tooting and Balham. This establishment is run by East African Asian Muslims, so no alcohol is allowed on the premises, but that doesn't deter a loyal clientele, who are packing the place out. Along with several other restaurants in Tooting Road, Maselash has had to expand, and has added another 25 covers. The food is fresh, well spiced and cheap – there are vegetable curries at £3.25 and meat curries for around £4 – and, to cap it all, you eat it in an elegant designer dining room.

Cost	£8–£20

Address 121 Upper Tooting Rd, SW17
T 020 8767 7676
Station Tooting Bec/ Tooting Broadway
Open Daily noon–midnight
Accepts MasterCard, Visa
W www.masaledar.co.uk

As starters, the samosas are sound: two meat (£1.60) or two vegetable (£1.60). Or try the chicken wings from the tandoor (five pieces £2.25), or the very tasty lamb chops (four pieces £3.50). You might move on to a tasty, rich chicken or lamb biryani (£4.25). Or perhaps try a classic dish like methi gosht (£4.25) – this is strongly flavoured and delicious, guaranteed to leave you with fenugreek seeping from your pores for days to come. Then there's the rich and satisfying lamb Masaledar (£4.75), which is disarmingly described as "our house dish cooked to tantalize your taste buds". In contrast the Masaledar daal (£2.95) is a less successful dish, unless you like your daal runny. The breads, however, are terrific, especially the wonderful thin rotis (60p). Look out for the various deals that range from "free naan and popadom with every main course Monday to Thursday" to "birthdays, parties, conferences … private parties of up to 120".

Sometimes the brisk takeaway trade, and the fact that all dishes are made to order, conspire to make service a bit slow. And despite, or because of, the absence of alcohol, you can have an interesting evening's drinking. Mango shake (£1.75) is rich, very fruity and not too sweet; order one before your meal, however, and greed will ensure that you have finished it by the time your food comes. Both the sweet and salty lassi (£1.50) are very refreshing, as is the "fresh passion juice".

Mirch Masala

INDIAN

You'll find Mirch Masala just up London Road from Norbury station. It may not look much from the outside, but it deserves a place on any list of London's top ten Indian restaurants – something South London's Asian community appear to have cottoned on to. As befits such a culinary temple, the chefs take centre stage; the kitchen is in full view and you can watch the whole cooking process, which culminates, as likely as not, in a chef bringing the food to table. They are certainly prone to wandering out while you are enjoying the last of your starters to ask if you're ready for your main course. What's more, at the end of the meal they are also happy to pack up anything you don't finish so that you can take it home. Take advantage; over-order; try a lot of different dishes. This is a very friendly place serving spectacular food at low prices. Both the food and the service are unpretentious in the extreme, which makes for very contented diners indeed.

Cost	£6–£16
Address	1416 London Rd, SW16
T	020 8679 1828
Station	BR Norbury
Open	Daily noon–midnight
Accepts	All major credit cards
W	www.mirchmasala restaurant.co.uk

Start with a stick each of chicken tikka (£2.50) and lamb tikka (£2.50), crusted with pepper and spices on the outside, juicy with marinade on the inside. Very good indeed. Or try the butter chicken wings (£3), cooked in a light, ungreasy sauce laden with flavour from fresh spices and herbs. Then move on to the karahi dishes, which are presented in a kind of thick aluminium hubcap. The vegetable karahis are exceptional. Go for the butter beans and methi (£3.50) – an inspired and delicious combination of flavours – and karahi valpapdi baigan (£4), aubergines cooked with small rich beans. Among the best meat dishes are the deigi lamb chops (£4.50), and the deigi saag gosht (£5) – spinach, lamb and a rich sauce. Even something simple like karahi ginger chicken (£5) proves how good and fresh-tasting Indian food can be. Rice (£1.50) comes in a glass butter dish complete with lid. Breads include a good naan (70p) and an indulgent deep-fried bhatura (60p) that will provoke greed in anyone who has ever hankered after fried bread.

A meal at Mirch Masala will be a memorable one. As they say on the menu, "Food extraordinaire. You wish it – we cook it".

Planet Spice

Planet Spice is a fish out of water. Even the presence of the latest transport innovation – the much vaunted tramway – cannot prepare you for the surprise you get when you arrive here. The restaurant (a sister establishment to the Babur Brasserie, see p.377) is located at the junction of two major roads and in premises that have been used for everything from a Greek restaurant to a dance school. Today the building houses an Indian restaurant of a very high order indeed – if Planet Spice were in the West End it would be showered with critical acclaim.

Cost	£15–£32

Address 88 Selsdon Park Rd, Addington, South Croydon
T 020 8651 3300
Station Croydon Tramway
Open Mon–Sat noon–2.30pm & 6.30–11.30pm, Sun 12.30–3.30pm & 6–11.30pm
Accepts All major credit cards
W www.planet-spice.com

INDIAN

The chefs have had to make certain compromises. The takeaway side of things is still dominated by old-style dishes – korma, Madras, chicken tikka masala – and any sit-down customers perplexed by the main menu can opt for these. The main menu, however, is agreeably sophisticated and really is the one you should work from. Start with the qutubshai (£3.75), chunks of saithi fish in a light batter, or ros-tos-crab (£4.95), a kind of crab gratin served in the shell. The ragda pattice (£3.50), a freshly made potato cake with a tasty chickpea curry, is also good. Main courses are distinguished by accurate and well-balanced spicing and unusually careful cooking. Try the tuna bulchao (£7.95), a classic spicy Goan dish applied to tuna. Team it with the lime and cashew nut rice (£2.25). Or there's seafood moilee (£10.95), a mild Keralan dish. Otherwise try a simple dish like kadhai lamb (£7.95), which is essentially tandoori lamb chops, or chicken Chettinad (£7.25), a South Indian dish famous for its fieriness (although it is somewhat tamed here). If all this sounds a bit fierce then there is always the Nilgiri chicken korma (£7.50) – named for the Nilgiri hills of tea-growing fame – this is a simple dish with a mild sauce made with mint and coriander.

These are ambitious dishes, handled well. It is undoubtedly due to the able chefs in the kitchen. Not what you'd expect of a curry house in Addington.

Le Raj

Le Raj was always a smart restaurant, and its proprietor and chef Enam Ali was always a good cook. Nevertheless, it entered the new Millenium refurbished and smarter than ever. This is not the food of the high-street curry house, but a fresh-tasting, thought-provoking cuisine. Granted, Mr Ali's obsession with presentation is still to the forefront and you will see triangular black

Cost	£12–£25
Address	211 Fir Tree Rd, Surrey
T	01737 371 371
Station	BR Epsom Downs
Open	Daily noon–2.30pm & 5.30–11pm
Accepts	All major credit cards
W	www.leraj.com

plates topped by silver domes, but overlook that, and the piped music, and you will have a great time. Ingredients are first-rate, flavours are exciting, and you'll wait as happily for each course as you would in a good French restaurant.

From the starters, try chot poti (£2.95) – a cone of masala popadom filled with chickpeas cooked in cumin, chilli and coriander. Delicious. Or tikka kerkere (£3.50), a superb chicken tikka variant, made with tender meat with a very thin, crisp coat. Or esa puri (£3.50), a well flavoured fried puri wrapped around spiced prawns. Everything looks elegant but, more importantly, everything tastes good. Main courses include some excellent Bangladeshi dishes – maacher tarkari (£11.50) is made with boal, a meaty fish, in a light tomatoey and creamy sauce. It's delicious, and gratifyingly bone-free. Enam Ali is not afraid to add to dishes and the chicken naga (£7.95) is a perfect example; the chicken, cooked with nutmeg and fresh herbs, is also tempered with hot African chillies. For good, intense flavours, order the kacchi (£9.95), a traditional Dhaka biryani, where the rice and lamb are cooked together in the pot slowly. The side dishes are good, as well. There's laau bhajee (£3.50), a very rich curry of pumpkin with bay leaf. And a first-class dhal (£3.50). Even the simple things are good, like the naans (£1.95) and rotis (£1.75).

Now that Indian restaurants have finally crashed through Michelin's "glass ceiling", the inspectors could do worse than make the journey to Epsom Downs. As a showcase for sophisticated Bangladeshi cuisine, Le Raj would be right up their street.

Shamyana

The rather good Indian food that you'll find in Tooting is gradually making its way south. At the forefront of this diaspora was the peerless Mirch Masala (see p.382); Shamyana followed suit and opened a few hundred yards up the road. What all these successful restaurants seem to have in common is well-made, unfussy, spicy food. In 2001 Shamyana has continued an inexorable march upscale. It now boasts a wine bar

Cost	£7–£20

Address 437–439 Streatham High Rd, SW16
T 020 8679 6162
Station BR Norbury
Open Daily noon–midnight
Accepts Amex, MasterCard, Visa
W www.shamyana-restaurant.co.uk

and dance floor and can seat two hundred, with a further large private room upstairs. And the menu breaks new ground too: it lists the calories and grams of fat involved in each particular dish. Trouble is, this often fiercely spicy Punjabi food is so good to eat that you may prefer not to be burdened with such information!

Start with chilli chicken wings (£2.50) or chicken tikka (£2.55) – tandoori dishes that are well spiced and well cooked. They're not at all dried-out, the man on the marinades knows his stuff. A sound option is the Shamyana mixed grill (£4.15) which includes everything from lamb chops to masala fish. As you move on to main courses there is an imposing array of vegetarian dishes – over a dozen to choose from (between £3.45 and £3.75) – tarka dal, karahi bhindi and zeera aloo stand out. Then there is an assortment of Punjabi favourites: ginger chicken (£4.50) or chicken jalfrezi (£4.95), rich with onions and capsicums. Another very good dish is the masala karella gosht (£4.50); the pundits will tell you that the flesh of the karella, or bitter melon, is very good for the blood and has a cleansing effect. But, medicinal or not, this is certainly an addictively good flavour – this lamb and karella curry is a real winner. Other stars are karahi gosht (£4.50) and karahi fish (£5.90). The "specials" are good, too, so look out for them.

The rotis are grand here. And there's an intriguing side dish you must order: mixed fried ginger, chilli and onion (£1) lives up to its description exactly, and is very handy for adding to rice or eating on its own with bread.

Tamasha

Tamasha, very roughly translated, means "a bit of a do", and this restaurant is a great place to come when you decide to push the boat out. From the moment you are greeted by the costumed doorman and shown into the mock-colonial interior, you know that this is no ordinary suburban curry house. Tamasha has a style all of its own which could be described as "Bromley elegant", as you can tell from the names of the dining rooms: the "Victorian", "Raj" and "India Club" rooms are light and airy, while the "Polo bar" is cosy and intimate, perfect for aperitif or cocktail; there is also a less formal room upstairs. The food lives up to these surroundings and is quite moderately priced (there's an all-in bargain Sunday buffet at £10.95). To wash it down, both ice-cold Cobra beer and Dom Perignon have a strong local following.

Cost	£14–£30

Address 131 Widmore Rd, Bromley, Kent
T 020 8460 3240
Station BR Bromley South
Open Mon–Sat noon–2.30pm & 6–11pm, Sun noon–2.30pm & 7–10.30pm
Accepts All major credit cards
W www.tamasha.co.uk

The menu lists dishes from all over India. Starters include well-known dishes such as the plate of mixed kebabs (£4.95) and king prawn puri (£4.95) – both good – and extend to unusual delights such as kheema khumb (£4.25), a dish of mushrooms that have been stuffed with minced lamb and then fried. The chicken manchoori (£8.50) is fiery with green chilli and tomatoes, although not overpoweringly so, and the raan Jaipuri (£9.95) is a grandstand dish made with leg of lamb, onions and almonds. Vegetarian dishes such as the vegetable jalfrezi (£5.50) – five different kinds of veg curried with capsicums – provide a simpler, fresher alternative, while the prawn-based raja jhinga silchari (£11.95) is richer and more highly spiced, and was apparently a very popular dish with East India Company officials. To round off your meal, try the Tamasha coffee (£4.50 per person, minimum four people). It sounds expensive, but the theatre of the preparation alone – caramelized glasses, grapefruit peel, brandy and lots of flames – is worth the price. And the coffee isn't bad either.

If the thought of the journey home seems too daunting, why not stay in one of rooms the Tamasha has maintained from its previous incarnation as an hotel? A double room costs £55 including breakfast – pukka English, of course.

Three Monkeys

In the West End and the City, cool restaurateurs are forever buying up old banks, ripping the insides out, slapping on a coat of ultra-chic frosted glass and reopening as the latest thing in slick designer restaurants. It's just a bit of a shock to see such an establishment – complete with a gangplank bridge over the basement bar – in sleepy old Herne Hill. And if that doesn't rock your imagination back on its heels, let's just add that Three Monkeys is an Indian restaurant. Albeit an unusual one. The well-written menu steers firmly away from clichéd Indian food. Since the last edition of this guide the prices here have abated somewhat, and while not cheap they now represent sound value. Perhaps it is just that in 2001 everywhere else has caught up a bit!

Cost	£19–£38
Address	136–140 Herne Hill, SE24
T	020 7738 5500
Station	BR Herne Hill
Open	Mon–Sat 6–11pm, Sun noon–3pm & 6–11pm
Accepts	All major credit cards
W	www.3monkeys restaurant.com

Starters range from shammi kebab (£4.95) – minced lamb rissoles the size and shape of a hockey puck – to a brilliant, messy-looking dish, palak palodi chat (£4.75) – small cubes of spinach mixture deep-fried until crisp and served with plenty of chunky raw veg and two sauces, sharp sharp tamarind and creamy yoghurt. Very nice. As is the vogue, there is an open kitchen, and the grills and bread are all visibly well made. The main courses run from simple dishes like lamb rojangosh (£8.95) to dishes like chicken tikka makhani (£8.95), which many curryologists assert is the parent of chicken tikka masala. Look out for a range of good fish dishes, and do not be put off by the fact that most of the curries have names unfamiliar to British curry houses; they are authentic for all that. Try the mean Colombo (£9.50), cod that has been given the fiery Chettiar treatment. Prices are always steepest anywhere you find the words "large" and "prawn". Prawns masala (£10.50) is a laconic title for prawns simmered in a sauce made with vinegar and a spicy Goan masala. Also in the good-but-expensive category is bhindi Jaipuri – a dish of okra cut very fine and deep-fried before being served with a seasoning of sour dried mango powder (£4.50).

Three Monkeys is a slick, fashionable, modern Indian restaurant serving commendably authentic food at prices that have to be taken seriously. It's not the monkeys' fault that they're in Herne Hill.

West

Barnes & Sheen

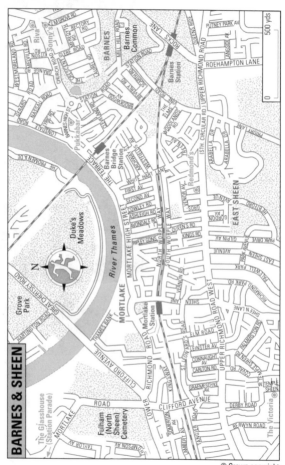

BARNES & SHEEN

© Crown copyright

The Glasshouse

Despite the boom of recent years, opening restaurants is still a precarious business. The Glasshouse, however, which opened in 1999, seems not only to have lived up to its admirable pedigree – chef Anthony Boyd honed his craft at the Michelin-bedecked Square (see p.85) and Chez Bruce (see p.331) – but also to have survived that difficult "be-patient-just-opened" period. What's more, the restaurant is on the doorstep of Kew Gardens underground station, which makes it easy for anyone who can get onto the District line. The interior has a clean-cut, modern feel to it and the chairs are worthy of lavish praise – they are blissfully comfortable, an aspect of dining which is all too often overlooked. The food is good. Very good. Boyd's style, which combines Square's sophistication and the rich flavours of Chez Bruce, is a sure-fire winner.

Cost	£20–£50

Address 14 Station Parade, Kew Gardens, Surrey
T 020 8940 6777
Station Kew Gardens
Open Mon–Sat noon–2.30pm & 7–10.30pm, Sun 12.30–3pm
Accepts All major credit cards except Diners

FRENCH

The menu is a simple one which changes daily and usually makes you choose from seven starters, seven mains and seven puds. At lunch, two courses cost £17.50 and three £19.50; for dinner the price is £25 for three courses. This is a snatch-their-hand-off bargain. The cooking, imaginative and straightforward, owes much to French cuisine. Starters range from Rossmore oysters with cucumber jelly through sauteed John Dory with spinach and Ricotta crespelle, cream of celeriac soup with celery salt croutons, and warm salad of wood pigeon with deep-fried truffled egg. Main courses vary from a classical Chateaubriand with all the trimmings (including a small supplement to the bill), to roast fillet of cod with creamed Savoy cabbage and crisp Bayonne ham. The roast guinea fowl with boudin blanc and grain mustard is good. Puddings have a deft touch and include old favourites like rum baba and savarin. The pear and almond tart with a poire William custard is particularly fine. The wine list is short and thoughtfully drawn up, with one or two unusual selections.

Service at Glasshouse is masterful, and will leave you feeling thoroughly cosseted. However, it's just as well to note the small print at the bottom of the menu that warns, "Please order taxis at least 25 minutes before they are required".

Pukkabar

INDIAN

Pukkabar, or "The Pukkabar and Curry Hall", to spell out its more fulsome title, started life in Sydenham. It was the brainchild of Trevor Gulliver, the mastermind behind that headquarters of nose-to-tail cuisine, St John in Clerkenwell (see p.199). Mr Gulliver's quaint theory was that curry is a very British dish, and that this British perspective is the one from which it is best approached. The Pukkabar offers well-made, well-spiced, good-value food in clean surroundings and with the minimum pretension and fuss. Curries are batch-cooked and the rest of the menu is made up of fresh food from the tandoor and, for starters, a range of tasty Indian street food. As with so many kinds of food, when it comes to curry, simple is good and, despite its English antecedents, the Pukkabar has ended up having a good deal more in common with clear flavours than most high-street curry houses.

Cost	£11–£28
Address	21 Barnes High St, SW13
T	020 8878 7012
Station	BR Barnes Bridge
Open	Mon–Fri 6.30–11pm, Sat 12.30–11pm, Sun 12.30–10.30pm
Accepts	All major credit cards
W	www.pukkabars.com

The menu changes regularly, but you can expect to find about eight starters listed, several of which are suitable for vegetarians. From the tandoor there's malai tikka (£3.95) – well cooked and tender chicken; or malayam sikhe (£3.95) – minced lamb kebabs; or tandoori salmon (£4.95). The presentation is accomplished here. As well as old favourites like onion bhaji (£3.95), there are moodier items like chicken pakora (£4.50) and deep-fried spiced prawns, which are served with salad and a mango sauce (£4.50). In addition to the mixed tandoori (£8.95) of chicken, lamb and salmon, the main courses are curries: chilli chicken (£6.95); a Goan prawn curry (£7.95); a tandoori salmon masala (£8.50); a mild aromatic lamb curry with yoghurt (£7.50); and even that all-British favourite, chicken tikka masala (£6.25). Rice dishes and breads are good; check out the garlic naan (£2). For pud there are Hill Station ice creams (£3) – better a reputable bought-in ice cream than a poorly made one from the kitchen.

In 2001 the Pukkabar launched a delivery service, although due to the small and steady Piaggio van used, it only operates if you live within a mile of the restaurant.

Redmond's

When Redmond and Pippa Hayward opened this small neighbourhood restaurant towards the end of the 1990s, it was head and shoulders above anything else the locale had to offer. A few years down the line and "Barnes & Sheen" may not quite be a match for Soho, but there are a good many very decent places to eat. Redmond's is one of the best. This place is propelled by a telling combo of very good cooking and reasonable prices. They

| Cost | £12–£45 |

Address 170 Upper Richmond Rd West, SW14
T 020 8878 1922
Station BR Mortlake
Open Mon 7–10.30pm, Tues–Fri noon–2.30pm & 7–10.30pm, Sat 7–10.30pm, Sun noon–2.30pm
Accepts Delta, MasterCard, Switch, Visa

tweak the menu on a daily basis, so it reflects the best of what the season and the markets have to offer. The dinner menu is not particularly short – about eight starters and mains – and proves astonishing value at £23 for two courses and £27 for three. There are also two lunch menus: the "express" at £10 for two courses and £12.50 for three, or the wider menu at £16.50 for two courses or £21 for three. What's even more astonishing is that the list is not splattered with supplements or cover charges. And the food here really is very good indeed: well seasoned, precisely cooked, immaculately presented.

If the terrine of chicken and foie gras is available when you visit, pounce. It's delicate, multi-layered, multi-textured – superlative-inducing in every way. There may also be a tartare of smoked haddock and sushi ginger, or perhaps a roast red pepper and red onion risotto. Main courses combine dominant flavours with elegant presentation. Roast sea bass comes with a Jerusalem artichoke and truffle-oil puree; duck breast with a gratin Dauphinoise; roast, crispy, spiced belly pork with crushed new potatoes. A fennel compote with tapenade and crab sauce partners roast red mullet fillets. The puddings are wonderful, too. Praline millefeuille of crème brûlée and poached peach with raspberry sauce makes an imposing tower out of luxurious dollops of vanillarey crème brûlée, peach segments and craquelin. The strawberry, raspberry and elderflower jelly comes with a delicate vanilla cream.

The short wine list is littered with interesting bottles at accessible prices. There are halves, magnums, pudding wines and just plain bargains. Splash out on the splendid Gigondas (£26), a perfect partner for the impressive all-British cheeseboard.

Barnes & Sheen

Riva

When Andrea Riva opened his doors some years ago, Hammersmith Bridge allowed easy access to devotees north of the Thames who doted on his straightforward Italian cooking. Then the bridge closed; then it reopened; and it is a testament to the pulling power of the kitchen that throughout this prolonged spell of planning blight the restaurant continued to be busy. It just goes to show – people will put themselves out for good food. Inside, this is a rather conservative-looking restaurant, with a narrow dining room decorated in a sombre blend of dull greens and faded parchment, and chairs which have clearly seen service in church. As far as the cuisine goes, Riva provides the genuine article, so first-time customers are either delighted or disappointed. The menu changes regularly with the seasons.

Cost	£25–£45

Address 169 Church Rd, SW13
T 020 8748 0434
Station BR Barnes
Open Mon–Fri noon–2.30pm & 7–11pm, Sat 7–11.30pm, Sun noon–2.30pm & 7–9.30pm
Accepts Amex, MasterCard, Visa

Starters are good but not cheap: the frittelle (£8.50) is a tempura-like dish of deep-fried Mediterranean prawn, salt cod cakes, calamari and artichoke, with a balsamic dip. If it is on the menu, you must try bocconcini di bufala – buffalo Mozzarella with roasted peppers, red onions, cherry tomatoes and capers (£7), vibrant and deliciously oily. The brodetto "Mare Nostrum", a chunky, saffron-flavoured fish soup (£7), is also superb – a delicate alternative to its robust French cousin. Serious Italian food fans, however, will find it hard to resist the sapori Mediterranei (£19 for two), which gets you crab and fennel salad; baccalà mantecato and polenta; poached pike in salsa verde; and eel in tomato sauce – a combination that is unlikely to be found on many menus outside the Po valley. Among the main courses, branzino al rosemary (£15) is a splendid combination of tastes and textures – a fillet of sea bass with rosemary and shallots is served on a potato tortina with fava beans. Battuta di pollo – chicken breast marinated in thyme and balsamic vinegar with spinach and pumpkin gratin (£12.50) – delivers a finely balanced blend of flavours.

If there's anybody out there who still thinks that pizza and pasta are the Italians' staple diet, Riva's uncompromising regional menu proves otherwise. The house wines are all priced at a very accessible £10.50. Of the whites, the pale-coloured Tocai is crisp, light and refreshing.

Sonny's

MODERN BRITISH

If the scientists are to be believed, we must evolve or die, and if they're looking for corroborating evidence they'll find it at Sonny's. This is one of those restaurants people describe as a "neighbourhood stalwart" but it has grown into something more polished. Barnes-ites have been supporting Sonny's since Modern British cuisine was just a twinkle in a telly chef's eye. The interior is modern but gratifyingly unthreatening and there is a busy, casual feel about the place. Sonny's shop next door sells a good many of those little delicacies that you would otherwise have to make the dangerous journey to the West End to procure. Leigh Diggins is chef here and he has a good grasp of just what his customers want. The menu is modern but not aggressively so, dishes are interesting but not frightening, and you will find the occasional flash of innovation.

Cost	£18–£38

Address 94 Church Rd, SW13
T 020 8748 0393
Station BR Barnes Bridge
Open Mon–Sat 12.30–2.30pm
& 7.30–11pm, Sun 12.30–3pm
Accepts All major credit cards

The menu changes on a regular basis to reflect the seasons, so you might find starters like watercress soup with Jersey Royals and truffle oil (£4.25), or chicken and sweetbread terrine with mixed leaves and sweet pickle (£6.50), or even, on a more whimsical note, maple-roasted quail with apple and red wine risotto (£6.75). Main courses may take classic combinations like pan-fried calves' liver with pancetta, and then add spatzle, pumpkin puree and grain mustard dressing (£11.50). There tend to be some attractive fish dishes, too: steamed fillet of halibut with Jersey Royals, broad beans and langoustine dressing (£14), say, or roasted zander with button onions, celeriac and bacon (£12.50). Or you could go much heartier with the haunch of venison, red cabbage, roasted salsify, butter chocolate and cep sauce (£12.50). The service is welcoming and the wine list provides some sound bottles at sound prices.

Puddings are comfortable: sorbets, jellies, baked Alaska with raspberries (£5.25). If Barnes is your neighbourhood, you will be glad that it has a restaurant like this, especially as there is a set lunch during the week – £13 for two courses, £16 for three. If Barnes isn't your neighbourhood, you could try one of Sonny's siblings: Parade, in Ealing (see p.417), or The Phoenix, in Putney (see p.357).

The Victoria

It would be nice to live in West Temple Sheen. The name has a good ring to it. The houses are palatial and pricey, both Sheen Common and Richmond Park are close at hand, and then there's The Victoria, a truly outstanding gastro-pub. The Victoria made the transition from pub to gastro-pub in late 2000, when a good deal of money was poured in. It emerged with a conservatory, squashy sofas and painted floorboards – very smart. As the distinction between restaurants and gastro-pubs becomes increasingly blurred, the Victoria just about hangs onto gastro-pub status by virtue of its accessible prices. What you're getting is restaurant cooking, a restaurant wine list and restaurant service, and you're getting it on the cheap.

Cost	£12–£30
Address	10 West Temple Sheen, SW14
T	020 8876 4238
Station	BR Mortlake
Open	Mon–Fri noon–2.30pm & 7–10pm, Sat & Sun noon–3pm & 7–10pm
Accepts	All major credit cards
W	www.thevictoria.net

The menu is blessedly short and changes daily – or even more frequently than that, should items run out. There are a handful of starters like piperade tart (£4), spaghettini with tomato parsley and lemon (£4.50), and moules marinière (£4). Or how about caldo verde (£3.50) – a stunning bowl of dark and satisfying cabbage soup, bolstered with an occasional chunk of pork, and rich with good oil? Very delicious indeed, but even so, it's not the most impressive starter, which is the chicken liver parfait served with toasted brioche and onion chutney (£4.50) – a large slice, perfectly seasoned and astonishingly light, almost fluffy. Remarkably good. Mains are also pretty triumphant – roast and confit pheasant, with cabbage and lentils, and green peppercorn sauce (£9.50) is excellent – the cabbage and lentils hearty enough to make a dish by themselves. Then there's a Jerusalem artichoke and rosemary risotto (£7). Or Irish stew (£8.50). Or skate wing with parsley salad and deep-fried capers (£7.50) – perfectly cooked, simple, and delicious.

Desserts are top stuff. It's a pleasure to watch punters savouring a lemon posset (£4) and to know that were they only to try your boca negra (£4.50) they would probably kill for it. A simple, dark, moist, rich, sinful, indulgent wedge of ultra chocolate cake.

Chelsea

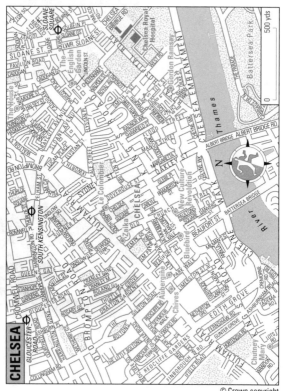

© Crown copyright

Aubergine

Aubergine deserves a prolonged burst of applause. It's a place that was once synonymous with Gordon Ramsay, who for five years built it into a serious restaurant in a neighbourhood what was a bit of a wasteland when he arrived. Then he left, but Aubergine had enough oomph to carry on without him. This restaurant has a pretty, elegant, airy

Cost	£24–£90

Address 11 Park Walk, SW10
T 020 7352 3449
Station South Kensington/
Earl's Court
Open Mon–Fri noon–2.30pm
& 7–10.30pm, Sat 7–10.30pm
Accepts All major credit cards

FRENCH

dining room and serves very good French food with panache and élan. This is top-drawer dining. The set lunch at £18 for two courses and £22.50 for three is an outrageous bargain. No wonder that, as in Ramsay's day, bookings at Aubergine are becoming hard to come by.

A lunch that comprises boudin of foie gras with toasted brioche followed by roasted monkfish with a fricassee of mussels in cider doesn't read, look or taste like £18's worth. Even at full throttle the main menu offers three courses for £45, which is not so very fierce for cooking of this calibre (although supplements hang on the coat tails of lobster, turbot, cheeses and the like). Starters may include red mullet escabeche; mousse of foie gras with girolles; warm salad of roasted vegetables with asparagus purée; and terrine of foie gras and confit of duck with pears poached in port. Main courses, which appeal greatly, include dishes like pan-fried sea bass with a bouillon of sweet peppers and tomatoes; best end of lamb with confit turnips and a thyme-scented jus; confit veal sweetbreads with a casserole of white beans and foie gras; and breast of chicken with Madeira-glazed ceps and roasted artichokes. Well-conceived, well-executed dishes, beautifully presented. It would be hard to suggest improvements. The Menu Gourmand at £60 will spin the experience out by presenting seven pixie portions and so allow you to make the kitchen brigade jump through a few extra hoops. Desserts are equally accomplished – coconut ice cream with chocolate caramel nougatine; pear Tatin with vanilla ice cream. The service is accomplished and unobtrusive.

The only cautionary note relates to the wine list, where the prices bolt swiftly out of reach for all but the most special of special occasions.

MODERN EUROPEAN

Bluebird

This is a slick place. If you like slick places, you'll like it a lot. Conran's Bluebird complex is large and sprawling: there is a food hall, a kitchenware shop, a cafe, a flower stall, a members-only club and the restaurant itself. The dining room is large, with a central bar, and manages to be both crowded as well as light and airy. The food is modern – Modern European, if that is in any way a meaningful description – and the Oriental twist to dishes which was a feature when the Bluebird started out has been tempered as the restaurant has matured. The service is professional to a T and the prices look fair – although when all is finally added up you may be surprised how high the total can be. There is, however, a good-value set lunch – two courses for £12.75, three courses for £15.75 – which also does service as a pre-theatre option (before 7pm).

Cost	£20–£40

Address 350 King's Rd, SW3
T 020 7559 1000
Station Sloane Square
Open Mon–Fri noon–3pm & 6–11pm, Sat 11am–3.30pm & 6–11pm, Sun 11am–3.30pm (brunch) & 6–10pm
Accepts All major credit cards
W www.conran.com

You might start with goat's Ricotta, olives and peppers (£8.25), or perhaps something more sophisticated, like pan-fried foie gras with fig chutney (£12.75). Wood-roast sardines, rosemary flat bread and olive oil (£7.50) makes good use of the wood-fired oven. The menu layout has been simplified, which makes for easier reading. Dishes are straightforward, in the best kind of way, and may include char-grilled tuna, potatoes and olives (£15.25); whole sea bass roasted in the wood-fired oven and served with tomato and fennel (£19.50); roast rump of lamb, gratin Dauphinois, glazed carrots and sauce soubise (£14); duck confit with parsley mash and roast garlic (£14.50); and wild mushroom lasagne (£11). Even that old trouper, steak au poivre (£21.50), makes a welcome reappearance. These are all dishes that people like to eat and are none the worse for being popular.

Puddings – tarte Tatin with caramel ice cream (£6) or chocolate tart with crème fraîche (£6) – carry on the theme and are generally successful. There is a classic brunch menu served on Saturday and Sunday at £17.50. Think eggs Benedict. Think chicken Caesar.

Chives

Chives is part of the Red Pepper Group, a restaurant chainlet that first made its reputation knocking out well-made pizzas from a wood–fired oven in the tiny Maida Vale restaurant of that name. Having taken this information on board, it's worth noting that Chives is nothing like a chain restaurant. As far as the room is concerned, Chives is all Chelsea Beach: blond wood floor, beige walls and soft lighting. The waiters are French. The menu is complex. The cooking is good. Strangely, the usual order of things is reversed, and there is an à la carte at lunch (starters around £5, mains around £12) with a prix fixe in the evening. The same dishes suffice for both menus, but there are a few more options at dinner.

Cost	£20–£60
Address	204 Fulham Rd, SW10
T	020 7351 4747
Station	South Kensington/ Earl's Court
Open	Mon–Wed 7–11pm, Thurs–Sat 12.30–2.30pm & 7–11pm, Sun 12.30–2.30pm & 7–10pm
Accepts	All major credit cards

The menu changes on a regular basis, but two courses will weigh in at £22 and three courses at £24.50. There are a few supplements on dishes featuring the usual suspects – mainly fish, fillet steak and foie gras. Starters can be highly original, like the dish of squid ink tagliatelle with braised rabbit and baby calamari, which is wholly successful. Or crisp roast salmon with herb gnocchi, pancetta and Parmesan emulsion – an interesting combination of tastes and textures. Or how about pan-fried foie gras with Jerusalem artichoke velouté and spiced duck ravioli? A dish that ends up more than the sum of its parts. There's a creative touch with the main courses too: osso bucco comes with caramelized sweet-bread and a lemon basil dressing – also successful. Herb-crusted red mullet is accompanied by a white bean, truffle and bacon cassoulet; and, in season, crepinette of lamb comes with honey roast winter vegetables. Puddings are also variations on a theme rather than merely replays of the classics – pear crème brûlée comes with a chocolate sorbet; or there's a lemon bread-and-butter pudding that would be more at home in a patisserie window and comes with a lemony-limy sorbet.

The wine list, which concentrates on France and Italy, strives – and largely succeeds – to be all things to all men, and runs from a Languedoc Chardonnay (£13.50) to a heavyweight Friulian red (£55).

Chutney Mary

For such a large, well-designed, elegant restaurant, the food at Chutney Mary is remarkably close to tasting home-made, which is perhaps the greatest compliment you can pay an Indian meal in London. Dishes here are not cheap, but the food is freshly pre-pared and the spicing is always authentic. A number of dishes change each quarter to keep the menu fresh. The

Cost	£20–£40
Address	535 King's Rd, SW10
T	020 7351 3113
Station	Fulham Broadway
Open	Mon–Sat 12.30–2.30pm & 6.30–11.30pm, Sun 12.30–3pm & 6.30–10.30pm
Accepts	All major credit cards
W	www.chutneymary.com

menu majors in regional Indian speciali-ties, and the restaurant hosts a succession of festivals which focus on the food of a particular region. You will have to book in the evening and for the very popular jazz brunch on Sunday, which comes in at the wholly reasonable price of £15 for three courses.

Starters are split into vegetarian and non-vegetarian, and can be con-veniently ordered as a selection (£6 or £7.50). The former brings samosas, papri chat and veggie kebabs; the latter brings crab cake, papri chat and calamari chilli fry. Both are tempting options, as are the crab cakes with a Goan spicing (£6.25). For mains, turn to the regional dishes, which tend to be complex and interestingly spiced: green chicken curry (£11.50) from Goa, for instance, with fresh coriander, green chilli, mint and tamarind; or a fiery Mangalore prawn curry (£15.75), cooked in an earthenware pot; or dum ka murgh (£11.50), a classic Hyderabadi chicken dish. There is also sarson batta murgh (£11.50), a chicken curry with mustard seeds, served with red pumpkin; or kosha mangsho (£12), a Bengali recipe for lamb braised slowly with onions, red chillies and cinnamon. Where applicable, dishes come with aromatic Basmati rice. As a side dish, look out for crisp-fried okra and banana (£3.75), a dish from Chettinad and Madras. Breads are also worth ordering, particularly the parata stuffed with spicy mashed potato with lime and herbs (£2.50), and the flaky, wholemeal lacha paratha (£1.75).

There is also a tasting menu that is only available in the evening. This offers four courses for £32 – papri chat, crab cake and calamari; then chicken tikka; then malai prawn curry, Bengali lamb curry, sag aloo, aubergine and rice dishes; and finally your choice of dessert.

Le Colombier

Viewed from the pavement outside on Dovehouse Street, you can see that Le Colombier was once a classic, English street-corner pub. But now it's a pub that has a small, glassed-in area in front that is covered with tables and chairs. How very Parisian, you may think, and you would be right. This is a French place. It is run by Monsieur Garnier, who has spent most of his career in the slicker reaches of London's restaurant business. With his own place he has reverted to type and everything is very, very French.

Cost	£15–£30

Address 145 Dovehouse St, Chelsea Square, SW3
T 020 7351 1155
Station South Kensington
Open Mon–Sat noon–3pm & 6.30–11pm, Sun noon– 3.30pm & 6.30–10.30pm
Accepts All major credit cards

The menu is French, the cooking is French, the service is French and the decor is French. When the bill comes, you tend to be surprised – first that it is no larger and secondly that they ask for pounds not francs. The cooking is about as good as you would have found in a smart Routiers in rural France during the 1970s – before slick places became hard to find. Starters include such bistro classics as oeufs pochés meurette (£5.80), soupe de poissons (£5.30), and feuilleté d'escargots à la crème d'ail (£6.80). And there's oysters, goat's cheese salad, duck liver terrine, and tomato and basil salad. Listed under "les poissons" there is lotte a la Catalane (£14.80), a simple dish made with monkfish tarragon and tomato cream sauce; and coquilles St Jacques aux champignons sauvages (£14.80), which is scallops with wild mushrooms. Under "les viandes" there is steak tartare pommes frites (£14.80) and lapin a la moutarde (£12.80). Under "les grillades" are the steaks and chops. Puddings include crêpes Suzette (£4.90) and omelette Norvégienne pour deux (£12), which is also described as "baked Alaska" – something of a geographical conundrum.

Service is as French as the menu itself, but Le Colombier is not some trendy retro caricature. None of the atmosphere is posed. If this seems like a provincial French eatery, it's because that's what it is. The fact that it is located in Chelsea makes the set menu for lunch and early diners (two courses for £13; on Sunday £15) very good value indeed.

The English Garden

When Searcy Corrigan Restaurants went shopping in Chelsea during the autumn of 1999, this is one of the places they bought (the other being The House, see p.408). The English Garden got the full make-over treatment: a maple-wood bar, lashings of soft, creamy and biscuity tones, and a judicious use of grey British slate. The new kitchen is headed up by Malcolm Starmer who worked with Richard Corrigan for five years at the Lindsay House, and before that in the Barbican. The service is slick, the room is comfortable, and Starmer's food is good. There are echoes of the Lindsay House, but only faint ones; this is well-conceived Modern British food which relies on good combinations of strong flavours.

Cost	£20–£45
Address	10 Lincoln St, SW3
T	020 7584 7272
Station	Sloane Square
Open	Mon–Sat noon–3pm & 6–11pm
Accepts	All major credit cards

MODERN BRITISH

The menu changes twice a day. For lunch there is a three-course set lunch at the derisory price of £19.50. Less than £20 for stuffed baby squid with Feta, chorizo, mussels and garlic, followed by rib of beef with roast root vegetables and aged vinegar, and then chocolate fondant with Bailey's mousse? This is a stellar bargain. Or perhaps parfait of foie gras and chicken livers with fig chutney, followed by fillets of mackerel with curried spinach, yoghurt and harissa, and finishing with toffee banana crumble with crème caramel? In the evening these dishes would be bolstered by one or two more serious numbers: starters like consommé of ceps with parsley dumplings and truffle oil; or potato and Taleggio gnocchi with shin of veal, parsley and lemon; and mains like beef Wellington with field mushrooms and watercress puree; loin of Gloucester Old Spot pork with black pudding, parsnip, apple and sage; leg of rabbit with roast sweetbread, Serrano ham, gratin potato and green beans; and seared scallops with smoked haddock croquettes, leeks and chive butter. At dinner the price moves up to £27.50 for three courses, with supplements kept to a minimum. Puds are indulgent: try anisée poached pear with Pernod ice cream.

Elsewhere in the Garden are two elegant private rooms that can be joined together, creating space for parties of ten, twenty or thirty. There is an irresistible temptation to say that everything in the garden is rosy.

Gordon Ramsay

2001 was the year that things came right for Gordon Ramsay. He achieved his third Michelin star, and dominion over a new restaurant within Claridges Hotel. At Chelsea the restaurant continues to be packed, while a smll extension to the kitchen means that things are not quite so crowded and frantic behind the scenes – this is a place

Cost	£35–£120
Address	68–69 Royal Hospital Rd, SW3
T	020 7352 4441
Station	Sloane Square
Open	Mon–Fri noon–2pm & 6.45–11pm
Accepts	All major credit cards

with a ratio of nearly one chef to every two customers. Thankfully, the prices are not as high as you might fear. There are two fixed-price cartes at both lunch and dinner (£60 for three courses, £75 for seven), and a steal of a set lunch (£30 for three courses). Even if you add £5 for a glass of good house wine, this offers the more accessible face of truly great cooking – as long as you can get a booking.

The menu here is constantly evolving and changing. On the main menus, look out for a tortellini of lobster and langoustine poached in a lobster bisque and served with a fine fennel puree and buttered cabbage; or a carpaccio of pigeon from Bresse with shavings of confit foie gras, baby artichokes and a creamed truffle sauce – this is a stunning dish of unusual delicacy; or a warm salad of caramelized calf's sweetbreads with crispy scallops, grilled asparagus and a sweet and sour vinaigrette, which is as robust and delicious as you could wish for. And those are just starters! Mains intrigue: fillets of red mullet cooked with saffron on a bed of marinated peppers and crab couscous, with lemon grass nage; poulet de Bresse poached then grilled with braised Savoy cabbage seasoned with marjoram, confit shallots, asparagus and thyme jus; fillet of Aberdeen Angus with caramelized pig's trotter and fried quail's egg cooked in goose fat and truffle sauce – think clichés like "cutting the steak with a fork", very tender, very rich. Pick a dish or even an ingredient you like and see how it arrives; you won't be disappointed. This is a class act through and through.

You will have to book at Gordon Ramsay, but, sensibly enough, reservations are taken only a month in advance, avoiding a potentially huge backlog. Book now, and count the days.

The House

🍴 Until 1999, this chintzy, tweedy, fussy little restaurant went under the sobriquet of "The English House", at which point in swept Searcy Corrigan Restaurants and everything changed ... except the chintzy, tweedy, fussy decor. There is nothing fussy or remotely old-fashioned, however, about chef/patron

Cost	£17–£40

Address 3 Milner St, SW3
T 020 7584 3002
Station Sloane Square
Open Mon–Fri noon–2.30pm
& 6–11pm, Sat 6–11pm
Accepts All major credit cards

Graham Garrett's food, which is strongly flavoured, well seasoned, straightforward and British. And after dining here you have to admit, albeit grudgingly, that the warren of little rooms and the "country-house-naff" wallpaper have a certain charm.

The menu changes on a weekly basis to keep pace with what the markets have to offer. It costs £27 for three courses at dinner, and there's a set lunch at a give-away £14.50 for two courses and £18 for three. In winter you could expect hearty starters like brioche, wild mushrooms and soft boiled duck's egg; warm carpaccio of swordfish with a caper and parsley dressing; or bresaola of beef and cured foie gras. The kitchen does a lot of home curing and home salting, and sensible regulars make a beeline for the resulting dishes. Main courses range from the super-straightforward – fried wing of skate with shrimp beurre noisette; risotto of asparagus with poached egg and Parmesan cheese; pan-fried rump skirt with oxtail sauce and watercress – and on to more adventurous stuff like venison turnover with red cabbage; red sea bream with roast new-season garlic, spinach, chorizo and beans; and roast belly of Gloucester Old Spot pork with scallops and pancetta. Puds are modern: grilled pineapple with chilli syrup and coconut sorbet; Sauternes and almond cake with marinated prunes; caramelized banana with vanilla waffle and maple syrup ice cream. But sometimes modern can be good!

The wine list is thoughtful. The front of house team know what they are doing. The cooking is accomplished and dishes have a remarkably satisfying quality about them. But you must either overlook or enjoy the decor. As well as owing ultimate allegiance to Richard Corrigan (see p.132), The House has a sister restaurant nearby in Chelsea – The English Garden (p.406).

New Culture Revolution

This is one of the latest in a series of noodle-bar chains to target London, and arguably among the best. New Culture Revolution brings Londoners noodles and dumplings in soup, with a North Chinese spin. They have recently changed the booking policy and now take reservations for parties of more than four people. If you haven't booked you may have to queue, but for only five or ten minutes, as tables turn around pretty fast. Once settled in, take time to peruse the menu, which gives you a chance to catch up with the philosophy of Northern Chinese cooking. There are a number of Confucius-like comments about the herbs and spices used, plus explanations about how wholesome this food is for the body. You'll find you feel better already.

Cost	£17–£40
Address	305 King's Rd, SW3
T	020 7352 9281
Station	Sloane Square
Open	Daily noon–11pm
Accepts	All major credit cards

The menu itself is divided into several sections, with starters "specially chosen to stimulate good digestion and cleanse the palate", and various combinations of soups, dumplings, noodles and rice dishes. Stimulate the juices with grilled prawns with chilli and garlic (£4.70), a "refreshing and energising" raw juice (£2.50 – a blend of carrot and apple), or the steamed qing kou (£4.50) – New Zealand greenlipped mussels. The main courses are filling stuff. The vegetarian tong mein (£4.90) is thick with writhing noodles at the bottom of a huge bowl of "mellow home-made" stock, together with enough vegetables to feed a small terracotta army. A Revolution extra chow mein with sha sha spices (£5.80) brings fried noodles and vegetables with a combination of beef, chicken and seafood – a good deal better than anything the local Chinese takeaway can deliver. Or there's kung po gai ding (£5.80), which is chicken with bamboo shoots and water chestnuts. Duck enthusiasts will find xiang su ya (£6.90) a happy solution – seasoned rice with crispy duck pan-fried with herbs and spices.

After 45 minutes you'll find yourself out on the street again, much to the relief of those waiting. It's not that you'll have been hurried or been made to feel unwelcome; rather that your tolerance of the lime green walls and uncomfortable seats will be running out. Good design feature, that.

Zaika

Zaika is an upmarket Indian restaurant that gives the lie to any snobs who still maintain that Indian food can never amount to anything. And in 2001 it became one of the first Indian restaurants in London to receive a Michelin star. Thankfully, in the face of such a temptation to go over the top with the frills and folderols beloved of the tyre chaps, Zaika still manages to be pretty unpretentious. The food is wholesome, it looks good and tastes good, and though your bill will not be a small one it will not be a West End wallet-breaker either. There are novel dishes to be sampled but they sit alongside classics – you can still enjoy an impeccable rogan josh served on the bone.

Cost	£20–£50
Address	259 Fulham Rd, SW3
T	020 7351 7823
Station	South Kensington
Open	Mon–Fri noon–2.30pm & 6.30–10.30pm, Sat 6.30–10.30pm, Sun 12.30–2.30pm & 6.30–9.30pm
Accepts	All major credit cards except Diners

Start with the dhungar machli tikka (£6.95). It is hard to praise this dish highly enough: a well-marinated chunk of salmon, cooked in the tandoor and served when just right. Wonder of wonders, not over-done! Or there is the outstanding kala murg (£5.95) chicken, cooked in aromatic black spices; and murghabi seekhe (£5.95), which are minced duck rolls. Some thought goes into the main courses. This is not a seasonal menu in the strictest sense of the term, but in summer the grey mullet will give way to sea bass and the cauliflower will be changed for broccoli. The nariyal jhinga (£12.50), made from prawns cooked in a coconut masala tempered with lime leaves, stands out. Or there's lal mirch murg (£9.95), a spicy chicken dish made with fennel and coriander seeds. The koh-e-rogan josh (£10.50) is very good. Samundri khazana (£21.50) is most interesting – this is a crispy, Hawaiian, soft-shell crab with spiced scallops and an Indian risotto. Inspirational stuff. The simpler dishes are also good – try the dubkiwale aloo (£4.75), a straightforward dish of potatoes with cumin. And the breads are splendid: try the malai nan (£2.50) with your starters – it's cheesy, sticky, self-indulgent.

On the dessert menu you may find the chocomosa. This is a dish that chef Vineet Bhatia has been toying with for a good while now, and one which finally seems to have come right: crisp samosas containing an admirably bitter melted chocolate.

Ealing & Acton

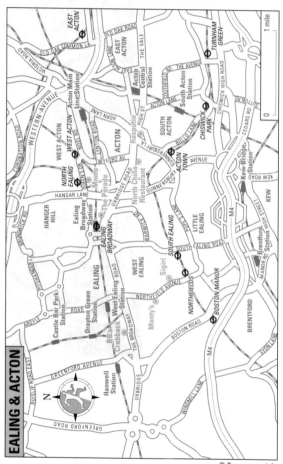

EALING & ACTON

© Crown copyright

BB's Crabback

Brian Benjamin (the eponymous chef at BB's) is from Grenada, but his food encompasses the whole Caribbean: classic dishes from Jamaica jostle those from Trinidad, as well as Grenada itself. The restaurant, hidden away behind the Uxbridge Road, can appear a rather charming backwater, an impression enhanced by the laid-back staff. But it is not undiscovered territory. The walls are papered with awards from various "salons culinaires" – and in 2000 Benjamin added the Afro-Caribbean Chef of the Year award for the second year running. This restaurant has a remarkable repertoire and everything is played in tune. Be sure to book if you want a table on a Friday or Saturday night.

Cost	£12–£28
Address	3 Chignell Place, West Ealing, W13
T	020 8840 8322
Station	Northfields
Open	Mon–Sat 6.30–11pm
Accepts	Amex, MasterCard, Visa

Start with ackee salt fish (£4.25). This is the classic Jamaican dish served with "bakes", which are like a kind of fried dumpling. Or try BB's crabback (£5.25) – a crabback is nothing more complicated than a crab shell filled with crabmeat and coated in a cheesy, creamy sauce. Or there's devilled salt-fish balls (£4.25) – spicy, irregular fish cakes. Or callaloo and okra soup (£4.25). Main courses all come with a choice of rice and peas, plain rice, or saffron rice. The rice and peas here is a revelation – rich, dark and spicy without being chilli-hot, and with a waft of cloves. The saffron rice is good, too – yellow and buttery. The main courses are half fish and half meat dishes: steak River Antoine (£12.95) is a sirloin steak flamed in Grenadian rum with a sweet relish sauce; while scampi Ashley (£11.95), named after Benjamin's son, has a sauce made with mushrooms, saffron and cream. Or there's Spice Island jerk chicken (£10.50), which is hot and spicy with a dozen herbs. Side dishes are good fun. Go for fried or boiled plantain (£3.25); dasheen (£3.25) – a root vegetable like a well-mannered parsnip; roti skins – which brings wafer-thin, dry, delicious bread (£4.50); or jumbie umbrellas (£3.25) – which translates as mushrooms.

If you're in inflammatory mood, try a dessert of banana flamed in rum and lemon (£5.20), which arrives at table quite seriously on fire. And to really indulge, finish with a cool slipper coffee (£5.95), described as "with cognac and a hint of rum. Topped with cream." It's enough to make the Irish look to their laurels.

Momo

The opening of a Japanese school in Acton led to widespread Nipponification of the local shops and services – there are Japanese food shops, Japanese estate agents, and even a mysterious Aladdin's cave called the Japanese Recycling Shop, which has shelf after shelf of repaired and refurbished electronic gadgetry – everything from rice cookers to typewriters. Nearby on Queen's Parade is this restaurant, a small establishment with 28 seats – it's a good idea to book. Service is smiling and helpful, and the long menu gives every opportunity to explore those less familiar dishes which may make you nervous in more intimidating, formal establishments.

Cost	£12–£40
Address	14 Queen's Parade, Ealing, W5
T	020 8997 0206
Station	West Acton
Open	Mon–Sat noon–2.30pm & 6–10pm
Accepts	All major credit cards
W	www.lamms.com

If you don't feel up to extensive menu exploration, go for the set menus – three or four dishes culminating in dessert may be had for prices ranging from £7.30 to £16 (lunch) or £15 to £25 (dinner). Assembling a meal yourself, you might start with yakitori (£3.80), three small, very good chicken kebabs; or kanisu (£6.30), a bowl of crabmeat and cucumber marinated in rice vinegar, which is delicate and fresh. Soups are very intriguing, especially dobin-mushi (£3.80), which comes in a small teapot with a tiny cup on top – a rich broth with chunks of shrimp and chicken to fish out with your chopsticks. Then there's buta shogayaki (£6.90) – thin strips of belly pork grilled with ginger and soy and served with a mound of ultra-thin coleslaw. If you want to try a grandstand dish, nigiri-zushi (£16) brings a box with a dozen pieces of assorted fish sushi, complete with gari – the amazingly delicious pickled ginger. Lovers of eel bow to the una jyu (£16.50), which is a box of rice topped with fillets of eel grilled with kabayaki sauce.

The operators at British Telecom's directory enquiries specialize in confusing this establishment with the larger, North African, restaurant of the same name in the West End (see p.103). Fortunately the staff here have the number of the other Momo and politely ask callers whether they want Momo W1 or Momo W5; the most frequent response, of course, is that the caller doesn't know.

Monty's

Once upon a time, the now defunct Ealing Tandoori held West London curry lovers in thrall – it was the undisputed first choice. Then, in the late 1970s, the three main chefs left to open their own place, which they called Monty's, on South Ealing Road. As business boomed, two of the chefs moved on to set up independently – but as all three co-owned the name Monty's, they all use

Cost	£10–£20

Address 54 Northfield Ave, Ealing, W13
T 020 8567 6281
Station Northfields
Open Daily noon–2.30pm & 6–11.30pm
Accepts All major credit cards
W www.montys.uk.com

INDIAN

it, and that is why there are now three different Monty's, all fiercely independent but each with the same name and logo. Unlike many small Indian restaurants, these are "chef-led", which is a key factor in making Monty's in Northfield Avenue an almost perfect neighbourhood curry house. You won't find banks of flowers or majestic staircases, the tables are too close together and you may be crowded by people waiting for a takeaway. But the cooking is class, the portions are good and prices are fair. This is a restaurant which has a fine grasp of what its customers want. And apparently they want more of it – Monty's Northfield has a new sibling on Ealing Broadway (T020 8576 4646).

A complimentary plate of salady crudités arrives with any chutneys and popadoms ordered, but starters are the exception rather than the rule here – perhaps because of the well-sized main course portions. Trad tandoori dishes are good, like the tandoori chicken (£4.50 for two pieces). Or there is hasina – lamb marinated in yogurt and served as a sizzler (£6.15). The boss here remembers introducing the iron-plate sizzlers at the Ealing Tandoori years ago and claims that his were the first in Britain. As you'd expect with a good tandoor chef, breads are delicious – pick between nan (£1.50) and Peshwari nan (£2.25). But the kitchen really gets to shine with simple curry dishes like methi ghosht (£6.95) – tender lamb (and plenty of it) in a delicious sauce rich with fenugreek; and chicken jalfriji (£6.95), which is all the dish should be. Vegetable dishes are also made with more care than is usual – both brinjal bhaji (£3.75) and sag paneer (£3.50) are delicious.

Monty's is one of very few local curry houses to serve perfectly cooked, genuine basmati rice. So the plain boiled rice (£1.95) – nutty, almost smoky, with grains perfectly separate – is worth tasting on its own.

North China Restaurant

The special Peking duck, which always used to require 24 hours advance notice, is now so popular that the restaurant cooks a few ducks every day regardless. So you don't always have to pre-order. But then you do, because it is SO popular that they cannot guarantee that you'll get one unless you order it. Inscrutable? The North China has a 24-carat local reputation: it is the kind of place people refer to as "being as good as Chinatown", which in this case is spot-on, and the star turn on the menu doesn't disappoint.

Cost	£14–£25

Address 305 Uxbridge Rd, Ealing Common, W3
T 020 8992 9183
Station Ealing Common
Open Daily noon–2.30pm & 6–11.30pm (midnight Fri & Sat)
Accepts All major credit cards
W www.northchina.co.uk

Unlike most other – upstart – crispy ducks, the crispy Peking duck here comes as three separate courses. Firstly there is the skin and breast meat, served with pancakes, shreds of cucumber and spring onion, and hoisin sauce. Then there is a fresh stir-fry of the duck meat with beansprouts, and finally the meal ends with a giant tureen of rich duck soup with lumps of the carcass to pick at. It is awesome. And the price, £42, is very reasonable, working out at just over £3 per person per course. If you're dull and just want the duck with pancakes the price drops to £32. So what goes well with duck? At the North China the familiar dishes are well cooked and well presented. You might start with barbecued pork spare ribs (£4.90), or the whimsically named lettuce puffs (£3.40 per person, minimum two), which turn out to be our old friend "mince wrapped in lettuce leaves". For a supplementary main course, prawns in chilli sauce (£7.25), although not very chilli, is teamed with fresh water-chestnuts, and tastes very good. Singapore fried noodles (£4.10) is powered by curry powder rather than fresh chilli, but fills a gap.

The genuinely friendly service at the North China stems from the fact that it is a family restaurant. If the genuine Peking duck does not appeal perhaps you should consider the North China's other high-ticket item. When lobsters are good at market they go onto the menu at a seasonal price – about £22.50 per lobster.

Parade

People who live in the better parts of Ealing drive Jaguars and live in million-pound houses. These are the sophisticated and leafy suburbs, but until the arrival of Parade in 1999 there was not a single proper restaurant to while away those evenings when the television disappoints. So when Parade opened (on a site that formerly hosted a rather arch Indian restaurant) you could hear the sighs of relief echoing around the neighbourhood. A sister restaurant to Sonny's in Barnes (see p.397), this is a modern, clean, keen sort of place, where neither the food nor the service will let you down. If you plonked this eatery down in the West End it would be run-of-the-mill, but here it deserves star billing. Which is why it is so amazingly busy every night of the week. Nowadays locals bemoan the fact that they cannot get in without booking.

Cost	£15–£45

Address 18–19 The Mall, Ealing, W5
T 020 8810 0202
Station Ealing Broadway
Open Mon–Sat 12.30–2.30pm & 7–11pm, Sun 12.30–3.30pm
Accepts All major credit cards except Diners

At lunchtime, when the restaurant is under a lot less pressure, there's a very decent set lunch, which costs £12 for two courses and £15 for three. In the evening everything goes à la carte. The menu changes regularly and is seasonally based. Starters are eclectic but well conceived, as the kitchen understands what the customer wants. Perhaps you'll find smoked haddock and whisky soup with Welsh rarebit (£5); chicken and foie gras boudin blanc with creamed beans and Madeira sauce (£6); or tempura tuna roll, vegetable salad and coriander cream (£7.50). Mains are grown-up versions of the starters, with dishes like poached ham hock, white bean stew, pancetta and salsa verde (£11.50); roasted sea bass with squid and sesame spring roll, and chilli, garlic and black bean sauce (£15); poached monkfish with fennel, mussels, tomato and rouille (£15); or rump of lamb with potato and aubergine galette, black olives and peppers (£15.50). The cooking is sound and the dishes are well presented. Service is generally slick, but has been known to creak under the intense pressure.

Parade's puddings are good: try rhubarb and vanilla parfait (£5.50), chocolate plate (£7.50) or banana profiteroles with hot chocolate sauce (£5.50). Why does a lemon grass crème brûlée (£5.50) sound so very Ealing?

Rasputin

You'll find the "Rasputin Russian Restaurant and Wine Bar" up at the Ealing end of Acton High Street. In 2001 the restaurant underwent a refurbishment and is now, in the words of the proprietors, "modern". It's still a jolly place, and the Russian specialities are homely and delicious, with an authentic emphasis on game in season. All this must be noted

Cost	£10–£25
Address	265 High St, Acton, W3
T	020 8993 5802
Station	Acton Town
Open	Daily 6–11.30pm
Accepts	MasterCard, Visa

before you have made any inroads into the twenty different vodkas, which come both as single shots and – take care here – "by the carafe".

With the menu comes a plate of cucumber, cabbage, green tomatoes and peppers, all markedly salty and with a good vinegary tang. For a starter, try pierogi – rich little dumplings that come stuffed with a choice of potato and cheese, meat, or sauerkraut and mushrooms; they are all priced at £3.85 a portion. The blinis – small buckwheat pancakes – are also good: try them with smoked salmon and sour cream (£4.50) or, if you enjoy the special thrill of finding a bargain, with 40g of Russian Sevruga caviar (£12.50). Sledzie (£3.45) is also delicious – pickled herrings with sour cream, apples, gherkins and dill. At Rasputin they are constantly tinkering with the menu and there usually seem to be several versions extant at once. Hold out for the golubtsy (£7.50), which is permanently under threat of banishment from the menu – this is a simple but satisfying dish of cabbage leaves stuffed with meat and rice. Very wholesome and very good. Or there's kotley po Kievsky (£7.95) – a chicken Kiev made with tarragon butter. Fish fans may want to try the losos (£9.95), which is a fillet of salmon cooked with artichoke hearts, capers and a white wine sauce. One of the desserts, "Charlotka" (£2.95), is none other than that classic old favourite, Charlotte Russe – a mousse cake surrounded by sponge biscuits. Welcome back. Also interesting is the Russian tea served in a glass and holder. It is made with tea, lemon and a splash of vodka (£1.95), with a small bowl of honey alongside for sweetening.

If you are of fearless disposition (possibly if you are a Russian exile) then the formidable game mixed grill is for you: wild boar chop, venison steak, pigeon breast, pheasant sausage and so forth, all for £14.95.

Sigiri

On the menu it says, "One of the main ingredients in Sri Lankan cuisine is coconut", presumably in response to the duty of care which has been imposed on restaurateurs, who must now save their customers from the dangers of nut allergies. In one respect it's sound advice, for if you are not partial to coconut you should think about eating

Cost	£12–£30

Address 161 Northfield Ave, W13
T 020 8579 8000
Station Northfields
Open Tues–Sun 6.30–11pm
Accepts MasterCard, Visa
W www.sigiri.com

elsewhere. Behind the somewhat industrial brick facade this restaurant is surprisingly spacious; the food is authentic and the service is charming. This is a very gentle place and it seldom seems very busy, but you will often hear Sigiri being praised within the Sri Lankan community.

The menu is long and complicated. For starters it is hard to oppose that Sri Lankan cousin of the masala dosa, the appa or hopper – bowl-shaped rice pancakes which are usually served with a sambol to add zing and flavour. Choose from plain (£1.50), egg (£1.60) or one with a dollop of coconut cream in the bottom (£1.60). The sambols are fun: pol sambol (£1.50) is made from onion and coconut with a seasoning of Maldive fish, while seeni sambol combines a kind of spicy onion jam with a sprinkle of dried fish. Very tasty. Also good is the malu miris (£3), which is a large, very mild chilli stuffed with minced lamb and deep-fried. For main courses, the fish dishes are good here: seer fish (£4.50) comes in rich tomatoey gravy. The basic curries are also splendid: chicken with potato (£4.50) is much richer and less austere than it sounds. The fried mutton (£5.50) is something of a disappointment, however, turning out a little on the greasy side; much better to leave room for some of the excellent vegetarian dishes like the green banana (£3) or the mallum (£3), which is finely shredded cabbage cooked with spices and coconut. The pickles are notable: try the achcharu pickle (80p), a red-hot combo of little pickled onions and little pickled chillies; and the amberella chutney, which is very like Italian mustard fruits.

Staff at Sigiri are very concerned that the food should not be too hot for you. Perhaps others have had trouble with some of the more tooth-melting dishes. Be brave, there are real flavours riding tandem with the chillies!

Earl's Court

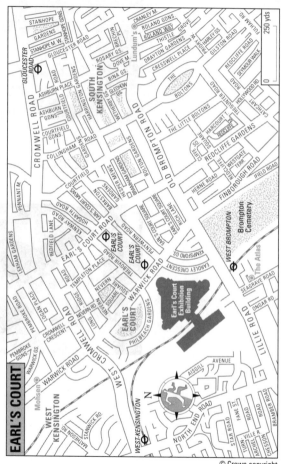

EARL'S COURT

© Crown copyright

MEDITERRANEAN/PUB

The Atlas

Once upon a time, pubs were for boozing. You got sarnies maybe, and pickled onions if you were lucky. The Atlas is as far away from that kind of place as it is possible to get. In a lively and informal atmosphere, brothers Richard and George Manners serve the kind of innovative, Mediterranean-inspired food that many full-blown restaurants would be proud of. George is the chef – he trained at gastro-pub headquarters, The Eagle in Farringdon (see p.195). The flavours come mainly from Spain, Italy and North Africa, and huge strings of dried peppers and bundles of cinnamon sticks vie for attention in the kitchen. But there are no concessions. The menu is chalked on a board twice daily, depending on what's in supply and on George's inspiration. You read, you remember, and you order at the bar.

Cost	£15–£30
Address	16 Seagrave Rd, Fulham, SW6
T	020 7385 9129
Station	Earl's Court
Open	Mon–Sat 12.30–3pm & 7–10.30pm, Sun 12.30–3pm & 7–10pm
Accepts	MasterCard, Switch, Visa

Starters may include pappa al pomodoro (£3.50), a rich Tuscan tomato and bread soup; verdura misto (£6.50), a salad made from grilled vegetables; or a saffron and wild rocket risotto with cherry vine tomatoes and Parmesan (£6.50). Main courses range from grilled Italian sausages, smashed parsnips with chilli and oregano, roast red onions with red wine and balsamic (£8); to grilled whole sea bass with spiced black beans and choricero peppers, tomato and chilli jam (£11.50). Or Catalan beef casserole (£9.50), an intriguing combination of flavours – chocolate, cinnamon, garlic, bay and marjoram. Or even poached smoked haddock, grilled new potato and green bean salad with shaved shallots and rocket, tarragon aioli (£8). The dessert selection is short and to the point, with dishes such as baked quince with maple syrup, cinnamon and cream (£4), or Donald's chocolate and almond cake with ice cream (£4).

The wine selection is also chalked up, and there are some unusual offerings served by the glass, which makes The Atlas a good venue for wine-lovers in search of a bit of impromptu tasting. Everyone else will be pleased to have found an eatery where you can get a decent pint. The Atlas is busy, noisy, friendly and young, and the food is good into the bargain. You're likely to end up sharing a table, so get there early.

Lundum's

DANISH

In 1999 the Lundum family (this is a genuine family restaurant – four of them work in the business) took over this site on the Old Brompton Road and set about turning it into London's premier Danish restaurant. The Lundums would be the first to admit that there is not a lot of competition; in fact this may well be London's only Danish restaurant, which gives them something of a head start.

Cost	£25–£65

Address 119 Old Brompton Rd, SW7
T 020 7373 7774
Station Gloucester Road/ South Kensington
Open Mon–Sat 10am–11pm, Sun (brunch) 10am–4pm
Accepts All major credit cards

There's nothing particularly Danish about the room, which is pleasantly light and airy with huge mirrors and a skylight, much the same as in previous incarnations – there has been some kind of a restaurant here for decades. What has changed for the better is the atmosphere. Now, all is fervent enthusiasm. They proudly produce interesting (and delicious) dill-flavoured aquavit, which is specially imported just for them. They also import the Danish sausages and all manner of other delicacies. The food is elegantly presented, competently handled and … Danish. At lunchtime it's trad Danish, in the evening modern Danish. You cannot help but be swept along by the tidal wave of commitment and charm – remember, there is a whole family working on you.

At dinner (£17.25 for two courses, £21.50 for three) the menu, which changes seasonally, reads like a lot of other menus – smoked salmon gravadlax, roast guinea fowl, steamed lemon sole. Best, then, to visit at lunch (£12.50 for two courses, £15.50 for three), when there are more Danish dishes on offer. Go à la carte and try the shoal of herrings (£3.25/£5.25) – simply marinated, or spicy, or lightly curried, or sour with dill. There are a dozen open sandwiches (£4 to £7.75): salt beef; smoked eel with scrambled eggs and chives; gravadlax with mustard dressing. There are two platters: Danish delicacies (£12.50); or all fish (£14.50). Or try the Medisterpølse (£7.25) – Danish sausage with creamed cabbage. Desserts are indulgent and the aquavit deadly.

"Gamle Ole – Danish Old cheese (18 months) served on rye bread and lard with onions, aspic and rum dripping" (£4.50). At first glance this dish, on the lunch menu, doesn't read well. But persevere, because it is really good, with tasty strong cheese and a seductive combination of tastes.

Mohsen

Just suppose that you are visiting Homebase on the Warwick Road. As the traffic thunders past, spare a thought for the people who still live here. For indeed, across the road you will see signs of habitation – two pubs, one a Young's house, the other selling Fuller's beer, and between them Mohsen, a

Cost	£8–£20
Address	152 Warwick Rd, W14
T	020 7602 9888
Station	Earl's Court
Open	Daily noon–midnight
Accepts	MasterCard, Visa

small, busy Persian restaurant. This shouldn't come as a complete surprise, as you are not so very far from the nest of Iranian shops on Kensington High Street, but for somewhere so hidden Mohsen tends to be gratifyingly busy. There is nothing better than a loyal core of knowledgeable Middle Eastern customers to keep up standards in a Middle Eastern restaurant. In this case the mission has been so successful that, as of spring 2001, there is a second Mohsen, puzzlingly called Mohsen I, at 1 Kensington High St, W8 (☎020 7937 0393).

In the window is the oven, where the bread man works to keep everyone supplied with fresh-from-the-oven sheets of bread. This bread (80p) is terrific – wholemeal, large and flat, but not too flat, with a perforated surface and a sprinkling of sesame seeds that gives a nutty crunch. The waiters conspire to see that it arrives in a steady stream and never has a chance to cool. The starters list is largely made up of things to go with the bread. You must have sabzi (£2.30), which is one of the most delicious and health-oriented starters in the world. It is a basket containing a bunch of fresh green herbs – tarragon, flat parsley and mint – plus a chunk of Feta. Eat it with your bread. Or there's koo koo sabzi (£1.80), which is rather like an under-egged Spanish omelette made with a bumper helping of parsley, dill, coriander, barberries and walnuts. Very tasty. Humous (£1.80) is good. The main courses tend to revolve around grilled meat – joojeh kabab (£6.20), for example, is a poussin, jointed, marinated, grilled and served on rice. Then there is chellow kabab-e-barg (£6.90), which is outstanding – a tender fillet of lamb flattened and grilled. It is traditionally accompanied by an egg yolk (50p extra).

Look out for the dish of the day. On Wednesday it is kharesh badenjan (£6), a stew of lamb and aubergines. And always be sure to finish with a pot of aromatic Iranian tea (£2.50), which is served in tiny, elegant, gilded glasses.

Fulham

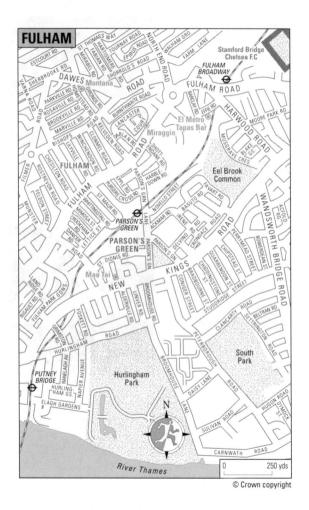

Mao Tai

Mao Tai is much more Chelsea than Chinatown, both in appearance and in the kind of food it serves. It's a pretty restaurant, cleverly lit, well-decorated and with brisk, efficient service. The food is Szechuan – sophisticated, but with a satisfactory chilli burn and a nice scattering of old favourites. The clientele is just what you would expect from an area that is the very apple of any estate agent's eye. Such surroundings – and, to be fair, such food – do not come cheap.

Cost	£20–£45
Address	58 New King's Rd, SW6
T	020 7731 2520
Station	Parsons Green
Open	Mon–Fri noon–3pm & 7–11.30pm, Sat 12.30–2.30pm & 7–11.30pm, Sun 12.30–2.30pm & 7–11pm
Accepts	All major credit cards
W	www.maotai.co.uk

CHINESE

Still, you'll leave well fed and well looked after, as both the cooking and service are slick and chic.

Start with steamed scallops (£7.85 for two). These are usually a pretty good indication of things to come and at Mao Tai they are well cooked – just firm without having become rubbery. Salt and pepper prawns (£7.85 for six) are very fresh but somewhat disconcertingly fried in their shells, so the lovely crispy bits end up on the side of the plate. Firecracker dumplings with Chinese chives (£6.40) are terrific – innocent-looking Shanghai-style dumplings with a reassuring belt of chilli lurking to surprise the unwary. Also good in the starters section are the salt and pepper soft-shell crabs (£6.50 each). For main courses, you have a choice of more than fifty dishes. Do not be too daunted: order Szechuan squid in a hot bean sauce (£9.50) – tender squid with, as it says, a hot, beany sauce. No disappointments here. Also good is the tangerine peel chicken (£8.50), a delightful and delicate dish. Or General Tseng's chicken (£8.50), which is diced chicken and peppers in Ma La sauce. "Mao Tai" duck (£11.50) is a variant of duck in plum sauce – this one is boneless and very tasty indeed, the ubiquitous chilli making only a small guest appearance.

In the vegetable section there's a choice of braised lettuce or broccoli in oyster sauce (£5.85) – opt for the lettuce. The still-crisp furls of cos are nicely wilted and make the perfect match for oyster sauce. Very good indeed. Alternatively, you can opt out of the decisions and order the Mao Tai feast – £24.70 per person for a minimum of two.

SPANISH

El Metro Tapas Bar

More taverna than tapas bar, El Metro resurrects memories of days spent meandering along the Costas, when atmosphere was the only consideration in choosing somewhere to eat. Pretentious it ain't. Asked about the origins of the pulpo gallego – "fresh octopus cooked in sea water" (£3.95) –

Cost	£8–£18

Address 10–12 Effie Rd, SW6
T 020 7384 1264
Station Fulham Broadway
Open Daily 9am–midnight
Accepts All major credit cards except Diners

the waiter replied in hushed tones, "Chelsea harbour". And as for the sea water? "It isn't." El Metro is a popular place, which means that reservations are essential to secure yourself a table, and even then you'll probably find yourself waiting. An amiable barman serving Cruz Campo Spanish beer (£2.50), or even a nostalgic glass of San Miguel (£2.70), and live music help pass the time. Full-blown mayhem surrounds the narrow dining area, which is presided over by a rather imposing bull's head.

The menu begins on an unintentionally authentic note with that Costa delicacy – the full English breakfast. Choose from egg, bacon, sausage, baked beans, tomato and toast (£3.95), or savour them with a nice cup of tea (£4.25). Generally accepted as the first meal of the day, breakfast here is served until 5pm. If you're ready for lunch or dinner, you can either go mainstream with a cheeseburger (£5.95) or lean towards the Spanish specialities. Perhaps start with sopa de ajo (£3.45), a spiced garlic soup with poached egg; or plunge straight into the calamares fritos (£3.95), crispy, fried, flour-coated squid rings which are deliciously tender to the bite. The albondigas (£6.45) – meatballs cooked in spicy sauce – are sound, the tortilla (£2.95) is solid and filling, and they do a nice dish of vieras gratinadas (£11.25) – grilled scallops and prawns, topped with Hollandaise sauce. Desserts (£2.75 to £3.25) consist mainly of flans and ice creams … more fond memories of the Costas.

House red and white Rioja (£9.95) is reasonably priced, but most parties – for which this makes an ideal venue – prefer Sangria (£9.95 per large jug), which makes a dangerously high-octane short-cut to merriment. You'll find more of the same at El Metro's other branch – which is usefully, if a little bizarrely, sited inside the underground station at Hammersmith – El Metro, The Metropolitan Arcade, Beadon Road, W6 (☎020 8748 3132).

Miraggio

Bright cafe-style gingham table-cloths and a simple rustic air belie the quality behind this family-run establishment. Your first sign of this is the appetizing display of antipasti in the window. There are mouthwatering wafer-thin strips of char-grilled courgette and aubergine, nutty little boiled potatoes with virgin olive oil and roughly chopped flat-leaf parsley, strips of grilled peppers, small and large mushrooms and an aubergine and tomato bake with tiny melted Mozzarella cheeses. It's enough to stop even the most jaded foodie in their tracks.

Cost	£15–£40

Address 510 Fulham Rd, SW6
T 020 7384 3142
Station Fulham Broadway
Open Tues–Thurs 12.30–3pm & 7.30–11pm, Fri 12.30–4pm & 7.30–11pm, Sat 12.30–4pm & 7.30–10.30pm, Sun 12.30–4pm
Accepts All major credit cards except Diners

For starters, choose the antipasti misti della casa (£8.50) and you'll get the window dishes. Otherwise, try sauté vongole (£10), sweet little clams sautéed until they are just open, or carpaccio di manzo (£8), a paper-thin raw beef fillet. Pastas include the usual suspects, with some less familiar dishes like rigatoni funghi e salsiccia (£8), which is rigatoni with sausages and mushrooms, or gnocchi crema scampi (£8.50). There are plenty of meat and fish choices, too, including spigola al forno con patate (£18), which is oven-baked sea bass with potatoes; calamari fritti (£15), a dish of perfectly cooked deep-fried squid; abbacchio scottadito (£9), simple grilled lamb; and filetto spinaci e patate (£15), a carefully cooked fillet steak with spinach and potatoes. If you're not already having spinach with your main course, try a side order of spinaci burro e Parmigiano (£4). Popeye would faint with pleasure. Puddings include what is claimed to be the best tiramisù in the area (£4) and zocolette (£4.00), a home-made profiterole with a Nutella filling. The kitchen is open to the dining room, so you can see your food being cooked, which makes for great entertainment. You can also be assured that ingredients like fish are fresh because Miraggio goes one step further than a lot of places and has the confidence to mark the few items that are frozen (like king prawns) with an asterisk.

Also remarkable is that Miraggio is currently a bring-your-own-bottle establishment, so your choice of wine is very wide indeed. This is a delightfully straightforward place, and a welcome addition if you want to enjoy good home-style Italian cooking in Fulham.

Montana

For atmosphere alone, Montana deserves the credit for livening up an otherwise dull corner of SW6. Hidden away down Dawes Road, it is certainly out on its own. An easy-going sort of restaurant with live jazz in the evenings (Tues–Sun), Montana serves quirky Southwestern food that has gained much praise despite a stream of critics pointing out that the dishes have little if anything to do with Montana – which in any case is not in the Southwest US. The decor is all ragwash and cowskin – remember Twin Peaks? Captured in two early sepia prints, Sitting Bull broods over the assembled diners – whatever would he have made of this "Southwest American" dining experience?

Cost	£15–£50
Address	125–129 Dawes Rd, SW6
T	020 7385 9500
Station	Fulham Broadway
Open	Mon–Thurs 7–11pm, Fri 7–11.30pm, Sat noon–11.30pm, Sun noon–10.30pm
Accepts	All major credit cards except Diners

Your opening move is to sample the two fresh house breads, which are strongly flavoured with herbs and chilli. Then perhaps a black and white seared blue-fin tuna, with cucumber slaw and sweet love sauce (£7) – how very Waltons! Or beef carpaccio with rocket and tomatoes (£6); or crab cakes with black bean and mango salsa (£7/£11). The menu changes with the seasons but is always on the adventurous side, certainly when it comes to the descriptions – voodoo stew (£15) comprises Creole prawns, mussels, clams, squid, chorizo, and jasmine rice. Duck! Duck! Goose (£14) translates as roasted leg, breast, smoked goose and dirty rice. Or how about Java crusted halibut (£14), which comes with roasted potato hash, and haricots verts. Also listed as a main course you'll find "chef's whim" (£22), two courses designed by the chef and available from Sunday to Thursday. Desserts can also prove exotic: how does a caramelized black cherry chimichanga sound? It comes with Brazil nut praline ice cream.

Montana has an interesting and wide-ranging wine list with bottles starting at around £12. There is a serious three-course set dinner priced at £25, but it is only available for parties of ten or more, and contrary to most current trends, Montana has discontinued its other set meal deals. Brunch, served on Saturday and Sunday until 4pm, is serious stuff.

Hammersmith & Chiswick

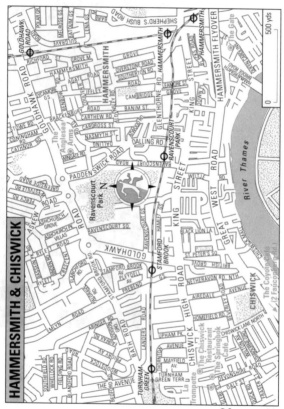

HAMMERSMITH & CHISWICK

© Crown copyright

The Anglesea Arms

🍴 Do not make the mistake of pigeonholing this establishment as merely a pub. The Anglesea serves very good food indeed, with a kitchen the envy of many more mainstream restaurants. The chef-proprietor is Dan Evans, a seasoned campaigner who was head chef at several of the brightest eateries of the 1990s. At The Anglesea, Dan runs the kitchen while his wife Fiona runs the bar and front of house. The menu changes at

Cost	£11–£27

Address 35 Wingate Rd, W6
T 020 8749 1291
Station Ravenscourt Park
Open Food served Mon–Sat 12.30–2.45pm & 7.30–10.45pm, Sun 1–3.30pm & 7.30–10pm
Accepts All major credit cards except Amex

least twice a day, dishes are crossed out as they run out, and, when you've achieved "favoured local" status, you can ask for something simple that's not even on the board. If they have the ingredients you can have the dish. Pitch up early, claim a seat, and not only will you dine well but you'll leave feeling good about the bill.

Who knows what Dan will have chalked up on the blackboard when you visit? The menu is both eclectic and attractive, and prices are held to a maximum of £5.95 for starters and £9.95 for mains. In the spring you might have to choose between a warm salad with rabbit, chorizo, dandelion and beans, and spinach and bean soup. Or between a Provençale fish soup and a pissaladière. Main courses may include venison and sage faggots, or honest, market-fresh fish dishes like skate, or cod in butter. You may find diver-caught scallops with pak choi, or something simple like Gloucester Old Spot ham, egg and chips, or saddle of lamb. To round things off, there is always one British cheese in perfect condition – like St Andrew's, a cow's milk cheese served with black grapes. Dan Evans has a very sure touch, and this cooking is about as far from the kind of grub you'll be offered in a thousand chain pubs as you can get.

As befits food such as this, there's a wine list to match. A dozen wines are on offer by the glass, and the choice is thoughtful. Not very many restaurants, and very few pubs, offer a range of pudding wines by the bottle, half-bottle and glass. Among them is a delicious pudding wine called de Pacherence from southwest France (£16.50 a bottle, £4.50 a glass) – a far cry from the builders' overalls and pints of Guinness that once ruled the roost here.

MODERN BRITISH

The Chiswick Restaurant

The menu here changes twice a day. Not completely – the puddings will probably stay the same and two or three dishes will carry over – but there's always something fresh for the large number of local regulars. And they're a lucky lot, for The Chiswick is quite simply one of the best neighbourhood restaurants in London. It serves delicious, well-presented dishes that major in strong flavours. Service is informal but

Cost	£12–£30

Address 131 Chiswick High Rd, W4
T 020 8994 6887
Station Turnham Green
Open Mon–Fri 12.30–2.45pm & 7–11pm, Sat 7–11pm, Sun noon–3pm
Accepts All major credit cards except Diners

with a steely edge of competence. Pricing is enlightened, with a lunch and early-evening menu (7–8pm) that costs £9.50 for two courses and coffee, or £12.95 for three. This goes up, but not extravagantly, to £12.95 for two courses and £15.50 for three after the witching hour of 8pm. You might get something along the lines of vine tomato soup and chicken confit and mash; or Greek salad and grilled mackerel and salsa verde. No wonder the place is packed.

Everything here is driven by the seasons and the markets, and with a menu changing twice daily it's hard to make very firm suggestions. The cuisine is generally Modern British, but when British produce is at its very best this means more British than Modern. Starters may range from spiny artichoke, broad bean and herb salad with crème fraîche dressing (£5.50); to Andalucian garlic soup (£4); or a warm salad of pigeon breast, bacon and fried potatoes (£5.25); or grilled squid, black bean dressing and coriander (£5.75). The inspiration for the main courses is similarly broad: octopus, mussel and chorizo stew (£9.50); linguine teamed with oyster mushrooms, ceps, parsley and garlic (£8.50); noisette of venison (£13.50) with red cabbage and roast, new season garlic. As an example of Anglo-French co-operation short-horn rib-eye steak with escargot butter and mash (£14.50) takes some beating. The wine list has plenty of good choices in the middle price range. Among the puddings, keep an eye out for apple fritter and vanilla ice cream (£4.50), or prune and almond tart with clotted cream (£4.50).

The arrival of dazzling newcomer, La Trompette (see p.440), will keep the Chiswick on its toes. Despite this restaurant's somewhat Spartan demeanour there has even been a brightening lick of paint in evidence.

The Coyote Café

When this outpost of American cooking changed hands in 2000, the new owners kept the decor, atmosphere and most of the menu the same (the new proprietor was a regular customer of some years standing). There is a new team in the kitchen, however, and the menu has been expanded. The best Southwest American cuisine, as can still be found here, is more delicate, intense and refined than most people associate with American food. The chilli flavours may prove hot but the tastes are also discernibly sweet, sour, fruity and rich. If you're not familiar with this kind of food, you should leave your preconceptions behind.

Cost £12–£30

Address 2 Fauconberg Rd, W4
T 020 8742 8545
Station Chiswick Park
Open Mon–Thurs 5–11pm, Fri & Sat 11am–11pm, Sun 11am–10.30pm
Accepts Amex, MasterCard, Visa

Alongside the main menu is a sheet of regularly changing specials, from which you might start with something genuinely out of the ordinary – how does Mozzarella and grilled mixed chilli salad served with cherry tomato dressing (£5.50) sound? From the main appetizers menu, try the Cajun angel in devil's blanket (£6.95) – prawns in bacon; or there's a nice mushroom and spinach quesadilla with melted cheese and barbecue salsa (£5.25); or Louisiana-style blue crab cake with garlic croutons, served with a smoked chilli sauce (£5.75). Among the entrées you'll see some familiar favourites: blackened rib-eye steak with chipotle gravy, skinny fries and tobacco onions (£12.75) is worth having for the chipotle gravy, which is a kind of tomatoey, tangy, fruity chilli sauce; the Howlin' chilli burger (£8.45) is large and delicious, topped with a ladleful of splendid chilli. Again, turn to the specials for even wilder and more exciting dishes like baked cod with a mussel and mixed herb butter sauce (£13.25). And last but not least, a "special" dessert – rich chocolate cherry gateaux (£4.25).

The Coyote Café is famed for its Saturday and Sunday brunch: corn beef hash (£6.95); Creole eggs Benedict (£6.95); Texas ham'n'eggs Alexander (£6.55); huevos rancheros (£6.25); American pancakes with molasses (£3.55). Good enough to make you howl, which will not endear you to the residents of Chiswick Park – unless, of course, they too are dining and howling.

The Gate

The extraordinary thing about The Gate, which is tucked away behind the Labatt's Apollo, is that you hardly notice that it's a vegetarian restaurant. This is enjoyable dining without the meat. It's not wholefood, it's not even healthy – indeed, it's as rich, colourful, calorific and naughty as anywhere in town. The clientele is a quiet and appreciative bunch of locals and pilgrims – it's unlikely that anyone could just stumble across this hidden-away, former artists' studio, which Adrian and Michael Daniel have leased from the nearby church since 1990. The airy decor and the high ceiling give it a serene, lofty feel, which may be The Gate's only nod to veggie solemnities. Basically this place is about good food and has been so successful that 2001 saw the opening of The Gate 2 (see p.247); this is one chain that we should be encouraging.

Cost	£16–£35
Address	51 Queen Caroline St, W6
T	020 8748 6932
Station	Hammersmith
Open	Mon–Fri noon–2.45pm & 6–10.45pm, Sat 6–11pm
Accepts	All major credit cards
W	www.gateveg.co.uk

The short menu changes monthly, but starters are always great. There's usually a tart, like the cherry tomato and blue Stilton (£5.75) which elsewhere, with its sophisticated salad, would be served as a main course. Also excellent are the green banana fritters (£5.50), which are served with a coconut, coriander and lime chutney. Portions are invariably hearty, so it's a good idea to share starters in order to pace yourself and sample all the courses. The mains are generally well executed. Mezzelune (£9.50) is a pasta crescent filled with goat's cheese and rocket, pan-fried in a light chive and leek sauce (£9.50). Or there's a dish of corn cakes (£9.25), which come with chilli-roasted baby artichokes, grilled vegetables, black bean salsa, avocado sauce and a pasila pepper sauce! Puddings are splendid: there may be rhubarb and plum crumble (£5.50), or the pressed chocolate torte (£5.50), which is a thinking person's death-by-chocolate. Those without a sweet tooth should go for the English cheeses (£5), where spiced fruit chutney and oatcakes accompany farmhouse varieties.

The drinks list is extensive, with all manner of freshly squeezed juices (£2.25), herbal teas (£1.25) and coffee (£1.25 to £1.75), while the wine list tops out at £22 (except for champagne) and has something for everyone: vegan, vegetarian, organic-only and carnivore alike.

The Springbok Café

As customers have got used to the idea of a South African restaurant, Peter Gottgens has been able to drift the menus towards more ambitious and exotic dishes. The Springbok Café is small and informal, with the open-plan kitchen centre stage. What's more, Peter – who trained as a chef in South Africa and Italy – is passionate about both the quality and authenticity of his ingredients. He gets his fish from Mossell Bay or Port St John's, and all the biltong, game and fresh herbs are flown in from South Africa. Due to EC regulations he can no longer import ostrich, but he does make sure to source English ostrich of South African stock.

Cost	£22–£38

Address 42 Devonshire Rd, W4
T 020 8742 3149
Station Turnham Green
Open Mon–Sat 6.30–11pm
Accepts All major credit cards
W www.springbok cafecuisine.com

The menu changes monthly, but you might start with Natal king prawn tails, purple potatoes, lowveld avocado and a red pepper oil (£6.25), zebra carpaccio with brandied apricots, rooibos onions and toasted Cape seed loaf (£5.25), or sautéed peri peri duck livers with a meal cake and tomato smoor (£4.35). For the main course, indulge yourself and try something that you have probably never had before – how about pan-fried Kammiebos guineafowl, roast pumpkin, mange tout and Mapumalaga chanterelles (£9.25)? Or maybe blesbok loin, butternut, roast green garlic and sweet peppers (£12)? Or go for something truly exotic – char-grilled zebra fillet, parmesan samp, butternut puree and wild garlic leaves (£14.50). The fish is particularly good here: try char-grilled Natal barracuda steaks, baby mielies, roast heirloom tomatoes and rocket (£10.25). The side orders are good too, try the peri peri potatoes (£2.50). By the time puddings come round, see if you have room to share a chocolate mielie meal pudding with crème fraîche and fresh raspberries (£4.50), or a granadilla panna cotta with naartjie shortbread (£4).

If you're the kind of person who only ever orders something that you are sure to like, perhaps consider having your meal elsewhere. Dining at the Springbok Café is a whole load of fun if you are interested in food. It is a place for "you'll never know until you've tried it". Take a few risks and discover something new.

FRENCH

La Trompette

La Trompette was one of the most eagerly awaited restaurant openings in 2001. Chiswick is among the more gastronomically sophisticated of the countless villages that lie within London, and the locals could read the signs – this is a restaurant from the same stable as Chez Bruce (see p.331), The Glasshouse (see p.393) and The Square (see p.85). For over a year Chiswickians had been spectators while the site underwent a radical refurbishment, re-emerging with a spacious and slick modern dining room. It's smart – more West End than W4 – and there's a good deal of light oak and chocolate leather. In opening week they hit it like a breaking wave and La Trompette has been seriously busy ever since. It deserves to be: the food is very good, the pricing is restrained and the service is on the ball.

Cost	£20–£50

Address 5–7 Devonshire Rd, W4

T 020 8742 1836

Station Turnham Green

Open Mon–Sat noon–2.30pm & 6.30–11pm, Sun 12.30–3pm & 6.30–10.30pm

Accepts All major credit cards

The prix fixe arrangements are straightforward: lunch is £17.50 for two courses, and £19.50 for three (rising to £23.50 on Sunday); dinner is £25 for three courses. The head chef is Ollie Couillard, who served time at both Chez Bruce and the Square. He is a very good cook. Dishes tend to have French roots and to be dependent on fresh, seasonal produce. The menu changes on a day to day basis. Presentation is simple but elegant. Starters may include such delights as chicken consommé with snail ravioli; an awesomely good, home-made charcuterie plate – including what may be a "best ever" chicken liver parfait; smoked haddock brandade with poached egg and Hollandaise sauce; sauté of sweetbreads and trompettes with grain mustard sauce. Mains are rich and satisfying: roast cod with a sage and onion crust; a steamed ballotine of red mullet with shell fish and herb vinaigrette; an extraordinary cassoulet Toulousain; daube of beef with Jerusalem artichoke puree; loin of venison with a celeriac gratin and ceps Bordelaise. The wine list is long and considered. This is a very good restaurant indeed.

Puds range from the classic – lemon tart, or gateaux Basque with rhubarb and orange compote – to an ultra trad blast from the past, like Baked Alaska (for two people). Enjoy!

Notting Hill

NOTTING HILL

N

WESTWAY

A 40(M)

HARROW ROAD

ALFRED RD

WESTBOURNE PARK

WESTERN ROAD

Galicia

A 40(M)

LADBROKE GROVE

Alastair Little W11

WESTBOURNE PARK ROAD

Cow Dining Room

WESTBOURNE PK. VS.

CHEPSTOW ROAD

LANCASTER ROAD

WESTBOURNE PARK ROAD

ARTESIAN ROAD

NEWTON RD

192

Osteria Basilico

COLVILLE

The Mandola

Ginger

WESTBOURNE GRO.

Rodizio Rico

Assaggi

KENSINGTON PARK ROAD

LADBROKE GS

NOTTING HILL

GROVE

LADBROKE SQUARE

PEMBRIDGE VILLAS

PEMBRIDGE SQUARE

MOSCOW ROAD

NOTTING HILL GATE

LADBROKE ROAD

Rôtisserie Jules

NOTTING HILL GATE

Black & Blue

Kensington Place

KENSINGTON CHURCH STREET

PEEL STREET

CAMPDEN STREET

HOLLAND PARK AVENUE

AUBREY WALK

The Churchill Arms

PALACE GARDENS TER.

0   500 yds

© Crown copyright

192

192 is a pretty restaurant and wine bar that attracts a young, moneyed crowd of local media, literary and music folk who treat the place as a house café. Most of them seem to know each other, which makes for a friendly atmosphere with much kissing and table-hopping, and you may well find yourself in conversation with singers fresh from their recording session seated at the next table. The bar section is always busy, and has a lively, clubby atmosphere.

Cost	£25–£40
Address	192 Kensington Park Rd, W11
T	020 7229 0482
Station	Notting Hill Gate/ Ladbroke Grove
Open	Mon–Thurs 12.30–3pm & 6.30–11pm, Fri 12.30–3pm & 6.30–11.30pm, Sat 12.30–3.30pm & 6.30–11.30pm, Sun 12.30–3.30pm & 6.30–11pm
Accepts	All major credit cards

The menu offers the kind of food that seems simple but is very hard to do well. It is based on best-quality fresh ingredients with little interference, and changes daily to reflect what is in season and at the markets. Things are basically set out as à la carte but there are a couple of deals – the two-course set lunch costs £10 from Monday to Friday and £12.50 on Sunday. Starters may include seared scallops with beetroot and cardamom reduction (£8.50), or crab and Jerusalem artichoke salad (£7). Or something simple like a cream of fennel soup (£4.75), or a smoked duck and mango salad (£6.50). Main course options may include tagliatelle with wild mushrooms (£6.50/£8.50), char-grilled chicken breast with polenta and braised lentils (£12), or pan-fried calves' liver with mash and red onion relish (£12.50). And there are always good fish dishes to be had: grilled swordfish with new potatoes, samphire and confit tomatoes (£13.50), or pan-fried salmon, roast peppers and grilled artichokes (£12.25). These are exactly what you want them to be, with flavours and textures all perfectly judged. Presentation is excellent at 192, with an eye for garnishes that enhance your anticipation. Leave room for pudding, as there are delights like coconut and pineapple millefeuille (£4.45), which features baked pineapple in a thin, biscuity pastry with coconut sorbet, and bitter chocolate tart with honey ice cream (£4.25).

192 is owned by the Groucho Club and the wine list features some of the club's wines. So if you can't wangle an invite to the Dean Street establishment, you can at least come here to see how the other half drinks.

MODERN EUROPEAN

Alastair Little W11

Alastair Little is a name that commands respect among restaurant-goers in London. Back in the 1980s, he was one of the main pioneers of the Anglo-Italian movement, a man without a professional catering background who wanted to serve real food – clean, fresh cooking, with home-made pastas and terrines – of the style and type that we all wish we could serve at home. Following the success of his clean-cut site in Frith Street (see p.119), he opened this much less expensive sibling in 1996. Notting Hill trendies rushed in hordes to try it out, but they have since moved on, returning Alastair Little to the foodies. Forget the trends. This is a top-class place and one that, even after a modest refurb and repaint, feels extremely comfortable.

Cost	£20–£50

Address 136a Lancaster Rd, W11

T 020 7243 2220

Station Ladbroke Grove

Open Mon–Fri noon–2.30pm & 6.30–11pm, Sat noon–3pm & 6.30–11pm, Sun 12.30–3.30pm

Accepts All major credit cards

The daily changing menu is short and sweet at lunchtime and middle-sized and sweet for dinner. At lunch, the price is fixed at £6 for first courses, £9 for a middling dish, £14.50 for full-blown mains and £5.50 for desserts – extraordinarily inexpensive for this quality. In the evening you'll find the same dishes plus a few others, and two courses cost £24.50, three £28.50. Starters might be the likes of baked new season's garlic soup with an egg; or capelletti in brodo; or gnocchi con sugo. Move on to middleweights like salt cod brandade with French beans and truffle oil; a mixed seafood bourride; or butternut squash and Ricotta ravioli with crispy sage; or even risotto nero, rich and black with cuttlefish and ink. Mains might include roast skate with chips and tartare sauce; a whole sea bass with black olives, roast tomatoes and potatoes; or a grilled pork loin chop with choucroute and a red wine sauce. But it is the apparently simple Italianate dishes that are Alastair Little's real strength, dishes like the soups, pastas and risottos that are fixtures on the menu. Don't miss out on them.

Desserts are the kind of rich, indulgent things that are so good that you almost feel embarrassed to be seen choosing them. Bitter chocolate torte comes with espresso ice cream, panacotta is served with caramelized blood oranges, and a £2 supplement will earn you a glass of vin santo with cantucci biscuits.

Assaggi

Assaggi is a small, ochre-painted room above The Chepstow pub. It's generally full at lunch and booked well in advance in the evenings. The prices are unforgiving and, on the face of it, paying so much for such straightforward dishes could raise the hackles of any sensible diner. But the reason Assaggi is such a gem, and also the reason it is always full, is that self-same straightforwardness. The menu may appear simple but it is littered with authentic and luxury ingredients, and the cooking is very accomplished indeed. Prepare yourself for a meal to be remembered.

Cost	£30–£65
Address	39 Chepstow Place, W2
T	020 7792 5501
Station	Notting Hill Gate
Open	Mon–Fri 12.30–2.30pm & 7.30–11pm, Sat 1–2.30pm & 7.30–11pm
Accepts	All major credit cards

You'll find a dozen starters – with the option to have the pastas as main courses – and half a dozen main courses. Start with pasta: maybe tagliolini bianchi alle vongole (£7.95/£9.95) – a dish of perfectly cooked pasta with small clams. Or a plate of sensational bufala Mozzarella (£7.95). Or grilled vegetables with olive oil and herbs (£7.95). Or zuppa di pesce (£9.75). Or there may be a dish like capesante con puré di finocchi e vinaigrette d'acighe (£10.75) – a simple plate of perfectly cooked, splendidly fresh scallops; or antipasto di salumi (£8.95). Main courses are even more pared-down: calves' liver (£15.95); a plainly grilled veal chop with rosemary (£17.95); fish of the day (£17.95); or filletto di manzo con galletti (£18.95) – a fist-sized lump of fillet steak with a mound of chanterelle mushrooms. All are memorable, while the side salad of tomato, rucola e basilico (£4.75) is everything you would wish for. Puddings change daily and cost £5.75. Look out for panacotta – a perfect texture – and the beautifully simple dish made from ultra-fresh buffalo Ricotta served with "cooked" honey. To accompany the short wine list features splendid and unfamiliar Italian regional specialities.

Assaggi is known for its bread. This is the famous Sardinian carta di musica – very thin, very crisp and very delicious. It's like a kind of Italian popadom, only better. The name came about because, when well made, the papery texture is reminiscent of the sheets of vellum on which music was first written.

STEAK

Black & Blue

🍴 Say the words "steak house" to a Londoner and they immediately conjure up a 1960s image – lots of tartan and red plush, with hapless tourists reaffirming their worst misgivings about British food. The time is right for a decent chain of steak houses. And Black & Blue may just be the first of a new breed. For a start, this establishment, which opened towards the end of 2000, has the very best provenance for its meat. All the steak here comes from Donald Russell of Inverurie – the company which is king of the Aberdeen Angus beef trade.

Cost	£12–£40
Address	215–217 Kensington Church St, W8
T	020 7727 0004
Station	Notting Hill Gate
Open	Sun–Thurs noon–11pm, Fri & Sat noon–11.30pm
Accepts	Visa, MasterCard

If you're looking for a smart modern restaurant, Black & Blue certainly looks the part. There are banquettes, a good deal of wood panelling, a stylish bar and some rather nice vintage Bovril posters – a restaurant designer has been hard at work here. Starters are predictable. There's a prawn cocktail (£4) which comprises half a dozen large prawns in a pink sauce that has a decent belt of horseradish in it. Or you could have butterfly prawns with a sweet chilli dip (£4). Or there's kiln-roasted salmon (£5). Thereafter there are burgers, salads, baguettes, two chicken dishes and tuna – ignore them in favour of the steaks. The steaks are good. Aberdeen Angus is well-flavoured meat, and each steak is cooked as requested (commendably enough, when you say rare you get rare). Each steak comes with a very decent mixed salad of watercress, flat parsley and rocket – steer clear of the proffered dressings – and tolerable fries. There are three kinds of steak: sirloin, rib-eye and fillet. Everywhere else in town, these three get in line with fillet as the most expensive, then the sirloin and finally rib-eye. But not here, where 6oz sirloin costs £9, 10oz £12; 8oz rib-eye is £14, 12oz £17; 6oz fillet is £15, 8oz £18 – why are Donald Russell's sirloin steaks cheaper than the rib-eye? This makes the 10oz sirloin the bargain buy. There's a small choice of simple desserts: chocolate cake and lime tart (both £5) are served with clotted cream.

The wine list is not long but is agreeably ungrasping. It makes a pleasant change to see simple reds priced at around £10 on a restaurant wine list.

The Churchill Arms

In the ever-expanding field of pub restaurants, The Churchill is something of an old stager. It was possibly one of the first in London to offer Thai food. Do you wonder why we see so few pubs selling Indian food, incidentally? Or Chinese food? Could it be because of the grand profit margins on Thai cuisine? Well, whatever the motivation behind it, The Churchill has nurtured its clientele (who are largely students and bargain hunters) over the years by the simple expedient of serving some of the tastiest and most reasonably priced Thai food in London. The main dining area is in a back room featuring acres of green foliage, but don't despair if you find it full (it fills up very quickly) – meals are served throughout the pub. Service is friendly, but as the food is cooked to order, be prepared to wait – it's worth it. If you really can't wait, pre-cooked dishes such as chicken with chillies (along with that other well-known Thai delicacy, Stilton ploughman's) are also available.

Cost	£7–£20
Address	119 Kensington Church St, W8
T	020 7792 1246
Station	Notting Hill Gate
Open	Mon–Sat 12.30–2.30pm & 6–9.30pm, Sun noon–2.30pm
Accepts	MasterCard, Visa

THAI

Dishes are unpronounceable, and have thoughtfully been numbered to assist everybody. The pad gai med ma muang hin-maparn (no. 15 – £5.50) is a deliciously spicy dish of chicken, cashew nuts and chilli served with a generous helping of fluffy boiled rice. Kwaitiew pad kee mao (no. 16 – £5.25) is pork, chicken or beef cooked with flat Thai noodles heated with red and green chillies – hot, but not unbearably so. The same cannot be said for khao rad na ga prao (no. 5 – £5.50), which is described as very hot. Not an understatement. This prawn dish with fresh chillies and Thai basil is guaranteed to bring sweat to the brow of even the most ardent chilliholic. For something milder, try the pad neau nahm man hoi (no. 17 – £5.25), beef with oyster sauce and mushrooms, or the khao rad na (no. 3 – £5.25), a rice dish topped with prawns, vegetables and gravy. Both are good. Puddings are limited in choice and ambition, but for something sweet to temper the heat try apple pie (£2.50) – a strange accompaniment to Thai food, but surprisingly welcome.

One of the refreshing things about The Churchill is you get restaurant-standard food with drinks at pub prices (an excellent pint), and they even do takeaways in traditional foil trays.

MODERN BRITISH

Cow Dining Room

The Cow is something of a conundrum. On the one hand it is a genuine pub – a proper pub, with beer and locals – and on the other it has become something of a meeting place for Notting Hill's smarter residents. Downstairs all is fierce drinking and cigarette smoke, while upstairs you'll find an oasis of calm and, at its centre, a small dining room. It is a good place to eat. The atmosphere is informal but the food is accomplished. The chef here is James

Cost	£20–£48
Address	89 Westbourne Park Rd, W2
T	020 7221 5400
Station	Westbourne Park
Open	Mon–Fri 7–11pm, Sat 12.30–2.30pm & 7–11pm, Sun 12.30–3.30pm & 7.30–10.30pm
Accepts	All major credit cards except Diners

Rix who formerly served time in Alastair Little's Frith Street establishment. The menu changes on a daily basis and delivers fresh, unfussy, seasonal food.

Starters put together tried and tested combinations of prime ingredients such as fresh pea and ham soup (£5); organic smoked salmon blinis with Sevruga caviar and sour cream (£9.50); rocket, pear and Parmesan salad (£6); ballotine of foie gras, grape chutney and toast (£8.50); and, looking somewhat self-conscious to be on such a menu, a Galician-style octopus salad (£6.50). Main courses cover most of the bases from ironbark pumpkin and Ricotta risotto (£12); through roasted brill steak, purple-sprouting broccoli and new potatoes (£16); grilled fillet of sea bass, lentil salad and gremolata (£15.50); to a brochette of lamb's kidney, pancetta and shallots with mash and mustard sauce (£13). The menu finishes triumphantly with pot-roasted rump of veal with braised root vegetables and salsa verde (£16.50). Puddings are a suitable mix of the comfortable and the desirable: crème brulée (£5); bitter chocolate tart with crème fraîche (£5.25); poached champagne rhubarb with custard (£5.25). Or you could go for cheese, which comes with the imprimatur that signifies well chosen and well kept cheeses – "Neal's Yard" cheeses with oatcakes (£5.25).

The menu encourages diners to commence proceedings with a glass of Black Velvet (£4.50) or "Prosecco di Conegliano e Valdobbiadene" (£4). But the staff will happily fetch you some of the excellent De Koninck beer from downstairs if these more exotic fizzies don't tempt.

Galicia

🍴 As you walk up the Portobello Road it would be only too easy to amble straight past Galicia. It has that strange Continental quality of looking shut even when it's open, and when it's shut it's invisible. Only make it through the forbidding entrance, however, and Galicia opens out into a bar (which is in all probability crowded), which in turn opens into a small, 25-seat restaurant

Cost   £12–£30

Address 323 Portobello Rd, W10
T 020 8969 3539
Station Ladbroke Grove/ Westbourne Park
Open Tues–Sun noon–3pm & 7–11.30pm
Accepts All major credit cards

SPANISH

(which is in all probability full). The tapas at the bar are straightforward and good, so it is no surprise that quite a lot of customers get no further than here. One regular once confided that some of the best Spanish dishes he had ever sampled were given to him as tapas at the bar while he was waiting for a seat, and that when he finally got the elusive table, he had eaten so much that he was forced to surrender it to someone in greater need. So, first secure your table…

…then cut a swathe through the starters – jamón (£4.25) is a large plate of sweet, air-dried ham; gambas a la plancha (£5.95) are giant prawns plainly grilled; and pulpo a la Gallega (£5) is a revelation – slices of octopus grilled until bafflingly tender and powdered with smoky pimenton. Galicia does straightforward grilled fish and meat very well indeed. Look for the chuleto de cordera a la plancha (£8.10), which are perfect lamb chops, or lomo de cerdo (£7.25), which are very thin slices of pork fillet in a sauce with pimenton. Or there's the suitably stolid Spanish omelette, tortilla (£4.90). And you should have some chips, which are very good here – thick and yet chewy, they taste just like those superior chips you get in Spain. The wine list is short and to the point, but also full of opportunities for exploration – you may find yourself the proud possessor of a Vega Grand Riserva for just £17.90. Or then again that bin may have run out.

Galicia is a pleasant place without pretension. The waiters are all old-school – quiet, efficient to the point of brusqueness, and with a slight tendency to grumpiness. The overall feel is of a certain stilted formality. The clientele is an agreeable mix of Notting Hill-ites and homesick Iberians, both of which groups stand between you and that table reservation – book early.

Ginger

(ॐ) Given that nearly every curry house on nearly every High Street in the land is owned and manned by Bangladeshi businessmen, you might think that Ginger, which opened in the spring of 2001, would be pretty run of the mill. Until you eat there. This is a restaurant that offers genuine Bangladeshi home cooking. Not the sweet and toma-

Cost	£25–£45
Address	115 Westbourne Grove, W2
T	020 7908 1990
Station	Notting Hill Gate/ Bayswater
Open	Daily 6–11pm
Accepts	All major credit cards

toey dishes worked up to suit the British palate, but the real deal. The restaurant is modern, and turquoise (*very* turquoise – if you don't like turquoise, don't go). There is attentive service, a thoughtful wine list, some slick cocktails … and, most important of all, the men in the kitchen really know their stuff. Genuine Bangladeshi cooking has long deserved a decent showcase, and at Ginger it has finally got one.

There are some stunning dishes. Start with the maach paturi (£5) – a fillet of pomfret, spiced, seasoned, then wrapped in a banana leaf and steamed. That's it. Fresh tasting fish, a citrus twang, heat from some mustard seeds. From the other end of the spectrum, try the shingara (£3.50) – imagine a solid vegetable samosa that has been made with shortcrust pastry, like a deep-fried pasty. The keema bhora (£4) are also good – flat cakes of minced lamb with plenty of fresh herbs. The difficult choices continue when it comes to the main courses: macher kofta jhol (£8.50) is epic – light, fluffy dumplings made with fish and herbs, in a rich sauce. Bangladeshis are besotted with fish – try the very traditional chingri chichinga (£11.50), which teams huge king prawns with a green Bengali vegetable called chichinga. Very tasty. Carry on to the murgh mooli (£7.50), which is spicy and good, the texture of the cooked giant radish contrasting well with the chicken. The kashimangsho bhuna (£9.50) is a thick, dark, satisfying goat curry with a good belt of heat to it. The kacchi biryani (£9.50) is rice flavoured with dried plums and almonds plus implausibly tender lamb, all with a contrasting cucumber and yoghurt glop to pour over it. Tok dal (£4.50) is a revelation: the creaminess of yellow split peas with balancing sharpness from green mango. The parathas (£2) are very good – flaky and suitably self-indulgent.

Puddings are sweet. If you think you're up to it, just attempt the mishti doi (£3.50), which is a lurid set yoghurt. Toothkind it is not.

Kensington Place

The first thing to know about Kensington Place is that it is noisy. The dining room is large, echoing, glass-fronted and just plain noisy. It's the racket of hordes of people having a good time. Rather than background music there's the busy hum of confidences, shrieks of merriment, and the clamour of parties. The service is crisp, the food is good and the prices are fair. The menu changes from session to session to reflect whatever the market has to offer, and there is a set lunch which offers a limited choice of three good courses for £14.50 during the week and £16.50 on Sunday. By way of example: you might have chicken liver crostini with truffle paste and rocket, followed by wild sea trout with capers and lemon, then poached mirabelles with vanilla cream. This is fine value for money. Regulars claim that the set lunch menu is the key to knowing just when head chef Rowley Leigh is cooking in person – apparently his handwriting is very distinctive!

Cost	£18–£50

Address 201–207 Kensington Church St, W8
T 020 7727 3184
Station Notting Hill Gate
Open Mon–Sat noon–3pm & 6.30–11.45pm, Sun noon–3pm & 6.30–10.15pm
Accepts All major credit cards

Rowley Leigh's food is eclectic in the best possible way. The kitchen starts on the laudable premise that there is nothing better than what is in season, and goes on to combine Mediterranean inspirations with classic French and English dishes. Thus you may find, in due season, starters like fish soup with croutons and rouille (£5.50), griddled foie gras with sweetcorn pancake (£9.50), tagliarini with crayfish and baby leeks (£6), or omelette fines herbes (£4.50). These are sophisticated dishes, and well-chosen combinations of flavours. Main courses might be smoked haddock Monte Carlo (£13.50), spiced grilled quails (£14), roast guinea fowl with tajine vegetables and saffron (£13.50), or cod with parsley sauce (£12.50).

The dessert section of the menu offers what may be one of London's finest lemon tarts (£5) and some well-made ice creams (£4.50). There are also traditional favourites with a twist: bread and butter pudding made with pannetone (£6), or panna cotta made with coffee and mascarpone (£5.50). And for hardened pudding addicts there is the ultimate challenge – the grand selection (£10). Indulge yourself (or share) and take a glass of Tokaji Aszu 5 Puttonyos (£5) alongside.

The Mandola

The food at The Mandola is described as "urban Sudanese", and as that means forgoing the doubtful pleasures of some of the more traditional Sudanese delicacies – strips of raw liver marinated in lime juice, chilli and peanut butter springs to mind – it seems like a pretty good deal. This would be a small, seriously informal, neighbourhood restaurant, but for the fact that it attracts people from all over town with its sensible pricing and often strikingly delicious dishes. They have not only had to expand into the shop next door, but also to institute two sittings a night. Despite such minor irritations there's much to praise. The staff are so laid-back as to make worriers self-destruct on the spot. The restaurant is unlicensed, so everything from fine wine to exotic beer is available – if you choose to bring it with you. Or you could try the deep-red, citrus-sharp hibiscus tea, which the proprietor describes as "sub-Saharan Ribena".

Cost	£12–£22
Address	139–141 Westbourne Grove, W11
T	020 7229 4734
Station	Notting Hill Gate
Open	Mon 6–11pm, Tues–Sun noon–11pm
Accepts	All major credit cards

To start there is a combo of dips and salads, rather prosaically listed as "mixed salad bar" for two (£10.50). There are a few Middle Eastern favourites here, given a twist, and all of them are strongly and interestingly flavoured. Salata tomatim bel gibna (£3.50) is made from tomatoes, Feta and parsley; salata tahina (£3.25) is a good tangy tahini; salata aswad (£4.20) is a less oily version of the Turkish aubergine dish iman bayeldi; salata daqua (£3.50) is white cabbage in peanut sauce; and tamiya (£4.75) is Sudanese falafel. All are accompanied by hot pitta bread. As for main courses, samak magli (£8.95) shows just how good simple things can be – fillets of tilapia are served crisp and spicy on the outside, fresh on the inside, with a squeeze of lime juice. Chicken halla (£8.50) is cooked in a rich, well-reduced tomato sauce that would be equally at home in a smart Italian eatery. Lovers of the exotic can finish with the Sudanese spiced coffee, scented with cardamom, cinnamon, cloves and ginger – your own flask and coffee set, enough for nine tiny cupfuls, for £4.

It is lucky that the bowl for the crushed green chilli with lime, onions and garlic (£1.75) is stainless steel, as the contents must be one of the hottest things in the known universe.

Osteria Basilico

Long before Kensington Park Road became the borough's hottest spot for outdoor dining, there was always a restaurant on this corner. When Duveen closed, the restaurant cat stayed on to have the next establishment named in its honour – Monsieur Thompson. Then, in its turn Monsieur T became Pizza by Numbers. Finally in 1992 came Osteria, which has flourished ever since. Daytime stargazing is enlivened by arguments between parking wardens, clampers and

Cost	£12–£45

Address 29 Kensington Park Rd, W11
T 020 7727 9372
Station Ladbroke Grove/ Notting Hill Gate
Open Mon–Fri 12.30–3pm & 6.30–11pm, Sat 12.30–4pm & 6.30–11pm, Sun 12.30–3.15pm & 6.30–10.30pm
Accepts Amex, MasterCard, Visa

their victims, while the traffic comes to a standstill for the unloading of lorries and for a constant stream of mini-cabs dropping off at the street's numerous restaurants. At dusk you get more of the same, with the street-lights struggling to make the heart of Portobello look like the Via Veneto.

Inside, pizza and pasta are speedily delivered with typical chirpy Italian panache to cramped, scrubbed tables. Go easy on the baskets of warm pizza bread, as the antipasti (£6) – various grilled and preserved tit-bits arranged on the antique dresser – are a tempting self-service affair. Of the other starters, frittura di calamari e gamberoni (£6.80) and carpaccio di manzo con pesto, rucola e Parmigiano (£7.50) are both delicious. Specials change daily and have no particular regional influence. Old favourites include branzino al forno con pomodoro, Mozzarella e salsa al funghi porcini (£16) or perhaps fettucine con tartufo bianco, Parmigiano e salsa al rosmarino (£13.50) – classic, well-prepared dishes. Among the permanent fixtures, spigola alla griglia con olio aromatizzato (£14.50) – is a simply grilled sea bass, while costolette d'agnello con pomodori freschi e melanzane (£12) is char-grilled lamb cutlets with fresh tomato and aubergine. Pizzas vary in size depending on who is in the kitchen – perhaps staff with shorter arms throw the dough higher, resulting in a wider, thinner base – but all are on the largish size. Pizza Diavolo (£7.50) comes with Mozzarella and a good, spicy pepperoni sausage.

There's a house Chianti at £9.50, but it's much better to opt for the Montepulciano d'Abruzzo (£13), a pretty decent wine at a pretty decent price.

Rodizio Rico

(ⓘ) If you're a lover of smoky grilled meat, Rodizio Rico will come as a godsend. In the south of Brazil this restaurant would be pretty run-of-the-mill stuff, but in W11 *churrascarias* are the exception rather than the rule. Rodizio can be a puzzling experience for first-timers. There's no menu and no prices – but no problem. "Rodizio" means "rotating", and refers to the carvers who wander about the room with huge skewers of freshly grilled meat from which they lop off chunks on demand –

Cost	£18–£25
Address	111 Westbourne Grove, W2
T	020 7792 4035
Station	Notting Hill Gate/ Bayswater
Open	Mon–Fri 6.30pm– midnight, Sat 12.30–4.30pm & 6.30pm–midnight, Sun 1–11pm
Accepts	Amex, MasterCard, Visa

rather like the trolleys of roast beef at Simpson's in the Strand. You start by ordering and then help yourself from both the salad bar and hot buffet to prime your plate. As the carvers circulate they dispense cheerfulness and bonhomie as they cut you chunks, slivers and slices from whichever skewer they are holding. You eat as much as you like, of whatever you like, and then you pay the absurdly reasonable price of £16.90 a head.

When you're up helping yourself to the basics, look out for the tiny rolls, no bigger than a button mushroom, called pão de queijo – a rich cheese bread from the south of Brazil. Also bobo, a delicious kind of bubble and squeak made from cassava and spring greens. Return to your seat and await the carvers – they come in random order, but they keep on coming. There's lamb, and ham, and pork, and spare ribs, and chicken, and silverside beef (grilled in a piece and called lagarto after a similarly shaped iguana!). Then for offal aficionados there are grilled chicken hearts. But the star of the show is picanha – the heart of the rump, skewered and grilled in huge chunks. Taste it and the arguments over the relative merits of rump and fillet are over forever – the "rumpers" would win by a landslide. Brazilians seem to revere the crispy bits, but if you want your meat rare you only have to ask.

South Americans rate the impossibly sweet soft drink Antarctica Guar-rana (£1.90) very highly. "Just like the guarana powder you can get in the chemist's shop", they insist. If the lure of alternative rainforest stimulants doesn't appeal, house wines start at a reasonable £10.50 a bottle. And, as you would expect of a Brazilian establishment, the coffee is very good indeed.

BRAZILIAN

Rôtisserie Jules

This rotisserie is one of a now diminishing empire set up by the eponymous Jules – the other remaining branch is at 6 Bute St, SW7 (☎020 7584 0600). They are admirably consistent: comfortable, modern dining rooms with the kitchen open and on show, and the rotisserie always a star. They operate a free delivery service, too, and have a constant stream of people calling in for meals to take home, but somehow they manage to avoid a takeaway atmosphere. Rôtisserie Jules makes the proud claim on the menu that, except for the bread and ice cream, everything is prepared on the premises from scratch and without using frozen ingredients. It seems believable.

Cost	£8–£18
Address	133a Notting Hill Gate, W11
T	020 7221 3331
Station	Notting Hill Gate
Open	Daily noon–11.30pm
Accepts	All major credit cards except Diners
W	www.rotisseriejules.com

ROTISSERIE

There is no evidence of wild flights of fancy on this menu. It has been simplified and now, rather than a separate starters section, you'll find side dishes and salads: corn on the cob (£2.50/£4.50); ratatouille (£2.50/£4.50); Caesar salad (£4.50); gratin Dauphinois (£2/£3.75); rather good fries (£2/£3.75). All are fair enough. But what to put with them? You are probably here for the chicken. Careful timing is the key, and the best time to visit is plumb in the middle of service, when things are at their busiest. That way you'll get your chicken freshly roasted and hot off the spit. There is nothing nicer. The chickens weigh about 3lb, and the pricing is complex: chicken (leg and thigh) with one side dish is £4.95; chicken (breast and wing) with one side dish is £6.25. A whole chicken, on its own, is £9.75. As well as chicken you could have tranche de gigot (£5.50) – lamb steak; or try the whole roast duck (£16), which weighs in at around 5lb – this feeds three or four people and they require half a day's notice. Even better, a whole leg of lamb (£23) weighs some 4¼lb, feeds between three and four people and needs two hours' notice. Confused? Don't worry – the key factor is honest food at reasonable prices.

The dessert menu is short: chocolate mousse (£2); apple tart (£3.25); Ben and Jerry's ice creams (£4.75). Rôtisserie Jules has that rare combination of simple food and sensible prices. Impressive for an establishment that is both a regular restaurant and upscale takeaway.

Richmond & Twickenham

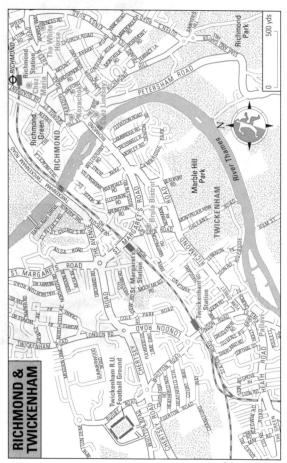

RICHMOND &
TWICKENHAM

© Crown copyright

Brula Bistrot

In 1999, two friends who worked in smart central London restaurants decided that the time had come to open their own place. They chose St Margarets as a locale and, as they were called Bruce Duckett and Lawrence Hartley, they called their restaurant Brula. It had a tiny, yellow-painted dining room about as wide as a railway carriage and an equally modest kitchen. It was very much a family affair. By 2000 Brula had become so successful that they had to move across Crown Road into larger premises. Now the Brula Bistrot (the name was enlarged in keeping with the new premises) is no longer a cramped affair. There are large windows with a profusion of rather elegant stained glass. Thankfully, the food and philosophy have endured – well-cooked French bistro food; limited choice; low, low prices.

Cost	£10–£20

Address 43 Crown Rd, St Margarets, Surrey
T 020 8892 0602
Station BR St Margarets
Open Mon–Fri 12.30–2pm & 7–10.30pm, Sat 7–10.30pm
Accepts Delta, Electron, Solo, Switch

FRENCH

You have to admire anyone who has the good sense not to mess with something that works really well. Lunch at Brula Bistrot will cost you £8 for one or two courses and £10 for three. Extra veg (should you want any) costs a further £1.50; an espresso to finish is £1. The menu changes on a weekly basis, so you might face a choice of celeriac remoulade, soft egg and chives, duck rillette with onion marmalade, and rustic fish soup with rouille. Then on to beef meatballs with thyme dumplings, fish of the day with soy and ginger dressing, or spinach and mushroom. Finally your pick of the puds. All very French, and all rather nostalgic, evoking that dimly remembered rural France when you could pitch up at any bistro de gare and be sure of a good, cheap, satisfying meal. In the evenings they go à la Carte (starters between £4.50 and £6; mains £9.50 to £11; puds £4) and add an extra dish to make four choices for each course – perhaps nine escargots de Bourgogne to start with, and venison steak with creamed endives and a red wine sauce to add gravitas to the main courses.

The Frenchness even extends to the list of suggested apéritifs at the top of the evening menu: kir (£3) or Pilsener (£2.50), Bellini or kir royale (£4.50). And if you spurn these blandishments the wine list is short and agreeable priced – a Chablis premier cru Fourchaume, 1998 was sighted at £25.

Richmond & Twickenham

Chez Lindsay

At first glance Chez Lindsay looks rather like Chicago in the 1920s – all around you people are drinking alcohol out of large earthenware teacups. The cups are in fact traditional Breton drinking vessels known as "bolées", the drink is cider, and Chez Lindsay lists a trio of them, ranging from Breton brut traditionnel to Norman cidre bouché. This

Cost	£7–£27

Address 11 Hill Rise, Richmond, Surrey
T 020 8948 7473
Station Richmond
Open Mon–Sat 11am–11pm, Sun noon–10pm
Accepts MasterCard, Visa

small, bright restaurant has had a loyal local following for a good many years. Most people are attracted by the galettes and crêpes, though the menu also includes a regularly changing list of hearty Breton dishes – especially fish. It's a place for Francophiles: both the kitchen and the front of house seem to be staffed entirely by Gauls, which in this instance means good service and tasty food.

Start with palourdes farcies (£5.95), where nine small clams are given the "snail butter" treatment – lots of garlic. Or the moules à la St Malo (£5.75), which are cooked with shallots, cream and thyme. Then you must decide between the galettes or more formal main courses. The galettes are huge buckwheat pancakes, large and lacy, thin but satisfying. They come with an array of fillings: egg, cheese and ham (£6.25); scallops and leeks (£8.75); Roquefort cheese, celery and walnuts (£6.50); and "Chez Lindsay" (£7.95) – cheese, ham and spinach. The other half of the menu is very Breton, featuring a good steak frites (£12.75) and lots of fish and shellfish. The "gratin de Camembert, flétan et crevettes" (£11.25) is an interesting dish: a gratin containing halibut, prawns and Camembert. Or there is the "bar grillé" (£15.75) – a whole grilled sea bass with salad and new potatoes. Ask the amiable staff about off-menu goodies, which, depending on the market and the season, might be anything from exotic fish to roast grouse.

At lunch, the menu de midi delivers two courses – a salad and a galette – for just £5.99, and there is always a three-course prix fixe at £10.99. Real pud enthusiasts will save themselves for the chocolate and banana crêpe (£4.50), topped with a scoop of gin and lavender ice cream (£1.30), a bizarre-sounding combination that ends up tasting strangely delicious.

Chez Maria

Michel de Ville has won his share of battle honours in his forty years in the catering industry, and his certificates and medals adorn the walls of this tiny restaurant he runs with Maria, his wife. The insignia of the Chevaliers de Tastevin is on one side and the gold medal he won as executive chef of the Playboy Club of America is on the other. This place is a

Cost	£20–£24

Address 5a Princes St, Richmond Market, Surrey
T 020 8948 1475
Station Richmond
Open Tues–Sat 6.30–11pm, Sun noon–7pm
Accepts MasterCard, Visa

FRENCH

"bistro du marché" of the kind that you would find in France, and they have added a particular quirk of originality – lunches are exclusively fish. Michel sees to the cooking; Maria, the service. You fetch your own wine from a nearby off-licence or wine merchant – Chez Maria is strictly BYO. There's also a sensibly simple pricing structure: £16.50 for two courses and £17.50 for three, with no charge for corkage. As there are only thirty seats you would be wise to book, especially at the weekend.

Maria is Portuguese and the menu claims that the restaurant offers "French and Portuguese Specialities", but the French side seems to have the upper hand. Michel cooks the kind of food that he is completely at home with, a sort of frozen-in-time bistro-favourites selection, but one where the dishes have been chosen to make the most sense of a single-handed kitchen. The pastrywork is good – try the tian des crevettes à la sauce Aurore et basilic, a sort of mini-quiche with prawns and a classic cream and tomato sauce. Fish of the day "façon du chef" is generally reliable. Or there might be a roast duck breast on a bed of braised cabbage. Recipes are traditional and none the worse for that: lamb might be paired with a rich haricot bean dish. This is good, honest, very unpretentious French food. Puddings continue the theme: tarte au citron, terrine au chocolat, and crème brûlée. Modernist gastronomes will not approve, but people who fondly remember cheap eats in France will feel pleasantly nostalgic. And here you can enjoy something very rare indeed in a world crowded with lattes, Americanos and tall-skinny-cappuccinos – a good cup of ordinary coffee for £1.

Michel is not above the occasional gastro-jest. To celebrate Burns night, you might be offered "Champignons farcis au Haggis et herbes fraîches", which somewhat gives the lie to the philosophical observation that life is too short to stuff a mushroom.

Kozachok

UKRAINIAN

Tourists will know Richmond as that funny little town on the Thames that cannot quite make up its mind whether it is in London or not. What is less immediately obvious is that it is also a good place to go and eat Ukrainian food. This is a significantly eccentric restaurant. Everything within is painted – bowls, decorative cruets, even the walls have naive cartoon murals. And bunches of twigs have been used to dec-

Cost	£18–£40

Address 10 Red Lion St, Richmond, Surrey
T 020 8948 2366
Station Richmond
Open Tues–Thurs 6.30–11pm, Fri & Sat 6.30–11.15pm Sun 6.30–10pm
Accepts All major credit cards except Diners

orate the ceiling. You will feel as if you have strayed onto a set during the filming of "Smiley's People". Service is more akin to treacle than quicksilver; the food is limited in choice and stolid in demeanour; "Why bother?", you will probably be asking. You should eat at Kozachok because you will enjoy yourself. The service is genuinely welcoming, the food is unfussed-about-with and the vodka (along with the excellent Obolon Ukrainian beer), will leave you giggling irresponsibly while the charm of the place and the people get to work.

There are half a dozen starters. Far and away the best is the blini – this is a large and fluffy creation, about 2cm deep and 8cm across, crisp outside, and very delicious – probably "best ever" when topped with aubergine ikra (£4.95), smoked salmon (£5.50), salmon caviar (£7.50), or – best of all – marinated herring (£5.75). Drunken salmon is also good (£6.95) – home-salted, vodka-cured salmon. Or there is ruletka (£4.75), which is sliced aubergine rolled around cheese. Mains include a Ukrainian speciality called varenki (£8.75), which is like grandparent ravioli filled with potato and cheese. From Siberia there are pelmeni (£8.75), thick dumplings stuffed with mince and served with sour cream – not for the faint hearted. Or there's shashlik (£8.95), a pork kebab which will seem a bit tame if you're drinking properly. Pud means mind-numbing and artery-clogging pancakes, as light as sandbags.

Vodka comes in a wide variety of guises here. And you will be fine right up to the moment when someone suggests beer chasers and you agree. Kozachok is further laid back than most of us can manage without a bed handy, but it is a charming place, run by genuine people who have a real grasp of hospitality.

Pallavi

(🍴) This is a small outpost of an Indian restaurant empire which also includes Malabar Junction (see p.13) – an impressive pedigree. Pallavi, the simplest and the cheapest, started its days as a large takeaway counter with just a few seats, then they moved over the road from the original site to these smart new premises. The cooking has travelled well, and still deserves the ultimate compliment – it is genuinely home-style. Unpretentious dishes and unpretentious prices. True to its South Indian roots, there is an impressive list of vegetarian specialities, but the menu features just enough meat and fish dishes to woo any kind of diner.

Cost	£10–£23
Address	1st Floor, 3 Cross Deep Court, Heath Rd, Twickenham, Middlesex
T	020 8892 2345
Station	BR Twickenham
Daily	noon–3pm & 6–11pm
Accepts	All major credit cards

INDIAN

Start with that South Indian veggie favourite, the Malabar masala dosa (£3.50). The huge, crisp pancake is made with a mixture of ground rice and lentil flour and is a perfect match for the savoury potato mixture and chutney. There's also a meat masala dosa (£4.95), described on the menu as a "non-vegetarian pancake delicacy" – full marks for accuracy there. Or try the delightfully named iddly (£3.50), a steamed rice cake made with black gram, which is eaten as a breakfast dish in India. Whatever you open with, have some cashew nut pakoda (£2.95), a kind of savoury peanut brittle made with cashew nuts, which is wholly delicious. The main dishes are simple and tasty, and are served without fuss. For unrepentant carnivores, chicken Malabar (£3.95), keema methi (£3.95) or kozhi varutha curry (£3.95) all hit the spot. But there are also some interesting fish dishes, including the fish moilee (£5.95). Veggies are good too: parippu curry (£2.15) – split lentils with cumin, turmeric, garlic, chillies and onions; kalan (£2.50) – a traditional sweet and sour dish of mango, yam, coconut and spices; cabbage thoran (£2.50) – sliced cabbage with carrots, green chillies and curry leaves. The pilau rice, lemon rice and coconut rice (all £2.20) are tasty, and parathas are even better; try a green chilli or a sweet coconut paratha (both £2.50).

In this posh new incarnation Pallavi is fully licensed, so you are no longer obliged to bring your own carryout. Thankfully, the lassi (£1) is still just as good.

Richmond & Twickenham

The White Horse

All over town, brave entrepreneurs are taking pubs away from the traditional breweries and transforming them into gold mines, but in this instance Fuller's brewery can be congratulated for encouraging quality themselves. The White Horse is a dark, spartan bar-restaurant with good, large tables that are well spread out – no sitting in your neighbour's pocket here. The food and pricing is also spot-on, as is confirmed by a steady trade and a note on the menu saying "we are now taking bookings for both lunch and early evening meals".

Cost	£12–£30

Address Worple Way, Richmond, Surrey
T 020 8940 2418
Station Richmond
Open Mon–Sat noon–3pm & 6.30–10pm, Sun noon–4pm
Address Amex, MasterCard, Switch, Visa

The menu is a short one, and all the better for it. Five starters and five main courses which change twice a day to accommodate whatever is best from the market. There might be a baby leaf salad with warm poached egg, shaved Parmesan and truffle oil (£5), which arrives with perky leaves and a suitably runny egg yolk. Or a watercress and pea soup (£3.75); or smoked mackerel pate with red onion compote, oranges and toast (£5.50); or sauté of scallops and bok choi with chilli and soy butter (£7.75). Main courses are also simple and well executed, like the wild boar sausages with roast apples, mashed potato and mustard (£8.75); or the roast pollack fillet with purple sprouting broccoli and beurre blanc (£9.50) – fresh fish, well cooked and well presented. Or farfalle with roast tomatoes, rocket and pine nuts (£6.75). The wide-ranging wine list tops out at £22 for a smart American Pinot Noir. What's more, there is the intelligent option of a 250ml glassful of any one of a dozen different wines (from £3.20 to £3.70). Puds are also seasonal, so you might be tempted by cinnamon bread pudding with stewed plums (£4.50), or prune and Armagnac tart (£4.50). And if they don't get you, then the dark chocolate pot (£4.50) probably will.

The last item in The White Horse's dessert section is Vivian's cheeses with wheat wafers and chutney (£5). The cheese in question has made the short journey from Vivian's, the superb delicatessen a few doors down the road – call in there for all manner of goodies. The White Horse cheeseboard proves how much more satisfying it is to sample two or three cheeses in perfect condition than to be faced with a huge selection of the unripe and overripe.

Shepherd's Bush & Olympia

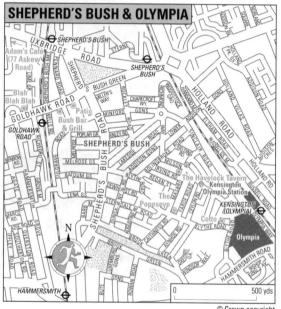

Adam's Café

Frances and Abdel Boukraa live a dual life. Each morning they run a respectable workers' cafe, and every evening they transform it into a North African restaurant. Bacon and eggs for breakfast; fish, grills, couscous and tagines for dinner. The kitchen here is run

Cost	£12–£20
Address	77 Askew Rd, W12
T	020 8743 0572
Station	Ravenscourt Park
Open	Mon–Sat 7–11pm
Accepts	All major credit cards

by a Tunisian chef with a Moroccan assistant, so all manner of North African delicacies are on offer, and the easy-going prices reflect the café heritage. You pick between three menus: rapide (£9.95 for a main course or two starters, plus mint tea or coffee); gourmet (£12.95 for main course and starter or dessert); or gastronomique (£14.95 for starter, main course and dessert). All exclude service, which you'll certainly want to reward. House wines start at £8.50, or you can bring your own (£1.50 corkage per person).

The Tunisian for amuse-gueule is "kemia" – complimentary saucers of wonderful home-made pickles, small meatballs and harissa, which arrive with the bread. Once you've got beyond the good home-made soups, such as the fish soup or the Moroccan spicy chickpea harira, you'll find that the starters are dominated by "briks" and "ojjas". Briks are deep-fried filo parcels filled with egg and herbs, egg and tuna, or peppers, mushrooms and potatoes. Ojjas are even more delicious. They come about when a pan of scrambled egg runs headlong into a pan of ratatouille, and are served with either spicy merguez sausages or shrimps. There are also briwattes – filo parcels of seafood. For a main course, you choose between grills (mostly brochettes – kebabs), couscous and tagine. The couscous arrives, as it should, with a tureen of vegetables in sauce, and choices of meats or vegetables. If you like a little fire, mix some of the red-hot chilli sludge – harissa – into a spoonful of the sauce and pour it over the couscous. Tagines, which hail from Morocco, are casseroles cooked and served in the eponymous pot with a conical lid; try the chicken with preserved Moroccan lemons. For puddings, place your faith in the Moroccan assistant chef; she produces brilliant almond and lemon tarts.

Beware, however, of the Tunisian digestifs. Thibarine is an aromatic liqueur made from dates which tastes of mothballs, while Boukha is an eau de vie made from figs which is faintly reminiscent of petrol.

Blah Blah Blah

The outside of Blah Blah Blah doesn't engender great excitement. It has a decent-sized shopfront, but the closed door and half-closed Venetian blinds over the windows make it look like a cross between a betting shop and a funeral parlour. Appearances can be deceptive – open the door and the first thing that hits you is the noise. There is

Cost	£12–£30
Address	78 Goldhawk Rd, W12
T	020 8746 1337
Station	Goldhawk Road
Open	Mon–Sat 12.30–2.30pm & 7–11pm
Accepts	Cash or cheque only

nothing in the room to absorb the sound. The floors, tables and chairs are wooden, there are blinds rather than curtains, and the only decorations of note are driftwood and old iron lamps. Add wallpaper music and the noise becomes formidable. This is the restaurant where Paul McCartney asked for the music to be turned down. Pricing is simple: at lunch starters cost from £3 to £4.50, and mains go for £5.95. Then, at dinner, starters range from £3.95 to £4.95 and mains from £7.95 to £8.95. Puddings are £4.50.

The little kitchen at the back of the room knows what it is doing. The boconccini is a dual dish: risotto-rice fritters are filled with Mozzarella and deep fried; semolina gnocchi are filled with dolcelatte cheese and given the same treatment. Californian sushi rolls are as good as you could hope to find outside a specialist establishment. The mushroom and Gruyère potato cake is an elaborate combination: the "cake" is made from pan-fried potatoes with leeks, sage and Gruyère, and it is topped with four different kinds of mushrooms that have been sautéed with shallots, garlic and white wine. Good, strident flavours. The roast fennel spanokopitta adds roast fennel and Feta cheese to the filling of the traditional filo parcel and is oven-baked to order. Main courses arrive on the huge side of large, but are moderately priced and obviously cooked to order. The desserts are ambitious and delicious – if it's on the list try the orange semolina cake that comes with orange syrup, almond cream and vanilla custard.

Blah Blah Blah offers well-prepared food that just happens to be vegetarian, rather than the kind of heavy, wholemeal and meaningful fare you would expect from a more "in-your-face" vegetarian restaurant. It is unlicensed, so bring your own. There is a very reasonable corkage charge of £1.25 per person.

Bush Bar & Grill

The rise and rise of Shepherds Bush seemed to culminate in the arrival, in late 2000, of the Bush Bar & Grill. The Bush end of the Goldhawk Road was once the preserve of curry houses, cafés, the street market and a pie-and-mash shop. Now they are joined by the Bush Bar, full of renegade stylistas who have travelled west from Notting Hill. This is a serious bar, complete with serried ranks of bottles, smart raised booths and smartly dressed punters. The large dining area is busy and the whole place has an agreeable buzz to it.

Cost	£12–£35

Address 45a Goldhawk Rd, W12
T 020 8746 2111
Station Goldhawk Road
Open Mon–Sat noon–3pm & 6.30–11.30pm, Sun noon–4pm & 7–11pm
Accepts MasterCard, Visa

The Bush Bar & Grill captures the informal, pacey bustle of a classic brasserie rather well. Service is brisk and with attitude, and the food comes flying out over the pass from an open kitchen that runs the length of the room. The menu changes on a monthly basis and is written in a way that encourages casual meals – there are three soups, salads, savouries and starters – all before you get to the mains, which showcase dishes from the wood-fired oven. The fish soup with rouille croutons (£4.75) is well made. The grilled squid with shaved fennel (£4.75) is a good combination of flavours. And the wild mushroom omelette (£5) is a really welcome sight on any menu. From the oven there's roast skate wing (£10.50), pork tenderloin (£12.75) and a grilled rib of organic beef (for two; £30). From the "other main courses", the daube of beef with celeriac puree (£12) is rich and well-seasoned. Puddings are a tad predictable: bread and butter pudding (£3.50); tart Tatin (£4); crème brûlée (£3.50). This restaurant has the measure of its customers, serves admirably unfussy food, and has prices that are grounded in reality.

The wine list at the Bush Bar & Grill is also extremely encouraging. In such a chic establishment, a reliable house wine (Armit's French Red or White) priced at £10 deserves a warm welcome. Seresin's Chardonnay 1998, from Marlborough in New Zealand, is a sound offer at £22, and even a top bottle like Chateau Gruaud Larose 1997 has an agreeably ungrasping price tag of £54.

Cotto

From the outside, Cotto, which stands on a corner site in a residential neighbourhood behind Olympia, is nothing special. Acres of plate glass frontage reveal a sprinkling of tables around a large central bar area. Once you have taken in the clean, white walls, the dark, ribbed carpet and the collection of

Cost	£15–£60

Address 44 Blythe Rd, W14
T 020 7602 9333
Station Kensington Olympia
Open Mon–Fri noon–2.30pm
& 7–10.30pm, Sat 7–10.30pm
Accepts All major credit cards

primary-coloured abstract paintings on the walls, there is precious little decoration. And therefore minimal distraction from the real purpose of this restaurant, which is to provide good grub for the discerning local residents.

The balance of the menu will strike a chord with foodies. Though the restaurant may have an Italian name (*cotto* means "cooked" in Italian), there is much drawn from English and French tradition in the make-up of the menu. It seems that the cooking is firmly rooted in the best of all approaches: treating ingredients with respect and striving to get the most out of each of them by judicious cooking and generous use of herbs. The menu – which changes regularly to follow the seasons – is not long, but there's plenty of variety. The five starters might include a fragrant new season's garlic and oregano soup (£4.95), or a somewhat heavier ox-tongue raviolo with tarragon broth (£5.50), the meaty, terrine-like "raviolo" offset by a delicate yet pungent herby liquor. Main courses may well include a proper vegetarian choice such as ragout of baby fennel, ratte potatoes and wild mushrooms (£11.50), as well as a couple of fish options such as monkfish with crab cannelloni and a basil bouillon (£15), or pan-fried John Dory with artichoke risotto (£14). Meat dishes include an excellent braised shoulder of lamb with turnips and marjoram (£13.50), and roast chicken with thyme and soft polenta (£14.50). Puddings, such as blueberry Pavlova (£6) and chocolate feuillatine with pear (£5.75), will please any sugar addict.

The food at Cotto is a satisfying experience, and it's served with good manners and grace. You should be aware, though, that the bill has a tendency to escalate, especially if you give the wine list full play. But a visit for lunch is much more affordable: two courses are offered at £12.50, three at £15.50. The menu may not be as interesting, but the same people will cook it with the same philosophy as at dinner.

The Havelock Tavern

Cost	£8–£20

Address 57 Masbro Rd, W14
T 020 7603 5374
Station Shepherd's Bush
Open Food served Mon–Sat
12.30–2.30pm & 7–10pm, Sun
12.30–3pm & 7–9.30pm
Accepts Cash or cheque only

The Havelock is one of those pubs marooned within a sea of houses; in this instance it's the sea of houses just behind Olympia. It's a real pub, with a solid range of beers as well as an extensive wine list. What is most attractive, though, is the attitude that lies behind the menu, which is chalked up daily on the blackboard. As the chef half of the proprietorial partnership says, "We're in the business of feeding people." And that's just what they do, serving up seasonal, unfussy food – the kind of fresh, interesting, wholesome stuff you wish that you could get around to cooking for yourself. The bar seats 75 and during the summer there's a terrific garden complete with vines and a pergola. Service involves stepping up to the bar and ordering what you want, so there's no service charge to bump up what are very reasonable prices indeed.

The menu is different every session, with more "one-hit" dishes served at lunch, when most customers are pressed for time. Starters might be field mushroom soup with parsley and croutons (£4), goujons of brill with mayonnaise and lemon (£5.50), or a plate of Spanish charcuterie and Serrano ham with piquillo peppers, olives and pickles (£5.50). Main courses range from leek, pea, potato and rosemary risotto with rocket salad (£5.50/£7.50) to char-grilled tuna, warm butter bean, celery, tomato and olive salad with oregano and lemon dressing (£10). Or a classic coq au vin served with mashed potato and green beans (£8.50) – the kind of sensible plateful that gladdens the heart in these days of ever-fancier food. Or maybe a large warm salad of sautéed calf's kidney, bacon, beetroot, green beans, shallot and mustard dressing (£10) appeals? Puddings are equally reliable – try the warm walnut tart with vanilla ice cream (£4).

A great deal of effort goes into selecting slightly unusual wines for the blackboard wine list. Many of them are offered at bargain prices but the biggest seller is still a glass of the house red. Popular rumour has it that the Havelock is one of Simon Hopkinson's favourite eateries. No wonder.

POLISH

Patio

The ebullient Eva Michalik (a former opera singer) and her husband Kaz have been running this Shepherd's Bush institution for more than a decade, and it's not hard to see why the show is still on the road. At Patio you get good, solid Polish food in a friendly, comfortable atmosphere – for a relatively small amount of money. And this little restaurant is a people-pleaser: you can just as easily come here for an intimate tête-à-tête as for a raucous birthday dinner. The food is always reliable and sometimes it's really excellent. There are two floors – downstairs feels a little cosier and more secluded.

Cost	£13–£26
Address	5 Goldhawk Rd, W12
T	020 8743 5194
Station	Goldhawk Road/ Shepherd's Bush
Open	Mon–Fri noon–3pm & 6pm–midnight, Sat & Sun 6pm–midnight
Accepts	All major credit cards

The set menu (available at lunch and dinner) is Patio's trump card. For £11.90 you get a starter, main course, petits fours and fruit ... and a vodka. The menu changes daily – ask Eva to tell you what's new in the kitchen and you could get something that's not yet listed. A dozen or so starter and main course choices are available on the set menu. Starters include plump and tasty blinis with smoked salmon; wild mushroom soup; Polish ham with beetroot horseradish; and herrings with soured cream. Everything is fresh and carefully prepared. For mains, there's a good selection of meat, fish and chicken dishes – the scallops in dill sauce, when available, are outstanding. Or you might try a Polish speciality such as golabki (cabbage stuffed with rice and meat), which is also available as a vegetarian dish; or chicken Walewska (chicken breast in fresh red pepper sauce); or sausages à la Zamoyski (grilled sausages with sautéed mushrooms and onions). Main dishes come with a hearty selection of vegetables such as roast potatoes, broccoli and red cabbage. Be prepared, too, for high-octane puds such as the Polish pancakes with cheese, vanilla and rum – the fumes alone are enough to send you reeling. Also good are the walnut gâteau, and the hot apple charlotka with cream. For those after more variety, including a scattering of non-Polish dishes, the à la carte offers further choice, and for not a great deal more money.

Patio is a good night out. The piano crammed in near the entrance is often put to use by a regular customer, and there are frequent sightings of a roving gypsy quartet.

The Popeseye

Just suppose you fancy a steak. A good steak, and perhaps a glass (or bottle) of red wine to go with it. You're interested enough to want the best, probably Aberdeen Angus, and you want it cooked simply. The Popeseye is for you.

Cost	£16–£50
Address	108 Blythe Rd, W14
T	020 7610 4578
Station	Hammersmith
Open	Mon–Sat 6.45–10.30pm
Accepts	Cash or cheque only

This quirky restaurant is named after the Scottish word for rump steak, and every week the proprietor buys his meat not from Smithfield or a catering butcher, but from the small butcher his family uses in the north of Scotland. The meat, of course, is Aberdeen Angus and the restaurant is a member of the Aberdeen Angus Society. The dining room is small, things tend to be chaotic, and the atmosphere is occasionally pretty smoky. As to the food, there is no choice: just various kinds of steak and good chips, with home-made puddings to follow. Oh, and the menu starts with the wine list. You choose your drink, and only when that's settled do you choose your steak – specifying, of course, the cut and the size (and they come very big here), and how you want it cooked. This winning formula is repeated at a second Popeseye at 227 Upper Richmond Rd, SW15 (℡020 8788 7733).

There are those times when, for nearly everyone, only a large piece of meat will do. You may have curry days, fish days, or pasta days, but for red meat days the Popeseye really hits the spot. Now, about these steaks. Popeseye comes in 6oz, 8oz, 12oz and 20oz (at £9.45, £11.45, £15.45 and £20.45), as does sirloin (£11.45, £14.45, £18.45 and £23.95), and fillet (£13.45, £17.45, £21.45 and £29.95). All prices include excellent chips, and a side salad is an extra £3.45. Puddings are priced at £3.95 and come from the "home-made" school of patisserie – such delights as apple crumble, sticky toffee pudding and lemon tart.

The wine list is an ever-changing reflection of what can be picked up at the sales and represents good value. There are eighteen clarets and half a dozen wines from Burgundy, plus others picked from the Rhône, Spain and Argentina – and there are also two white wines on offer for people who have lost the plot. Ask advice. People have been seen here happily drinking Château Palmer 1987 for £53 a bottle, which, despite being a tidy sum, is also a bargain.

Southall

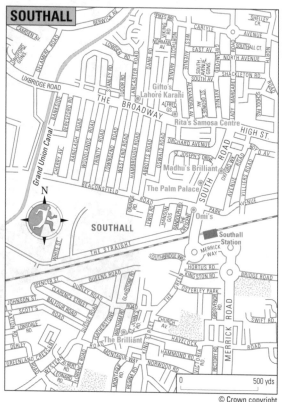

© Crown copyright

The Brilliant

🍴 The Brilliant is a Southall institution. For more than twenty years the Anand family business has been a non-stop success and it is now a bustling 250-seater. For twenty-five years before that, the family's first restaurant, also called the Brilliant, was the toast of Kenya. The food at The Brilliant is East African-Asian, and very good indeed. D.K. Anand (known as Gulu) rules the kitchen with a rod of iron and, to quote him, "there's no frying-pan cookery here".

Cost	£15–£30

Address 72–76 Western Rd, Southall, Middlesex
T 020 8574 1928
Station BR Southall
Open Tues–Fri noon–2.30pm & 6pm–midnight, Sat & Sun 6–11.30pm; closed Aug
Accepts All major credit cards
W www.brilliant restaurant.com

INDIAN

A relatively small number of dishes are freshly cooked in bulk, and if a curry needs to be simmered for three hours then that's what happens. The resulting sauces are incredibly rich and satisfying – and yet Gulu won't countenance any cream, yoghurt, nuts or dried fruit.

To start with, you must try the butter chicken (£8 half, £16 full). A half-portion will do for two people as a starter. This dish is an enigma: somehow it manages to taste more buttery than butter itself – really delicious. There's also jeera chicken (£8/£16), rich with cumin and black pepper. And chilli chicken (£9/£18), which is very hot. If you're in a party, move on to the special meals section – these come in two portion sizes, suggested for three people and five people. Methi chicken (£17.50/£32), masaladar lamb (£17.50/£32) and palak chicken (£17.50/£32) are all winners. Alternatively, choose from among the single-portion curries, which include masala talapia (£9), a fish curry of unimaginable richness with good firm chunks of boneless fish. Well-cooked basmati rice costs £3.50 and, as well as good rotis (£1), the breads list hides a secret weapon – the kulchay (£1). This is a fried, white-dough bread, for all the world like a very flat doughnut. Hot from the kitchen they are amazing – it's best to order a succession so that they don't go cold.

Ask to try Gulu's pickles – carrot, sharp mango and hot lime. They are splendid. Also try the Kenyan beer Tusker (£2.50), with its label rather engagingly designed like a bank note. Unfortunately, enjoyable though it may be, it doesn't cut much ice with the chilli chicken!

Gifto's Lahore Karahi

In Southall they know a good thing when they taste it. Gifto's Lahore Karahi specializes in freshly grilled, well-spiced meats and exceptionally good breads, backed up by a few curries and one or two odd dishes from Lahore. They do these superbly well and consistently. It is a sign of the towering success that 2001 saw a major renovation and refurb but the emphasis is still on a no-frills operation. A row of grinning chefs seem to juggle with the three-foot skewers as meat goes into the tandoor caked in a secret marinade and comes out perfectly cooked and delicious. Despite having a hundred seats downstairs and the same again upstairs, there is a still a queue outside at the weekend.

Cost £8–£16

Address 162–164 The
Broadway, Southall,
Middlesex
T 020 8813 8669
Station BR Southall
Open Mon–Thurs
noon–11.30pm, Fri–Sun
noon–midnight
Accepts All major credit cards
W www.gifto.com

Whatever else you order, you need some bread. Peshwari nan (£1.60) is a triumph, hot from the oven, flavoured with garlic and fresh herbs, and liberally slathered with ghee and sesame seeds. It's hard to imagine it bettered. To accompany it, you might start with an order of chicken tikka (£3.60), which is juicy and strongly spiced. Or go straight for a portion of five lamb chops (£5.20) encrusted in tandoori paste and grilled until crisp. Or try pomfret fish (£6.90) from the tandoor, a worthwhile extravagance. Curries include sag gosht (£5.90), which is chunks of lamb in a dark-green, velvety spinach base; Nihari lamb (£5.90), cooked slowly on the bone in a rich gravy; and, more unusually, batera – quail – curry (£5.90). The menu describes paya (£5.90) as "lamb trotters in thick gravy" – a gravy created by three hours' cooking in a pot with ginger, onions and garlic. For specialists only, perhaps. Very delicious, and supposed to "purify the blood", is the karela gosht (£5.90), a telling combination of bitter melon and lamb. The side dishes will tempt all comers, especially the tarka dhal (£3.90), which is rich and buttery.

You can specify your seasonings for all the Lahore's dishes – mild, medium or hot. Hot is very hot and will have you calling for a large mango shake (£2). All drinks at the Lahore are soft, though you can bring your own beer or wine (no corkage).

Madhu's Brilliant

In the beginning was the Brilliant Restaurant and Nightclub in Nairobi. Then there was The Brilliant restaurant in Western Road, Southall, run by the Anand brothers (see p.477), and then their nephew Sanjay set up Madhu's Brilliant, which is in South Road. These are the dynastic entanglements behind the continuing debate as to whether the original Brilliant or Madhu's serves the better food. Madhu's is a tad more sophisticated than The Brilliant, and it has recently been refurbished and offers fancier service. But the East African/Punjabi food served at both has always been stunningly good and a real eye-opener to those accustomed to more standard curry house fare.

Cost	£10–£25
Address	39 South Rd, Southall, Middlesex
T	020 8574 1897
Station	BR Southall
Open	Mon, Wed & Thurs 12.30–3pm & 6–11.30pm, Fri 12.30–3pm & 6pm–midnight Sat & Sun 6–11.30pm
Accepts	All major credit cards

INDIAN

As at The Brilliant, you'll find all the Anand family signature dishes: butter chicken (£6.50 half-portion, £12 whole), jeera chicken (flavoured with cumin, £6.50 and £12) and chilli chicken (hot as Hades, £7 and £13). Also very good at Madhu's is the masala fried tilapia (£3), which is chunks of fresh fish fried in a splendidly exotic batter. On the chef's speciality list there are some interesting dishes such as boozi bafu (£18). This is a cauldron of thin lamb chops, stewed for a long while in an improbably rich curry gravy. It is cooked and served on the bone, which means that not only does the sauce improve tenfold, but there are all those delicious bones to suck. Machuzi kuku (full cauldron, for up to six people, £30; half cauldron, for three people, £16) applies the same principle to chicken. From the single-portion curries list, the chicken curry with methi (£6.50) is well spiced, and there's a very respectable chicken tikka masala (£6.50) for when you're feeling unadventurous. Breads are exemplary, the keema nan (£2.50) being particularly delicious.

Choosing between The Brilliant and Madhu's Brilliant remains a challenge. They both have their strengths, they are both streets ahead of your average run-of-the-mill curry house and they can both be wholeheartedly recommended. Visit both and decide for yourself.

Omi's

Omi's is a small, no-frills eatery with a kitchen that seems at least as spacious as the dining area. The explanation for this lies next door, where you'll find one of Southall's larger banqueting and wedding halls. Omi's is a thriving outside-catering operation and has never been purely a restaurant – until some years ago the food shared a

Cost	£5–£12
Address	1 Beaconsfield Rd, Southall, Middlesex
T	020 8571 4831
Station	BR Southall
Open	Mon–Thurs 11am–9pm, Fri & Sat 11am–9.30pm
Accepts	All major credit cards

counter with a van-rental business. Now you'll find tasty, Punjabi/Kenyan-Asian dishes, lots of rich flavours and great value. The dining room is hardly prepossessing, and the menu is one of those back-lit neon display boards, but there is a refurb in the offing and, as the notices proudly boast, it is "Fully Licensed". Don't miss out on a bottle of Ambari (£3.35), a Goan beer which sports an intriguing injunction on the back label: "For real fun drink chilled". This is one restaurant where your wallet will enjoy the trip as much as you. The idea of opening for a bit longer each day and even on Sunday is often discussed – best ring and check.

The food is cooked by a formidable line-up of chefs in the back, doubtless knocking up dishes for diners with one hand while masterminding the next Indian wedding for eight hundred with the other. And, while you eat, a constant stream of people come and go to pick up their takeaways. Start with some of the starters, which are behind the counter. Chicken tikka (£3) is good and spicy. Aloo tikka (50p) is a large and savoury potato cake, rather like a fish cake without the fish, fried until delightfully crisp on the outside. Or try the masala fish (£2.75), a large slab of cod thickly encrusted with spices. Go on to sample a couple of the specials – aloo methi (£3.50), potatoes cooked with fenugreek, is very moreish indeed. The chilli chicken at Omi's shows influences from Chinese cuisine – the flavours are a kind of Punjabi sweet and sour. All the curries are commendably oil-free and strongly flavoured. They thrive on the cook-and-reheat system in operation here, and are best eaten with breads – parathas (£1), rotis (40p) and the mega-indulgent puffy fried bhaturas (50p) are all fresh and good.

If you feel a sudden tightening of your fist, you'll warm to the multi-course set meal on offer here – it costs a miserly £4, either vegetarian or non-vegetarian. West End emporia please note these prices!

Palm Palace

The Palm Palace may be short on palms, and it is not palatial by any manner of means, but the food is great. This is the only Sri Lankan restaurant among the restaurant turmoil that is Southall, and the menu features a great many delicious and interesting dishes. As is so often the case with Sri Lankan food, the "drier" dishes are particularly

Cost	£9–£18

Address 80 South Rd, Southall, Middlesex
T 020 8574 9209
Station BR Southall
Open Daily noon–3pm & 6–11.30pm
Accepts All major credit cards

appealing, and there is a good deal of uncompromising chilli heat. The dining room is clean and comfortable in a sparse sort of way, and service is friendly and attentive.

Starters are very good here. Try the mutton rolls (£1.50), long pancake rolls filled with meat and potatoes. Or there's the fish cutlets (£1.50), which are in fact spherical fish cakes very much in the same style as those you find in smart West End eateries, but better spiced and a tenth of the price. Move on to a "devilled" dish: mutton (£4.50), chicken (£4.50) or, best of all, squid (£4.95). With a dark tangy-sweet sauce with chilli bite, these dishes combine spices with richness very well. There was a time when every curry house in the land featured Ceylon chicken, usually just a standard chicken curry with an additional dollop of coconut milk. Here you'll find a short list of real "Ceylon" curries including mutton (£3.95) – they're good, if straightforward. Try the chicken 65 (£4.50), whose name is said to refer to the age of the chicken in days: any younger and it would fall apart during cooking, any older and it would be tough. Whatever the provenance, it is a name worth noting, getting you delicious chunks of chicken with a rich and spicy coating. The hoppers (Sri Lankan pancakes) are good fun – string hopper (£2.50); egg hopper (£1.25); milk hopper (£1). Try a simple vegetable dish as well – the saag aloo (£2.50) gets you fresh spinach and thoughtfully seasoned, well-cooked potato, and heavens be praised, with no pool of surplus oil.

Beer-lovers must order a big bottle of Lion Stout (£3.50), which is dark, dangerous and delicious. As well as being 8% alcohol, it brings with it a ringing endorsement from Michael Jackson, the "beer hunter" himself. Look at the back label and you will find not only his portrait, but also a short eulogy – "chocolatey, mocha, liqueurlike" and so forth. This beer is surprisingly good with spicy food.

Rita's Samosa Centre

Those diners with an artistic bent will be disappointed by the refurb at Rita's, which has meant the loss of the garish, other-worldly murals (and also the little paan shop by the doorway). This place is now light and bright and has a good many more seats, but business continues much as before. It is still noisy, busy and bustling, and if you are a shy, retiring type, this isn't a place for you – indeed, you probably won't get served. To eat here you must go up to the counter where all the dishes are set out in giant trays, choose your meal, pay, and then seat yourself. The food will eventually arrive. There's no sign of a system but everything seems to turn up in the end. And when it does it is simple, tasty and cheap. Who could ask for more? Perhaps a few bright murals…?

Cost	£3–£12
Address	112 The Broadway, Southall, Middlesex
T	020 8571 2100
Station	BR Southall
Open	Daily 11am–10.30pm
Accepts	Cash or cheque only

The dishes are divided into sections – curries, bread and rice, chaats (street food) and snacks. Snacks make good starters, as do chaats. Try an onion bhaji (£1) – huge, and opened out flat so that it's all the crisper. Bhel puri (£2.25), alu tikki (£2) and dahi puri (£2.50) are all street-food items – tasty and good value. Or how about half a pound of chicken tikka (£3.50)? Or a superb, half-pound fish tikka (£3.50)? They both eclipse the samosas (40p each) after which this diner is named. Main course curries are rich and simple. Try lamb (£4.50), lamb saag (£4.50) or a deadly chilli lamb or chilli chicken (£5.50), both of which arrive scatter-bombed with halved fresh green chillies. And despite the demise of the paan shop, there is still the kebab roll section by the door. This place offers really good, freshly cooked, delicious, reasonably priced fast food.

You can take your own beer or wine to Rita's, but it is much more fun exploring the (non-alcoholic) drinks section. A pint of salty lassi (£2) is wonderfully cold and pleasantly sharp, with a savoury dusting of fine-ground cumin seed. And then there's faluda. Faluda is very thin, very soft vermicelli which comes in a glass of milkshake. The sensation of these "worms" slithering up the straw and into your mouth is most disconcerting. Furthermore, you can have faluda with a scoop of ice cream in it (£2). What a way to end a meal.

Further West

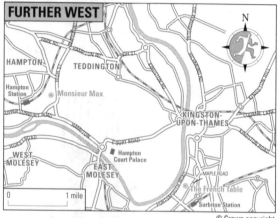

FURTHER WEST

HAMPTON

Hampton
Station

PARK ROAD

HAMPTON ROAD

BRIDGE ST

TEDDINGTON

⊙ Monsieur Max

UPPER SUNBURY ROAD

HURST ROAD

HAMPTON

WEST
MOLESEY

COURT ROAD

EAST
MOLESEY

■ Hampton
Court Palace

TEDDINGTON ROAD

KINGSTON-
UPON-THAMES

LOWER HAM ROAD

PORTSMOUTH ROAD

LORDALE LANE

HAMPTON COURT ROAD

MAPLE ROAD

⊙ The French Table

■ Surbiton Station

| 0 | 1 mile |

N

The French Table

A collective shudder ran through Surbiton's gastronomes when they heard that Luca was to be no more. Quickly followed by a sigh of relief, in June 2001, when they saw the restaurant at 85 Maple Road reopen with new owners, a new name and a new menu. The French Table serves well-cooked, modern French/Mediterranean food. The new owners are Eric and Sarah Guignard;

Cost	£18–£40

Address 85 Maple Rd,
Surbiton, Surrey
T 020 8399 2365
Station BR Surbiton
Open Tues–Thurs 7–10.30pm,
Fri & Sat 6.30-10.30pm Sun
noon–3pm
Accepts MasterCard, Visa

MODERN EUROPEAN

he cooks and she runs the front of house. Aside from getting a signwriter to paint the new name, the Guignards have done little to change the premises – it's still minty green with a slate floor. But the new menu is a more radical departure, as despite modern influences Guignard's food is rooted in the French classics – as befits a cook who has served time in various Michelin-starred establishments.

Flavours are upfront and the seasoning spot on. There is a deft handling of different textures and presentation is commendably unfussy. Starters like roast asparagus with almonds, fried garlic and leek sauce (£4.80) are well handled - crisp asparagus, softer leeks, buttery sauce and not over-powered by the garlic. Or salad of marinated beef, baby onions, carrot spaghetti and foie gras carpaccio (£5.50) - the carrot spaghetti has a welcome tang of vinegar, and a thin sliver of foie gras is allowed to melt over the pan-fried beef. It's not often that you see the words "foie gras" and a price like £5.50 in the same sentence. Main course dishes are robust and delicious. Pork belly caramelized with confit tomato ravioli, roast shallots and red wine jus (£12.20) is a grand dish - the pork cooked to melting point. Or there's pan-fried skate, crushed new potatoes, red peppers, tomatoes and chives (£11.20). Or rump of lamb served with wild mushrooms and gnocchi fricassée, Parmesan dentelle and its own jus (£13.80) - the Parmesan biscuit adding a savoury crunch. The wine list here is largely French and gently priced, the service is friendly and everybody seems to be trying very hard indeed - as befits an "owner driver" establishment.

The "dark chocolate soufflé (£4.95) – allow 20 minutes" is the real thing. A difficult dish perfectly judged: fluffy outside with a dark and dangerous heart of runny chocolate goo, this is not one of those "twice-cooked" cheats' soufflés.

VERY FRENCH

Monsieur Max

You know those tabloid stories about people being trapped in the wrong bodies? Well, Max Renzland is a Frenchman trapped inside an Englishman. Monsieur Max is the latest – and most critically acclaimed – in a succession of restaurants from which Max and his late twin brother Mark struggled to dispense authentic French food and Gallic culture to appreciative Londoners.

Cost	£24–£45
Address	133 High St, Hampton, Middlesex
T	020 8979 5546
Station	BR Fulwell
Open	Tues–Fri noon–2.30pm & 7–10.30pm, Sat 7–11pm, Sun noon–2.30pm
Accepts	All major credit cards

It embodies all the best bits of those legendary small French restaurants. Service is cheerful and unashamedly biased towards regulars. The short menu changes every day. Dishes range from stunningly simple to French classics. And, joy of joys, Monsieur Max is in London – well, nearly.

Max is also a bit of a bargain. Dinner (or Sunday lunch) is £24.50 for three courses; the midweek lunch is £19.50 for two courses or £25 for three. Starters range from the simple – finest Cantabrian anchovies, cured and served with shallots, or home-made rillettes of pork and duck – to more complex dishes such as terrine of dill-marinated salmon layered with crème fraîche and cucumber salad. For a main course, if it's on the menu, you should jump at the poulet de Bresse in two services (for two). This takes 25 minutes: first you get the breast – simply roasted, with potato Dauphinoise and a vin Jaune and morel cream sauce – and then the legs, served with a mixed leaf salad and truffle jus. Max has a new source of French chickens that supplies exclusively to this restaurant. He is very picky about his chickens, and once you taste one you'll see what all the fuss is about. His fish, duck and Scotch beef offerings are equally impressive. Puddings are of the order of rum baba, or an old-fashioned rice pudding with Madagascan vanilla, Agen prunes and cognac caramel. Push them aside and go for the cheeseboard – twenty French farmhouse cheeses in perfect condition. As for wine, there are about 250 bins – enough for the choosiest oenophile.

If you are a West London Francophile, you're probably already a regular here and will be unfazed by the minor eccentricities of the menu and service.

Index

Index of restaurants by name

A–Z note: The Eagle appears under E not T, La Trompette under T, and Al Duca under D. But Café Pacifico is a C, San Daniele an S and Alastair Little an A. Well, you have to have rules.

1 Lombard Street, The Brasserie   **181**

1 Lombard St, EC3
ⓣ020 7929 6611
Modern French

192   **443**

192 Kensington Park Rd, W11
ⓣ020 7229 0482
Modern British

Abeno   **5**

47 Museum St, WC1
ⓣ020 7405 3211
Japanese

Abu Ali   **89**

136–138 George St, W1
ⓣ020 7724 6338
Lebanese

Adam's Café   **467**

77 Askew Rd, W12
ⓣ020 8743 0572
North African

Al Waha   **111**

75 Westbourne Grove, W2
ⓣ020 7229 0806
Lebanese

Alastair Little   **119**

49 Frith St, W1
ⓣ020 7734 5183
Modern European

Alastair Little W11   **444**

136a Lancaster Rd, W11
ⓣ020 7243 2220
Modern European

Alounak   **112**

44 Westbourne Grove, W2
ⓣ020 7229 0416
Iranian

Anatolya   **209**

263a Mare St, E8
ⓣ020 8986 2223
Turkish

Andrew Edmunds   **120**

46 Lexington St, W1
ⓣ020 7437 5708
Modern British

The Anglesea Arms   **435**

35 Wingate Rd, W6
ⓣ020 8749 1291
Modern British/Pub

Anglo Anatolyan   **291**

123 Stoke Newington
Church St, N16
ⓣ020 7923 4349
Turkish

Arancia   **361**

52 Southwark Park Rd, SE16
ⓣ020 7394 1751
Italian

Arkansas Café   **171**

Unit 12, Old Spitalfields Market, E1
ⓣ020 7377 6999
North American/Steak

Aroma II   **21**

118 Shaftesbury Ave, W1
ⓣ020 7437 0370
Chinese

Artigiano   **241**

12 Belsize Terrace, NW3
ⓣ020 7794 4288
Italian

L'Artista   **242**

917 Finchley Rd, NW11
ⓣ020 8731 7501
Pizza/Italian

Assaggi 445

39 Chepstow Place, W2
☎020 7792 5501
Italian

The Atlas 423

16 Seagrave Rd, Fulham,
SW6
☎020 7385 9129
Mediterranean/Pub

Aubergine 401

11 Park Walk, SW10
☎020 7352 3449
French

The Avenue 97

7–9 St James's St, SW1
☎020 7321 2111
Modern British

Babur Brasserie 377

119 Brockley Rise, Forest
Hill, SE23
☎020 8291 2400
Indian

Il Bacio 292

61 Stoke Newington
Church St, N16
☎020 7249 3833
Pizza/Italian

Bah Humbug 325

The Crypt, St Matthews
Church, Brixton Hill, SW2
☎020 7738 3184
Mostly Vegetarian/
Modern British

Bank 31

1 Kingsway, cnr of
Aldwych, WC2
☎020 7379 9797
Modern British

Banner's 255

21 Park Rd, N8
☎020 8348 2930
Caribbean/Modern British

Baradero 203

Turberry Quay, off Pepper
St, E14
☎020 7537 1666
Spanish

Barcelona Tapas Bar 182

1a Bell Lane, E1
☎020 7247 7014
Spanish

Base 243

71 Hampstead High St,
NW3
☎020 7431 2224
Modern British

BB's Crabback 413

3 Chignell Place, West
Ealing, W13
☎020 8840 8322
Caribbean

Belair House 378

Gallery Rd, Dulwich
Village, SE21
☎020 8299 9788
French

Belgo Centraal 32

50 Earlham St, WC2
☎020 7813 2233
Belgian

Bengal Village 172

75 Brick Lane, E1
☎020 7366 4868
Indian

Bibendum
Oyster Bar 143

Michelin House, 81
Fulham Rd, SW3
☎020 7589 1480
Seafood

Bierodrome 271

173–174 Upper St, N1
☎020 7226 5835
Belgian

Bistro Daniel 90

26 Sussex Place, W2
☎020 7723 8395
French

Black & Blue 446

215–217 Kensington
Church St, W8
☎020 7727 0004
Steak

Blah Blah Blah 468

78 Goldhawk Rd, W12
☎020 8746 1377
Vegetarian/British

Index

Index

Index of restaurants by cuisine

Categories below are pretty self-explanatory, though note that "Indian" includes Bangladeshi, Indian and Pakistani restaurants.